# Make Your Own Music Videos with Adobe® Premiere®

# Make Your Own Music Videos with Adobe® Premiere®

**Pete and Maura Kennedy**

Best-Selling Books • Digital Downloads • e-Books • Answer Networks • e-Newsletters • Branded Web Sites • e-Learning

New York, NY ✦ Cleveland, OH ✦ Indianapolis, IN

**Make Your Own Music Videos with Adobe® Premiere®**

Published by
**Hungry Minds, Inc.**
909 Third Avenue
New York, NY 10022
www.hungryminds.com

Library of Congress Control Number: 2002103280

ISBN: 0-7645-3676-1

Printed in the United States of America

10 9 8 7 6 5 4 3 2 1

1O/QT/QW/QS/IN

Distributed in the United States by Hungry Minds, Inc.

For general information on Hungry Minds' products and services, please contact our Customer Care department within the U.S. at 800-762-2974, outside the U.S. at 317-572-3993 or fax 317-572-4002. For sales inquiries and reseller information, including discounts, premium and bulk quantity sales, and foreign-language translations, please contact our Customer Care department at 800-434-3422, fax 317-572-4002 or write to Hungry Minds, Inc., Attn: Customer Care Department, 10475 Crosspoint Boulevard, Indianapolis, IN 46256.

For information on licensing foreign or domestic rights, please contact our Sub-Rights Customer Care department at 212-884-5000.

For information on using Hungry Minds' products and services in the classroom or for ordering examination copies, please contact our Educational Sales department at 800-434-2086 or fax 317-572-4005.

For press review copies, author interviews, or other publicity information, please contact our Public Relations department at 317-572-3168 or fax 317-572-4168.

For authorization to photocopy items for corporate, personal, or educational use, please contact Copyright Clearance Center, 222 Rosewood Drive, Danvers, MA 01923, or fax 978-750-4470.

**Hungry Minds**™ is a trademark of Hungry Minds, Inc.

# About the Authors

**Pete and Maura Kennedy** met in Austin, Texas and began a musical collaboration that resulted in six critically acclaimed CDs, a number of successful national tours, and an appearance on Nanci Griffith's Grammy-winning *Other Voices, Other Rooms* CD and video. Maura first began editing in Adobe Premiere after the duo returned home from a month-long tour with over 40 hours of raw video footage. Her first editing project, a music video for the duo's song "Free," won the Washington Area Music Award for Best Music Video in 2000. The following year, the duo received the same award for their "Nickeltown" video. The Kennedys remain active in both audio recording and music video production, while still finding time to tour the nation in their Dodge van. Pete and Maura married in 1994 and renewed their vows in 1999 at the Graceland Wedding Chapel in Las Vegas, NV. They currently reside in New York City, directly above a Seattle-based coffee shop. Their latest CD, *Get It Right,* is available on the Jiffyjam label.

# Credits

**Acquisitions Editor**
Michael Roney

**Project Editor**
Timothy J. Borek

**Technical Editor**
Alan Ford Hamill

**Copy Editor**
Beth Taylor

**Editorial Manager**
Rev Mengle

**Senior Vice President,
Technical Publishing**
Richard Swadley

**Vice President and Publisher**
Barry Pruett

**Project Coordinator**
Maridee Ennis

**Graphics and Production Specialists**
Gabriele McCann
Kelly Hardesty
Heather Pope
Jacque Schneider
Kathie Schutte
Jeremey Unger

**Quality Control Technicians**
John Bitter
Andy Hollandbeck

**Permissions Editor**
Laura Moss

**Media Development Specialist**
Angela Denny

**Illustrator**
Rashell Smith

**Proofreading and Indexing**
TECHBOOKS Production Services

*To Richard Lester, the man who invented music video.*

# Preface

If you are a music lover and have always thought that you could make a music video if only you had the right tools, this book is for you. If you or someone you know is in a band, and you want to make a video for your Web site or as a promotional tool, this book is for you. If you have great stacks of pre-video vinyl, and you always wanted to make your own video for your favorite song, this book is for you. If you saw a video on TV and said, "I could make a much better video than that," this book is for you. If you want to become a professional music videographer, this book is a great place to start. In this book, we show you how to shoot, edit, and export music videos using only your video camera, your computer, a CD, tape, or even vinyl record (you supply the record player!) and Adobe Premiere. We walk you through the steps to make a simple video sequence, and we explain the powerful tools available to you in Premiere. We also give you tips on how to make your homemade videos look like the professional, high-dollar ones you see on TV. We suggest resources you can go to for further information. Finally, we even offer some ideas on how to promote and distribute your music video. There's no reason why you can't compete with the pros!

## The 3½ Minute Music Video: Have You Got What It Takes?

To create your own music video, you need three main elements: video footage, audio footage, and an Adobe Premiere computer workstation. The following sections discuss these building blocks in detail.

### Video source material

Because Adobe Premiere 6.0 supports FireWire/i.LINK connections (also known as IEEE 1394), you get the most out of Premiere if your video camera is digital, complete with a FireWire/i.LINK port. If your video camera is a VCR, that's okay because we show you in Chapter 6 how to import analog video and convert it to digital data. Later in the book, we direct you to stock footage libraries, which can provide you with all styles of footage, from sports and landscape footage to Vintage TV commercials and historic films. The footage is there, but it usually comes at a price.

# Audio source material

You can use a CD of your band's original material for your video, or if it's for private use (we call it *fun*), you can use any music in your video. You must, however, convert your audio into a file format that Premiere can read. When you import your video through FireWire connections, the audio signal is captured along with the video. If you are planning on using music from a CD, you need to convert the Compact Disc Audio file, or CDAs, to WAV or AIFF files by using a third-party audio converter application. We prefer Sound Forge, but you may want to use another program. If you're using a Mac, you can import CD files as WAV or AIFF files without having to use a third-party converter.

# Computer hardware requirements

Requirements vary by platform and the type of operations you want to perform with Premiere. Read on to learn about hardware requirements specific to Macintosh and Windows computers.

## Windows

If you are running the Windows operating system, your system will need to meet the following minimum requirements to effectively run Adobe Premiere:

✦ Intel Pentium II processor (300 MHz or faster)

✦ Microsoft Windows 98, Windows 2000, Windows ME, Windows NT 4.0 with Service Pack 6, or Windows XP

✦ 64MB of RAM (128MB or more recommended)

✦ 85MB of available hard-disc space required for installation (40MB for application)

✦ 256-color video display adapter

✦ Large-capacity hard disk or disk array

✦ CD-ROM drive

Additional requirements for DV:

• Intel Pentium III 500MHz or faster (Pentium III 700MHz recommended)

• Windows 98 Second Edition, Windows ME, or Windows 2000

• 128MB RAM (256MB or more recommended)

• Dedicated large capacity 7,200 rpm UDMA 66 IDE or SCSI hard disk or disk array

• Microsoft-certified OHCI IEEE-1394 interface

• Microsoft DirectX-compatible video display adapter (for Windows XP)

• DV Devices Compatibility Matrix

Additional requirements for third-party capture cards:

- Adobe Premiere-certified capture card

### Macintosh

If you are running the Macintosh operating system, your system will need to meet the following minimum requirements to effectively run Adobe Premiere:

- ✦ PowerPC( processor
- ✦ Mac OS software Version 9.0.4
- ✦ 32MB of available RAM (128MB or more recommended)
- ✦ 50MB of available hard drive space required for installation
- ✦ Apple QuickTime 4.1.2
- ✦ Large-capacity hard disk or disk array

Additional requirements for DV:

- PowerPC processor (at least 300 MHz)
- Apple FireWire 2.4
- QuickTime-compatible FireWire (IEEE 1394) interface
- Large-capacity hard disk or disk array (capable of sustaining 5 MB/sec)

# How The Book Is Organized

We've written this book so that you can either read it straight through from start to finish or jump around from chapter to chapter as needed. We include many step-by-step exercises throughout the book that help explain Premiere's capabilities. *Make Your Own Music Videos with Adobe Premiere* is divided into four main parts.

## Part I: Video Killed the Radio Star: Planning Your Masterpiece

Part I serves as an introduction to Premiere as well as an overview of the music video art form. Chapter 1 is a QuickStart video tour, which walks you through the steps you will take to assemble a music video, apply basic effects, and view your finished product. You use video and audio clips available on the CD-ROM for this project. Chapter 2 describes the steps involved in creating a music video, from gathering music and video and using your Premiere software, to finally exporting your video file to various formats. It discusses the hardware you need. Here, we also discuss what it costs to make a video from the basic, bare-bones budget, to optional extras you may consider. Chapter 3 gets you started on conceptualizing your music video. Pete reviews various music videos and tells you what makes some of them great and others not so great. We try to get you brainstorming, and we also point you to places where you can find archived videos for study.

## Part II: Start Me Up: Beginning Your Own Music Video

Part II really gets you going with your own music video project. Chapter 4 helps you tap your creative energies and helps you think more like a cinematographer, recognizing great opportunities for shooting and giving you basic camera techniques. Chapter 5 shows you lighting tricks, slow and fast motion shooting tips, shooting with neutral backgrounds that can later be filled, and other tips for creating special effects while shooting. Chapter 6 shows you how to import your own video clips into your Premiere project. Chapter 7 explains where you can obtain video clips from outside sources.

## Part III: I Want It That Way: Editing Your Music Video

Part III covers everything you need to know about assembling your video. Chapter 8 tells you how to set up your Workspace and Monitor settings and familiarizes you with Adobe's powerful Timeline. Chapter 9 gets you familiar with transitions, including cuts, and various types of fades. Chapter 10 covers adding titles for professional-looking music videos. Chapter 11 shows you how to add sound overdubs in the event that you want your music video to have narration or other special audio effects not present in the music file. Chapter 12 introduces you to all of the built-in special effects available in Premiere.

## Part IV: It Ain't Over 'Til It's Over: Formatting and Distributing Your Video

Part IV covers what you need to know to format and export your video, after you've finished editing it. Chapter 13 shows you how to save and format the video for videotape. To prepare your video for distribution on CD-R, DVD, and the Web, read Chapter 14. Finally, Chapter 15 takes you a step further by sharing the secrets of promoting and distributing your video!

## Part V: Valuable Information

The *Make Your Own Music Videos with Adobe Premiere* appendixes provide a guide to the CD-ROM, a hardware overview, and a list of optional video equipment you might consider owning. They also include a resource guide including recommended reading, Web sites, contests and festivals, stock footage library information, and ideas for distribution.

## Road Diary sidebars

Road Diary entries, in the form of sidebars, recall our personal experiences with the topic discussed in that chapter. They also provide insight into related topics. Think of Road Diary entries as fun "side trips" from the task at hand.

# Conventions Used in This Book

The following conventions are used throughout this book.

## Windows and Macintosh conventions

For cross-platform instructions, the Windows command or key precedes the Macintosh command or key, which is enclosed in parentheses. For example: *Press Enter (Return) to preview the movie.*

## Key combinations

Any Windows combination key commands are indicated with a + connecting the two or more keys. For example, Ctrl+S is how we indicated the Save key combination. For Mac key commands, we connect the keys with a -, as in Shift-T.

Some commands use a single keystroke. In those cases, we put the keyboard key in parentheses, after the button command. For example: Click the Mark In button (I) to mark the in point of the video clip you want to capture.

## Button commands

The first time we refer to any Premiere button, that button appears in the left margin. For example, when we first tell you to click the Play button, you'll know what that button looks like in Premiere, because you'll see it in the margin.

## Menu commands

In this book, two words joined by the character ⇨ represent actions you perform in sequence. For example, if you read File⇨Open, you should click the File menu and then click the Open command in the resulting menu list.

## Typographical conventions

In general, *italics* introduce new terminology. When a word or words are italicized within a quote, it indicates stress on those words. **Bold** type indicates text or numbers that you should type on your keyboard. We have capitalized terminology specific to Premiere's functions, that is: Timeline, Dual View monitor, and so forth.

# Navigating Through This Book

Various signposts and icons are located throughout Make Your Own Music Videos with Adobe Premiere for your assistance. Each chapter begins with an overview of its information and ends with a quick summary, or Chapter Replay.

Icons are placed in the text to highlight important or especially helpful items. Here's a list of the icons and their functions:

 **Tip**        Tips provide you with extra knowledge that separates the novice from the pro.

 **Note**       Notes provide additional or critical information and technical data on the current topic.

 **Cross-Reference**    Cross-Reference icons indicate where you can find more information on a particular topic.

 **Caution**    The Caution icon is your warning of a potential problem or pitfall.

 **On the CD-ROM**    This icon indicates the CD-ROM contains a related file.

# How To Contact Us

We're forever on the road, which means that we stay in touch with just about everyone through e-mail and our Web site. To e-mail questions or comments regarding the material in this book or music videos in general, you can reach us at videokennedy@aol.com. To see our videos as we finish them, click the TV icon on our Web site at www.KennedysMusic.com. While you're there, you can read more entries in our road diary as they come out, hear sound clips from our various CDs, check out our touring schedule to see when we're coming to your town, sign up for the monthly newsletter, buy our CDs, or join the JanglePoets discussion group! To reach us via snail mail, write to The Kennedys, P.O. Box 8461, Reston, VA 20195.

# Acknowledgments

Thanks to Mike Roney for his support and encouragement, and to Tim Borek, Beth Taylor, and Alan Hamill for their fine editing.

Thanks also to Al Smith, Dan Rosenbaum, Rich Stumpf, Jen Balfus, Amy Manegold, Mike Connelly, Peter Primont, Aida Gurwicz, and everyone at Cherry Lane Music; Glenn Dicker, Stephen Judge, David Alston, and everyone at Redeye Distribution; JJ Rassler and everyone at Rounder Records; Anna Borg, Abby Stahlman, and all the staff at Jiffyjam Records; Paula Amato, and Jon Peterson.

Thanks to Danny O, illustrator/artist/ lover of guitars, for creating our sidebar icon.

Thanks to Joe Hansard, Harry Keates, Larry Seese, and Erik Lundblade for their technical advice. Thanks to Greg Lukins for consultation on mixing audio.

Special thanks to Frances and Dan Allman, Brendan Paul, Beatle Bob, Vinnie Santoro, Steve Hansgen, Ron Campbell, and all extras for appearing in our videos.

Thanks to all the writers in our families for setting such a high standard.

Thanks, finally, to Battista's in Las Vegas, NM, The Amphora Diner in Herndon, VA, and Starbucks on Astor Place in New York City for keeping us supplied with sustenance while we wrote this book.

# Contents at a Glance

# Contents

## Part II: Start Me Up: Beginning Your Own Music Video 69

**Part III: I Want It That Way:
Editing Your Music Video**                                    **163**

# Introduction

## The MTV Generation: The Marriage of Music and Video

The MTV generation actually traces its roots back to the very beginnings of cinema. Music was an integral part of the silent movie experience. It was performed live in the theater by brilliant organists and pianists who could improvise soundtracks on the spot. They knew what musical devices would call up feelings of love or loneliness, anger or despair, fear, or determination. They could evoke the pride of a nation or the downfall of a dictator. In movie theaters around the world, music and the on-screen image formed an inseparable alliance early on.

With the coming of sound to films, music became an even more vital part of the movies. Filmmakers, and even animators, could use full symphony orchestras to convey emotion. This is the theme of Walt Disney's animated classic *Fantasia,* a film that has been a major influence on music video.

Musicians also performed on-screen, and if you isolate the performance clips from the rest of the movie, you wind up with something very similar to a modern video. For example, in the classic *Cabin in the Sky,* a moralistic story about a slacker husband and his church-going wife, the band at the local honky tonk is none other than Duke Ellington and his orchestra. The amazing vitality of their performance, complete with wild dancers who foreshadow modern rock dancing, is very close in spirit to the videos favored by today's rock and pop bands. The group is performing live, in their natural element, and the audience is every bit as important as the band. Production techniques have changed, but the basic elements of a great video were already in place in the 1930s.

Many of the earliest jukeboxes featured short film clips, called *soundies*. They had the same purpose as an MTV video. That is, they promoted the visual appeal of the act in the hope that viewers would buy the record. The rise in popularity of rock 'n' roll in the 1950s coincided with the explosion of television as a predominant form of family entertainment. The 1950s were a time when many mothers started working, and teenagers had a window from 3 p.m. to 5 p.m. when they had complete control of the family TV set. The networks began offering shows aimed specifically at teens. Dance parties, especially the phenomenally successful *American Bandstand,* became known as a way for record labels to create overnight stars. The movies picked up on this trend as well, and two films in particular — *The Girl Can't Help It,* featuring Little Richard, and *Rock Around the Clock,* featuring Bill Haley and the Comets — had an impact on rock music's popularity. Some parents were outraged by the unconventional appearance and demeanor of these artists, but a lot of kids fell in love with this new, fun way of looking at life, and a revolution was born.

Why do we picture Buddy Holly with black horn-rim glasses? Why do we imagine Jerry Lee Lewis sliding his foot up and down the piano keyboard? And why do we do the "duck walk" when we imitate Chuck Berry? We recall these things because the television and movie screen imbedded these images in our psyche. As great as their music is, it's the visual image that we recall first when we think of classic rock stars. This is what modern-day record labels are hoping for when they vie for airtime on MTV — a visual image that will become part of youth culture.

The Beatles redefined the on-screen image of the teen idol. What they lacked in traditional stage skills, such as dancing and script reading, they made up for with quick wit and natural screen charisma. In early 1964, after their first round of appearances on *The Ed Sullivan Show*, there was a push in the industry to produce a commercial film with them as the stars. The film, *A Hard Day's Night,* is in many ways the template for all rock video. It's not drama. It's not storytelling. It's about capturing the excitement of rock on the screen.

No one understood the power of television better than former Monkee Mike Nesmith. He produced the first national cable TV video show, *Popclips.* The show was successful enough to give the parent company the confidence to greenlight a full-time video channel, Music Television, or *MTV*. This new content-hungry channel opened its arms to any innovative artist who could fill up four minutes of airtime. MTV made a strong statement by airing, as their very first clip, the Buggles' song "Video Killed the Radio Star." MTV challenged the rock establishment, based as it was on radio and touring. They were airing clips by unknown artists, and clips that wouldn't meet the technical standards of the big-budget networks. The good ones were concept pieces that brought the director in as a member on the band, someone who extended the meaning of the lyrics, and the visual image of the act, beyond their own conception of themselves.

Many people initially viewed MTV as a novelty that would fold up as soon as teens moved on to the next arcade game. But highly stylized, high-quality videos by artists, such as Madonna and Duran Duran suggested a new paradigm. These artists sought to combine the visceral appeal of rock with the visual appeal of fashion, post-modern pop art, and cutting-edge independent film. MTV issued an invitation to creative artists from these media to get involved in this new form of visual rock. When Steve Barron directed Michael Jackson in the "Beat It" video, all the pieces came together. A superstar became a megastar overnight; a cable channel leaped to the forefront of the new information frontier; and a young, wobbly art form found its legs.

# Adobe Premiere: The Best Music Video Production Tool Yet

Why is Adobe Premiere so special, you ask? Premiere contains everything, short of raw footage and music, that you need to make a music video, including capture capabilities, effects, transitions, and export modules that make exporting to the Web, videotape, or CD-ROM a snap.

Premiere provides user-friendly workspaces and palettes, and a creative environment to assemble, edit, and export your videos. Although you may use third-party effects, Adobe provides you with 74 effects (29 of them are Adobe After Effects effects) and 75 transitions! In short, you get all the tools you need in one powerful program.

Because we're equally concerned with audio capabilities when making music videos, Adobe Premiere's audio effects beat those of other video-editing programs, hands down. Adobe offers 21 audio effects including band-pass filters, panning options, compression, EQ, chorus, flanger, echo, delay, and reverb. We love this newer feature mainly because we know we have to compensate for the fact that most people still listen to music through tiny speakers on their computer or on TV. Now we can adjust the EQ for each application! We can also compress the sound files so that our music is at optimum volume.

# Let's Get Ready To Rock

You've got the book. You've got the CD-ROM. We assume that you have access to a computer that meets the system requirements. You probably have some type of video camera. As you begin down your path of music video production, remember this: The sky's the limit, and the best way to get your video noticed is to make it as fresh and unique as you can. You don't necessarily need a lot of money, a big crew, and Michael Jackson to do it (although all three would help)! Use your imagination and shoot for the stars!

# Video Killed the Radio Star: Planning Your Masterpiece

❚

◆ ◆ ◆ ◆

◆ ◆ ◆ ◆

# QuickStart: Producing Your First Music Video Segment

CHAPTER

✦ ✦ ✦ ✦

**In This Chapter**

Making music video tutorial

Importing clips from the CD-/DVD-ROM

Importing audio from the CD-/DVD-ROM

Specifying project settings

Creating a new project

Arranging clips in the Timeline

Adding transitions and effects

Playing back your video segment

✦ ✦ ✦ ✦

**W**elcome to the wonderful world of music video production! We'll waste no time getting you started. The CD-ROM in the back of this book contains all the clips you need for the tutorial in this chapter. For optimal results, copy the *Nickeltown Tour* folder from the enclosed CD-ROM onto your hard drive. If you have two separate drives, copy the folder to an empty drive or a different drive from the one storing the Premiere program. If you need help installing the CD-ROM contents, see Appendix A. Now fire up your computer, load the trial version of Adobe Premiere, and follow these steps!

We advise that you follow this chapter step by step from beginning to end. By doing so, you'll gain enough of a basic working knowledge of Premiere that will enable you to refer to the other chapters out of sequence if you wish to do so. Thus, *Make Your Own Music Videos with Adobe Premiere* can serve you as both a basic primer and an everyday reference manual.

## Starting a New Premiere Project

Premiere refers to each video program you create as a *project*. You must create a project before you can import and edit footage. Follow these steps to start a new project:

1. **Start the Adobe Premiere program.** The first time you start Premiere, the Select Initial Workspace dialog box appears. Select A/B Editing. To find out about other workspaces you can use, see Chapter 8.

2. **The Load Project Settings dialog box appears on your screen.** Click to expand the DV-NTSC folder, and select the Standard 48 kHz preset, as shown in Figure 1-1.

3. **Click OK.** A new Premiere project opens on your screen, consisting of three windows and three floating palettes, as shown in Figure 1-2. Premiere refers to each of the videos you produce as a *project*.

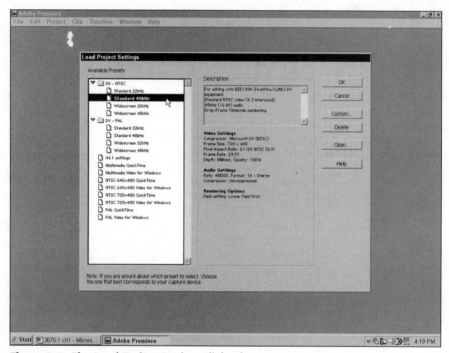

**Figure 1-1:** The Load Project Settings dialog box

Because you selected the A/B Editing workspace in Step 1, the following elements appear on your screen:

✦ Project window

✦ Monitor window

✦ Timeline window

✦ Effects Controls palette

✦ Navigator palette

✦ Transitions palette

Each of these windows can be resized or moved about the screen. To *resize* a window or palette, click the bottom-right corner and drag diagonally, either outward to enlarge it or inward to reduce it. To *move* a window or palette, click its title bar and then drag it with your mouse to its new location in the Premiere application window.

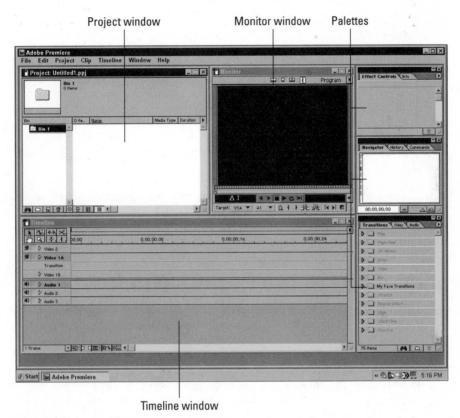

Project window    Monitor window    Palettes

Timeline window

**Figure 1-2:** Each Premiere project displays a Project window, a Monitor window, a Timeline window, and several floating palettes.

# Loading Clips Into Your Project's Bin

Premiere defines the audio, video, and still image footage that make up your project as *clips*. The Project window contains one folder, or *bin,* in which to store these clips. When you produce your own video, you will need to *capture* (that is, transfer from video source to computer) your video clips. Chapter 7 describes the capture process in detail. However, for this tutorial, you need only the clips provided on the CD-ROM.

To import the clips to your project's bin, follow these steps:

1. **Choose File⇨Import⇨Folder.**

2. **Select the Nickeltown Tour folder, which you should have copied from the CD-ROM to your hard drive and click OK.**

3. **The Nickeltown Tour folder, or bin, appears in the Project window (see Figure 1-3).**

4. **Save the Project now, by choosing File⇨Save.** A Save File dialog box appears.

5. **Type** Nickeltown Tour **in the File Name text box and click Save.**

Your project's name now appears in the Project window's title bar. You can open and close any window in your Project, except the Project window, without losing any information. Be sure to save your work before closing the Project window. If you don't, you'll lose any work you've done since the last time you saved your project.

**Tip**   Unsaved information can tax the computer's processor and causes jittery playback. If you experience jitter as the clip plays, optimize the data by saving the project. This bit of housekeeping usually makes ornery clips play back smoothly.

# Opening Clips in the Project Window

You can preview clips before adding them to your Premiere project. Premiere lets you do this easily by opening the clips directly from within the Project window.

Follow these steps to open clips in the Project window:

1. **Double-click the Nickeltown Tour bin in the Project window.** The bin opens to reveal the ten files inside, including eight movie files (.avi), one audio file (.wav), and one title file (.ptl). If you want, you can click and drag the lower-right corner of the Project window to expand it. Figure 1-3 shows the different parts of the Project window

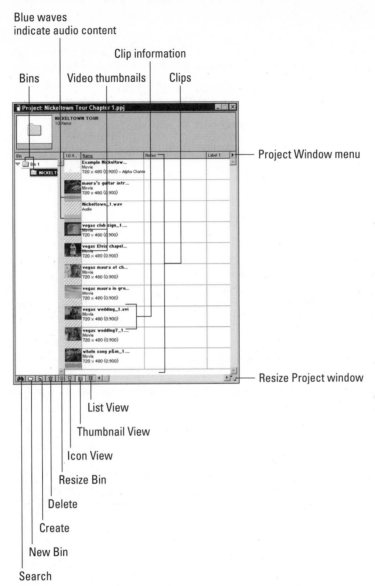

Blue waves
indicate audio content

Clip information

Bins    Video thumbnails    Clips

Project Window menu

Resize Project window

List View

Thumbnail View

Icon View

Resize Bin

Delete

Create

New Bin

Search

**Figure 1-3:** The Project window

2. **Click the Project Window Menu button and then select Thumbnail view.** In
   this mode, a thumbnail icon represents each item.

3. **Look at the Name column.** Each item has a name and is identified as either a movie or an audio clip.

4. **Now look at each thumbnail. Three of the items have a blue audio wave along the bottom, indicating that the clip includes audio.**

5. **Double-click the thumbnail of the file titled** `maura's guitar intro.avi`. The clip opens in its own Clip window.

6. **Press the L key on your keyboard to play the clip.**

7. **Close the Clip window when you've finished.**

You can open each clip in the bin following these same instructions.

## Creating a storyboard

A *storyboard* isn't actually part of your music video, but we've found it to be a great tool for outlining your video, based on the clips you have on hand. Professional cinematographers and videographers use hand-drawn storyboards all the time. Premiere offers storyboards that use stills from your clips as visual aids. What's more, you can add text to each image to further describe what your final video will look like.

## Loading clips into a storyboard

Follow these steps to place clips into a storyboard:

1. **Choose File⇨New⇨Storyboard.**

2. **Drag the Nickeltown Tour bin from the Project window into the Storyboard window.** Figure 1-4 shows what the Storyboard should look like.

Each clip in the storyboard contains a still, or poster frame, from the clip, the name and duration of the clip, and an area where you can type in descriptive information. The Storyboard window can be resized by dragging the bottom-right corner of the window in or out.

Duration of clip

Name of clip

Space for descriptive text

Filmstrip and speaker together indicate both audio and video content

Storyboard window menu

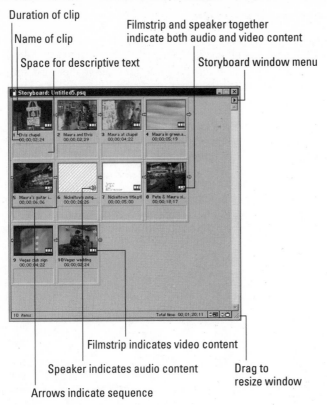

Filmstrip indicates video content

Speaker indicates audio content

Arrows indicate sequence

Drag to resize window

**Figure 1-4:** The Storyboard window

## Adding text to storyboard

When creating a storyboard, we usually type in the song lyrics below each clip. If a clip is more suited for an instrumental section of the song, we type a note suggesting that as well. You can add any kind of text to your storyboard that will help you organize your clips.

1. **Double-click the rectangular area below the clip named** `Nickeltown` `title.ptl`. The Edit Note dialog box appears.

2. **Position your cursor inside the Edit Note dialog box and type** Nickeltown Title. You can type any kind of description in this area.

3. **Click OK.**

## Determining contents of clips

Each clip in your Storyboard window contains an image in the bottom-right corner indicating whether the clip contains video, audio, or both. A small filmstrip icon indicates video material, as in the `Elvis chapel.avi` clip. A speaker icon indicates audio material, as in the `Nickeltown song.wav` clip. When a clip contains both video and audio material, both icons are present, as is the case with the `maura's guitar intro.avi` clip.

## Arranging clip order

Rearrange the clips within the Storyboard by dragging and dropping them. Don't worry about overwriting Clip 1. The clips know to move forward a space. By using Storyboards before actually arranging your clips to make your video, you visualize what you have in the can already, and you can determine if you need more footage to complete the story. Now, drag the clips around within the Storyboard so that they're in the order shown in Figure 1-5.

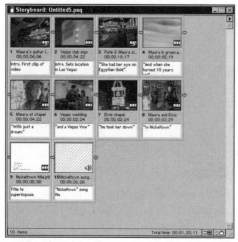

**Figure 1-5:** Arrange clips in the Storyboard window as seen here. Note the descriptive text that was added.

## Printing, naming, and saving your storyboard

You can print your Storyboard the way you would print any document by choosing File➪Print. To save your Storyboard, choose File➪Save and specify the filename and location.

# Arranging Your Clips in the Timeline

You sequence your clips in the Timeline to assemble your music video. You can move a clip into the Timeline by dragging it from the Project window or from the Storyboard window.

## Placing the audio clip on the Audio track

Locate the `Nickeltown song.wav` file in either the Project window or the Storyboard window, and drag it to the Audio 1 track on the Timeline, as shown in Figure 1-6. Make sure that the clip snaps to the beginning of the Timeline by dragging it flush left.

You will build your video clips to this audio track, so you don't want to accidentally change or move it. To prevent inadvertent changes to the Audio 1 track, click the Lock/Unlock Track button of the Audio 1 track, just to the right of the speaker icon at the left edge of the track in the Timeline. You should see a padlock icon when this option is turned on.

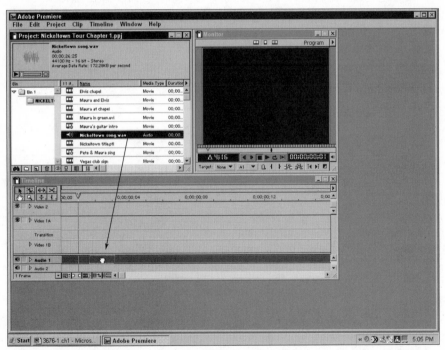

**Figure 1-6:** Drag the audio clip from the bin to the Audio 1 track on the Timeline.

## Understanding the Timeline

The Timeline shows the audio track you just dragged and dropped as a blue rectangle. The name of the clip appears in the rectangle. Figure 1-7 shows all the significant parts of the Timeline. When you drop the clip onto the Timeline, a yellow bar appears along the top of the Timeline. It's exactly as long as the audio clip, and it has a little arrow at each end. This is called the Work Area bar, and it delineates the borders of the beginning and the ending of the video. The bar automatically extends as you add more clips.

Just below the Work Area bar is the Time Ruler, which measures time along the Timeline like a ruler. If you look toward the bottom-left corner of the Timeline, you should see the Time Zoom level. You can zoom in to see a clip frame by frame or zoom out to see an entire song on the Timeline. For now, click the Time Zoom Level menu and select 2 Seconds from the resulting pop-up menu.

The Edit Line marker is the pointer that sits on the Time Ruler. By moving the Edit Line marker along the Timeline, you can easily navigate around your video. Find the Edit Line marker and drag it forward along the Timeline to see and hear the video and audio material in the Timeline. Dragging in this manner, as opposed to playing the Timeline smoothly in real time, is called *scrubbing*. To play the video in real time, press the spacebar. The spacebar works as an on/off switch for playing the sequence of clips in the Timeline.

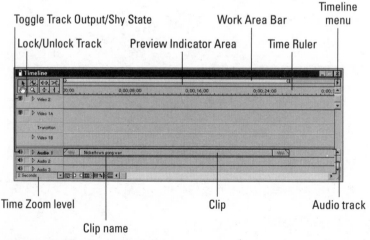

**Figure 1-7:** The Timeline window

# Placing the first video clip on the Video track

Now that you've given the music video a song, you can add visual content, such as video clips and still images, from your bin or Storyboard window. To place a video clip in the Timeline, follow these steps:

1. **Locate** maura's guitar intro.avi **in the Storyboard window and drag it to the Video 1A track.** (Place the clip at the very beginning of the Timeline.)

After you've dropped the video clip onto its track, another clip of the same title and duration appears in the Audio 2 track. This happens because this clip contains both audio and video material. In this case, the audio and video material is separated in the Timeline. The video information is placed on a Video track, and the audio information is placed on an Audio track. If you click and drag either clip up and down the Timeline, the corresponding clip is dragged with it. The tracks are linked in this way. If you delete the audio clip from the Timeline, you also delete its corresponding video clip. When you delete a clip from the Timeline, you do not delete the actual clip; you delete the placement of the clip in the Timeline.

2. **Drag the Edit Line marker to the beginning of the Timeline.**

3. **Press the spacebar to play the video.** The video plays in the Monitor window, and you'll hear both audio clips play at the same time. The audio portion of the video plays later than the music on the Audio 1 track. In other words, the clips are out of synch, and you have to put them in synch with each other (covered in the following section).

## Synching video to audio

Use the audio portion of the maura's guitar intro.avi clip as a tool to line up or *synch*, the video to the Nickeltown song.wav audio clip. There's no real scientific way to do this; you just have to use your ears and your eyes.

Follow these steps to synchronize video to the audio clip:

1. **Delete all clips from the Timeline except** Nickeltown song.wav.

2. **Drag the Edit Line marker to the beginning of the Timeline.**

3. **Press the spacebar to start playback of the Timeline.** Notice that the music volume doesn't fade in; the guitar strums right away at normal volume.

4. **Press the spacebar again to stop.**

5. **Double-click** maura's guitar intro.avi **in the Project window.** A Clip window opens, which displays the first frame of that clip. See Figure 1-8 to identify the elements of the Clip window.

6. **Play the Clip window's clip by either pressing the spacebar or by clicking the Clip window's Play button.**

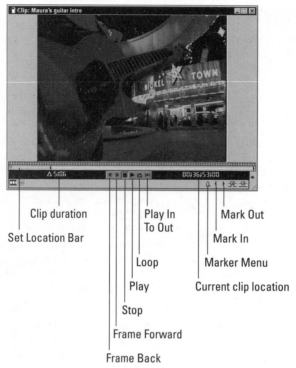

Clip duration

Set Location Bar

Play In
To Out

Loop

Play

Stop

Frame Forward

Frame Back

Mark Out

Mark In

Marker Menu

Current clip location

**Figure 1-8:** The Clip window

## Editing the in point

Most of the time, your clips will contain superfluous material, that is, more footage than you want to use in your Premiere project. You can edit the clips to create new starting points, or *in points*. In the audio portion of the `maura's guitar intro.avi` clip, you can hear a little pause before Maura starts strumming the guitar, so you'll need to edit that part out. The desired effect is to have the guitar strum in the video track at the same time it's strummed in the audio track.

Follow these steps to edit the beginning of the clip:

1. **In the Clip window, drag the Edit Line marker to where you first hear the guitar strum (00;36;54;00).**

2. **Mark this as an in point by either choosing Mark⇨In from the Marker Menu or by pressing the I key.**

 3. **Click the Play In To Out button to play the clip starting at the new in point.**

4. **Drag the clip from the Clip window to the Video 1A track in the Timeline, flush left.** You may need to resize the Clip window to see the target video track. Premiere automatically places the audio portion of `maura's guitar intro.avi` on the Audio 2 track.

5. **Close the Clip window.**

6. **Drag the Edit Line Marker to the beginning of the Timeline and press the spacebar to play the video.**

What you hear is a combination of the `Nickeltown song.wav` audio clip and the audio portion of `maura's guitar intro.avi`. The clips are much more in synch now than they were before you edited the in point. When the Edit Line marker moves beyond the range of the first video clip, you'll hear the volume drop as the audio clip on the Audio 2 track drops out.

Because the audio is close and only needs slight adjusting, at this point, editing without hearing the Audio 2 track is easier. You started out putting these two tracks together by using your ears to locate the beginning of the song. Now you'll use your eyes to match up the visual of the guitar strumming to the sound of the guitar on the Audio 1 track. *Remember, the sound on the Audio 1 track is the only sound that will be in the final video.* You should use the music on the Audio 2 track only as a guide.

## Deleting unwanted audio

If you try to erase an audio track that is linked to a video track, both tracks will be erased, unless you first take the video and audio out of synch by pressing the Toggle Synch Mode button at the bottom of the Timeline window to take the Audio and Video tracks out of synch.

Follow these steps to delete unwanted audio from a video clip:

1. **Click the Toggle Synch Mode button to take the video and audio tracks out of synch.** See Figure 1-9.

2. **Select Maura's guitar intro clip on the Audio 2 track.**

3. **Press the Delete or Backspace key on your keyboard.** The corresponding clip on the Video 1 track was not deleted because the video and audio tracks are no longer linked.

4. **Check to see how the video and audio is synched at this point by pressing the Play In To Out button on the Monitor window.** The video is now in synch with the audio!

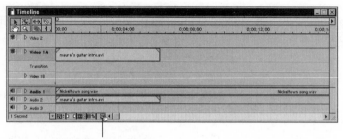

Toggle Synch Mode

**Figure 1-9:** Take the video and audio tracks out of synch by clicking the Toggle Synch Mode button on the bottom of the Timeline.

5. **Now drag the Edit Line marker to the beginning of the Timeline.**

6. **Click Play.**

## Editing the out point

Just as you can edit the in point of your clips, you can also edit the clips to create new endings, or *out points*. Because the acoustic guitar strums to the beat of the song, it will help you to think of this song in "beats." Because the acoustic guitar plays each beat with a *downstroke* on the guitar, you can use that as a guide to the beats. A downstroke is each time the hand strums the guitar from the top downward. You will see an *upstroke* in between each downstroke. The very first sound on this audio track is a downstroke. It's your job to match the downstrokes of the video with the downstrokes of the audio.

We used the first nine downstrokes of this clip as our first clip of the video. This clip contains eleven downstrokes, so you need to edit out the last two downstrokes by changing the out point. Here's how:

1. **Double-click the** `maura's guitar intro.avi` **clip on the Video 1A track.** The Clip window opens.

2. **Click the Play In To Out button.**

3. **Count the downstrokes as the video clip plays.**

4. **When you count the ninth downstroke, press the spacebar to stop playing the clip.** The actual frame that we stopped on is 00;36;58;05.

5. **To mark the same out point that we used, drag the Edit Line marker to 00;36;58;05.**

6. **Press the O key to set this out point.** After you set the out point, the Apply button appears below the transports.

Apply

7. **Click the Apply button to apply the changes to the clip in the Timeline.** If you close the Clip window without applying the out point, you will lose your out point and have to reset it.

**8. Close the Clip window.**

**9. Click the Play In To Out button on the Monitor window.**

You have successfully synched your first clip to the audio track and edited the clip's duration.

## Look for the light

**Road Diary**

It has been said that good lighting makes the difference between a good video and a bad one. If that's true, then we should have given up at the start, because we didn't have any lights, good or bad. But ignorance and lack of funds worked in our favor. Because we couldn't set up elaborate gear, we just traveled to places that had interesting existing light and shot there! Our early experience taught us to always look for the available light first and then add to it if we needed to. If the existing light was sufficient, we stuck with it, and we still do.

Our friend Kate Wolf wrote a song about an elderly man who lived on a farm in Oklahoma. She was visiting him, and when she was leaving the house one day, he pulled her aside. His hearing was weak, so he spoke in a loud voice. "Look for the light," he said. "You gotta look for the light!" He wasn't speaking figuratively. He really meant it. And it was good advice. Everything that we see, we see because light is falling on it. Thomas Edison opened up the nighttime to new possibilities by making light readily available at all hours, and film made illuminated images portable. When we shoot video, it is the light falling on objects that we are shooting. So light is the essence of visual art. Get in the habit of looking for it. When you walk into a room or into a natural environment, keep in mind that you can see things because light is coming from somewhere. Where's it coming from? What is the source? What direction is it coming from? Is it shining directly or reflecting off of something? Where does it make shadows fall? When you look at a face, is it completely or partially lit? What mood does the light create?

Master painters have spent centuries studying light, and present-day cinematographers study painters to see how light can bring objects to life. During the Renaissance, painters began portraying real people in real situations, and they drew their subjects lit by light from a believable source. Rembrandt, for example, did a number of self-portraits, and he lit his own face from above and to the right. Doing this created a realistic character, with shadows falling across parts of his face. We can see that he is "one of us," but we don't know everything about him. He has emotions, he has a complex personality, and his face conceals as much as it reveals. The 17th century Dutch painter Jan Vermeer painted many of his subjects in their homes, and he used the natural light coming in through windows to illuminate them. Study how he uses shadows, stained glass, and reflections to bring his characters to life. When you look at a painting, look for the light, just as you would in a "real" situation. Then, when you look through your viewfinder, especially if you use an LCD screen, think of the shot as a painting and consider how the light is helping you tell the story. What does it reveal about your subject and what does shadow conceal?

*Continued*

*Continued*

In the film *The Godfather,* cinematographer Gordon Willis used two basic lighting schemes. When the gangsters were with their families, the shots were brightly lit with sunlight and overexposed to look like 1950s era family photos. When the heavies went behind closed doors, they were in shadow, with yellow filtered light creeping in. The lighting reinforced the basic images of good and evil. The gangsters' faces, in these darkened scenes, were lit from directly above. This angle is not normally used because it puts the subjects eyes in shadow. This creates a feeling of unease in the viewer. When we communicate with some- one, we take signals from their eyes. But in this film, we can't tell what Marlon Brando is thinking, because we can see the set of his jaw, but we can't read his eyes. The shadows tell us that he's in control, and he's probably up to no good. Consider how you would light the face of Katrina and the Waves singing, "Walking on Sunshine" versus "White Wedding" by Billy Idol. How would you use light and shadow to make the singer in your band look friendly or mysterious to reinforce a lyric?

# Placing the vegas club sign.avi clip on the Video track

Drag the `vegas club sign.avi` clip from the bin or storyboard onto the Video 1A track, flush left to the first clip. You've just created the simplest type of transition — the cut. There is no fade-in or fade-out in a cut. One clip ends and the next begins right away. Play the video through the first two clips.

## Changing the speed of a video clip

We love timing visuals with rhythmic beats in our videos. You may decide that this is your style too, but it's not a rule, by any means. The three lights that comprise the sign in this clip turn on in sequence. In the clip's unedited state, the sign lights up at a quicker tempo than the beat of the song. Your goal here is to match each light to consecutive downbeats. Premiere offers the option of adjusting the speed of a video clip.

To synch the speed of the light sequence to the tempo of the downbeat, follow these steps:

1. **Select the** `vegas club sign.avi` **clip in the Timeline.**

2. **Choose Clip⇨Speed.**

3. **Type in** 70.

**Note**

A number lower than 100 slows down the clip, adding length to the duration. A number higher than 100 speeds up the clip, shortening its duration.

4. **Click OK.**

A red bar appears directly under the Work Area bar, along the length of the clip whose speed you just adjusted. The appearance of this red bar means that you made an adjustment that has yet to be processed or rendered. The next section shows you how to render your edits.

## Building a preview

Premiere builds previews for all the clips to which you apply effects. Before you can view the effected clips fully processed, you need to render the effects by building previews. To build a preview of all the material in the Timeline, press the Enter (Return) key on your keyboard. After you do that, a Building Preview status bar appears, indicating how many frames and how much time the Preview will take to build. The video then plays automatically from the beginning when the preview is complete. A green bar replaces the red bar when Premiere finishes building the preview.

## Editing the in point of the clip

The tempo of the lights now matches the tempo of the music, but they come in *behind the beat*, or after the downbeat. You need to line up the visual "beat" of the first light coming on to the musical downbeat.

To remove some frames from the beginning of the clip, follow these steps:

1. **Double-click the** `vegas club sign.avi` **clip on the Video 1A track. The Clip window opens.**

2. **Use the right-arrow key to move to frame 00;10;53;27.**

3. **Press the I key to set the in point.**

4. **Click the Apply button below the transport buttons in the Clip window.**

5. **Close the Clip window.**

6. **Drag the** `vegas club sign.avi` **clip flush right to the** `maura's guitar intro.avi` **clip in the Timeline.**

7. **Press Enter (Return) to build the preview.**

## Editing the end of the clip

The `vegas club sign.avi` clip is still running when the vocal line comes in. The objective here is to stop the `vegas club sign.avi` clip from displaying just before the vocals start.

To edit the out point of the clip, do this:

1. **Drag the Timeline's Edit Line marker to where the vocal comes in (around 00;00;08;06).** Use the arrow keys on your keyboard for precision placement.

2. **Position the cursor over the right edge of the clip in the Timeline window so that the Selection tool turns into a Trim tool.**

3. **Drag the end of the clip to the left, stopping at the edit line.**

4. **Release the mouse button.**

5. **Build the preview by pressing the Enter (Return) key.**

## Cropping a clip

The `vegas club sign.avi` clip was filmed in "old movie mode" on our camcorder. Aside from adding a cool sepia effect to this clip, it also gives the clip the illusion of being wide-screen, by adding areas of black on the top and bottom of the moving image. If your entire video is shot in this mode, you could just leave it alone for a continuous old-time effect, but because it's the only clip in this video that was shot in old movie mode, you'll have to crop the clip with a video effect to make it uniform with the surrounding clips.

To crop the clip, perform the following steps:

1. **Choose Window⇨Show Video Effects.**

2. **Click the Find Video Effect button, represented as a binoculars icon, at the bottom of the Video Effects palette, as shown in Figure 1-10.** Premiere provides nearly 100 different video effects in the Effects palette. You can either look through them all by hand — which we recommend you do at some point to familiarize yourself with the available effects — or you can search for the effect you want using this find feature.

Find

**Figure 1-10:** The Video Effects palette find tool enables you to quickly search Premiere's video effects.

3. **Type the word** crop **in the Find Video Effect text box that appears on your screen.**

4. **Click the Expand Folders box, so that a check mark appears.**

5. **Click Find.**

6. **The folder containing the Crop effect (the Transform folder) expands, and the searched effect is selected.** Click Done.

7. **Drag the Crop effect from the Video Effects palette to the** `vegas club sign.avi` **clip.** A green bar appears at the top edge of the clip in the Timeline, indicating that an effect has been applied. The Effect Controls palette opens on your desktop, and the Crop effect controls are displayed.

8. **Resize the Effect Controls palette by dragging the lower-right corner of the palette to reveal all the controls for this effect.**

9. **Crop the top of the clip by dragging the Crop Top slider in the Effect Controls palette from 0 to 10 and crop the bottom of the clip by dragging the Crop Bottom slider from 0 to 10, as shown in Figure 1-11.**

10. **Render the work area by pressing Enter (Return).**

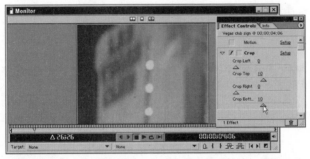

**Figure 1-11:** The Effect Controls palette displays different controls for each applied effect.

# Synching the Pete & Maura sing clip to the audio

Drag the `Pete & Maura sing.avi` clip from the bin or Storyboard to track Video 1A in the Timeline, flush left with the last clip. You need to synch this clip with the music. It has audio material that will help you do this. Synching is most important in the placement of this clip, because the subjects are actually singing, and you want to make it look realistic. Make sure that the Toggle Synch Mode button is switched on.

## Setting the in point

Here, you should use the same techniques you used earlier when synching up the guitar intro in the section "Synching video to audio."

1. **The vocal starts right up at the end of the preceding clip, so the best way to synch this clip to the audio is to first toggle the Audio 1 track output to shy state, which mutes the track's audio.** Click the speaker icon at the left edge of Audio 1 track, so the icon disappears to make the audio track shy, as illustrated in Figure 1-12.

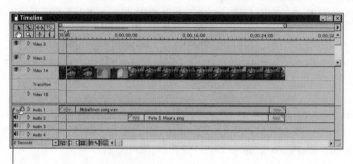

Toggle Track Output/Shy State

**Figure 1-12:** The Toggle Track Output/Shy State button turns a track on or off, without deleting the track from the Timeline.

2. **Drag the Edit Line marker just to the left of the** `Pete & Maura sing.avi` **clip and then press the spacebar to play.**

3. **When you hear the vocal entrance, press the spacebar to stop.**

4. **Position the cursor over the left edge of the clip until it turns into the Trim tool.**

5. **Drag the in point to the Edit Line. Slide the clip flush left with the previously placed clip.**

6. **Toggle the Audio 1 track back out of its shy state.**

7. **Make the Audio 2 track shy.**

8. **Make the necessary placement adjustments to make the video and audio synch up perfectly.** (You may need to resize the Monitor window to see if the lip-synching works. If so, drag the lower-right corner of the Monitor window downward.)

If the video seems to be ahead of the audio or rushing, you need to add frames to the beginning of the clip. Slide the clip to the right by clicking the clip and dragging it to the right in the Timeline, and use the Trim tool to click and drag the in point to the left. If the video seems to lag behind the beat of the audio, you need to remove frames by dragging the in point to the right and sliding the video flush left to the preceding clip.

### Setting the out point

Although the `Pete & Maura sing.avi` clip contains an entire verse, you'll only use the first line of the song: "She had her eye on Egyptian gold." You need to set the out point to truncate the clip.

1. **Drag the out point of the `Pete & Maura sing.avi` clip to the left to include only the portion of the clip that ends with the word** *gold*.

2. **When the clip is in synch, take the video and audio tracks out of synch by clicking the Toggle Synch Mode button.**

3. **Delete the corresponding audio clip from Audio 2 track.** (See the section "Deleting unwanted audio" earlier in this chapter.)

## Placing the Maura in green.avi video clip into the Timeline

The next clip further establishes the wackiness of Las Vegas by showing Maura in a head-to-toe, lime-green polyester bellbottom pantsuit! To add this clip to the Timeline, follow these steps:

1. **Double-click the `Maura in green.avi` clip to open it in a Clip window.**

2. **Drag the Clip window's Set Location Marker left or right so that the Current Clip Location reads 00;46;47;07.**

3. **Press the I key to set the in point.**

4. **Drag the Set Location Marker to where the Current Clip Location reads 00;46;50;25.**

5. **Press the O key to set the out point.**

6. **Drag the clip from the Clip window to the Video 1 track of the Timeline, flush left with the last clip on that track.**

**Tip**    You should save your work periodically as you edit your video to avoid the risk of accidentally losing work if either Premiere or your whole system crashes.

## Cross-dissolving into the next clip

The next transition is not a cut, like the transitions so far. The clip you just placed in the Timeline *cross-dissolves* into the next clip. To apply a Transition, you must first have two video clips that overlap on two different video tracks on the Timeline. You then apply a Transition onto the Transition track.

## Positioning clips

Follow these steps:

1. Double-click the `Maura at chapel.avi` clip to open the Clip window.

2. Edit the clip's in point to be 00;53;53;01.

3. Edit the out point to be 00;53;55;22.

4. **Drag the clip over the Timeline's Video 1B track so that it slightly overlaps with the previous clip on the Video 1A track.** You want the clips to overlap because in a cross dissolve, which is the transition you will apply, you blend one clip with the next.

5. **Click and drag the Edit Line Marker to be placed over the overlapping clips.**

6. **Select 1 Frame in the Time Zoom Level.**

7. **Click and drag the** `Maura at chapel.avi` **clip to overlap by between 15 and 20 frames.**

## Applying the transition

After overlapping the video clips, you're ready to choose a transition from the floating Transitions palette.

To select and apply a transition to a clip, follow these steps:

1. **Click the Transitions tab on the Video Effects palette, as shown in Figure 1-13.** If the Palette is not visible, choose Window⇨Show Video Effects.

2. **Click the Search icon (binoculars) at the bottom of the palette.**

**Figure 1-13:** The Transitions share a palette with the Video Effects.

3. **Type** Cross Dissolve.

4. **Click Find.**

5. **When the Cross Dissolve transition is located, click Done.**

6. **Drag the Cross Dissolve transition to the Transition track between Video 1A and Video 1B tracks.** Position it exactly where the two clips overlap. It should be flush left with the beginning of the clip in the Video 1B track and flush right with the end of the clip in the Video 1A track. Premiere automatically sizes the Transition to fit the overlapping clips. (See Figure 1-14.)

7. **Build the preview by pressing Enter (Return).**

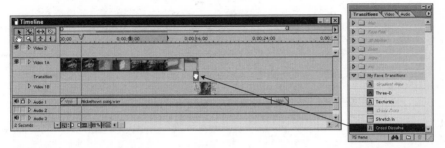

**Figure 1-14:** Drag transitions to the Transition track, between two overlapping Video 1A and Video 1B clips.

If you don't render the work area, the monitor screen goes black, and a small white *x* appears, indicating an effect that needs to be rendered.

Why some transitions are straight cuts and others are dissolves is a matter of personal style. In this video sequence, we used cuts at the beginning of the video to establish the style and location of the song. Almost immediately, the lyrics flash back to "... when she turned 18 years old, with just a dream and a Vegas vow...." That flashback, along with the dream-like lyrics suggested a dreamier transition, and Cross Dissolve was our transition of choice.

## Raiding the rag and bone shop

**Road Diary**

We never pass a vintage clothing store without grabbing the camera. To some, it might be a junkshop, but to us, it's a storehouse of potential free props. Ask for permission to shoot some video. The person at the register is usually the owner. They don't make enough money to hire staff. We've been turned down, usually in places where they figure they can make money renting out the stuff for movies. That's okay; they're eking out a living in the alternative world, so more power to them. Most times, though, they get behind the idea. We usually start by interviewing the owner. Most of them are people who have traveled a lot. You cover a lot of miles in the search for vintage kitsch. Some of them are people who lived for years in the straight world and then chucked it all for a life selling polyester shirts to fledgling rock bands. Like I said, more power to them. They let us spend the day shooting in their store, and we give them a plug on stage at our next gig.

*Continued*

*Continued*

Anyway, with the interview in the can, we start looking through the racks for cool stuff. Polyester shirts from the 1970s are great on-screen, providing instant color. Groovy wigs abound, and other props are often scattered around. Basically, we co-opt the ambience of the place, which usually could be summed up in one word: *Groovy*.

We were shooting our video for "Free" on the streets of Athens, Georgia, when we came across a great thrift shop. The owner was glad to give us the run of the place, and we scored a lot of shots there. She had a super-cool 1960s-era eight-track player, with a built-in mirror ball! We found that, by shooting close-ups of the mirror ball, we could get great retro looking lighting effects, with the colors changing randomly as the orb moved around. Some of the cheesier shots were reminiscent of Peter Fonda's seminal film *The Trip*, one of the first hippie movies. Fonda's film would meander away from reality into lens-filling kaleidoscopic effects, a technique we frequently find useful, especially when we don't have any good clips left in the bin. There was also a great old velvet couch, and Maura started grabbing vintage clothes. I recall a lot of leopard skin. We started lip-synching "Free." I remember wearing a huge cowboy hat at one point. Budget for costumes and effects on this shoot — zero. Thank heaven for the quirky nationwide network of thrift shop gypsies. By the way, avoid any place with the word Antique out front. They'll call the police if you even look like a musician, a guerilla filmmaker, or anything other than a rich potential customer. Look for the words "thrift," "vintage," or "junk," and avoid the A-word.

## Placing the remaining clips in the Timeline

The remaining clips will round out the video segment by introducing the Las Vegas wedding scenario into the story. To add remaining clips to the Timeline, follow these steps:

1. **Drag the** `Vegas wedding.avi` **clip to the Timeline's Video 1A track and overlap it with the** `Maura at chapel.avi` **clip by about the same margin.**

2. **Apply the Cross Dissolve transition between the Vegas wedding clip on track Video 1A and the** `Maura at chapel.avi` **clip on track Video 1B.** (See the section "Cross-dissolving into the next clip.") Figure 1-15 shows a detail of this cross dissolve transition.

3. **Build the preview.** (See the section "Building a preview," earlier in this chapter.)

4. **Drag the** `Elvis chapel.avi` **clip to the Video 1A track, flush left with the last clip.** This is another cut, as opposed to a cross-fade transition.

5. **Drag the** `Maura and Elvis.avi` **clip from the bin or Storyboard window to the Video 1A track, flush left with the** `Elvis chapel.avi` **clip.** This is another cut.

6. **The end of this clip jumps to a useless shot of the back of our van.** Edit the out point so that the clip ends just before this, when Elvis gives the thumbs up.

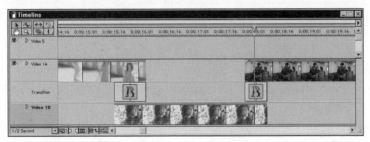

**Figure 1-15:** Detail of Cross Dissolve transition between two clips

# Adding Video Effects

The video tour is now in sequence, with the proper cuts and transitions all in place. You can give this sequence more life with a few simple video effects.

## Adjusting brightness and contrast

The `Pete & Maura sing.avi` clip is nice, but it's quite dark. We can, however, use one of Premiere's Video Effects to brighten it up. Here's how:

1. **Click the Video tab on the Video Effects palette.**

2. **Expand the Adjust folder, by clicking the right-pointing arrow to the left of the Adjust folder in the Video Effects palette.**

3. **Select the Brightness and Contrast effect and drag it to the** `Pete & Maura sing.avi` **clip on track Video 1A in the Timeline.**

4. **The Effect Controls palette opens to reveal the available controls for this effect.**

5. **Set the Brightness by dragging the triangle-shaped slider to 60.**

6. **Set the Contrast, this time by clicking the underlined Contrast value number.**

7. **Type in** 60.3.

8. **Click OK.** You can set Brightness and Contrast by using either of the two above procedures.

## Changing the color balance

Because the first lyric sets the stage with, "She had her eye on Egyptian gold," we wanted to reflect the magic of the dream of Las Vegas riches, by having the clip's overall hue turn to gold. You can do this by adjusting the color balance and then applying a *keyframe*. A keyframe changes an effect over time. You may define as many keyframes as you want in each clip. Premiere automatically sets two keyframes — one at the beginning and one at the end of each clip. By defining an effect's values at the beginning of the clip and changing the values at a later point in the clip, you give the effect motion.

Follow these steps to adjust color balance:

1. **Locate the Color Balance video effect in the Adjust folder of the Video Effects palette.**

2. **Drag the Color Balance effect over the** `Pete & Maura sing.avi` **clip in the Timeline.**

3. **The Effect Controls palette now adds the Color Balance effect, below the Brightness and Contrast effect you applied in the last exercise.** The Effect Controls palette reflects the effects of whichever clip is currently selected.

4. **Click the Enable Keyframing box of the Color Balance settings in the Effect Controls palette, as shown in Figure 1-16.**

Enable Keyframing

**Figure 1-16:** The Enable Keyframing box enables you to change video effects on a clip over time.

5. **Expand the Video 1A track by clicking the arrow on the left side of the Video 1A track.**

6. **Drag the Edit Line marker to where you hear the word "gold."** We want the gold video effect to be fully in place by this point in the clip.

7. **Adjust the Color Balance controls in the Effect Controls palette as such: Red = 100, Green = 178, and Blue = 0.** You may need to scroll down to display settings. These settings result in an overall yellow hue.

8. **Click the Next Frame arrow on the left edge of the Timeline, as shown in Figure 1-17.** The Edit Line marker then moves to the next keyframe.

9. **Set this keyframe's parameters to the same values you set in Step 7 to apply the gold effect throughout the rest of the clip.**

10. **Build your preview.** (See the section "Building a preview" earlier in this chapter.)

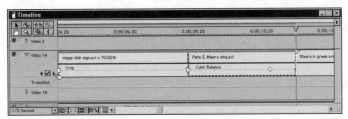

**Figure 1-17:** Advance to the next keyframe by clicking the Next Frame arrow in the expanded video track.

# Hyping colors with Brightness and Contrast

*Hyped color*, also known as color saturation, is very important in music videos. You have three and a half minutes to capture your viewer's attention, and hyping the colors is a proven way to do just that. After you set the parameters of an effect that you are going to use over and over, you don't need to redefine the settings each time. We used the same Brightness and Contrast settings in several of our clips.

1. **Drag the Brightness and Contrast effect to the** `Maura in green.avi` **clip on the Timeline.**

2. **Set the Brightness for 19.7.**

3. **Set the Contrast for 45.9.**

4. **Build your preview.** Notice that the greens are much more vivid, reflecting the flashiness of Las Vegas.

5. **While the** `Maura in green.avi` **clip is still selected, choose Edit⇨Copy.**

6. **Select the** `Maura at chapel.avi` **clip.**

7. **Choose Edit⇨Paste Attributes.**

8. **Select Settings and check only the Filters box, as shown in Figure 1-18.**

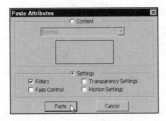

**Figure 1-18:** The Paste Attributes feature enables you to apply settings you frequently use, without having to go through all the setup steps each time.

9. Click Paste.

10. Select the `Vegas wedding.avi` **clip.**

11. Choose **Edit**➪**Paste Attributes Again.**

12. **Press Enter (Return) to render the work area.**

13. The `Vegas wedding.avi` **clip still seems a little dark. Select that clip.**

14. **In the Effect Controls window, set the Brightness value to 45.9 and the Contrast value to 65.6.**

## Blurring a clip

We wanted to give a slight blur to the `Maura at chapel.avi` clip, suggesting the dream that's reflected in the lyrics.

Here's how you blur the clip:

1. **Open the Blur folder in the Video Effects palette.**

2. **Select Antialias and drag it to the** `Maura at chapel.avi` **clip.** Antialias is one of the few Premiere video effects that is either on or off — it offers no other settings to configure.

## The best Elvis on the Vegas strip

**Road Diary**

By the way, you're probably wondering who portrays the groovy Elvis in our Vegas clips. It's Brendan Paul, the top Elvis interpreter on the scene today. If you've ever seen the 1968 Singer TV special, you know the intense dynamism that Elvis generated when he was at his best, and Brendan embodies that excitement and charisma. He's usually jetting around the country doing high-priced gigs, so weddings aren't normally his thing, but we lucked out. He happened to be in town and he had an hour free the afternoon we renewed our vows, so we were able to snag him. He not only gives the coolest reading of the wedding vows, but he sings several songs as well, including, "It's Now or Never." Because we knew the Jordannaires' parts we joined right in on the background vocals. It was a day we'll always remember, and the video footage is one of the gems of our collection. In fact, we were in Los Angeles a few weeks after the ceremony, and our van disappeared, towed away by the LAPD. Our first reaction was, "Oh, my gosh! The Elvis video!" We didn't care about the van, but we didn't want to lose the video, especially the footage where Maura's crying. The ceremony ended with a dynamic rendition of "Viva Las Vegas," with all three of us singing and dancing our hearts out. Check this performance out on the complete "Nickeltown" video on the CD-ROM. If you need an Elvis, and you can afford the best, Brendan Paul's your man. See Appendix D for his contact information.

# Fading Out the Audio

Most music videos follow the fade on the recorded music. Because this tutorial only uses a portion of the song, you can fade the rest of the song out.

Perform the following steps to fade out the music:

1. **Unlock the Audio 1 track on the Timeline by clicking the Lock/Unlock Track button at the left-hand edge of the Track.**

2. **Expand the Audio 1 Track by clicking the triangle at the left of the track, as shown in Figure 1-19.**

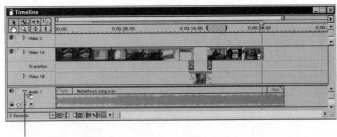

Collapse/Expand Track

**Figure 1-19:** The Collapse/Expand Track button can expand the track to reveal further information about your track.

3. **Notice the red line that runs the length of the** Nickeltown song.wav **audio clip.** This line is called the Volume rubberband. (If the line is blue, click the red Display Volume Rubberbands button.) Each Volume rubberband contains two handles, which are movable volume controls — one at the beginning of the clip, and one at the end.

4. **Position the Selection tool over the Volume rubberband until the arrow turns into a pointing finger.**

5. **Position the pointing finger over the Volume rubberband at a point even with the beginning of the last video clip.**

6. **Left-click the Volume rubberband to create a volume handle, as shown in Figure 1-20.**

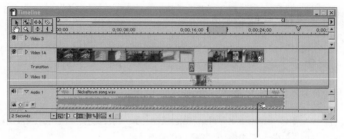

Create Rubberband Handle

**Figure 1-20:** Add Volume handles by clicking the Volume rubberband.

7. **Move the cursor to the handle at the very end of the** `Nickeltown song.wav` **audio clip.** Click and drag it to the bottom of the clip, as shown in Figure 1-21.

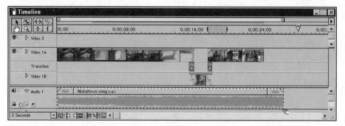

**Figure 1-21:** Drag the Volume rubberband down to create an audio fade-out.

## Adding a Title

Titles contain text, which is opaque, and an *Alpha Matte*, which is the transparent area around the text. The Alpha Matte enables the underlying video to show through between and around the text. Music video titles often fade in and out. Your last task in this tutorial is to create an MTV-style title for your music video.

Use the following steps to create an MTV-style title:

1. **Position the Edit Line at 00;00;07;23 by clicking and dragging the Edit Line marker.**

2. **Drag the** `Nickeltown title.ptl` **clip from the bin or Storyboard onto the Video 2 track of the Timeline, flush left to the Edit Line.**

3. **Expand the Video 2 track to reveal the Opacity rubberbands.** Opacity rubberbands in the Video track are similar to the Volume rubberbands in the Audio track. You can think of it as a volume control for the opacity of the clip.

4. **Position the Edit Line marker at the left edge of the** `Nickeltown title.ptl` **clip.**

5. **Move in ten frames by pressing the right arrow key on your keyboard ten times.**

6. **Hold the cursor over the red Opacity rubberband at the point where the Edit Line is located.**

7. **Click the Opacity rubberband to create a new handle.**

8. **Hold the cursor over the first Opacity rubberband handle at the very beginning of the clip.**

9. **Click the handle and drag it all the way down.**

10. **Move the Edit Line marker to the end of the title clip.**

11. **Move back ten frames by pressing the left arrow key on your keyboard ten times.**

12. **Hold the cursor over the Opacity rubberband where the Edit Line lies.**

13. **Click the Opacity rubberband to create another handle.**

14. **Click the very last Opacity rubberband handle and drag it all the way down.** Your title clip should look like the one in Figure 1-22.

15. **Render the work area.**

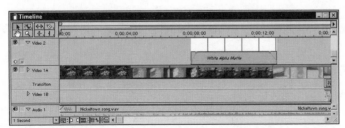

**Figure 1-22:** The Opacity rubberbands enable you to set fades on your titles.

You may want to keep the title clip handy to modify and use in your own videos. It's set up like a standard MTV title. Of course, you're not limited to using this style; you can be as creative as you like. (See Chapter 10 for more on titles.)

You've just completed the tutorial. Premiere is simple and easy to use! Of course, we couldn't possibly cover all of Premiere's powerful tools in this chapter, and that's why you need to read the rest of this book and follow all the step-by-step examples.

# Chapter Replay

After reading this chapter and following along with all the step-by-step instructions, you should:

✦ Have a general understanding of how a video is assembled

✦ Be familiar with some of the issues inherent to music video, including synching video to audio, and using the beat of the song to help you align clips

✦ Understand the concepts of adding video effects and transitions

✦ Understand how to add titles

Chapter 2 describes all the steps involved, the resources required, and the costs associated with making music videos with Adobe Premiere.

✦   ✦   ✦

# Making a Music Video: An Overview

◆ ◆ ◆ ◆

**In This Chapter**

Steps to making a
music video

What you need

◆ ◆ ◆ ◆

**S**o you want to make music videos? Ten years ago,
your best bets would have been to volunteer at a local
community-access TV station, enroll in film school, a school
for visual arts, or intern at a large commercial TV station.
These avenues were the only way for you to get access to the
sophisticated, expensive gear used in TV production.

Now, all that has changed. Due to the miraculously rapid
growth of microchip technology, video production is one of a
growing number of formerly arcane crafts that have come into
the eager hands of consumers. With the right software and
hardware, and this book, you'll be making your own music
videos in no time. This chapter provides an overview of the
entire process including obtaining music, gathering video
footage, editing in Adobe Premiere, and exporting your project so people can view it without a computer. We conclude
the chapter by listing all the required gear and what you can
expect to pay for it.

## Step 1: Obtaining Music

We're guessing that you want to make music videos because
you love music, just like we do. Beyond that, what do you
want to accomplish? Do you want to make a video of your
own garage band? Your friends' band? Do you want to make
an artsy video to go along with your all-time favorite song? Do
you just want to shoot a live band and be able to edit your
footage in a professional way? Today's digital video technology provides numerous applications. Premiere doesn't care
where you get your music, and this book will show you how to
import all kinds of source music into your video, including:

✦ Live concert audio, captured on your DV camcorder

✦ Analog recordings, including vinyl and cassette

✦ Digital CD recordings

## Live concert music video

When we were kids, before we started performing professionally, we haunted every live music nightclub that we could get into with a fake ID. We weren't interested in underage drinking — the big draw for us was the music. Seeing and hearing a tight knit group of pals earnestly pumping out rock 'n' roll in some dingy, flat black-painted basement club was the ultimate escape! If only we could have captured those seminal shows on videotape. See Figure 2-1. Maybe then we'd have a way to convey visually the moments of inspiration that were the source of our passion for music. Good news! In the new paradigm of digital video, you can easily and relatively inexpensively obtain the gear needed to capture these moments, and you can give the editing technology a home on your desktop!

**Figure 2-1:** Capture the energy of a band with live concert footage.

## Using DV audio for music track

Using a digital video camera not only provides you with a crystal-clear image and low-cost medium, doing so also provides you with CD-quality audio. What's more, most DV camcorders give you the choice of using the built-in microphone or an external one, which is usually not included in your DV camcorder purchase. You also have the option, depending on your make and model, of either relying on the camcorder's built-in volume settings and compressor/limiters or setting and controlling the volume manually.

### Gaining permissions

If you're interested in shooting a live band, you need to obtain permission from the band. Obtaining a release form never hurts; you want to have something in writing. Any entertainment lawyer would be able to provide you with an appropriate release form.

If the band is signed—that is, they have an exclusive record company or management contract—you need to contact the band's manager and/or record label first. Many artists sign contracts that restrict them from recording for anyone other than the label (this includes you). However, local, unsigned bands often welcome the opportunity to have a videographer commit their performance to tape. Offer to tape a band's live performance and give them a copy of your edited project. If they like what they see and hear, the band may decide to sell the video to their friends or shop the video to record labels and TV stations and give you a proper credit and a cut of the proceeds.

Let the club owner know your intentions. The owner probably won't have a problem with you shooting a video — hey, it's free publicity for the club — but you may need to follow a few rules. The owner's concern is for the happiness of his clientele and may not allow you to obstruct anyone's view. You may also be required to use only the stage lighting, or you may have to come early and mount your camcorder on an existing beam or some other non-obstructing location.

## Paying royalties

You won't have to pay royalties for simply shooting a music sequence, but if the finished project is ever shown in a commercial outlet (TV, movie, convention, Web), you need to know about financial responsibilities.

A *mechanical royalty* is a payment due to a songwriter whenever their song is reproduced on a commercial CD, film, or video. In addition, royalties must be paid to the copyright owners of master recordings when those masters are used for commercial purposes. In other words, if you make money by selling a product that features someone else's song or master recording, you need to pay them for using it. Consult an entertainment lawyer before making commercial use of anyone else's song or recording.

What about paying the performer? In many recording contracts, record labels think of music videos as promotional tools. If they're lucky, they'll get the video aired on MTV or VH-1, and the repeated showing of that video will result in bolstered CD sales. If, however, music videos are sold, as opposed to shown on TV, the performing artist has a right to a chunk of the income. In addition, the songwriters may be entitled to performance royalties every time their song plays on the radio or television. A fledgling band is frequently willing to waive these fees in the early stages of their career. However, when the band is no longer fledgling, they may have lawyers and managers who will require payment whenever their music is used. Protect the band and yourself by spelling out in writing what license and royalty fees will be paid and when such payments will kick in. For example, a new band may be willing to waive their royalties until they get a major label contract or until your video is commercially distributed. At that point, when real money is being made, everyone should be entitled to his or her statutory fees. Talk to a lawyer about generating a standard contract for baby bands that protects the rights of both the band and the videographer.

## Original band video

If the local garage band or your own band (garage or otherwise) wants a video to accompany their studio recording, all you need is a copy of the CD. You can load the CD track onto your computer and use that track as the audio track to your song. If the recording is in analog form, such as vinyl LP or cassette tape, you first need to convert it to a digital format, typically a WAV file. If your computer is a Mac, you can directly import the song from CD (CDA file) as is. If you're using a PC, you must first convert the CDA file to a WAV file or other Premiere-compatible sound file by using third-party software, such as Sonic Foundry Siren or Vegas.

See Chapter 6 to learn about converting analog audio to digital.

## Favorite song video

In the confines of your own home, you can do just about anything you want. It's a great country! Perhaps you're just a huge fan of the Fountains Of Wayne. The only video you've seen of theirs is "Radiation Vibe," but you have a great concept for "Amity Gardens." Maybe you want to create a music video for a group that was around before the art form was invented. As long as these videos don't air publicly, you won't have to worry about permissions or royalties.

# Step 2: Gathering Video Footage

Okay, you have the music you need. What images do you want to use in your video? This section describes the different types of footage most often used in creating music videos.

## Live concert footage

If you're shooting a live concert, you already have music and video that's synchronized. But how many live concerts have you seen where just one camera is trained on the act? You'll get a more professional look and a larger set of editing options if you use more than one camera. Ask around to see which of your neighbors has a DV camcorder. Maybe he could lend you the second camera in this two-camera shoot. If you can't find another camera, see if the band is willing to play the song you want to capture during the soundcheck. Set your camera up in one location and then move it to a different angle for the concert.

## Shooting digital video footage

If you're putting together a traditional music video in which the band lip-synchs, set up a time and a place with the group and make sure that you have a boom box and copy of the CD to play while the band members sing along.

## Using analog archives

You may have old analog video of the band from a county fair performance back in the 1980s, before the digital format was in place. You can use analog video, but you must first convert it to digital. We explain this process in detail in Chapter 6.

## Tapping stock footage libraries

You can obtain stock footage from stock footage libraries. Many DV-geared magazines have classified ads in the back that list stock footage outlets. Stock footage can be expensive, but you can find some inexpensive or even free sources.

 See Appendix D for other sources of stock footage.

## Still photographs

Still photography can be used in your video to create elaborate slide shows. Check out one of those *Behind the Music* shows that air on VH1. If the artist is no longer alive, the videographer often relies on still photography to tell the story. You can use this technique in music video as well. If you're creating a video of your sister's high school band but you only have still photos, think of how you can use these stills in conjunction with motion shots to tell the song's story.

# Step 3: Editing Video in Adobe Premiere

After you have all the audio and video material sources figured out, your next step is to put it all together. The editing process is pretty straightforward and can be as simple as placing video clips back-to-back over a single audio track. Premiere, however, offers editing tools, effects, and transitions that enable you to express yourself in a new, creative way.

Premiere enables you to arrange your clips on up to 99 video and 99 audio tracks. You can add creative transitions to overlapping video clips, and add multiple video effects to any video clip, using any of the 74 available effects. Premiere supplies all the tools you need to give your music video a professional look.

# Step 4: Exporting Video

After you complete the editing process, you need to export your video so that people can view it on a device other than your personal computer. You have the choice of exporting your video to VHS, CD-R, or DVD-R with no reduction in quality. You can even export it to film if you have a use for that format. These days, the World Wide Web serves as one of the most convenient and widely used outlets for music videos. Use Premiere's powerful compression tools to format your video for viewing on your own Web page, your friendly neighborhood band's Web page, or any number of Web servers that host independent music videos.

## Premiere's Web output file options

Premiere offers three export options for Web-based video, where you can export a clip, a portion of the Timeline, or the entire program to be viewed on the World Wide Web. These options include:

✦ Save For Web

✦ Advanced Windows Media

✦ Advanced RealMedia Export

See Chapter 14 for detailed instruction on exporting your video for the World Wide Web.

## Exporting for video

You can export your finished video to tape simply by playing the Timeline and recording the output to a VCR for an analog tape, or back to your DV camcorder for a digital copy. If you record from the computer to your DV camcorder, you can then use that tape as your *master* tape and hook your camcorder up to your VCR whenever you need to make a dub. All DV Camcorders have built-in digital-to-analog converters.

## Burning to CD

You can export your music video as a file that you can burn to CD-R. CDs containing videos are called VCDs (Video CDs), and they're a fun and inexpensive way to distribute your music video. If a band wants to include video material with their next CD release, but isn't ready to go the DVD route, packaging the music CD with a bonus disc of video material would be a reasonable alternative.

Bands can sell VCDs at their concerts, distribute them to their fan clubs, or send them out as calling cards. And unlike copying to VHS, there's no generational loss in data, so your hundredth CD-R is as clear as your first.

## Exporting for motion picture film

If your music video will be ultimately viewed on motion picture film (many contests and film festivals require that entries be submitted on motion picture film rather than video), you will need to arrange to use a motion picture recorder from a postproduction facility. You will need to customize the frame size and resolution according to the postproduction facility's standards.

## The lessons of Roger Corman

**Road Diary**

We've learned a tremendous amount about shoestring production by studying the career of the great low-budget filmmaker Roger Corman. He shot classic cult films, such as *Little Shop of Horrors* and *Bucket of Blood* (the latter about a crazed beatnik poet, the former about a man-eating houseplant) in a matter of days. Less than a week, in fact, for each of these two films. How did he do it? By using the right people, by working very efficiently, and by being resourceful. For example, one day he heard on the news that a forest was on fire near Los Angeles. Without hesitating, he rented a horse and hired an actor who could ride it. He dressed him in medieval garb and had him ride slowly through the burned out forest with the smoke still rising from the ashes. No movie yet, but a really cool and evocative scene. This scene later became the opening of his classic film, *The Masque of the Red Death.* Another time, he heard that a large barn was going to be demolished, so he paid the farmer to let him film the flames leaping and the timbers crashing. Then he incorporated clips from that shoot into a whole series of films, all of which ended with the villain's castle burning down. By doing this, he saved thousands of dollars in production costs, insurance, and so forth. Corman routinely bought out the last few days of the contract on a set, when a major film was going to wrap a little bit early. He hired carpenters to do a few cosmetic changes and then did a few days shooting on the set, again saving thousands in production costs.

From this philosophy, we have developed the motto, "If you build it, we will shoot there." Once, while we were driving across Texas, we came across a partially restored Western town. About a third of the town was finished, and the rest was in various stages of construction. We pulled the van over, jumped out and lip-synched a few songs, taking care to keep the bulldozers and dump trucks out of the frame. Then we took a few shots of us walking around with guitar cases, kicking up dust. By the time the owners happened by, we had plenty of stuff in the can. The owners didn't seem to mind us being there. We played a couple of tunes for them and talked about music for a while, and then we wished them luck with the restoration and took off. Location, location, location. . . .

# What You Need

We don't like to assume anything, so here is a complete list of all the hardware and software you need to make your dreams of editing music video a reality. Figure 2-2 illustrates the basic hardware and software you need.

**Cross-Reference** For a detailed discussion of using and upgrading DV editing computer hardware, see Appendix B.

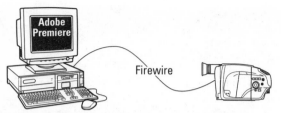

**Figure 2-2:** All the hardware you need to make music videos is a computer with appropriate hard drive, RAM, processing speed, a FireWire port, and a CD-ROM drive. Connect your DV camcorder via FireWire.

## Computer with AV-ready hard drive

Because you'll be working with memory-intensive video and audio, you need to have a computer whose hard drive has the capacity to store the video and audio clips and can spin fast enough. Your system should also have enough RAM to keep up with the demands of Premiere.

You can expect to spend around $2,000 on a computer (if buying new) capable of smoothly and efficiently processing audio and video data. When purchasing a computer for video editing, keep three things in mind:

✦ The bigger the hard drive, the better.

✦ The bigger the RAM, the better.

✦ The faster the processor, the better.

You should also make sure that your computer is equipped with a FireWire port. If you plan on exporting your music videos to CD, or archiving your project clips to CD, you will also need a CD-RW drive.

### Hard drive

Try to get a computer that has at least a 15GB hard drive, partitioned into two sections, with a hard disk speed of at least 7200 rpm. Two hard drives or two hard drive partitions allows for faster, smoother processing of your video. Our computer has a partitioned 30GB drive, and it's more than enough space. Our desktop computer has only 13GB in a partitioned drive, and we're able to edit one music video at a time on that machine. You need 85MB to install Premiere on a PC and 50MB for Mac. If your computer has everything but enough drive space, you're in luck. A 60GB 7200 rpm hard drive currently costs less than $200.

### RAM

*Random access memory (RAM)* serves as temporary storage. The minimum system requirement for Premiere on both the Mac and PC is 32MB, but Adobe recommends

128MB. The more RAM you have, the smoother the software processes your project data. Most new computers are shipped with room for RAM expansion. At the current cost of around $40 for a 256MB module, you can noticeably enhance the performance of your computer.

### Operating system

Running Premiere requires Mac OS Version 9.04 on a Mac and Windows 98, Windows ME, Windows NT, or Windows 2000 on a PC. We run Premiere on Windows XP with no problems. You can purchase Windows XP Home Edition for $200, or get the upgrade, if you qualify, for $100. If you're currently running Windows 95, you don't qualify for the upgrade, but if you run Windows 98, you can purchase Windows XP as an upgrade. Mac's latest OS X v10 retails for around $130.

### IEEE 1394 connectivity

To edit digital video, you need a way to transfer video to your computer. Your video and audio material does not necessarily have to begin in the digital domain — you can use LP audio, analog video, and even photo snapshots — but all material must end up as digital data on your computer. The best way to achieve this transfer is through an *IEEE 1394* (commonly called *i.LINK* or *FireWire*) port. Many computers sold today have this type of port, and even if yours is not equipped with FireWire ports, you can upgrade. For as little as $30, you can purchase a new FireWire PCI card with two or three ports to upgrade your current computer for handling digital video. See Figure 2-3 for different types of IEEE 1394 cables.

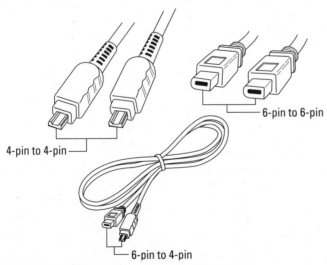

6-pin to 6-pin

4-pin to 4-pin

6-pin to 4-pin

**Figure 2-3:** IEEE 1394 comes in both 6-pin and 4-pin varieties. 6-pin to 6-pin, 6-pin to 4-pin, and 4-pin to 4-pin cables provide all the configurations you need to connect any IEEE 1394-ready gear.

### CD-ROM drive

You need a CD-ROM drive to install the Premiere software. If you have the choice of getting a CD-RW or CD-RW/DVD combo drive, opt for the combo. If upgrading your current computer, you may want to install an aftermarket drive, available in both internal and external models. Depending on the drive's speed and whether it's internal or external, new CD-RW drive street prices range from as little as $70 to $200.

## Stalking the wild western shirt

**Road Diary**

Okay, your band realizes that they need a cool look, one that will give them a unique identity. They also realize that they can't afford expensive costumes, unless they're a KISS tribute band, in which case they'll just have to bite the bullet. They should also realize that they can't just go down to the local mega-discount store and get some stuff off the rack. Heck, people watching the video on TV would look down and notice that they're wearing the same shirt as the guy on the screen! So where do you find cheap, unique costumes without busting your nonexistent budget? The kind of stuff you launder before you wear it, not just after? At stores that sell old, funky, used stuff. Here are a couple of good ones:

In New Orleans, take the streetcar up Carrollton Avenue and past the Camillia Diner to Thrift City. This is a really big thrift store; in fact it occupies a former supermarket. Prices are low and here's the coolest part. During the 1970s, polyester shirts and bellbottoms were the uniform of the day in New Orleans, the "city that care forgot." After all, this is the home of funk! The groove came from here and spread worldwide, and those dudes wore the funkiest of duds. Check out an old Meters album cover to see what I mean. Anyway, Thrift City is a great place to score '70s funkwear. Next door is the world's grooviest bowling alley, Midtown Rock 'n' Bowl. Here, live bands play while you bowl, and you dance between turns to the best in Crescent City R&B, Blues, and Zydeco. This place really rocks. Ask the shoe rental guy about the time Mick Jagger stopped in to bowl a few frames.

Now, if it's western shirts you want — and what Americana band doesn't need a trunk full of them — boot-scoot over to Texas. Rockers, such as Lenny Kravitz, Ben Harper, and even Madonna know the video value of these beauties. Austin prices are high, because a lot of collectors are around. Head for the hinterlands for the real bargains. We take the bus to Lubbock, Texas, the home of Buddy Holly. Across the street from the bus station is an AMVET thrift shop with a good supply of Western yoke shirts — classic cowboy stuff. In Texas, these aren't rock band accoutrements. They're the everyday shirts worn by working-class cowdudes young and old, so the thrift shops are well stocked. Stay away from the big cities when you're looking for cheap used video wear. Collectors keep the prices high, so go where collectors aren't!

## Premiere software

After you place the digital video and audio data on your computer, Adobe Premiere is the only software you need to create professional-quality music videos. Premiere enables you to arrange your video clips on up to 99 video tracks, and your audio on up to 99 separate audio tracks. You can create video composites of two or more tracks. You can also create elaborate transitions between tracks. Premiere's video and audio effects give you the tools you need to spice up your video.

A trial version of Adobe Premiere is included on this book's companion CD-ROM, but you will need to purchase the full version if you want to export your finished video or use many of Premiere's advanced features. You can purchase Adobe Premiere from the Adobe Web site at `www.adobe.com/products/premiere/main.html`. Pricing for the full version starts at $549, and upgrades cost around $150. You can also get Premiere bundled with other video editing software, such as After Effects, as well as FireWire cards, for a discounted rate. If you're purchasing a new computer, check to see which models bundle Adobe Premiere with the included software bundle.

## Video camera

If you happen to have a DV camcorder with FireWire, you're ready to transfer your digital video directly into the computer. When you transfer digital video from your DV camcorder to your computer via FireWire, your video never leaves the digital domain, and you lose no signal in the transfer. When you capture your video this way, the video material is not compressed, so you keep your video images and sounds at full quality.

If your camcorder does not have FireWire, you can choose from several options. You can transfer your video through a third-party capture card, which is a hardware device that provides a connection between your analog camcorder and your computer. If you have a DV camcorder, but you want to use old footage from an analog videotape, you can first record the analog tape onto your DV camcorder through its analog inputs, thus using the camcorder as a capture card. After you've recorded from the analog source to your DV camcorder, you can then capture the newly converted digital video to a computer through the FireWire cable.

The price of DV camcorders continues to fall while the number of features increases. Today, you can buy a DV camcorder for less than $1,000. If you plan to broadcast your video, however, we recommend a professional-quality model, which typically costs between $1,000 and $2,000.

Higher-priced camcorders are *three-chip* units, which means that three computer chips, or *charge coupled devices (CCDs)*, convert the light into digital signals. These cameras use a separate chip to process red, green, and blue information, and the resulting video quality is superior to that of a single-chip camcorder, which has only one chip. If you intend to distribute your music videos to TV or use them in any professional setting, consider spending the extra money on a 3CCD camcorder. Most consumer models are single-chip units. The price difference can be around $500 to $1,000 more for a 3CCD camcorder. Many manufacturers and dealers differentiate between single- and three-chip camcorders by using the terms *consumer grade* for single-chip models and *professional quality* for three-chip models. You can also tell whether a camcorder is a single-chip camcorder if the description includes *RGB filter*. This filter is included with single-chip camcorders to compensate for inferior color clarity.

Surf the Web and visit manufacturers' Web sites to compare current prices and features.

## Videotape

A few years ago, you had to go to a specialty shop to buy DV tape. Now you can buy tapes at your local drugstore, and they cost about $10 each. DV tapes can be taped over, so as soon as you have used all the footage you want to, you can reuse your DV tape.

## Optional extras

Technically, all you need is video material, either shot on a digital video camera or obtained from other sources, an audio track, your computer, and Adobe Premiere. You may also want to consider using lights, a VCR, and a CD burner.

### Lights

Shooting in natural or available light is the simplest way to shoot video; however, sooner or later (probably sooner), you'll find yourself in a great shooting location with less-than-appropriate light. You can easily improve this type of situation by using a three-point lighting system.

You can invest a lot of money in a *three-point lighting* system, but if you're just starting out, we recommend that you buy an inexpensive one. By using a cheap system, you'll discover the features that you like, the ones you wish you had, and the ones you don't really need. Three-point lighting systems are a combination of two lights that can provide diffused light, either with umbrellas or other types of diffusers, and a spotlight. Some spotlights have one setting, and others are adjustable. An inexpensive three-point lighting system can cost as low as $300.

You should use a tripod to obtain steady shots. They're absolutely necessary if you want to shoot the band in front of a neutral background or use a Background Matte to replace the scenery with something more exciting later.

**Cross-Reference** Chapter 4 describes techniques for using a three-point lighting system. See Chapter 12 to learn about using a Background Matte.

## VCR

Most people already have a VHS-format VCR as part of their home entertainment system. If your VCR has video and stereo audio inputs, you have all you need to export your final music video to VHS tape. Many new VCR models cost less than $100. See Chapter 13 for full details on how to export your Premiere project to VHS tape.

## CD burner

Blank CD-R media enable you to cheaply and easily distribute music videos. CD-distributed videos are commonly referred to as VCDs (Video CDs). You can either format them as compressed files, such as QuickTime or Windows Media files or keep them at full resolution for better-than-VHS quality videos. These CD video files can be played only on computer screens. If your computer is equipped with a CD burner, you can easily write, or *burn*, music videos to CD-R media. If your computer is not equipped, you can install a CD burner in your computer's empty drive bay, or you can purchase an external CD burner drive. External drives are typically slower and more expensive than internal drives. Many internal CD burners cost less than $100.

## DVD burner

DVD burners are finally available! Just a year ago, blank DVDs cost around $10 each and the burners themselves cost well over $1,000; but the price has dropped dramatically over the past few months. New DVD burners currently go for under $500, and blank DVD-R media cost as little as $3.00.

## DSL or other high-speed Internet connection

Although it's not necessary for you to have high-speed access to the Internet, we recommend it if you plan on uploading videos to the Web or viewing or downloading videos for study. You can upload, download, or view videos over a telephone line, but you'll have to wait a long time (at least twenty minutes to download a three-minute compressed music video), and the quality will be highly compromised.

These days, if you have cable TV, chances are good that you also have access to a DSL line or high-speed Internet. Downloading a video by either of these means takes only seconds rather than a half-hour, as does uploading your music video to your site or to a host site.

If you want to study archived music videos on the Web, you should seriously consider getting a high-speed Internet connection. Check with your local carriers. You should be able to get high-speed Internet access for less than the cost of a second telephone line.

# Chapter Replay

After reading this chapter, you should be able to:

✦ Know the steps involved in making a music video

✦ Understand the resources needed to shoot, edit, and export a music video

✦ Have a good idea of what your initial budget is for getting set up to produce music videos

✦ Understand the formatting choices available for exporting your final project

Now that you know all that's involved in creating a music video, you're ready to start conceptualizing. Chapter 3 explores music video forms and discusses different techniques you can use to brainstorm your first music video.

✦     ✦     ✦

# Conceptualizing Your Video

The number one rule in the craft of video making is that there are no rules! It's sort of like being a cowboy out west of the Pecos, when there weren't any lawmen around. Although this nascent art form has developed a few standard methods, most of which have been borrowed from cinema and photography, there is no codified rulebook for music video. Basically, it's always been okay to be new, fresh, and innovative.

But if the playing field is level, why is it obvious that some videos are more entertaining, exciting, even thought provoking than others? If there aren't any rules, aren't there at least guidelines to help a neophyte get started? Well, you can simply aim a camera at your band, press record, and play a song, but if you're investigating the processing power of Adobe Premiere, you probably want to do more than that. The best way to learn about video is to watch videos. It's a visual medium. You do it with your eyes. The rest of this chapter takes a close look at some videos that stand out from the rest and explains why.

## Video Forms

Music always resists categorization, and many musicians don't want to be restricted by labels. But if you view several hundred videos, as we did in writing this book, you will begin to recognize recurring characteristics. As these techniques and concepts become familiar, the videos divide themselves up into groups based on visual form and musical style. For convenience, we present them here in groups that emerged as we watched.

## Funny videos

One great thing about the anything-goes attitude toward rock video is that it works great for comedy. The early directors, following in the footsteps of TV pioneers, such as Milton Berle and Spike Jones, found that they could get away with almost anything, as long as it made people laugh. Humor lives on as an essential element in popular music, as evidenced in a rich history of funny videos.

### The Beatles: *A Hard Day's Night*

The Fab Four burst on the American music scene with a single, dynamic television appearance on *The Ed Sullivan show*. The Beatles were a visual band from the beginning. In fact, most of the early press coverage of them was focused on their hairstyle that was deemed to be extremely radical and unruly. Kind of hard to believe now! Serious consideration of their music didn't happen until three years into their career, when newspapers hired college journalists to write reviews of the "Sergeant Pepper" album, thus giving birth to the field of rock journalism. But in 1964, the Beatles made teenage girls scream and fork over cash for records every time they shook their bemopped heads. That's all industry execs knew, and there was a rush to get a film into theaters that would capitalize on the *head shake = scream* equation while it still had its effect. American comedy veteran Richard Lester directed a film, a black and white rave-up called *A Hard Day's Night*. How did this low-budget quickie kick-start the video revolution, anyway?

*A Hard Day's Night* could easily have been a throwaway. The film was mainly an excuse for United Artists, the distributor, to get the rights to release a Beatles album because the contract called for a number of new songs. Lester, however, wasn't satisfied with that. After rejecting a number of scripts, he hired Alan Owen, another comedy veteran, to put together a truly witty story that would reflect the Beatles' own brand of caustic Liverpudlian humor. The next layer was Lester's addition of touches borrowed from the French new wave — a hand-held documentary style, deliberately stark black-and-white sets, lots of location shooting, and moments of pure surrealism. At one point, early in the film, the Beatles are talking to a surly, upper-crust-type old man on board a train. In the very next frame, they are running beside the train, looking at him through the window. Then, without explanation, they are back inside the train talking. Surreal moments like this didn't happen in Elvis movies.

Owen wrote the script with very clear direction from Lester. The Beatles are placed, in the early part of the film, in very tight, confined spaces— a train, a car, and a hotel room. They are prisoners of their own fame, but at a certain point, their native energy overcomes this confinement, and they literally burst forth, from the back door of a theater into a vacant lot. With no fans nearby, they are able to go crazy, and they do. In the clip, "Can't Buy Me Love," Lester and the band make no attempt to re-create a live concert. The clip is all about concept, and the concept is wacky, surreal comedy, in the style of the British comedy troupe The Goons, for whom Lester had also directed films. This marriage of music, fashion, comedy, and surrealism set the standards for all rock video to come.

### *The Monkees* television series

Here they came, walkin' down the street. Hollywood's answer to the Fab Four was a transparent attempt to turn *A Hard Day's Night* into a weekly comedy series, minus the real Beatles. After all, the mop tops weren't full-time actors, and they made more money from their concerts and records than they could earn playing themselves on TV. But what if you could hire real actors to portray wacky, witty creative types with teenage sex appeal? What if you could sweeten the deal by hiring Hollywood's top songwriters to write actual hit songs and promote them on the radio? Add in dolls, trading cards, magazines, and other paraphernalia that accompanied '60s pop mania, and you could cash in big time.

This was the thinking of music publishing executive Don Kirshner, who was looking for a way to position himself and his stable of ace songwriters in the lucrative teen television market. His plan worked. *The Monkees,* goofy comedy aside, was a weekly showcase of cutting-edge techniques, such as sudden jump cuts, surreal inserts, preposterous props, and actors suddenly addressing the camera. Until the age of digital effects, you couldn't do much to a music video that hadn't been done somewhere on an episode of *The Monkees.*

## The Buggles: "Video Killed the Radio Star"

Appropriately enough, this was the first video ever aired on MTV. The title is a powerful manifesto, and the quirky effects, so radically different from the straight concert footage of the 1970s, clearly spelled out what video was all about. This was a new medium, descended from but not the same as the rock 'n' roll movies of the past. Many devices used in this video turn up again and again through the 1980s up to the present day. The solid white background is a nod to *A Hard Day's Night*, and is still in common use. The clips in which the band is seen on a TV screen are a standard effect even now. Most importantly, director Russell Mulcahy imbued the video with a gloss of novelty that spelled out the code of music video — young, fresh, and new.

## The B-52's: "Song for a Future Generation"

This video contains an interesting little study in eyeline perspective and mask editing technique. At about 1:33 into the song, the band sings a little bridge consisting of the word "now" repeated seven times, followed by "la" repeated five times. They sing the "las" in unison. For the "nows," one girl sings two, one guy sings two, and another guy sings one. The other two are sung in unison. From this simple musical bridge, the director created an interesting sequence. First, he shot each of the five band members in a variety of head shots (looking up, looking down, looking right and left, and looking diagonally down and up to the right and left). Then he picked up shots of the singers mouthing "now" straight into the camera. Finally, he got shots of each band member mouthing the "la las" straight into the camera. With ten shots per band member, this created a bin of fifty clips. Next, he created a mask overlay with five vertical ovals. By giving each band member a "home" oval, he was able to orchestrate their head movements so that the current singer would always face forward with the other members looking at her/him. When the singer changed, all the heads reoriented. When they sang in unison, they all faced forward. (See Figure 3-1.) The transitions are simple jump cuts. The effect recalls the opening credits of *The Brady Bunch*, and the fact that some of the head angles aren't quite right just adds to the charm. Try this one at home.

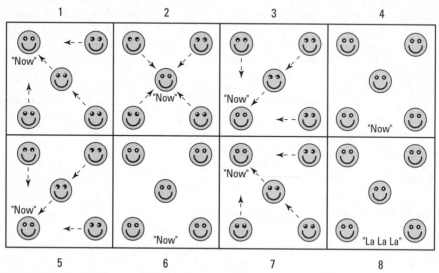

**Figure 3-1:** This B-52's clip recalls *The Brady Bunch*.

## Weezer: "Buddy Holly"

This Ric Ocasek-produced power-pop gem was turned over to comedic visionary Spike Jonze. This skateboard punk/technical wizard, who adopted his alias in tribute to an equally outrageous pioneer of early television, Spike Jones, went above and beyond the call of duty to create a comic masterpiece. The video recreates a segment of the 1970s sitcom *Happy Days*. Jonze compresses a simplified plot into three minutes and reprises all the main characters from the show. The amazing part is that they are the real characters not modern-day look-alikes! He apparently nailed down the rights to use their images and interpolated real footage of the show with a master shot of the band members, who seem to be entertaining the guys and dolls at a sock hop. It's utterly realistic. Jonze's masterful use of reaction shots makes it appear that the band members and the cast are interacting. Try this at home using matte technique; however, if you use a real TV show, make sure that you have the right to show it in public, or else keep it for your own private use. Check out Woody Allen's film *Zelig* for more examples of this advanced matte work. In addition, the video version of the 1960s comedy film, *It's A Mad, Mad, Mad, Mad World* features behind-the-scenes footage that clearly explains matte technique.

### The Beastie Boys: "Sabotage"

Spike Jonze strikes again, with another re-creation of that mother lode of pop kitsch, 1970s TV. This time, he casts punk/rap trio the Beastie Boys as detectives in an action-packed cop show, complete with title credits announcing their TV names. Wigs and fake moustaches come into play as Jonze effectively turns our 1990s heroes into 1970s nerds. Jonze is a master of disguise and has been known to accost strangers, including movie stars, in a variety of makeup devices and props, playing assorted strange characters. He rarely gives a straight interview, preferring to create absurd scenarios that make it impossible for a reporter to get much information out of him. For all these traits and for his technical brilliance, he's rightfully considered one of the greats of music video.

## Artful videos

MTV intended from the beginning to establish an identity separate from the live footage rock concert network TV shows of the 1970s. They sought out videos that gave equal weight to musical and visual aesthetics. This idea brought to the forefront acts who understood concept and weren't afraid to take chances. Like rockers of every generation, the cutting-edge artists were initially considered eccentric novelty acts. But as the audience accustomed not only their ears but also their eyes to the new wave of rock artists, hit videos began to happen when an act combined a really strong song with a really striking visual image.

### Eurythmics: "Sweet Dreams Are Made of This"

"Sweet Dreams" is a series of unusual shots that reveal their logic only after repeated viewings, and only after we realize that the sets and props help tell the story. As the action begins, vocalist Annie Lennox is dressed in men's clothes, and her face is expressionless. She looks like a dictator, slapping a riding crop in her hand. She points to a video screen in some kind of underground war room. She's not your laid-back rock chick of the 1970s. Her "assistant," duo partner Dave Stewart, appears to be creating the music by impassively pushing buttons on a computer. The action switches to a scene that seems to be borrowed from turn of the century Surrealist Marcel Duchamp. The couple is seen, blindfolded, playing cellos in a bucolic pasture. A cow appears to take a liking to them and when the duo returns to the war room, the cow also shows up there. The duo returns to the cow pasture, but now they have the computer and a large table from the war room. Shooting in just two locations, they've created a video that takes us into the realm of surrealism, but with a simple logic — scene A, followed by scene B, then scene A with props from scene B, and winding up in scene B with props from scene A. It's very effective because of the juxtaposition of elements not usually seen together. A cow next to a computer grabs our attention!

The video ends with two new scenes. In the first, the duo sails off in a boat, Dave bowing on his cello. In the final scene, you suddenly see a "reality" shot of Annie waking up. On her bedside table rests a book, and the camera dollies up to show us the title, *Sweet Dreams Are Made of This*. We've been inside her dream the whole time. From the well-rested look on her face, she doesn't remember a bit of her dream. Only at this point do we realize that, in her dream, she's been resolving the two sides of her personality — the dominant, aggressive side and the gentle artistic side. This was the first but not the last rock video to draw on the ideas of dream psychologist Carl Jung.

The Eurhythmics' video actually opens up the meaning of the lyric. The words alone are deliberately oblique and minimalist, but the video paints a compelling dreamscape. After you've seen the video, the song is never quite the same without it. This transformation is a primary goal of music video. The visual dimension should expand the meaning of the lyric, not compress it. This video masterfully achieves that.

### Smashing Pumpkins: "Tonight, Tonight"

The video's directors, Jonathan Dayton and Valerie Paris, based this remarkable video on a film by cinema pioneer George Melies. Melies's 1902 movie, *A Trip to the Moon*, astonished audiences with its advanced special effects. Dayton and Paris decided to pay tribute to Melies by re-creating, as closely as possible, his original sets and real-time effects. Needless to say, digital post-production wasn't around in 1902, so this 1996 video achieves most of its unique quality through highly imaginative set construction and a cleverly played out story line.

In the video, a young couple takes off in a hot-air balloon, destined for the moon. Surprisingly, they reach it with no problems and are soon surrounded by high-jumping aliens who resemble a malicious version of the Blue Man Group. Catapulting back to the safety of earth, they find themselves under the ocean, where a pot-bellied Poseidon presents a mermaid-studded floorshow. They eventually bob back to the surface, where a ship christened the S.S. Melies, rescues them. Visually, this video can't be compared with any other, because the director shot it by using a hand-cranked camera from the turn of the twentieth century. It simply looks different from anything else. Part of the archaic quality is the blinking effect characteristic of silent films. In addition, the colors resemble watercolors, in striking contrast to the hyped saturations of modern video. Even if you mute the audio to this great song, the video is very enjoyable as a modern silent film.

### Aterciopelados: "El Estuche"

Visually lovely and thought provoking, this video is filled with subtle symbols and dreamlike effects. A series of beautiful, mysterious images suggests an enigmatic earth mother, who initiates the unending motion of nature. On the first viewing, this video appears as a sequence of unconnected, impressionistic shots, but further viewings reveal an interesting structure.

Part one begins with a black-and-white shot of a man walking down a side street. An antiquated poster of a woman, posed like a saintly icon, distracts him. The poster comes to life, in color, and the man goes into a trancelike state. The camera switches to his point of view. Through his eyes, we see the icon begin to sing and move.

Part two consists of a dozen shots of the woman, in a glass enclosure, such as the ones used to house dolls of saints in the old world. She is lit in a warm golden light. In every shot, she is rotating slowly on a pedestal, from the right side of the screen toward the left. The shots cross-fade smoothly into one another, interrupted only by jump-cuts to fuzzy black-and-white clips of inanimate objects, including a nude statue, a gyroscope, and classroom atoms that snap together to form elements.

In part three, the woman disappears, and the black-and-white objects take over. A toy boat fights the waves in a hot bathtub, and a series of animated stills of empty plastic containers marches across the screen.

In part four, the woman reappears in a flowing blue gown. She is holding containers made of beautiful glass and ceramic. She is the carrier of life. Once again, she is rotating slowly to the left.

In part five, the woman appears again, dancing in a short hippie-style dress. She has developed from a detached icon to a symbol of life and youth. Once again, she is rotating slowly to the left.

In part six, the boat reappears, followed by images of seahorses and manta rays.

In part seven, the director merges symbols from the various sections. The woman, by use of a striking matte technique, pulls aside her skin to reveal the sea inside her breast. The message, that she is the mother of life, is complete, and she morphs back into the golden-lit poster icon.

In the final shot, we change back to our original black-and-white point of view, and the man comes out of his trance. He continues down the street on his errand, probably forgetting his brief encounter with these primal symbols of life. We realize that the entire action of the video may have taken place in a split second, as he glanced at the evocative poster.

This is a wonderfully conceived and beautifully shot video. The director, Marina Zurkow, plays with time, expanding the man's momentary reflection as he glances at the poster into a three-minute exploration of his thought process. The consistency of the shots carries viewers along on the journey. Out of 45 basic clips, 33 are images that rotate slowly to the left. Six more move to the right, and six do not move. This basic symmetry gives us a feeling of never being lost, even as we explore the inner, impressionistic reaches of the man's mind. The look and concept of this work compare with the finest art films and set a high standard for music video.

## Coldplay: "Trouble"

This video is appealing for its clever story, which features an altruistic bird/wizard and sparkling visuals. It's an editing tour de force, featuring a dazzling combination of matte effects, transparent overlays, sped-up time-lapse photography, miniature props, and stock footage. Director Tim Hope artfully blends these elements to create an alternative world where plants grow immediately and fireflies flicker all day long.

In the simple narrative, a girl lives in a tiny cottage atop a towering rock. Her only connection with the world below is a bird that flies freely from her lonely outpost down to the farmlands, across which the band members ride in an antique wagon, playing a strange keyboard like the one the Beatles used in "Strawberry Fields Forever." The bird, which is free to ride on the wagon or sit on a tree branch in the girl's garden, seems determined to set her free as well. As night falls, he summons a tornado (it seems to be made out of tissue paper) that grabs her house and rockets it on a dazzling rainbow highway, depositing it in the middle of a small town high in the sky. The visuals never suggest that the action is happening on earth and complement the story's fantasy quality. Check out the director's use of subtle rectangles around all the human characters, just one of many small touches that make this video interesting.

### Michael Jackson: "Billie Jean"

Anyone who is at all familiar with music video has seen this one. Along with its companion piece, "Beat It," this video did more than any other to put MTV on the cultural map, sparking the music video revolution of the 1980s. These two groundbreaking videos convinced record labels that video was a valid selling tool and set a new artistic standard for the medium.

"Billie Jean," directed by Steve Barron, perfectly balances the elements of a great video. It tells a story without being too literal. It showcases the star's best qualities and leaves no doubt about his talent. The video is visually beautiful, and it creates a unique world different from our day-to-day existence. Jackson's dancing and singing would have been enough to make a great video, but Barron goes beyond the call of duty to create a video in which each frame is unique and colorful, without ever overpowering the star's natural talent. In addition, through the use of repeated devices, such as the panels that light underneath Jackson's feet wherever he walks, Barron cast the singer as a mystical, shape-changing fantasy character. This enigmatic quality became Jackson's trademark, which is a far cry from the slick tux-wearing image that preceded this video. So Barron created four minutes of great TV, a new image for a major talent, and a new credibility for a much-maligned infant medium.

These artful videos don't try to relate to other videos, and they don't try to fit into a certain marketable genre. They may be influenced by cinema, photography, painting, or even psychological theory, but in the best cases, they are simply the creations of original thinkers.

## Star-Power videos

The simplest formula for an exciting video can be summed up in one phrase: interesting people doing interesting things. If your star has irresistible charisma and does something that lifts the popular concept of entertainment to the next level, then your job is easy. Just shoot them, arrange your clips in a sequence, and you're done. Unadulterated charisma enabled Elvis to make his name simply by singing and dancing on TV. Charisma also explains why Michael Jackson just had to moonwalk during Motown Records' 25th anniversary special in the early 1980s. The Beatles' first performance on *The Ed Sullivan Show* consisted of the group singing in front of a simple backdrop with three camera angles and a couple of dolly-up shots. No special effects or slick editing was used in any of these epochal performances, yet each one of them started a revolution that defined the music of a decade. Why? Because the performers were charismatic, and they were doing something that viewers hadn't seen before.

Are you lucky enough to be shooting the next Elvis or Michael Jackson? Then keep it simple. Here are some videos where the director wisely kept to a minimal concept — letting the artists do what they do best.

### Bob Dylan: "Subterranean Homesick Blues"

This excerpt, from the documentary film, *Don't Look Back*, introduces the birth of the rock star as antihero. Emulating his idol James Dean, Dylan refused to adopt the slick trappings of stardom. Instead of lip-synching the lyrics, he performed a sardonic parody of the practice by flipping large cue cards instead. In direct contrast with the teen idols of the previous generation, he dressed in street clothes and sang in a decidedly funky location, an alley in Greenwich Village. His costar, beat poet Allen Ginsburg, also epitomized this new generation of antihero. Dylan's refusal to buy into the traditional star system had a tremendous impact on artists of the day, including the Beatles, and his antiheroism is still the accepted image for rock stars today.

### Bruce Springsteen: "Born to Run"

This video is a compilation of clips of the legendary live performer. Springsteen has done plot-driven concept videos, including "I'm on Fire," in which he plays a soft-spoken auto mechanic, but he's at his best giving a rocking performance onstage. "Born to Run" captures Bruce and his band at various moments spanning their 25-year career, and it certainly evokes pangs of nostalgia among his longtime fans. He even autographs the final freeze frame. This video needs no special effects or tricky editing. Springsteen's dynamic stage moves provide the motion, and the camera simply captures him in his natural element.

### Michael Jackson: "Beat It"

This video is one of the best known of all time, and it certainly did much to make millions of new viewers aware of MTV. The action is loosely based on the rumble scene from Leonard Bernstein and Stephen Sondheim's Broadway play *West Side Story*. The video depicts Jackson as a streetwise teenage superhero who lives alone in a one-room New York City walk-up. Although his surroundings are Spartan, his charisma is such that he can break up gang fights with the overpowering rhythmic impetus of his dancing. The early part of the video shows him only in cutaway shots. It takes a few minutes for him to get the vibe that a rumble is brewing. He gets dressed and arrives at the scene of the action. When Jackson comes on-screen for good, the final minute of the video is given over to a choreographed dance, with him leading the gang members in a series of steps rarely seen outside of the streets of the Bronx. This moment conveys the triumph of Jackson's charisma and dancing ability over the negativity of gang warfare and successfully blends the dance-driven vitality of classic R&B with the gritty "mean streets" cinematic style of contemporary filmmakers, such as Martin Scorsese.

### Chris Isaak: "Wicked Game"

If you've ever turned the pages of *Vogue* or *Cosmopolitan*, you've seen the black-and-white photography of Herb Ritts. His shots typically place a single figure against a bright, white background. Ritts occasionally translates this uncluttered but striking style to video, as he does here with Isaak and his mysterious costar. Many of the clips from this video could be captured as stills and used to advertise upscale cologne or accessories. The plot is very simple. Isaak pursues and catches a dream woman on a windswept beach. But does he really catch her? Even as they embrace, she never looks into his eyes. Static shots of Isaak standing on the beach, as clouds move unnaturally fast above him indicate that he is a passive participant in events that he can't control. Ritts keeps the plot uncomplicated and focuses on Isaak's matinee idol face, which recalls James Dean. In this way, "Wicked Game" harks back to the "moody, handsome star" vehicles of the 1950s, especially Dean's *East of Eden, Rebel without a Cause,* and *Giant.*

## Effect-driven videos

When *2001: A Space Odyssey* was released, legendary film director Stanley Kubrick was criticized for including long sections with no dialogue or plot development. The critics said he relied too much on beautiful and startling images. Kubrick answered them, saying that film is a visual medium. It was a great art form before it even had sound. Motion pictures are all about the images on the screen. This certainly is true of video, as well, because most music videos have no dialogue. We frequently study videos with the audio muted. If the images hold our attention for four minutes in silence, then we know it's a good video. Try watching MTV with the sound down. You may be surprised at some of the videos that capture your imagination, when musical bias is out of the equation.

All of the videos in this category are visually captivating, sound or no sound. To work in this realm of cutting-edge effects, you have to develop your editing and effects application skills to a high level. Some of these videos are so effect-heavy that the musical artist doesn't even appear on-screen. In others, the effects heighten and enhance the excitement that is essential to a great performance.

### Peter Gabriel: "Sledgehammer"

This 1980s tour-de-force is still a technical marvel today. It's an editing masterpiece. After an opening sequence of extreme close-ups, the frame widens to include Gabriel's entire face and the real fun begins. A series of blindingly fast edits continues for a full three minutes before finally slowing down slightly. The shot list is long, because of the extreme editing speed. An animated train circles Gabriel's head. His hair turns into cotton candy. His head turns into an ice sculpture, and then it turns into a fruit bowl. In the space of four minutes almost every effect available at the time is used.

The 25 basic scenes in this video contain many rapid-fire jump cuts. A sequence of lightning-fast edits of Gabriel's face takes up three of the four minutes of the video. Even the editor may not know how many total cuts there actually are, but here's a rough estimate. If Gabriel's shirt, in one scene, changes eight times in a two-second interval, than each shirt clip would be about a quarter of a second, or 250 milliseconds, long. If the editor decided to keep up that rate for the full four minutes of the video, doing so would result in about 1,000 clips being used to construct the entire piece. That's a lot of clips to string together in four minutes of tape. And here's the brilliant part. It's not a mishmash! This video can be viewed frame by frame, and each frame is an interesting, thought-provoking shot. In a word — wow!

## A Tribe Called Quest: "Scenario"

This clever video creates a simulated software interface that lets the viewer feel like she is editing and adding effects to the clips in real time. It's a must-see for anyone interested in video editing. Here are a few of the highlights:

The rappers appear in headshots inside typical PC-style windows. One window sits on top of a stack, and the stack can be shuffled around. Smaller windows can be on-screen along with large ones. Sometimes the main rapper appears in the large window, with the next crew member on deck in the smaller window. When his turn comes, the windows flip-flop. Control panels also appear on the screen. When zoom is illuminated, the shot zooms in. Eyeline tricks are played. At one point, Q-Tip raps and then looks to his left. Busta Rhymes is in his own window, looking to his right at Q-Tip. Q introduces Busta, and he takes over, as his window zooms up in size.

This video also contains lots of funny moments. For example, a small window appears with a whirling head inside. When the whirling stops, you see the face of filmmaker Spike Lee. A salon control panel appears. It controls the hairstyle of the rapper on-screen. The settings include Nappy, Long, Curl, and Troll. That's right, as in the little plastic dolls.

At another point, a flashing user command appears: "Check the house now!" The follow up command is "Blink 'em . . . Really . . . Try it!" The headshots on the screen cut in rapid-fire succession from one tribe member to another, and if the viewer blinks at the right speed, a new screen seems to pop up with every eye opening.

## Psycore: "I Go Solo"

Director Markus Manninen presents a well-constructed animated video with the look of a video game. The video depicts band members as action figures whose mission is to bust the lead singer out of an evil castle, where futuristic aliens are holding him. The fearless band members pull off the rescue by using space age weaponry, and a high-speed chase ensues. This chase is similar to the canyon race in *Star Wars: Episode I — The Phantom Menace* and is not unlike any number of video game programs. The lead singer shoots down the pursuing helicopters, and the band reaches its goal, an outdoor rock festival.

This video is an example of the close connection between music video, animation, and action-oriented computer games. The notion of band members as cartoon characters stretches back to *Josie and the Pussycats* in the 1970s and *The Archies* and *The Beatles* cartoon series in the 1960s.

If your act is willing to share the spotlight with the latest in digital technology, then you have the freedom to experiment to the fullest potential of your editing software.

## Videos that balance effects and performance

This is the broadest category of music video. Because most videos intend to promote the band as real people who exhibit charisma and star quality, it's rare that technology completely takes over. Most music videos are, rather, a marriage of effects and traditional performance. These videos show the musicians doing what they do best with digital enhancements that lift their visual image above the rest of the pack.

### Remy Zero: "Save Me"

This video has two basic elements. The first is a master shot of the band, performing in front of a solid background. In the editing process, many moving shots of graphic effects, explosions, and even wildlife footage are matted in behind them. The second element has a simple but very clever effect. The lead singer spent an entire day walking backwards around the streets of Manhattan, through the normal crowds of people on the street. When this footage is run backwards, as it is here, he appears to be the only person in New York who walks forward, while everyone else is in reverse. You see many interesting shots, including one where he gets out of a taxi as one of the "backward walkers" climbs in. Later on, we discover that little children share his secret. In the end, he finally notices, shrugs, and starts walking backward like everyone else.

Director Phil Harder definitely wasn't snoozing on the day of this shoot. A lot of advance planning was involved in the creation of this video equivalent to a backward guitar solo.

### Apex Theory: "Shh . . . (hope diggy)"

If video is all about motion and color, this one could define the medium. Every frame is filled with super-fast movement and saturated color. The edit tempo is similar to Peter Gabriel's landmark "Sledgehammer," but this is a more straight-ahead performance video. Like Gabriel's piece, it's interesting to note that the singer's mouth stays in synch with the lyrics, although everything else in the frame, including his eyes and hands, seems to be going at a hundred miles an hour. The crowd spins around the band like a carousel on steroids, and removed frames make the band members leap like digitized dervishes.

This is a high-energy band, and through lightning-fast editing, directors VIM and Tony have upped the quotient even higher.

# Urban video styles

All the visual elements in a video, including the sets, the props, the costumes, the editing tempo, and the use of effects, contribute to an overall look that reinforces the musical content. For example, long, slow shots of a guy pouring brandy for his girl would probably be inappropriate for a Rage Against the Machine video, but they may be entirely correct for a Brian McKnight slow jam. Conversely, the rapid fire staccato edits that would match the assault of Lenny Kravitz may seem way out of synch against a laid back hip-hop groove. Urban musical styles have developed a variety of looks that compliment the vibe, be it a late night slow jam or a streetwise rap.

## Angie Stone: "Brotha"

Angie Stone's songs usually feature a positive message, and this one is no exception. The theme is role models, and director Chris Robinson uses simple and effective techniques to bring it across in a powerful way. The basic master shot is Angie singing the song on a hillside in Los Angeles. Throughout the video, you see quick cutaways to still photos of positive African-American male role models. Martin Luther King, Jr., Jesse Jackson, Colin Powell, Bill Cosby, Bob Marley, Will Smith, and many others appear. At the end, the video rewinds through a series of these stills, just to bring home the message of hope.

## Maxwell: "Fortunate"

The lush visual quality and thematic symmetry of this video would seem to qualify it for a place in the Museum of Modern Art, if they ever have a video gallery. Director Francis Lawrence's use of understated technique combines a slightly disturbing dream sequence with a sheen of muted color and subtle motion.

There is only one set, an ultramodern, starkly furnished apartment high above Manhattan. There are only two characters, Maxwell and a female companion, who may be dream generated. There are only two colors, blue and red. The list of red objects is short: a bottle of ink, a dress, a pair of lips, a pair of sunglasses, the iris of an eye, and a couple of roses. Everything else is translucent blue. The action takes place at night, lit by the source light of soft lamps, which frequently cause flares in the camera lens. Lawrence lingers on these flares for a long time and uses some of them as whiteout transitions.

The most striking compositional technique is the use of semitransparent rectangular panels, added in the editing process, that resemble smoked glass. Lawrence uses these over and over, combining them with a camera technique that shifts the shot slightly, while the subject stays in place. Doing this makes the rectangle shift so that a face that was obscured becomes exposed, and vice versa. The rectangles also create impressionistic walls that separate the characters and can also bring them together. This technique is so essential to "Fortunate" that of 80 basic cuts, 40 of the clips feature the shift. The effect is usually executed in time with the tempo of the music; Beat one, hold. Beat two, shift. The blue light, the floating rectangles (which the characters don't see), and the subtle camera shifts all combine to create a hypnotic effect which is very consistent with the mellow groove of Maxwell's music. This video is state of the art.

### Lauren Hill: "Everything Is Everything"

Director Sanji creates an amazing illusion that serves as the central visual theme of this video. The entire island of Manhattan becomes a huge turntable, with the Empire State Building as the spindle. A massive cartridge drops into the grooves: Fifth Avenue, Park Avenue, and Broadway. There's even the big hand of the divine DJ that occasionally does a little scratching by shuttling the whole island back and forth. In dramatic scenes, everyday people notice the shadow of the giant tone arm pass over them, and the whole city develops a feeling of unity. We're all spinning on the same turntable! This video is great in both technique and message.

### Mary J. Blige: "No More Drama"

This video, directed by Sanji, is a serious treatment of urban problems, and it underscores the power of hip-hop to shed light on disturbing realities. There are three subplots, each set in different parts of the city. A mohawked drug addict, a gang member, and a battered wife all arrive at the point where they realize that it is up to them to change their lives and take responsibility for their own survival. As Mary J. walks past a bank of TV screens that show the latest world news, she pleads, with tears in her eyes, "No more drama." This is a moving video that would translate well into a feature-length film.

As in other genres, the only rule in urban video is that there are no hard and fast rules. Romantic slow jams do tend to have longer clips, (about three seconds is average), and they do tend to use slow blackouts as transitions. Oh yeah, they do tend to have subplots that depict couples fighting or falling in love. But hey, there's somebody in Brooklyn right now coming up with a new concept that will set the video world on its ear.

## Live videos

Slow jams revel in subplots, hip-hoppers include the whole crew as a show of solidarity, and special-effects-driven videos can take your mind just about anywhere, but nothing showcases a great rock 'n' roll band like a live performance. Band members interact with each other and with the audience. If you can capture that feeling on videotape, you don't need any special effects. All the magic is in the performance, as demonstrated by the charismatic Bruce Springsteen's "Born to Run" video discussed earlier in the chapter.

### James Brown: "Night Train"

This video is an excerpt from a remarkable mid-1960s film called *The TAMI/TNT Show*. With a great cast, including Chuck Berry, Bo Diddley, The Miracles, The Beach Boys, The Rolling Stones, The Ronnettes, and Marvin Gaye, this live concert from Los Angeles defined the sound of a generation. It's now available on video under the title *That Was Rock*.

All of the performers were reportedly humbled and intimidated by James Brown's incendiary set, which established a new standard for entertainment. Funk was an unknown concept to the general public, and Brown unleashed it in a dazzling display of dance moves and soul shouting that set the world on its ear. The story of hip-hop, from Sly Stone to Stevie Wonder to George Clinton to Grandmaster Flash and Kurtis Blow, begins here.

### The Beatles: "I Saw Her Standing There"

This film clip, from their first live show in America at Uline Arena in Washington, D.C., is a true document of what Beatlemania was all about. Amazingly, as they come onstage, they have to rearrange their amps and drums by themselves before they can begin playing. Roadies weren't invented yet. The band is more audible in this relatively small arena than they are in later clips, and they are rocking beyond anything you've heard on their albums. This feels like the moment when they realized that they had actually made it, and the struggle was worth it. The joy comes across in every riff. Furthermore, anyone who has ever doubted Ringo's credentials as a hard-rocking drummer should check out this footage. It's available on videotape as part of a Maysles Brothers documentary film called *The Beatles First Visit*. After you've viewed this film, see if you don't think that Richard Lester studied it closely as he prepared to shoot *A Hard Day's Night*.

## Our very own cavern club

**Road Diary**

Have you ever seen early photos of the Beatles at the Cavern Club, their home base in Liverpool? The shots are always gritty, grainy, and very dark and yet filled with vitality. They capture a black-and-white world of leather jackets, sweat, and loud music. You feel like part of the crowd, jammed into the small subterranean space to dig on these new sounds that were unraveling the restrictions of prewar Victorian culture.

We decided to pay tribute to this primal rock photography at a gig in, of all places, Nebraska. Out there on the Western plains, we loaded into a Knights of Pythias Hall. The building was a former car dealership, and it still had a lot of the 1950s furnishings intact, including a great candy-apple red vinyl couch straight out of *Happy Days*. When we looked at the stage, we immediately flashed on the Cavern Club. It was small and had an archway built around it that gave it an enclosed feel. The lighting was minimal, and the vintage furniture completed the vibe. We set up the DCR-TRV900 on a tripod in the back of the room, set for old movie mode. Then we shot a master of the whole show. Of course, we deliberately threw in a few Beatlesque moves, including headshakes and duo harmony vocals on a single microphone. From the distance that we were shooting, about 30 feet, we got a good approximation of the old grainy photos of the Fab Four at the Cavern Club. The audio was pretty rough, but it didn't matter. From that distance, lip-synch was unimportant. We've been dropping short clips from that shoot into lots of different songs whenever we want to suggest a Liverpudlian vibe.

# Compilation videos

MTV's sister channel, VH1, was founded to cater to an audience that didn't necessarily want a steady diet of the latest, newest videos. Many viewers wanted their cutting edge vids seasoned with some of the classic stuff. Y'know, a little Hendrix, a little Doors, maybe some Joplin. For those viewers, VH1 created VH1-CL (classic). Only problem was, none of these artists made videos, because the form wasn't invented yet. Fortunately, they all made at least a few TV appearances. Some, the Beatles and the Rolling Stones, for example, even made feature films with plenty of live footage.

For the artists who exist mostly on old kinescopes of TV shows, sound quality is not up to today's standards, and the TV footage may need plenty of massaging to bring it up to modern specifications. You do the best you can, by finding out what vintage material is available, and being resourceful. Here's how one director made a modern looking video out of old source material.

## The Allman Brothers: "Statesboro Blues"

The Allman Brother's live cover of Taj Mahal's version of this Blind Willie McTell gem is certainly a Southern rock classic. And fortunately for blues lovers, it exists in pristine audio form. The Bro's recorded it as part of their *Live at the Fillmore East* sessions, in the early 1970s, with their original lineup, including the great slide guitarist Duane Allman. Tom Dowd, one of the recording industry's most brilliant pioneers, engineered these sessions. His craft was such that you could pull those tapes out of the vault today, remaster them, and they would sound like a modern record. In fact, that's exactly what Atlantic Records did a couple of years ago. With the remastered album coming out on CD, it seemed appropriate to air a video of this classic performance. Unfortunately, concerts weren't routinely videotaped in the early 1970s, and footage of "Statesboro Blues" at the Fillmore didn't exist. There was scattered film footage of the group on stage, however, and it was assembled into a performance of this song.

One of the basic notions going into the project was that most people can't tell exactly what a guitarist is playing by looking at his hands. They hear licks. They see fingers moving. It all adds up. That made the guitar parts of this guitar-heavy song fairly easy. When the slide guitar plays, they show a clip of Duane playing slide. Doesn't have to be in synch. Vocals were a different matter. There were clips of younger brother Gregg singing, but he wasn't singing "Statesboro Blues." This problem was gotten around through a simple technique. During the vocal lines, a clip plays of another band member, right up until the last word. On that word, there's a cut to a quick clip of Gregg's mouth closing. He has a way of pulling away from the microphone at the end of lines, so this added a little extra punctuation. The viewer believes that he just got through singing one of the lines of Statesboro.

Drums also posed a problem. Viewers can tell if the drummer is hitting the cymbals and drumheads in time with the music, so whenever the band's two drummers are shown, they are in slow motion. The viewer enjoys the effect and doesn't expect them to be in synch with the track. Voilà! You see a *live* performance of the founders of Southern rock, playing one of their signature tunes.

# Storyboards and Music Video Concepts

You can use a few simple tools and exercises to bring even the fuzziest of concepts into focus. The more time you spend visualizing your final edit and considering what details will be involved in making it happen, the less frustrating the process of video creation will be for you and your donut-paid crew.

## Storyboards: Putting your video down on paper

A *storyboard* is a cartoon, similar to the ones in the Sunday comic section. It provides a visual map for you to follow as you shoot your video. You don't need to be an artist to create a storyboard. Some of the top directors draw simple stick figures. Even with primitive graphics, a storyboard can give a useful rough sketch of who will be in a shot, where the actors will stand in relation to one another, and what other objects may be in the frame with them. The storyboard can also indicate what direction light will be coming from and, through the use of simple arrows and dotted lines, can show the direction in which actors will be looking and moving. Most importantly, the storyboard enables you, the director, to look at the beginning, middle, and ending of your video before you actually shoot anything.

If your video involves subplots or different locations, you may be shooting several full-length master takes that will later be edited together. In this case, you may want to create several storyboards. The first is your master storyboard. The master storyboard is a cartoon of your eventual vision of the final edit. It's like the outline of a book, and it can alert you to potential problems. Is that crane shot of the car crash in panel 23 really possible within your budget? Is the transition from Times Square to the Amazon jungle too abrupt? It's good to resolve these questions at the storyboard stage, before you spend real time and money. See Figure 3-2 for an example of a master storyboard.

Your master storyboard serves as your roadmap all the way from your first concept right through to the final edit. Feel free to revise it. At least you know from the outset that you have four minutes worth of good ideas that hang together. If you are shooting in different locations, you may also want to create shot-specific storyboards. Storyboard number two might map out the master shot of the band playing at the Steak and Sausage, with the lead singer jumping into the mosh pit on the third chorus. Storyboard number three would map out the shots for the subplot where the bass player falls in love with the cocktail waitress, and so on. Here are a couple of sample storyboards. See Figure 3-3 for an example of a shot-specific storyboard.

Most experienced directors caution against becoming enslaved by these planning tools. They are great for making sure that your concept is organized and doable before you start, but if something spontaneous happens, go with it. If you're shooting in Union Square and a pigeon lands on the drummer's head, don't yell, "Cut!" Even though that wasn't on your storyboard, it may turn out to be the best moment in the video.

Panel #1 / Scene 1
Establish shot of town

Panel #2 / Scene 2
Wide shot of club

Panel #3 / Scene 3
Wide shot of band

Panel #4 / Scene 3
Big Joe enters

Panel #5 / Scene 4
Big Joe sings c/u

Panel #6 / Scene 3
Big Joe throws harmonica

**Figure 3-2:** The master storyboard is a road map of your entire video. This excerpt shows the opening scene of "I Flip For You."

Panel #1 / Subplot #2
Waitress brings beer

Panel #2 / Subplot #2
Bass player hugs her

Panel #3 / Subplot #2
They kiss

Panel #4 / Subplot #2
Big Joe watches, c/u

Panel #5 / Subplot #2
Big Joe interferes

Panel #6 / Subplot #2
Bass, Big Joe fight

**Figure 3-3:** The shot-specific storyboard is a guide to shooting lengthy clips that will later be incorporated into your video. This excerpt shows a subplot that will be used for cutaways.

## Symbolism

A feature film has a 100-page script and at least an hour of screen time to get its message across. In contrast, a music video has three or four minutes and usually no dialogue at all to convey its message. To increase our chances of conveying complex ideas in such a limited time, we rely heavily on symbols. Symbols are visual cues that trigger associations in the viewer's mind. By using them, we can put across a lot more information than the three-minute format allows us to in real time.

On a simple level, a mohawk haircut is a symbol. If Johnny the bass player has a mohawk, we know some things about him. He doesn't work at a bank. He doesn't intend to apply for a job there. This tells us that he's committed to his music. It also tells us that, if he has an alternative haircut, there may be other ways in which he doesn't buy into society's concept of "normalcy." So just by appearing on-screen, before he has played a note, Johnny has caused some of us to identify with him and others to be alienated. A definite statement has been made with one shot of a haircut. By utilizing visual symbols, we give the viewer more information than we could normally present in a short time, and we have the creatively liberating chance to do so in a metaphorical, rather than a literal, way.

## Brainstorming ideas

One great thing about storyboards is that you can create imaginary videos and work on your concepts, with nothing more than a sketchpad and a marker. Go down this list of basic concepts, and if an idea catches your attention, or you see one that you can improve upon, grab your pad and sketch out a quick storyboard. Start with just a dozen panels. If the idea looks promising, develop a more detailed sketch. Consider how your own resources, including your camera, lights, locations, and the editing power of Premiere may contribute to the project. Keep these sketches in a portfolio. As time goes by, you'll develop a list of your own, and you can trace the development of your directing style by paging through this file.

If you're at a loss for your first music video concept, use the following scenarios and tips to jumpstart creativity:

✦ A live concert by a visually exciting band. How would you accentuate their strongest features?

✦ A live concert by a visually boring band. How would you use lighting, camera angles, editing tempo, and effects to make them appear to be exciting?

✦ A band lip-synchs onstage at a club with a live audience. A subplot appears in quick cutaway shots and gradually takes over the video. How would you control the ratio of band/subplot shots so that the transition happens gradually?

✦ A band lip-synchs onstage at a club. A subplot appears in cutaway shots, at a location on the other side of town. Events in the subplot bring the characters closer to the club, and in the final scene, their action happens in the club while the band is playing.

✦ Shoot a punk rock band interacting with a live audience. Edit with extremely quick cuts that convey the excitement and near-anarchy of their live performance.

✦ Shoot a psychedelic band. Introduce cutaways of computer graphics of multicolored fractal images. Create a gradual takeover of the video by these images, including a transitional shot in which the band gradually disappears behind a curtain of shimmering colors.

✦ Write down your dreams as soon as you wake up in storyboard form.

✦ Shoot a live band by using lens flares from the source lights as a major compositional element.

✦ Create a video using fast motion for onstage footage and slow motion for a subplot about a prisoner. Edit to bring out maximum contrast.

✦ Shoot a band in front of a solid background and then matte in a variety of textures behind them. How can this device make a boring band seem more exciting or create a comedic or surreal situation?

Hopefully, by now you're saying, "I've got better ideas than that!" Well, don't just sit there. Storyboard them! After you've storyboarded a video, the next impulse is to go out and shoot it. Hopefully the list above will give you a kick-start. Many of the above video effects are described in Chapter 12.

# Chapter Replay

Now, after reading this chapter and following along with all the examples, you should be able to:

✦ Identify music videos by genre

✦ Identify specific techniques used in music videos

✦ Construct a storyboard to help organize your video concepts

✦ Understand the use of symbolism in video

In the next chapter, you use your skills in creating and storyboarding concepts by applying cinematic camera and lighting techniques to give your videos a truly professional look.

✦    ✦    ✦

# Start Me Up: Beginning Your Own Music Video

# Shooting the Raw Footage

The more great footage you shoot, the less time you'll spend polishing so-so shots. Adobe Premiere can accomplish a lot in post-production. However, if you start with great footage, you'll be ahead of the game. In this chapter, you learn basic techniques for making your raw footage look great.

So how do you create great footage? Well, as we love to say, video is a visual thing. You create great footage with your eyes. Special effects can go a long way to enhance the visual quality of your footage, and skillful editing sets the tempo for your three-minute opus. However, having great raw footage before you go into the editing workspace has no substitute. Even though videotape is cheap, you want to maximize your ratio of good quality shots, and you will benefit from the technical know-how to produce certain effects. Best of all, by learning some basic cinematic techniques, you won't always have to say, "We were goin' for that home movie vibe, y'know?"

## Working with Light

Available light is a wonderful gift given to us courtesy of the sun and then improved upon somewhat by Thomas Edison. Shooting using available light only is a wonderful experience, and doing so can take you to some interesting places, but sunlight won't always provide everything you need for a great shot. Shoots often call for the use of artificial light, but before you turn on a light, you must effectively position your subject. This is the first step in the overall composition of the shot.

# Positioning your subject

Imagine that you're shooting a folksinger in front of a waterfall. She's singing a song about the environment, and the afternoon sun is hitting the waterfall in such a way that, with the tripod placed exactly ten feet away, a rainbow forms in the spray. By putting your artist four feet from the lens, and six feet in front of the falls — don't try this at Niagara — you get a rainbow over her shoulder. You want to shoot quickly, before the sun moves (well, the earth, actually). But you notice that the perfect spot for her to stand is directly under a huge oak tree, and the tree casts a shadow right over her eyes. Artificial light is needed.

To arrange artificial light on a subject, in this case, the singer, you need to position her correctly. Here's how:

1. **Put a piece of duct tape on the exact point where she's standing.** This point is called a *mark*. You're not shooting her feet, so the mark won't show up in your footage. During breaks, she can get a sip of coffee, check messages, and still return to the same spot over and over.

2. **Put another piece of tape at the point (a tree, for example) where you want her to focus her eyes.** Later on, when you edit, you need the relationships of the guitar, her head, her eyes, the falls, and the rainbow to be consistent from clip to clip.

3. **If you want her to move during the shot, place another mark where she should stop.** Then you can record several versions, or *takes,* of the same shot and edit the best parts later.

# Using the three-point lighting system

Cinematographers use three basic lights to set up a scene. The three lights are defined by the way they are used. In a low-budget system, all three lights can be the same type of hardware. This three-point lighting system is a flexible method for taking care of common problems in scene composition. The three elements of the system are:

✦ **The key light**. This is used to illuminate the most important feature in the shot, usually the subject's face.

✦ **The backlight**. This is used to create a sense of distance between the subject and the background.

✦ **The fill light**. This light, which may actually be several lights, is used to smooth out the overall composition, and to control shadows.

## Using the key light

After you've positioned the singer, you can light her face. You need a lamp and a bulb that are optimized for digital video not still photography, because digital video cameras take in much more light than still cameras. A shop that specializes in video gear can guide you to the right equipment. Before shooting, mount the light on a stand and look at her face. Does she look like she's being interrogated on *Law and Order*? If so, the light's too bright. If you use a light stand, make sure that it provides a clip for mounting an inexpensive reflective umbrella, available at most pro camera shops. In addition, lamps frequently feature *barn doors*, moveable flaps that control the intensity and direction of the illumination. Aim the light away from your folksinger, into the umbrella and move the stand a little closer to her. She should now be bathed in diffused, indirect light. Diffused light makes her face glow, without bringing out every detail. Finally, angle your light slightly to give the shot realism. Because you're shooting in the afternoon, the background will have shadows. Give her nose a gentle shadow by adjusting your light a little off center. Make sure that the light comes into the frame from the same direction as the sunlight — from the west in this case. Finally, make sure that the key light is not overshooting her face and washing out the natural rainbow in the background. Now that you have the face effectively lit, you can use the other two lights in the system to clear up any problems in the shot.

## Using the backlight

Notice that the rainbow and the singer's face both look great, but the waterfall looks like it's falling directly onto her head! The camera tends to flatten distance out a bit, which results in the classic tree-growing-out-of-head shots that you can find in most family photo albums. To eliminate this problem, you apply the depth of field concept by creating a sense of distance between the singer and the falls. You want the viewer to sense that there is a real distance from the lens, where the viewer's eyes are, all the way back to the waterfall. You can create depth of field in two ways:

✦ Position your subject properly between the background and the camera lens.

✦ Use backlighting.

With the subject positioned effectively in the shot, you can enhance the overall sense of depth in the scene by using a *backlight*. Because both her hair and the waterfall are dark, they blend together as one object. With the backlight in place, viewers can tell that she is not *in* the falls. Simply aim a light at her head and shoulders from outside the frame of the shot and behind the singer, but not spilling directly into the camera lens. This lighting angle creates a subtle halo around her head. Viewers can sense the distance, and the shot becomes deeper and richer. This technique was perfected during the era of black-and-white movies.

 **Tip**     Study the interior shots of vintage Humphrey Bogart flicks to see how subtle backlighting makes a dark figure stand out from a dark background.

## Using the fill light

The third light you need is a *fill light*. Having a fill light on hand when shooting your footage helps to smooth out the overall composition of the video. You can use the fill light to solve any problems that the first two lights may cause. For example, in adjusting the key light to give the singer's nose a little natural shadow, you cast a long, distracting shadow on the front of the guitar. Ignore this shadow when you're setting the key light. Get the lighting on her face perfect, and then use a fill light to take out the guitar shadow. Film crews may keep a number of fill lights on hand to solve little problems. Be creative. Sheets of cardboard covered with tin foil work well as low-budget reflectors, a technique called *bounce lighting*. If you can talk a couple of friends into serving as your crew, appoint one of them to be *gaffer*, the person who sets the lights, and the other one to be *grip*, the person who moves stuff, including reflectors, around. And remember, coffee and donuts ensure a happy crew. Figure 4-1 shows the *three-point lighting* system in action.

**Tip**

You don't need a truckload of gear to set up a three-point lighting system. Three 250-watt lamps, with stands and umbrellas, should do. We splurged and spent a little extra on one light with adjustable intensity. We use this for our key light. Working indoors, this light gives us complete control, and we just plug the lights into a generic power strip, the kind with it's own on-and-off switch. Outdoors, we run the power strip to a heavy-duty extension cord and then run that to an AC adaptor that plugs into our van's cigarette lighter. The van acts as our mobile generator. Of course, keep your lights turned on for as short a time as possible to avoid draining your car's battery!

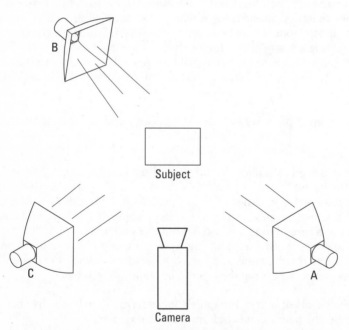

**Figure 4-1:** The three-point lighting system, set up and ready for use. The elements are: A. Key light; B. Backlight; C. Fill light.

# Incorporating source light into your shot

In the world of music video, we frequently find ourselves in situations that are already lit. Shooting live bands on location often involves the use of *source lights.* A source light is any light that is actually present in the shot. Not only is the light fixture a part of the set but so is the light that it gives off. This applies to lamps, candles, lit matches, lanterns, and so forth. When a band plays onstage, it deliberately uses lights to create an environment that is more intense than natural lighting. Most stage lighting gear consists of theatrical lights with different colored gel inserts. In addition, one or more spotlights may be used. High-powered theatrical spots are designed to illuminate the featured performer's face in such a way that she seems close to the patrons in the last row. This amount of lighting is much more than you normally use to light a camera shot from ten feet away. But the extra intensity usually works in your favor. The reason for shooting a band live is to re-create their onstage excitement, so the overexposure of powerful lighting can be a good thing, as long as you don't let it get out of hand. Tina Turner's live video of "Proud Mary," for example, serves as a great example of the effective use of source lighting. Hundreds of source lights illuminate the stage, and director David Mallet, a pioneer of rock video, uses them to pump more and more energy into the video as the song builds to an exciting climax.

Beyond the basic stage lighting, the venue may use anything from computer-controlled rotating beams to an oil-slide light show. Take advantage of these resources, and if the venue has a lot of special lighting effects, try to get some shots of the effects as they illuminate the backdrop. These shots can be used later for cutaway inserts and overlays, and are useful in creating chroma key effects in Adobe Premiere. For example, imagine you're editing footage of a band called, The Exploding Universe performing live at the 9:30 Club. The club had some dynamic lights on the backdrop, framing most of the band members nicely in your footage, but the bass player was standing in front of a nine-foot amplifier with gray grill cloth. Plus, he was wearing jeans and a white t-shirt, while the rest of the band was decked out in Hendrix-inspired velvet. During a live show, you can't direct the band members to stand where you want them, and you can't use Premiere to retroactively change their outfits (maybe on a later version . . .), but you can use the chroma key feature to bring the bass man into the same lighting environment as the rest of the group. By keying out the color of the amplifier and blending a good still of the backdrop lighting using a chroma key, the bass player's background is as exciting as the rest of the band. In the editing process, when you switch between clips of band members, you can keep your transitions smooth. The lighting backdrop remains consistent.

**Cross-Reference**    See Chapter 12 for step-by-step chroma key directions.

## The Boy Scouts were right

**Road Diary**

"Be prepared" is as good a motto for videographers as it is for pocketknife-wielding scouts. One way to avoid unforeseen circumstances is to foresee them, through your viewfinder. Here's a tale of disaster averted and another tale of a plain-old disaster.

I picked up an afternoon gig at a local Thai restaurant. The owner is a jazz and blues fanatic. Posters of Miles and Coltrane and B.B. King and Howlin' Wolf cover the walls. One wall has a big portrait of the sax-playing king of Thailand. Because the gig was a reunion, of sorts, with some swing guitar buddies whom I hadn't played with in a long time, Maura decided to shoot the show.

We got situated on stage, and she set up the perfect shot. Because it was a one-off gig, and we would only play each song once, it was a single-camera/single-take shoot. The angles had to be right, because we wouldn't have any alternate clips. Fortunately, she rolled some tape while we were warming up, and a problem appeared as soon as the first customers drifted in. The pathway from the front door to the tables crossed right through the shot! Because we loaded in our gear through the back door, and set up while the club was empty, it never occurred to us to think about the audience roaming around. So after setting up for 30 minutes, Maura had 5 minutes to find a spot on the other side of the room, check the light, control the shadows, and get a great angle. Of course, the video turned out great. The Pad Thai was darn good, too.

A couple of weeks earlier, we went to a wedding, and we volunteered to shoot it. May as well get some experience, we figured. If our music gig ever goes down the tubes, we can always shoot wedding videos for a living! Anyway, we set up meticulously, getting the perfect angle on the marks where the bride, groom, and minister would be standing. To get every word of the nuptials, we ran stereo remote microphones up to the edge of the stage. We were set. But again, we didn't account for those pesky real people who tend to show up at these events. As soon as the doors were opened, the crowd pushed their way up to the very front, leaving just a small semicircle for the wedding party. Our beautiful medium tripod shot was now an extreme close-up of the back of a balding man's head. Oh well, we sighed, at least we'll get audio, and we can burn a lovely keepsake CD. At that point, the wedding march began, and two little flower girls came shyly down the aisle, cute as a button. The girls deposited their flowers and sat down at the edge of the stage — directly on our microphones! Goodbye, audio. So we wound up with a close-up of a guy's head, with some muffled dialogue, interrupted only by the deafening rustle of starched crinoline. Oh well, you win some; you lose some. Maybe we can convince everybody to come back and do a retake.

On concert shoots, keep in mind that the band is performing for a live audience. If you insist on hijacking the lighting or the stage layout for your video, you may defeat the very excitement you have come to capture. Don't try to override their lights by aiming your own powerful white light across the stage. Don't mount tripods or light stands in the space where the band members move around. And never come directly between the lead singer and the audience. These intrusions create an uncomfortable vibe and may actually get people angry. Thus, you wind up shooting the band at a not-so-great show. On a live shoot, make yourself invisible, and the band will love you.

Because the venue's lighting person is controlling the lighting at a live show, you will want to be able to tweak your video's lighting in post-production. You can accomplish this by using Video Effects when working with Adobe Premiere. If your band members look underexposed or overexposed, which can change as the live lighting changes, the easiest way to compensate is by applying the Brightness effect. Premiere also provides a Contrast control slider within this effect. Try using both of these to keep your lead singer lit, and to lift her out of the background. If the live lighting was extremely dynamic, and there are problems with both too much and too little light, try isolating the problem clips and treat each one separately. If possible, shoot several shows, or borrow an extra camera and operator for the night. That way, if you need to chop up your lead singer clips to process various lighting issues, you'll have plenty of alternate shots to work with. Read more about using Adobe's built-in video effects in Chapter 12.

# Using Basic Camera Techniques

If your lights are well set, you've won half the battle. Now, on to the other half — rolling tape!

When we first started using our digital video camera, we simply held it in front of our eyes and looked around. In theory, doing this sounds fine, but when translated to the screen, we had viewers reaching for the Dramamine. Here's why. When you move your eyes to look from one object to another, the brain sends a message to the rest of our senses to let them know that this will be happening. If you look up from your desk toward the ceiling, you don't feel like your entire body is being upended, because your sense of balance, situated in the inner ear, has been forewarned that the eyes are about to look up.

The video viewer, however, doesn't get these warnings. Detached from the camera, they can't sense that the camera is about to move. Motions that seem smooth to the camera operator can seem jerky and disorienting to the viewer. For example, suppose that you and a partner are on the Staten Island ferry; it's a beautiful day, and you're shooting a static shot of the Statue of Liberty. Suddenly, your partner yells, "Hey, look at the blimp over Brooklyn!" You immediately swing the camera overhead, rotate 180 degrees, and start searching around the sky for a blimp. Does doing this give your viewer a smooth transition from a statue to a blimp? No! From their point of view, it's like being seized by Godzilla and thrust high into the air, with the Manhattan skyline swirling in the background, and then shaken in the giant's fist, high in the sky over Brooklyn. This experience is not one that your viewers want over and over. To cite another example, we recently watched a charming home video of a couple of kids playing by a pool. Most of the time, the kids were jumping up and down in a very cute way. Their dad must have thought it was cute, too, because whenever they would stand still, he would jerk the camera up and down! Did this create the illusion that the kids were still jumping? Not on your life! After the first couple of times, we learned to look away quick whenever the kids stopped jumping, or risk nausea.

## Understanding the basic shots

From the two tales above, we can derive a couple of simple rules. First, set up transitions so that the viewer travels along with you. Additionally, don't move the camera too much or too fast. Learn a few basic shooting techniques used in the film world, because knowing them helps you to avoid common pitfalls.

### The establishing shot

The establishing shot tells the viewer the location of the action he or she is about to see. For this reason, the establishing shot is frequently the opening shot of the piece. A feature film may have several establishing shots, as the action moves from Paris to Moscow to Mars or to the Sahara Desert. Two of the most common establishing shots used in music video are the Manhattan skyline shot (see Figure 4-2), for videos shot in New York, and the desert shot, for videos shot near Los Angeles. The rest of the video doesn't have to actually be shot in the same location. Remember the establishing shot of the Brooklyn row houses at the beginning of each *All In the Family* episode? The rest of the show was shot on a soundstage, but as soon as Meathead walked in the front door, you believed that he was walking into one of those row houses.

**Figure 4-2:** A typical establishing shot

### The wide shot

Effective shooting moves from the general to the specific. After your establishing shot gives the viewers a sense of place, you bring them in closer to the action with your next shot. For example, if your establishing shot is the Manhattan skyline, your next shot might be the rooftops of a few buildings on Central Park West. The viewers already know that they are in New York, so the wide shot (Figure 4-3) narrows the story down to a neighborhood. One rooftop seems to have some activity going on, but it's a little too far away to see clearly. By using this shot, you create a desire in the viewer to find out what's going on up there. That desire creates curiosity and gives momentum into the next shot.

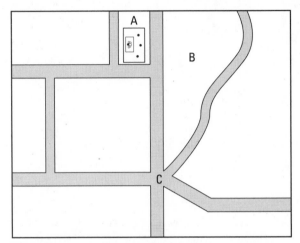

**Figure 4-3:** A typical wide shot with a band playing on a rooftop (A), with Central Park (B) visible in shot as well as intersection (C).

## The master shot

The master shot is the main shot of your video. This shot is the artist performing the song all the way through, as shown in Figure 4-4. If you have one camera, you want to do several versions of this shot from various angles. Many videos feature a band playing on a sound stage or in a live performance situation. Videos sometimes feature other elements, including subplots in other locations, actors who are not in the band, supermodels gazing into the camera, and so forth, but the basic shot of the band playing the song is the master. If the song is four minutes long, this shot should be four minutes long. Other elements are cut into this shot. You may want to shoot a fairly wide master of the whole band and then another tighter take of just the lead singer. Later on, the band members may complain about the lead singer getting too many shots, but you'll be long gone by then!

**Figure 4-4:** A typical master shot, showing the full band onstage

You may have noticed that some videos use several master shots to show contrasting backgrounds, clothing, or instruments. This concept achieves variety but sacrifices focus. Would Sinead O'Connor's video have been more effective if she'd sung "Nothing Compares 2 U" in a dozen different locations? Sometimes less is more. Punk rock bands lean toward stripped-down videos of the group playing for a live audience. The feeling is that the energy and motion of the band and their crowd provide the necessary fuel to drive the video. In that case, the master may be the only shot you need. Run a couple more takes, just to make sure that you record a variety of shots. Always get at least two takes so that you can show the band from a variety of angles, without having to rely on panning and zooming shots in the final edit.

## The medium shot

The medium shot depicts an individual character in your video. As shown in Figure 4-5, the medium shot shows the actor from the waist up. The viewer gets to know this person without the forced intimacy of a close-up. A medium shot can also further the action by including an important prop, such as a gun in a mystery movie or a guitar in a music video. If you're shooting a band, get a master of the song first and then have the band play again and get medium shots of each member. If you're shooting a solo artist, get a medium shot master and then go back and get close-ups. For a band with a featured lead singer, get a wide master shot and then a take of medium shots, followed by a take of close-ups of the lead singer. Speaking of singers, when Elvis first appeared on *The Ed Sullivan Show,* the producers insisted on nothing wider than a waist-up medium shot so that the audience wouldn't see his scandalous swiveling hips.

**Tip**

To smoothly transition out of a medium shot of a band member, direct him or her to look to the right or left of the frame. The viewer assumes that the actor is looking at someone off screen, who will then react. This expectance of interaction gives momentum into the next shot.

**Figure 4-5:** A typical medium shot shows the lead singer from the waist up.

## The reaction shot

This shot, typically a medium shot, shows an actor reacting to a look or statement by another actor in the preceding shot. In other words, if you come out of a shot with the lead singer smiling to the left, than a good next shot would be the guitarist smiling to the right, as shown in Figure 4-6. One shot could be done in January, the other in March, but the viewer doesn't know that. To the viewer, the singer smiled at the guitarist on her left, and he smiled back. If the guitarist also smiled to the left, then it wouldn't be an effective reaction shot. The shot would simply look like they were both smiling at a yet-to-appear third party. Of course, check the wide shot of the band first to make sure that the guitarist is actually standing to her left.

**Figure 4-6:** A reaction shot should have a realistic angle relating to the previous shot.

Trained actors are good at isolated reaction shots. They don't need to be looking at a real person. With band members, getting your reaction shots while they are actually onstage playing together is more effective because their interaction will be real.

Even if the final audio track will be a dubbed-in studio version of the song, have the band play and sing live for the camera. Use this time to pick up two-shots as well.

## The two-shot

Viewers love to see interaction. The chemistry of two actors on-screen together has an added dimension that doesn't happen in any other shot. Do you think Bogart and Bacall would have had the same sparks if they only appeared in separate reaction shots? How about Laurel and Hardy? In music video, two-shots are underused, because an effort is being made to promote one individual as the star or to foster a notion of equal star power — boy bands or girl groups, for example. But this shot can be very powerful in reinforcing the notion of band camaraderie (see Figure 4-7). Think of the three frontline Beatles. Even after the band could obviously afford three microphones, they still continued to use two, so that two of them would always double up on one mic. This gave the audience an opportunity to see them not only sing together, but also goof around, laugh, and do their patented head shake. The same holds true for the Rolling Stones' Mick Jagger and Keith Richards and Steven Tyler and Joe Perry of Aerosmith.

**Figure 4-7:** The best two-shots capture interaction.

Of course, a two-shot with more than two actors becomes a group shot. The group shot may be referred to as a three-shot, a four-shot, and so on, if the title will help the director keep shots sorted out later on. Professional actors work on group shot scenes for days, trying to get the kind of chemistry that many band members have naturally. If your act actually gets along make sure that their chemistry shows up on tape.

## The close-up

The most frequently used close-up is a shot of a main character's face, as shown in Figure 4-8. Handle this powerful shot with care. Keep in mind that a viewer perceives a close-up shot of the subject's face to be just a few inches from his or her own. Consider how rarely this occurs in normal conversation. Consider also that on a TV screen, a close-up face is seventeen inches high, or about twice as large as a normal face. On a home theater system, the close-up is even larger. Although your lead singer may be thrilled with the idea of lots of close-ups, he may not like the way they actually look on-screen, so use close-ups sparingly. Any imperfections in the subject's face are magnified by a factor of two on a 17-inch screen.

**Figure 4-8:** The face is the most common close-up.

The close-up is a very effective shot when you want to express an intimate but very strong emotion. Think of the few times in normal conversation when one speaker would put her face only inches away from the listener. Thus, urban, slow-jam videos use a lot of close-ups to express the vibe of mellow, after-hours love. In a different application, punk bands that specialize in protest songs use close-ups to express anger and deliberately bring the viewer uncomfortably close to the song's topic.

One way to script your close-up shots is to listen to the audio mix. The mixing engineer in a recording studio uses *reverb*, an effect that emulates the sound reflections of various rooms, to create a depth of field on the CD. When he wants the singer to seem far away and majestic, he applies a heavy mix of reverb. When he wants to suggest that the singer is only a few inches from the listener's ear, he applies less reverb. Sound engineers use the term *dry* to describe a signal with no reverb, and they use the metaphor of relative *wetness* to describe increasing levels of reverb as it is applied to the signal. For an example, consider Nirvana's video for "Smells Like Teen Spirit." The songs verses are mixed dry, and the choruses, the more general statement, are mixed wet. The listener is pulled in close to singer Kurt Cobain during the dry, quiet verses, and is pulled out into the dancing crowd during the louder, wet choruses. To coordinate your shots with the audio mix, use wide shot when the singer's reverb is wet and use close-up shots when the reverb is dry. Medium shots work with medium reverb. This technique creates a believable overall experience for the audience.

## The extreme close-up

The extreme close-up turns a part of the singer into an object. The most common extreme close-up is of the eyes, because the eyes can carry the full expressive content of a dramatic line or a song lyric (see Figure 4-9). Footage of lips can also serve as an effective shot, particularly to reinforce a pivotal lyric. In music videos, the guitarist's fingers are frequently the subject of this shot, as the song's focus shifts momentarily from the singer to the guitar solo. You can also use an extreme close-up for an important drum fill. Think of the song "Born to be Wild." If you were shooting a video for that song, where would you place an extreme close-up of the snare drum?

**Figure 4-9:** The extreme close-up objectifies part of the body.

You may sometimes find it effective to reverse the usual wide-to-close-up order of shots. If the song begins with a guitar riff, your opening shot could be an extreme close-up of the guitarist's hands, followed by a medium shot of the vocalist singing the first line, followed by a wide shot of the band, followed by an even wider shot of a thousand fans dancing around a makeshift stage in the desert. We used this technique for our "Nickeltown" video. The opening shot shows Maura's right hand playing the guitar. As the images expand out, you can clearly see that we are in Las Vegas.

On the CD-ROM    This book's CD-ROM contains QuickTime versions of a few of our videos, including "Nickeltown."

Extreme close-ups can create powerful symbols. For example, imagine a country song about a very elderly woman. She's lived a long and full life, and she's worked very hard. For your visual concept, simply run an extreme close up of her hands for the first part of the video. The calluses and wrinkles tell a story, and they let the viewer imagine scenes covering a whole lifetime. Because the song is about the past, you don't need a wider shot to establish where she is right now. Let the hands serve as a symbol. On the last line of the song, switch to her eyes in another extreme close-up. With only two shots, you can imply an expansive story by using extreme close-ups to objectify parts of the body as symbols.

## Insert shots

Insert shots divert the viewers' eyes away from the main action for a short period of time. These shots can be very effective in moving the concept along by giving the viewer additional information, or introducing a subplot. For example, suppose you're shooting a band, The Electric Watchband, at a street concert in San Francisco. You get your master shot of them performing onstage, and then you put a number of insert shots in the can. You don't need to shoot everything on the same day. Take day two and get shots of the Golden Gate Bridge, Alcatraz, the Haight-Ashbury street signs, and so forth. By inserting these, you don't need to announce, "Here they are, live from San Francisco!" The insert shots tell that part of the story.

Inserts can be used in this way to establish place as well as to portray symbols. If your act plays kickin' country, inserts of NASCAR-style racing and soft-focus pickup trucks are positive symbols for the band's audience. In our own videos, we frequently drop in inserts of wacky vintage guitars, because those images reinforce the carefree side of rock 'n' roll that our music projects. Getting to know your subjects and your location is the best way to plan your inserts.

## Cutaway shots

*Cutaway shots* are shots that are not part of the main action. As part of the development of the video, a cutaway shot can struggle for dominance with the main action and eventually take over. For example, U2's video for "New Year's Day" begins with a basic master shot of the band playing the song. The band is standing in a snowy forest, and they look very cold. This master shot is interrupted every ten seconds or so by a very short clip of stock footage of Russian tanks rolling across snowy fields during World War II. (The album *War* contains this song.) These two elements, the master and the stock footage, roll along until the keyboard solo that occurs mid-song. At this point, a new shot enters. Four horseback riders are riding through the same snowy forest. We never see the faces of the riders. But we understand that they are the band members, or at least represent the band members. The original master clips of the band playing are now very short, and the clips of the riders take over the video. The riders are carrying white flags, and they seem to be on some kind of anti-war mission. Symbolically, they convey the idea that the band's sense of political purpose has transcended their identity as rock musicians. It's now more important for them to be depicted as the four horsemen of the apocalypse than it is for them to finish the song as a band, and eventually the live performance clips disappear entirely. As the video ends, the band rides off into the woods. They still haven't found what they're looking for, but they have reaffirmed their solidarity. This simple, one-day shoot is really stirring and defines what the group is all about. When you choose your cutaway shots, consider how they should move the concept forward, and how they should define the identity of the act.

## Pickup shots

While you are assembling your clips, you may come up with a wish list of shots that you didn't get. You may have orphan points in the song that just don't have an appropriate clip. If the band has resumed touring and are now on a different continent, you're out of luck. Make do. But if the group is local, and your crew people don't hate you after the first shoot, arrange a day for pickup shots. You only need to call the people necessary for the shots on your list. Keep the list short and work efficiently. Now isn't the time to experiment. Be familiar with the basics of continuity when doing pickup shots because continuity errors are most likely to creep in at this time.

## Planning the route

**Road Diary**

Route the locations and provide directions so that your unit person can drive logically from one place to another without wasting time. Here's an example:

✦ 6 a.m. Top of Mt. Bonnell, facing east. Wide shot from hilltop, as sky lights just before sunrise. Try to get all of downtown in shot. Alternate shot: Begin with shot of north end of town and pan slowly left to right, finishing the shot looking south of town.

✦ 8 a.m. — Breakfast at Starbucks. Keep receipt.

✦ 9 a.m. — North end of Congress Avenue Bridge, facing north. Shoot state capitol dome. Static shot. Use polarizing filter to contrast pink sandstone with hyped blue sky. See Chapter 5 for more on using polarizing filters.

✦ 11 a.m. — Interstate 35, 10 miles north of Town Lake Bridge, facing south. Shoot Austin city limit sign with Capitol dome in distant background.

✦ Noon — Lunch at Threadgill's. Keep receipt. Shoot exterior.

✦ 2 p.m. to 5 p.m. — Cruise around the hill country. Get the following shots: an armadillo, a longhorn steer, a couple of old barns and windmills, and a small country store. Shoot the buildings in "old movie" mode and in regular color.

✦ 6 p.m. — Return to Mt Bonnell. Repeat this morning's shots. Take alternates until the sun goes down.

✦ 7 p.m. — Dinner at El Azteca. Keep receipt. Shoot exterior.

✦ 8 p.m. — South Congress Avenue. Shoot exterior of Continental Club.

✦ 9 p.m. to 10 p.m. — Park at the corner of Congress and Sixth. Walk east. Shoot exterior of Driskill Hotel. Continue walking east and shoot neon signs, partying college kids, handheld. Wrap.

✦ 11 p.m. — Magnolia Café. Meet with director and hand over tape and log of shots with tape locations. Get reimbursed for meals and gas.

### Second-unit shots

Inserts and establishing shots frequently don't involve live actors or musicians. To save time, the video director may hire (the pay might be donuts) a second unit to shoot these. This unit may be only one person. The important thing is that you get the shots that don't require precise placement and lighting of real people. For example, let's say that you're shooting an Americana band in Austin. You have your permission from the Continental Club to shoot there from 10 a.m. until 6 p.m., when they have to kick you out and set up for the nighttime show. Anticipating that you will need all that time to load in, set up, aim the lights, get the band in their clothes, shoot the master, shoot retakes for medium shots, two-shots, close-ups, and alternate angles, you realize that you won't have time to take any exterior or location shots. Here's where your second unit comes in. If you and your second unit have the same camera so much the better, because at the end of the day she can hand the tape off to you. You can load it in at the same time as your band footage by using your camera as the playback deck. So what does your second unit shoot? Well, consider your concept. These guys are a classic Austin band, and you want to really evoke Texas. Plan a route for your second unit so that she can shoot all the location shots for your video. See the "Planning the Route" sidebar for an example of how to plan a direct route.

Notice that none of these shots involve live actors or musicians. All of them use available natural light. None of them involve direction, per se, so you, the director, don't need to be present. These shots happen while you are shooting the band at the club. By using the second unit, you have your cutaway shots at the end of the same day as your master shots. You can start editing right away.

## Shooting techniques

Now that you have a repertoire of basic shots, you can look at ways to get the most out of them. In this section, you can discover how to use the same techniques that cinematographers use to make your low-budget videos look professional.

### Tripod shots

You need a tripod for any shot that shouldn't look deliberately shaky. Handheld footage that looks steady through a small viewfinder appears shaky on a larger screen. Additionally, a camera mounted on a tripod stays in its adjusted position until you move it. Even the slightest movement of your hand will destroy all the work you have put into setting up the perfect lighting and camera angles. When you select your tripod, keep two rules in mind:

✦ **Don't buy a very lightweight model.** The reason that you're getting it is to stabilize your camera, right? And what's more stable, an economy car or a semi truck? Get the tripod that more closely resembles a semi truck, and you won't have to worry about light breezes giving your camera the shakes.

✦ **Get a tripod with a fluid head.** Tripods without this feature hold your camera in one place, but they aren't capable of executing any non-jerky moves. Get a moderately heavy tripod with a fluid head, and use it for all of your shooting, unless you deliberately want the handheld look.

## Handheld shots

You probably grew up making handheld shots with the family Polaroid camera. The shots probably looked all right, too, unless the Airedale happened to jump on you just as you were shooting. Consumer still cameras are very forgiving in this respect, because the shutter is only open for a fraction of a second. If you can hold still for that long, you'll get a clear shot. No such luck with video, however. In a video clip, the viewer has lots of time to realize how shaky the camera is.

A look that was pioneered in the 1960s was based on the exciting, immediate quality of newsreel footage. A reporter running beside a group of armed rebels doesn't have time to set up a tripod. Doing so would be pointless, because the rebels are running, and she's close to them — they'd be out of her shot in no time. So the intrepid reporter pulls her camera off the tripod and runs alongside the action, steadying the lens as best she can. The resulting footage is not pristine in quality, but it captures the dynamic energy of the rebellion as it actually happened. Energy has no substitute, so handheld technique is perfectly fine when it's the best way to capture an exclusive moment.

When Richard Lester directed *A Hard Day's Night*, one of his intentions was to show the Beatles fleeing from hordes of rabid fans. He didn't have to stage this footage. Hundreds of fans showed up at the first day's shooting in a railway station. As Lester began to shoot, the police lines broke, and the fans bore down on the group like a herd of runaway buffalo. As the fab four ran for the safety of the train, Lester grabbed the camera and ran along with them, shooting their flight with the shaky motion of a running cameraman. In his first shot, he had captured the electric mania that surrounded them, and he caught the mixture of joy and desperation on their faces as they ran for their lives. This scene, the opening of the film, is a great commentary on pop stardom, and it could have only been shot unrehearsed, with the handheld camera. So make sure that you have a quick-release mechanism on your tripod and a good pair of sneakers.

## Zoom shots

The zoom button is the most misunderstood control on the camera, and "zoom abuse" is the most obvious emblem of amateur video. The zoom button has one very useful function. For example, you are on the balcony of your hotel in Hawaii, shooting the activity out on the beach. First, you start with a wide shot of the whole area. Get into the habit of starting with this type of establishing shot. After you get that shot, you start to focus on different things that are happening. To the left, a guy is doing the limbo dance under a flaming torch. To the right, a group of girls are doing a hula dance. On the terrace below, you see a huge feast of tropical fruit. You decide to shoot all three of these scenes, but you encounter a problem: You're stuck on the balcony. Each scene is a different distance away. So you begin by shooting your spouse, who is standing on the balcony, four feet away. No problem. Now you look out at the fellow limbo dancing. He's 50 feet away, and he looks pretty small. Frame him in your viewfinder and then zoom in on him until his scale is compatible with your previous shot. Now begin your shot of limbo man. The important point here is that you used the zoom button to set up the distant shot. You don't use it *during* the shot. As you continue to shoot activities on the beach, you use the zoom to set up each shot and make them all compatible in scale, should they later be seen in sequence. When you go to edit your Hawaii travelogue in Adobe Premiere, you don't use the zooming footage; you use the clips between the zooms.

Feature films generally don't use zoom shots. When the director wants to move closer to a subject, she uses cuts of shots that move progressively nearer. You can create these from a zoom shot, but only if you zoom, then stop, then zoom, then stop, until you are at the closest point. Then, in your edit, you can capture the stopped parts of the shots. You won't be able to edit mid-zoom shots together realistically. Another way of coming in closer is to use a dolly-in shot, which we describe next.

## Dolly shots

In a dolly shot, the distance from the subject changes by moving the camera. This shot is far more effective and less cheesy than the zoom. In a zoom, the lens is adjusted to make the subject appear closer. In a *dolly-in* shot, the entire camera moves toward the subject, which is similar to how your eyes function naturally. For example, say you're a general reviewing a line of troops. If you want to look directly into the eyes of a private 20 feet to your right, would you maintain your position, turn your head toward him, and then "zoom" your eyes up to his? Of course not. You would walk 20 feet to your right, and stand directly in front of him. The tricky thing about dollying is keeping the motion smooth. If you simply walk forward, every step you take will seem magnified on the screen, and the viewer will think, "Okay, now they're walking forward." To keep the motion transparent, wheels are much better. Professional dollies are expensive pieces of rental gear but, like everything else in low-budget production, improvised alternatives can be used. You can make a dolly out of plywood and casters for your tripod. This will work well for indoor shots, as long as the way is cleared of cables, coffee cups, and so on. For handheld dolly shots, a wheelchair is the preferred low-budget alternative. You can find a used one in the want ads. Simply sit in the wheelchair, steady the camera on your lap, and have a grip wheel you around. For exterior shots, particularly street scenes and building exteriors, the car is your best dolly. Have a grip drive, of course!

If you can dolly in, then it follows that you can also *dolly out*. Furthermore, you can dolly left and dolly right (see Figure 4-10). Smooth dolly shots are a sign of professional-quality film and video. Great directors, such as Orson Welles and Alfred Hitchcock are known for their dollying skills.

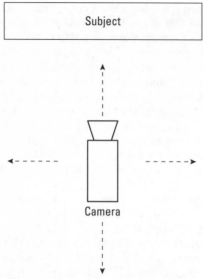

**Figure 4-10:** In a dolly shot, the entire camera moves forward, or backward, left, or right.

## Panned shots

A *pan shot* occurs when the cameraperson stays stationary, but moves the camera laterally to take in a panorama, as shown in Figure 4-11. After zooming, panning is the most abused shot in amateur video. When we first got our camera, we were never content with a simple wide shot of, say, the New York City skyline. We would start by focusing on the Empire State Building and then jerk the camera sideways up to the Bronx, bringing it back down slowly all the way to Battery Park. We didn't realize that we were robbing our viewers of the pleasure of looking at our first wide shot of the island, and then using their own eyes to move from left to right, taking in the Bronx down to the Battery at their own pace. Filmmakers learned long ago that when shooting something static, such as a large city, letting the shot sit long enough for the viewer to take it all in is preferable to directing their eyes around to specific points. Overuse of this type of panning makes the viewer feel that you are afraid the shot is boring without extra camera movement.

Another type of panning to avoid is moving back and forth between two actors who are talking to one another or singing a duet. Either use a two-shot of both of them or cut to medium shots of each individual. In the edit, don't cut right between each line of dialogue or lyric. Doing so gets predictable. For variety, use some reaction shots. Sonny smiles while Cher is heard singing a line on the audio track, then Sonny sings the first half of his line, and we cut to Cher reacting to the second half. This type of shooting has much more momentum than does panning the camera back and forth between the two singers.

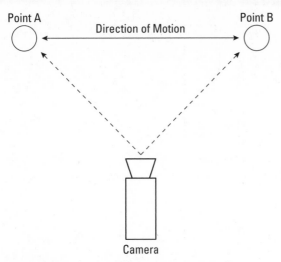

**Figure 4-11:** In a panned shot, the camera is stationary. The lens is aimed from point A to point B along a horizontal plane.

So when do you use panning? When doing so is essential to the action. Thelma and Louise are speeding across the desert, pursued by police. The shot opens with their car against the bleak background of the arid desert. As the camera dollies back, the shot widens, and we see police cars in hot pursuit. Because all of the cars are moving fast, they will soon be out of this part of the desert, which means that they'll be out of our shot if we don't start panning. The pan follows them, then speeds up and pulls ahead of them, and in our widened shot, we can see the canyon coming up. Use panning when a moving object is about to exit the frame, and you don't want to lose it, even for a second. Remember OJ Simpson's famous SUV ride down the freeway? The news helicopters that followed him were executing an *extremely* long pan shot.

## Tilt shots

This shot occurs when the cameraperson stays in one place and moves the camera up and down, as shown in Figure 4-12. Tilt shots are the equivalent of looking someone over from head to toe, or vice versa. You can use a tilt shot on a stationary object, such as the Empire State Building, but first ask yourself if showing a static shot of the building would be more effective. A static shot lets the viewer get a sense of its immense scale by looking at it from top to bottom and comparing it with nearby buildings.

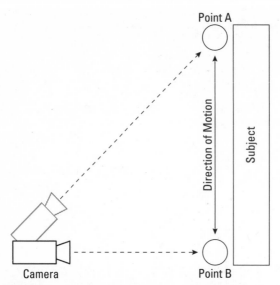

**Figure 4-12:** In a tilt shot, the camera remains stationary. The lens moves upward or downward along a vertical plane.

A better use of the tilt shot would be in a "crocodile hunter" type situation, where a python is slithering up a tall tree. Because it's impractical to stay close to the python and follow it up the tree, the cameraperson wisely stays on the ground and executes a tilt shot that follows the snake on up. In this case, I would definitely recommend a zoom shot rather than a dolly-in to get a close-up of the subject!

## Canted shots

Sometimes called a "Dutch Angle," a canted shot occurs when the camera is tilted at a diagonal angle along a horizontal plane (see Figure 4-13). The center line of your subject would lie between two corners of the shot, rather than between the bottom and the top. This suggests upcoming motion, because the viewer hopes to see the subject back in normal perspective. This shot suggests that the subject is eccentric and maybe a little goofy. It also looks kind of gimmicky, so use this shot sparingly. Better yet, save this effect for your experimentation in Adobe Premiere. If you apply it and don't like it, you can always undo it.

**Figure 4-13:** A canted shot

## Stylin' on a shoestring budget

**Road Diary**

As a shoestring video pioneer, you usually work without a crew. That is, unless you have friends who are crazy enough to stand for hours in the heat and/or cold while you make tiny adjustments in the length of a boom they've been holding in the air since 7 a.m. Friends like that are frequently no longer friends after a long shoot. And that's just location crew. Finding preproduction help is hard, too, unless your dad owns a donut shop and you can offer really spiffy incentives in lieu of cash. So you need to be able to develop your own storyboards, write any script material, come up with a concept, and generally brainstorm in the days leading up to the shoot. One thing you won't have the money for is a professional stylist.

Who needs a stylist? Anybody who's gonna appear in a video, that's who. Why did Hendrix look so cool all the time? Why did the Beatles have those groovy collarless jackets? Why did Motley Crue wear jeans ripped in exactly the right places, and why did all of the above use a case of hairspray before every gig? Because they all had stylists. A stylist isn't necessarily a beautician or a makeup artist, although all the artists mentioned above did wear makeup in public. A stylist is someone with a great visual eye who understands that the audience isn't just listening to the band — they're watching the band. Musicians who have practiced their instruments for years may not always place a high value on the visual aspect, but if they come to you to make a video, they know the importance of it.

*Continued*

*Continued*

Are you the one to advise them? Well, look in a mirror. Would you take fashion advice from yourself? If the answer is no, then seek professional help, preferably the free kind. Now, who gives fashion advice and actually knows what he or she is talking about? The answer is simple: a clothing salesperson. We're not talking Hugo Boss or Donna Karan, unless you're shooting a video for Julio or Barbra. Think about the act you're shooting. Are they a punk band, whose fans like surfing and skateboarding? Then go to shops that sell clothes to that particular subculture and look for a salesperson who seems to be really into it, not just coasting through the minimum wage world. People who work in trendy boutiques are into fashion, just like you're into music and video, and they hope to advance their career beyond sales. Let this aspiring designer know that you're shooting a low-budget video, and that the guys in your band are willing to spend $100 each at the store if she can pick out their clothes and come up with a cool look for them. Offer a credit and a free copy of the video. This stuff can help her with her own aspirations. If your act is hip-hop or metal, find the right shop for their look, although bands in these genres usually have a lot of visual smarts. For jazz artists, a classy retro period look may be right. Putting together this look involves finding some unusual clothes, such as vintage gowns, double-breasted suits, silk ties, and wing-tipped shoes. You could rent clothes from a costume shop, but finding the right pieces at thrift shops is less expensive.

If you have a really enthusiastic stylist, do a thrift-shopping trip. With luck, this excursion can yield unique vintage. Do you think Smashmouth went down to the local mall to get their clothes for the "Walking on the Sun" video? Heck no, they spent a whole day on Melrose Avenue in L.A. (with a stylist from the label, no doubt), finding the tackiest stuff on the racks, and in doing so they created a unique look for their band. Hey — find some really loud shirts, and you can save a bundle on lights!

If your act balks at the idea of someone telling them how to dress, just call her a "visual advisor" and let them know that it's just for this shoot. However, band members need to get used to the idea that, when they're working in the television medium, they will receive advice about how they should look on-screen. If you're lucky, of course, you'll be working with artists like David Bowie who are highly visual as well as musical. Keep in mind, however, that even the Beatles had to be told by a photographer friend to comb their hair down over their foreheads. They protested but thanked her later on. Video is a visual medium. If your band is only into the audio part, tell 'em to stick with radio!

# Putting Action in Your Footage

As you edit more and more video, you may find yourself constantly making note of ideas that you wish you had used during the shoot. As you load clips into Premiere, think about the footage you are passing over. In many cases, footage is rejected because there is no action that might pique the viewers' interest and move the concept along. Think of this while you are shooting, and try to conceive each shot as a portrayal of an action instead of a still portrait.

# Find the motion in each shot

Moments of static inactivity are typical of amateur video. To some extent, this mistake is understandable, because only recently has editing gear been available to consumers. Now that you have Premiere, you can trim these dull bits out of your videos.

In preparation for loading a clip into Premiere, leave footage at the beginning and at the end. You want to have some slack so that you can trim later, after you've seen how the whole piece flows. Suppose that you are using a shot of a man playing poker. He looks his cards over and then turns his head toward the camera and gives a thumbs up sign. This motion moves the story along, and is the one that best identifies the shot. In your edit, you want to focus on this movement and cut out any dead air around it. When you place this shot on the Timeline, cut out the early frames where the man looks at the cards and start the clip after he has already started moving his hand. After he gives the sign, cut the end of the shot as he is turning back to the table. This way, you never have a moment when your subject is simply sitting still.

# Shooting with the edit in mind

After you have your master shot of the whole band playing the entire song, you move on to your secondary shots. These include medium shots, two- and three-shots, and close-ups. In each case, make sure that the shot has a reason. The reason, in video, will usually be a movement of some kind. If the act incorporates dance, you're obviously in luck. Just make sure that you get lots of footage of all of their best choreography from various angles.

Specialized genres of music have their own informal choreography. Rap artists typically interact directly with the camera, and their trademark moves are as much a part of the music as their rapid-fire rhymes.

Punk bands frequently include a live audience in their shoots. Communal solidarity with their fans is an essential element in the music, and the dancing/moshing of the crowd is a form of spontaneous choreography. Make sure that you devote lots of tape to these moving symbols. When you go to edit, you may find that the clips you can't wait to load in are the ones with distinctive motion.

As you edit, cut the end of each shot with the subject moving, and cut the beginning of the next shot with that subject moving. If your band members look at each other, cut while their heads are moving, not before and after they move. When you shoot, make sure that every shot involves motion. This is video, not painting!

# Lip-synching

Unless you do only single-camera, single-take live performances with live sound, you will get involved with *lip-synching*. This process was long associated with cheesy lounge singers on 1960s TV, but with the advent of video, it opened up new horizons, as directors moved away from literal portrayals of stage performance. Lip-synching has been used in film for years. On a location, actors are reciting lines while the director shouts instructions to them and to the crew. Machinery is whirring; fans may be blowing. Airplanes go by overhead. Microphones may not be able to get close enough without interfering with the shot. In addition, actors may get their moves down perfectly, but flub a line in an otherwise perfect take. For all these reasons, dialogue is frequently dubbed in after the shoot. Other sounds may be dubbed in as well. Doing so is frequently accomplished on a Foley stage, a type of studio that specializes in reproducing any type of sound, from a butterfly's wing flapping to the Titanic hitting an iceberg.

In the editing process, you deal with lip-synching issues constantly. Keep in mind that the viewer wants to believe that the singer is singing live. This desire works in your favor. Fans who have grown up on music video are willing to believe that Bono is singing to them from the top of a statue ten stories above Berlin. Would we actually be able to hear him? Doesn't matter. This is video, not reality. So put him in the spectacular setting and dub in sound later.

Check out the Jimi Hendrix video of "Are You Experienced." The video was created decades after his death, so no video shoot happened, per se. The video features a montage of many clips of him playing and singing, shot over a period of years. There is no master shot of him singing the song "Are You Experienced." He does, however, seem to be singing the song at certain points. The editor made skillful use of lip consonants to re-create the lyrics of the song.

# Using Continuity Guidelines

Getting good raw footage is essential to any video, but there's more to it than that. A really effective music video has pacing, rhythm, and a certain believability that carries the viewer out of his everyday existence and into the world of the song. But if your clips are shot as separate bits to be pieced together later on your Premiere Timeline, how do you make sure that all of the pieces flow together? The way to ensure this is by following the guidelines that filmmakers refer to as *continuity*. Take a minute to learn some of the basics and consider how they apply to music video.

## Placement continuity

As you set up to shoot your master take of the whole band playing the song all the way through, lay down marks for every person and prop that will be included in the scene. Amps and drums count as props. Make yourself a diagram of the set. That way, if you need to come back for a retake later on, you can reproduce the set accurately enough to be able to cross-cut between the two shoots without the viewer catching on. For example, if you need to retake the second verse, and the bass player puts his SVT amp two feet to the left of its old position, the giant amp will seem to jump around whenever a clip from take two is inserted. Giant jumping amps may be part of your concept, but if they are not, observe the rules of prop placement continuity to avoid this unintentionally comic effect.

Your musicians may move from one specific position to another during a shot. For example, the guitarist and singer may move together to interact during a solo, and you want to hit them with a red light at that point. You will need to mark their spots, so that when you turn on the light, you won't have to move it around to get it right. Color code the player's marks, so the lead singer will go from red duct tape to red duct tape, and the guitarist will go from blue to blue. This doesn't detract from spontaneity — it actually enhances it. You can do one or two run-throughs and set the marks and then shoot the move in a single take. The tiresome alternative is to do many retakes, hoping to hit the right camera and light angles by luck.

In the '80s, music video directors frequently used deliberately discontinuous placement to make items disappear and reappear. For example, consider this shooting script: Take one, full band. Take two, same thing without the bass player. Take three, full band and bass player standing on roof of nearby BMW. Get the picture? By inserting quick clips of takes two and three into the master, the wacky bass man seems to disappear, and then reappear later on the roof of his car, while the rest of the group plays on, unruffled. This cheapo effect was usually used for no apparent reason, except perhaps that the band looked boring without it. As the decade faded, this effect did, too.

## Costume continuity

The performers in your video should get used to the idea that their appearance will be scrutinized much more closely on-screen than in a typical live gig situation. If you saw the Beatles once, live at a large arena in 1964, would you remember that they were wearing collarless jackets? Probably not. But most of us, whether we were alive then or not, have seen video footage of the group on *The Ed Sullivan Show* so many times that it's easy to recall what they were wearing. Had Ringo's jacket been at the cleaner's, and had he worn an NYPD jacket to the arena instead, who would remember now? But had he committed that lapse of haberdashery on TV, they would always be remembered as the group with the drummer dressed like a New York City cop.

On video, small details of dress are magnified and preserved for anyone who wants to keep them, freeze-frame them, and analyze any inconsistencies. If your lead singer gets tired of his Docs after take seven, and switches to a pair of Nikes, you won't be able to use any footage from then on, unless you decide to incorporate a magical shoe change. This doesn't mean your musicians have to wear slick, theatrical clothes. If the drummer wears a torn Ramones t-shirt for day one, and you need to re-take the same shot on day three, just make sure he's got the same shirt on. Small details matter. If you are using close-up shots of your singer, and he has a two-day five-o'clock shadow, make a note of that. If you need to call him in a week later to get a few pickup shots, make sure he knows two days in advance about the five-o'clock shadow. Otherwise, his beard will magically grow or recede during the final edit of the song.

This consistency applies to hair and makeup, too. When your folk singer finalizes her hair and makeup for the coffeehouse take, she forfeits the right to "improve" on that look until the scene is in the can. When a film director calls for "Hair!" and "Makeup!" he's not saying, "Make the star look better." He's saying, "Make the star look the same as she did at the beginning of the shoot." He's thinking ahead to the editing process, when he needs to be able to mix and match clips.

## Lighting continuity

When you shoot indoors using a three-point lighting rig, or any kind of artificial light and/or reflectors, make a diagram of where your lights are placed for each shot. That way, when you come back for a retake, you can re-create the shot. This information should be logged in your continuity notebook, along with set diagrams and wardrobe notes. Lights that are placed in different areas will produce shadows that seem to move mysteriously when clips are edited together.

If you are shooting several shows on a tour, contact the venues in advance to find out which ones have the most similar lighting rigs. If you only shoot three gigs, and one is at Joe's Tavern, the next one is opening for Cheap Trick at the Beacon Theatre, and the third one is a backyard barbecue in Red Bank, it will be very hard to assemble a credible concert video that will resemble a single contiguous show. The exception to this would be a "tour" video, where the night-to-night disparity in production values might be part of an interesting sidebar to the story of an aspiring band on the road.

Lighting continuity is much more difficult to control outdoors, because Mother Nature puts in her two cents in the form of clouds and daytime changes in light. A shot done at an easily recognizable time of day, such as dawn or dusk, will have to be reshot at the same time. Cloudy days can be okay for shooting if the sunlight is gently diffused. If you need pickups on that shoot, however, don't go back on a bright, sunny day. The unpredictability of outdoor light is one of the reasons why the film industry is based in Hollywood. Los Angeles has a great number of days per year with identical weather, and a lot of money rides on feature film shooting schedules.

## Motion continuity

When a character will be moving, sketch out in simple form what direction they will be moving in. Is it from the left side of the frame to the right? Make sure that this stays consistent as you shoot several versions of this motion. A storyboard will help, especially if the takes are separated by hours or days.

Picture a horseman in a classic Western movie. He's galloping across the plains, on his way to rescue a pioneer girl tied to a railroad track. He's moving from the left side of the screen to the right, showing the audience the right side of the horse. During the shoot the director decides, "Y'know, that's a beautiful horse. I really ought to shoot it from both sides." So he hauls the camera to the other side of the trail, and does another take. If the cowboy repeats his ride, he will now appear to be riding from the right side of the screen to the left. The director is happy, because he's got both sides of the lovely horse. What the audience sees in the theatre is the cowboy riding bravely toward the damsel in distress, then chickening out and heading back the other way. His direction changes every time the director wants to switch sides of the horse.

Another variation on this bit of misdirection involves two moving subjects. Are they both going the same way? Then they must move the same way within the frame. Imagine the same inept Western. Slim is riding from the left side of the frame to the right, to rescue another damsel. He shouts to his buddy, Tex, to follow him. Now, our friend the director shoots Tex's scene a few weeks after Slim's and he didn't bother to write down which direction Slim was riding in. "Doesn't matter," he figures, "I sure like the left side of Tex's horse." So he shoots Tex riding from the right side of the frame to the left. What's the final edit look like? You guessed it. Poor old Slim and Tex, riding furiously toward each other. Thank heaven for the digital age! With Premiere Horizontal Flip feature, in the Transform folder, you can easily correct this type of error, saving our two cowboys from an embarrassing collision on the range.

Deliberate motion discontinuity can be used to create the impression of confusion, or searching. In U2's "New Year's Day" video, four horsemen ride through a forest. In some clips, they ride from left to right, in others, from right to left. It's obvious to the viewer that they are searching for something. For a comedic example, check out the film "It's a Mad, Mad, Mad, Mad World." As the eight main characters travel across the country in search of a buried treasure, shots of their vehicles are jump-cut, moving in all directions, indicating their general confusion. But keep in mind that if you create confusion on screen, you only want to do it deliberately!

## Eyeline continuity

When a character looks off to one side of the screen, the audience wants to know what he's looking at. And when he looks at another character, the audience expects the other fellow to react in a believable way. *Eyeline continuity* helps create the illusion of characters interacting, even though the editor may be placing a variety of separate clips on the Timeline. For example, suppose that you have your wide shot of the band, with the guitarist standing to the singer's left, or *stage left*. He appears, to the viewer, to the singer's right, because the band is facing us on-screen. If you follow up, perhaps days later, with medium shots of individual band members, and you want the lead singer to smile at the guitarist, make sure that she smiles to the right of the frame, from your perspective, and he smiles back, in the next shot, to the left. Of course, if he's standing *stage right*, the medium shots are reversed. You can accomplish these shots without both subjects being present at same time if you observe the rules of continuity. Of course, if both the guitarist and the lead singer were to smile to the right of the frame, they would appear to be smiling at a third, unseen person, perhaps the drummer. Because two band members rarely smile at the drummer, this sequence would detract from the credibility of your video!

## Centerline continuity

Basically, *centerline continuity* means keeping things straight. If you shoot your lead singer in a medium shot from the waist up, and she is a little to the left of the centerline of the frame, make a note of her position before you shoot a retake of the same shot. If you just place her somewhere in the frame, you won't be able to cut take one and two together, unless you luck out. The same thing applies when you have more than one subject in the frame. If you cut clips together with centerline inconsistency, they appear to do the "old soft shoe" on-screen. Of course, if that's their act . . . .

# Composing Your Shots

The total composition of a shot involves everything you have learned about lighting, shooting, and continuity. *Composition* is simply what the shot looks like. Some film directors have very distinct compositional signatures. As you channel surf, you can always tell when you land on a Hitchcock film, or something directed by Jim Jarmusch. Certain video directors have their own distinct compositional styles. Hype Williams' depiction of female R&B artists is an exciting update of George Clinton's notion of African American space heroes. Williams places his subjects in sets that recall Kubrick's *2001: A Space Odyssey,* but with the pulsating, over hyped lighting of Times Square. This combination of street and space is a unique, recognizable visual style. Check out Williams' videos for TLC and Faith Evans for examples of this distinctive style.

## Learning from the masters

Cinematographers study the work of master painters. Painting has been around a lot longer that film and video, and the great practitioners have had centuries to develop theories for the use of light and color. Take a look at how Dutch master Jan Vermeer uses light coming in through windows to illuminate his interiors. Compare that with Edward Hopper's light coming in through the smoky windows of a late night diner. These two examples of light streaming through glass produce very different feels. How would you translate these two feels to videotape?

## Applying black-and-white techniques

To really get a feel for the subtleties of lighting, study black-and-white films. In this genre, the director can't depend on color to pump energy into a shot. Everything must come from motion and shades of gray. Black-and-white shot composition is an art form in itself. Cinematographers before the age of color were expert in the use of shadow and backlighting to create dramatic effects. Classics in the genre include two Humphrey Bogart films, *Casablanca* and *The Maltese Falcon*, and Orson Welles's 1941 masterpiece, *Citizen Kane*. Alfred Hitchcock's *Psycho* and Richard Lester's *A*

*Hard Day's Night* are instances where a modern director chose black and white over color to achieve a visual effect. The Police's "Every Breath You Take" video demonstrates the influence of moody, atmospheric black-and-white film noir on music video.

## Mastering montage

A *montage* is a series of shots that are juxtaposed in a way that ignores the conventions of visual continuity and evenly paced story telling. In traditional, storytelling cinema, montage was used to represent a dreamlike state of nostalgia, where images flood a character's thoughts, rushing back in nonlinear fashion, overlapping each other like unconscious, Jungian dream symbols. Picture a World War I soldier, lying on the battlefield with his whole life passing before him as he succumbs to his wounds. The images may overlap, but they don't have to flow in a continuous way. Lighting and shadow can change radically from scene to scene, and individuals can appear in a variety of clothing and hairstyles with no context. Montage sequences were usually short — no longer than a couple of minutes — because they lacked plot and character development to carry the story along.

"Great!" I can hear you exclaiming. "I'll adopt montage as my style, and then I won't have to worry about all these rules of continuity." You wouldn't be the first to do so. Montage is one of the most common forms of music video. Unlike feature films, videos don't have large budgets, and they are usually shot and edited in a time span measured in days not weeks or months. In a time crunch, get as much footage as you can, and sort it out later. Videos usually involve nonprofessional actors, namely the musicians, and their enthusiasm can suffer greatly if they are overdirected. Many videographers feel that encouraging the musicians to be natural produces the best video. By giving the musicians total freedom, consistency is compromised. However, a lot of great energy shows up on tape. In this working environment, montage starts to look a lot more feasible than a coherent narrative.

From a creative standpoint, montage co-exists comfortably with music. Literal images that convey the exact lyrics of the song can hijack the viewer's imagination. When you hear "So What" by Miles Davis, do you really want to picture an individual saying the words, "so what?" Of course not. Davis probably thought that the opening horn riff sounded like that phrase, so there isn't a literal interpretation of the tune. If a videographer tried to apply a literal interpretation, more harm than good might be done. Narrative story lines have a tendency to weigh down music video. Four minutes is not long enough to develop a story comparable to *Citizen Kane,* and a too-easy-to-get story line is worse than none at all. Keep in mind that most videos are made with the intent of someday being aired in heavy rotation somewhere, and a simplistic story line bears up under repetition about as well as an obvious joke.

Since the '60s, montage has been a staple of music video. Montage need not be dreamlike or fantastic. Any sequence of shots that is strung together without a unifying narrative thread is a montage. Some examples are technical tours de force.

For instance, Peter Gabriel's "Sledgehammer" video is a dizzying collage of effects, with the singer's digitally manipulated face in the eye of the hurricane. Madonna's "Ray of Light" updates this same technique by using high-speed edits of matte and mask effects, as the singer dances in front of a solid background that's been transformed into a maelstrom of motion and color in the editing workspace.

Because videos usually don't include dialogue and are too short for extensive character development, one can theorize that they are exempt from the traditional restrictions of storytelling cinema. In this way, videos are closely related to TV commercials. Many of the top videographers are involved in the making of TV commercials, which have become a cutting edge art form. Commercials attempt to present enough visual imagery and color to make the viewer remember the spot and want to see it again in a short amount of time. That's certainly what music video is all about as well. As an aspiring video director, however, take the time to learn the lighting, shooting, and continuity guidelines that cinematographers have used to capture images on film. When the time comes to direct a smoothly edited, well-paced narrative, you'll be able to do it well.

## Chapter Replay

After reading this chapter, you should be able to understand the following:

✦ The use of the three-point lighting system

✦ The use of the basic camera shots

✦ The use of continuity guidelines

✦ The basics of shot composition

Now that you know how to shoot your footage, you can do just that. Go to it and have fun! Chapter 6 shows you how to move footage into Premiere for assembling and editing your music video.

✦　✦　✦

# Shooting for Special Effects

If you've invested in a good DV camera and sophisticated editing software, you undoubtedly want your finished product to look like more than a home movie. You may want to produce music videos that have the sleek polish of a Herb Ritts supermodel clip or the techno-glitz of a Hype Williams sci-fi mini-epic. You may just want to capture the kinetic energy of a great rock band on tape. Whatever your vision, you will use some kind of special effects to achieve it. Effects are applied at two stages in the making of a video. *Production effects* are techniques used during the actual shooting, and *post-production effects* are refinements applied during the editing process. Both types fall into the general category of special effects. In this chapter, we take a look at some of the ways you can use effects while shooting.

## What is a Special Effect?

Let's think of some obvious examples of special effects: Godzilla knocking down a city, King Kong climbing a building, and the *Terminator II* cop morphing into the mercurial T-1000 robot. Now let's go to the other extreme. Imagine the local school board is on a public access cable program, discussing its annual budget. There aren't any aliens, hopefully, and no giant gorillas either. There's no special lighting, no treatment of shadows, no makeup, no edits, no graphics; in fact, nothing that would entice the viewer to choose the TV screen over reality, unless you're specifically interested in the education budget. To convince viewers to sit on their sofa for hours at a time, staring at a box, TV must offer a heightened, novel version of life — something more than what viewers can see by simply walking around the neighborhood. To do this, directors use a wide range of effects, some obvious, many subtle, that lure their viewers away from reality. In fact, *effects* could be defined as any treatment that is applied during production or post-production to create a departure from the literal documentary depiction of reality. The possibilities range all the way from using lipstick and hairspray to creating starships, with myriad variations in between.

# Types of Special Effects

Limitless variations of possible effects exist, so we've broken them down to a few types for you to explore further.

## Mattes and chroma keys

These effects involve steps that take place in both the production and post-production stages. During the shoot, actors and objects are filmed in front of a solid color background that does not contain tints found in their skin color. Blue and green are used most often. In post-production, these colors can be identified and effectively "removed" from the clip, leaving space for another layer to show through. In general terms, a *matte* is any post-production process that defines a portion of the clip as transparent, allowing another image to show through. A *chroma key* is a type of matte in which a color is selected as the defining characteristic of the effected region.

The Hollywood blockbusters of the 1950s, such as *The Ten Commandments* and *Ben Hur* made liberal use of mattes by creating sweeping deserts and grandiose Roman cityscapes behind Charlton Heston and his casts of thousands. Actually, the cast was frequently dozens, with a few thousand more painted on matted-in backgrounds. Hollywood still has a thriving subindustry of matte painters who create the dramatic backgrounds for *Star Wars* and other epic scale, otherworldly productions. Computerized animation now makes it possible to create lifelike environments that blend seamlessly with the foreground action. They can also be used to create mythic worlds that don't exist in reality, like the fantasy city in Michael Jackson's "Billie Jean." The backgrounds can be stationary, or they can be motion clips or animation. The next time you watch *Jurassic Park*, keep in mind that the actors may be gazing in awe at a herd of herbivorous dinosaurs that were actually matted in later by computer-generated-imagery (CGI) artists. The director simply put the actors in front of a blue background and said, "Stare in awe." Rent the movie *Wag the Dog* for a detailed sketch of how matte assembly takes place.

 **Cross-Reference**    See Chapter 12 for a walk-through of the matte and chroma key tools available in Premiere 6.5.

Decades ago, filmmakers dealt with the problem of shooting characters riding in a car by using *chroma keys*. It was impractical and dangerous to perch on the hood of a moving car, especially in a chase scene, only to end up with shaky footage marred by windshield reflections, assuming that the cameraman survived the trip! In addition, the car would be moving through all kinds of uncontrollable shadows, making it impossible to effectively light the characters. To shoot this type of scene, the actors sat in a stationary front seat, with a blue background in place of the rear windshield. At a later time, a pickup truck, specially outfitted with a secure tripod, would cruise the route that the car travels in the scene, aiming backwards, of course. By laying in this background and adding controlled windshield highlights and shadows, plus the reflection of stoplights and streetlights for realism, the scene would look convincing. In Premiere, we have smoothing tools that enable us to get even closer than Hollywood could back in the day. So experiment with mattes and chroma keys. And remember, if you use this type of effect, make it look really convincing, like *Star Wars: The Empire Strikes Back* or really fake, like the B-52s' "Roam." Anything in-between qualifies you for "accidental comedy" status! Figures 5-1 and 5-2 illustrate this process.

**Figure 5-1:** Soldier in front of blue screen

**Figure 5-2:** Soldier with painted mountain background matted in

## Miniatures and models

Remember the wonderfully jerky movements of the original *Godzilla* as the lumbering monster gleefully knocked down buildings, terrifying platoons of soldiers on the ground? A full size 200-foot monster would have been hard to create in the 1950s, so the producers settled for a two-inch version. By moving the beast's arms and legs by hand and then painstakingly shooting each new position, they were able to create action when the bits were spliced together. Projected on a big screen, the two-inch model became a terrifyingly huge monster. But what about the soldiers? They were real guys! How did they look so much smaller than the Big G? Of course, their scenes were shot *sans* monster in front of a chroma background. When *close-ups* of the tiny creature were layered full screen behind *long shots* of the soldiers, the scale suddenly became frighteningly realistic to the 1950s audience. See Figures 5-3 through 5-5.

**Figure 5-3:** Two-inch beast in front of small painting

**Figure 5-4:** Real-life soldiers in front of blue screen

**Figure 5-5:** Composite of beast and soldiers. The beast now towers over the men.

Even though CGI labs create today's monsters, models and miniatures are still used extensively. The ship in *Titanic* is actually several models, none of them near the size of the original ship, and many of the space vehicles in *Star Wars* are the size of glue-together hobbyist models, combined with multiple layers of matte and chroma-key paintings, animations, and live-action clips.

The multilayering features of Premiere make these sophisticated visuals available to us, but careful planning at the shooting stage is essential to get the most out of these powerful features. Skillful directors are adept at placing actor's marks and eye-lines and setting up camera points-of-view in such a way that live action shots appear synchronous with matted in action. In addition, lighting and shadow must appear consistent when mixing matted layers, unless you are going for a deliberately unreal effect. If you shoot your band being threatened by an Alaskan brown bear during the synth solo, get your stock footage of the bear first. Study the angle of sunlight, the clouds in the sky, and the direction of the breeze blowing the leaves in the bear footage. Make sure that you reproduce these conditions when you shoot the band in front of your green screen, cowering behind the Ryder truck. Inconsistent lighting between the forefront action and the matte background is a dead giveaway.

## Spectacular backgrounds on a shoestring budget

**Road Diary**

Editing in Adobe Premiere enables you to shoot action — singers singing, drummers drumming — in front of a solid background and then insert a different background as you edit. Thus, the guy playing guitar in your rec room can be placed by a fjord in Norway, and the folksinger strumming at the Common Bean Coffeehouse can be put in front of the Statue of Liberty. We shoot backgrounds on the road, whether we have an immediate use for them or not. Our philosophy is "How often do we happen to be in front of Mt. Rushmore?" If we ever do a remake of *North by Northwest*, we'll save ourselves a lot of money by having backgrounds already in the can.

Because music videos tend to be *impressionistic,* evoking a feeling rather than spelling out a linear story, we love backgrounds that involve lots of color and texture but don't include specific objects that bring the viewer down to earth. You can achieve this by shining active lights on a white background, but it's way cool if you can shoot actual objects that are moving. One of our best shoots for background and fill shots was at Mardi Gras a few years back. We got up at dawn and made our way over to one of the streets that would soon be the scene of the joyous mayhem that is the Zulu parade. This parade has the best floats, the most colorful costumes, and by far the funkiest music at Mardi Gras. As the last float goes by, the crowd pours into the street and dances in the second line behind the brass bands. This is really big fun.

We decided to shoot most of the parade in really distorted, color-hyped modes because straightforward video of the floats is readily available. In fact, my parents had 8mm films from the 1950s that resemble the present day parade. We wanted footage that wouldn't be a home movie of Mardi Gras. We wanted lots of streaming lights, lots of motion, and lots of texture. These are all things that get expensive in the world of special effects, but we gambled that by using the floats as raw material, we could morph the floats into abstract shapes that would blend into all kinds of musical situations later on. We shot the effects *in camera,* that is, while we were running tape, but we had lots of options, in Adobe Premiere, to add colorizing and "good" distortion later on. When we use these as short clips, as we do here and there in the "Free" video, they don't evoke Mardi Gras. They are just abstract splashes of color and motion that pump energy into the edit. When you see color in motion, shoot it and keep a library of these "vitamin C (C for color)" clips to liven up your mix.

## Stunts

A *stunt* is a live action that is physically impossible or too dangerous for actors to perform in real time on the set. Stunts are effective because they show humans doing things that don't seem possible. The earliest post-production stunts were achieved by using reverse action and slow and fast motion, and these effects still get a laugh. Buster Keaton roller skating backwards in fast motion was funny in the 1920s, and it's still funny now. Moe whacking Curly on the head with a hammer combined with an overly loud sound effect is still shocking, and it was considered pretty violent in those innocent, pre-*Bonnie and Clyde* times.

Real people can perform stunts, or stunts may be executed by the manipulation of props by the crew. The real people are known as *stunt doubles,* a special breed who relish getting shot, falling off of rooftops, and getting into car crashes. They are specially trained and licensed, and their employers pay massive insurance costs to use them for just a few seconds of action. Their services are outside the scope of amateur video, and it's not advisable to persuade normal actors — or even drummers — to perform any action that qualifies as a stunt. A friend of ours who toured with The Who told us that Keith Moon once jumped off the Asbury Park pier into the ocean, just as the group was about to go onstage. The show was held up while the roadies swam around looking for him in the surf. If you want to recreate this wonderful moment in rock history, you can use a mannequin dressed in drummer's clothes (Zildjian® t-shirt, headband, and so on) and don't endanger anyone's life.

# Sound Effects

Music videos differ from films in that the music bed runs all the way from the beginning to the end of the piece. Normally, it's not combined with additional tracks of dialogue, sound effects, and ambient/action sound as it is in film. Keep in mind, however, that Premiere offers up to 99 tracks of audio, and your stereo song uses up two of them. The creative potential is there to add additional sound, but it must be used judiciously, if at all, to avoid distracting the viewer from the song. In certain creative situations, however, the act may feel that a cinematic-style collaboration featuring additional dialogue and sound can enhance the impact of the song. This concept has been explored by such big-budget artists as Michael Jackson and Reba McEntire, who both have created mini-movies to frame their songs. It's also an option for avant-garde videographers who work outside of the restrictions imposed by major-network airplay. If your creative impulses suggest added sound, and the act is agreeable, you should feel free to explore the techniques used by filmmakers in the field of sound design.

## Wild sound

A *wild sound* isn't the sound of Jimi Hendrix at Monterey, although that was pretty wild. It's a film term for sound shot on location, capturing live audio in an unprocessed, documentary style. You would not use this sound for an MTV-style video. That genre features studio recordings, synched with video footage shot at a later time. Wild footage may be used for a realistic live rockumentary, although even in this case, multitrack recordings are usually made and remixed for optimum quality. Wild footage is always used for the making of videos that show the activity that takes place behind the camera and feature spontaneous commentary by the cast and crew. The *Making the Video* series on MTV features wild audio recorded along with behind the scenes footage, followed by studio audio at the end of the program when the final clip is aired. Listen to this show to compare the difference in quality between the wild and studio footage. Which is fuller and richer sounding? Which is more realistic and evocative of place?

## Studio sound

A complete description of the techniques used in recording, mixing, and mastering modern CDs is beyond the scope of this book. You should note, however, that your audio should be of the highest quality to reinforce the impact of your video. Modern CD producers use digital mixing techniques that are similar to the layering options available to videographers to optimize the sonic impact of each individual track/instrument used in a song. *Audio compression* is a type of a level-controlling technique that maximizes the volume of each instrument so that it stands out clearly in the mix, and *equalization* is a form of selective volume control over select frequencies of the audio spectrum, imparts the highest sonic quality to the tracks. In addition, recording engineers use *reverb* to create depth. The engineer, working on a *mixing console* (see Figure 5-6 for a typical mixing console), combines all of these elements in the final mix and then adds compression and equalization again to the final stereo mix in a process called *mastering*. Mastering sets the overall level of the song at a volume comparable to that of other commercial releases so that when the final cut airs on radio or television, it doesn't sound too weak or too loud in comparison with other programming and so that it meets federally established output levels for communications media. If you want to venture into the world of professional broadcast, make sure that an experienced mastering engineer prepares your final audio. Adhering to professional standards avoids the possibility that TV stations can't play your great video because its playback level is too low or too high for their broadcast gear.

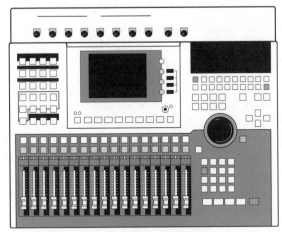

**Figure 5-6:** A modern mixing console features hardware controls for reverb, equalization, compression, and individual channel volume. The console, pictured here, blends 16 separate tracks down to a two-channel stereo mix.

# Dubbed-in sound

If you decide to go beyond the stereo tracks of your song and add additional sounds, you will encounter the same problems dealt with by early filmmakers. Shooting on location, a very common situation in music video, involves many uncontrollable elements. Let's say that you're shooting on the streets of New York, for example. Can you predict exactly when a loud siren, honking cab, or noisy bus will pass by? Can you control the idling eighteen-wheeler across the street? Probably not, unless you want to risk getting your nose broken by a teamster from Red Hook. Consider some of the other sounds that happen while you're shooting video. Planes fly overhead, crew members clear their throats and sneeze, singers flub lyrics, drummers drop sticks, and so on. All of these sounds will be present on your wild audio, and when you want to capture the lead singer shouting, "Take it away, Justin!" to the guitarist, you can't control things so that a cab won't beep at the same time. Instead of doing ten takes of "Take it away" while you hope for ambient silence, you can easily record that line later and dub it in on your Premiere Timeline.

Feature films *dub in* much, if not all, of the dialogue after scenes are shot on location, and low-budget films use the technique to get footage in the can when the actors don't have time to memorize their lines and deliver them perfectly. They get as close as they can, and the director uses a cutaway shot whenever they mess up. Later, when the time pressure of location shooting is off, they simply read the lines off the script while watching the footage. Of course, films are routinely dubbed in other languages by using this technique — sometimes convincingly, sometimes not. In the world of vintage TV, *Mister Ed* certainly comes to mind as a classic use of dialogue replacement!

For a film, just re-recording dialogue is not enough. All of the other sounds, including footsteps, doors opening and closing, crickets chirping, and so forth, must be convincingly reproduced. Specialists known as *Foley artists* create this reproduction. Working in their studio, which is called a Foley pit, they study the film carefully and make judgments on which sounds will be reproduced. Some are done electronically, and of course samplers and synthesizers are used, but true Foley artists still do much of their work in the old-fashioned way, by manipulating real materials; a floor full of sand or gravel, pieces of iron and wood, bolts of fabric, and so forth, to create a controlled version of nature. They don't always strive for complete realism. If the main characters are talking in a whisper in Times Square, the level of noise from passing cars and cabs will be reduced to suggest reality without interfering with the dialogue. *Stems*, or submixes are created to give the director control over these elements in the final mix. The clarity of the dialogue is all-important, so realism may be sacrificed to bring the script to the forefront; just as realistic lighting may be compromised to bring forward an important facial expression. On the other hand, they may strive to heighten reality. Hollywood gunshots, first created long ago for early action movies, haven't changed in decades. Even though they don't sound at all like a real gun, they still serve to draw the viewer into the world of cinematic illusion.

Since the earliest sci-fi radio dramas, sound designers have created sounds that don't exist in our world to transport listeners away from reality. Think of *The X-Files* theme or the wonderful dialects of the talking creatures in the *Star Wars* movies. You may want to follow this path if your musical artists agree to let you manipulate their audio in a creative way. Techno, house, and other forms of electronica are elastic musical genres that lend themselves to remixing techniques. Offer to combine creative video concepts with sonic manipulation and form partnerships with cutting-edge audio artists in your area. A good Digital Audio Workstation (DAW) program like Sonic Foundry's Sound Forge gives you extra flexibility. Be creative and remember, your camera works as a remote audio recorder even when you're not shooting specific footage. If you record a cow mooing and then lower the pitch 200 percent and lengthen the duration another 200 percent, you may end up with the sound of the Titanic hitting an iceberg. It's been done that way. Crank it up 200 percent and you may have the chirp of an ewok sizing up Luke Skywalker. Video has guidelines but no hard and fast rules. Let your imagination be your guide.

# The Videographer's Toolbox

Throughout a videographer's career, she compiles techniques that yield the best results and discards those that don't work. She relies on this ever-growing toolbox for creating special effects in music videos.

## Portals

Have your viewers see some of the video through another opening "inside" their TV screen. The most famous example is Hitchcock's *Rear Window*, in which much of the action takes place as Jimmy Stewart looks through his window into the window of his neighbors across the courtyard. In a current-day video of the Turtles' classic, "Happy Together," the group appears only on the TV set at a groovy hippy party. In Alanis Morissette's video for "Hands Clean," she appears throughout on the screen of a vintage TV set that fits neatly inside the frame of the viewer's actual set. At one point, her set is seen on the screen of the inside set, so the viewer seems to be looking at three screens at once. Portals of this kind are great for putting a modern band in a vintage period setting or a vintage band in a modern setting. Figure 5-7 illustrates a typical portal composite. This effect can be achieved in Premiere, using a matte effect. Starting with a static shot of a vintage television, the video editor would define the TV screen as the determining shape of the matte. The action clip would be scaled to fit neatly inside the screen, creating the portal effect. See Chapter 12 for a complete explanation of Premiere's matte effects.

**Figure 5-7:** This portal image appears on a screen within a screen.

## Illusory points of view

You can fool your viewers into thinking you spent a fortune — well, at least $100 — on effects with a few simple camera tricks. Let's say the band is playing. They get to the guitar solo, and a large, mothership-scale spaceship passes by overhead. Happens all the time, right? The hardest part about this shot would be rigging a fake spaceship to pass above you while you aim the camera at it from below. Aliens have busy schedules, and they don't always show up when you need them. Pulley and scaffold systems are impractical for rebels without a budget. Wouldn't it be great to just accomplish this shot in the rec room? Maybe during a good *Star Trek* rerun such as "The Trouble with Tribbles?" Let's use a few simple tricks to get a good bit of cheesy video.

First, shoot a steady tripod shot straight up at the almost-dark sky just after dawn or just before dusk, if you sleep late like we do. Then spread a large green screen flat on the floor and pull a model spaceship slowly across it as you shoot from a ladder up above. Mount the spaceship upside down, belly facing up, on a simple dolly with fishing line attached. Finally, shoot the band members in medium shots, looking up and doing double takes in their best B-movie style. Throw the whole mess of clips onto your Timeline, with the long, slow spaceship pull as your master. If the pull is uneven, loop the most even section by copying and pasting it repeatedly until it lasts for the duration of the shot. Enlarge the ship image so that it almost fills the screen. Then enable a green-excluding chroma key and lay the sky in underneath it. Once again, if the shot is shaky, sample a short edit, and copy and paste to increase its length. If needed, sample a bit of sky and use it to cover up any visible fishing wire. Finally, cut away to the band member's reaction shots wherever your edit points are visible. See Figures 5-8 through 5-11.

**Cross-Reference**    To find out about using chroma key effects, see Chapter 12. To find out more about copying and pasting clips, see Chapter 8.

**Figure 5-8:** Band member reaction shots, looking upward

**Figure 5-9:** The night sky

**Figure 5-10:** Shooting the space ship as it's pulled across a green screen

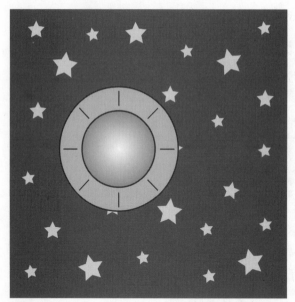

**Figure 5-11:** Composite shot of the ship "flying" across the sky

This kitschy sequence won't earn you any Oscar nominations, but it gives you practice at several basic techniques: directing (the double takes), chroma key (inserting the sky), using miniature models (the plastic mother ship), and fooling the audience into thinking that they are looking up at something that you actually aimed down at.

## Deep in the heart of Texas

**Road Diary**

When Maura and I are in Austin, Texas, we stay at the Austin Motel. It's our home-away-from-van. This south Austin institution features groovy theme rooms. Once we stayed in the "Great Wall of China" room, which featured bamboo trim and a wall-sized mural of the imposing edifice. On another trip, we stayed in a simpler, non-themed room with textured walls that resembled stucco. I noticed that the light from the east side window created cool little shadows on the wall, similar to the hand painted backdrops used for the cover shots of upscale magazines. I also noticed as I was talking to Maura near the window that her face was being lit with a clean dividing line down the middle. The east side of her nose was in sunlight, and the west side was in shadow. This reminded me of the cover of "Meet The Beatles," and I remembered reading an interview with their photographer, Robert Freeman. He simply shot them in a hotel room with the natural window light hitting their faces half-way for the famous cover that looks like a laboriously set-up studio shot.

I had Maura stand in one spot, and I shot her head and shoulders in black-and-white mode, while she sang several songs. I directed her not to move her head. The lighting was providing the interest. When you set up a good head-and-shoulders shot like this one, have the singer perform the song the whole way through. You know the shot works, so when you discover problems with your location and action shots, for example a dog running across the set, or the appearance of the ever-present jogger in the background, you can always cut to your reliable head-and-shoulders shot. Besides, people always like to see a face, full on. Look how successful TV news is with little more than talking heads. So look for the light and get the whole song.

## Rain

In a hard rainstorm, visibility is greatly reduced, so movies usually depict rain as a general hosing-down of the set and a lighter drip on the actors, just before the camera rolls. Shooting in actual rain is not advisable if you value your gear, and the friendship of your actors. Our friend Joe Hansard made us act for several hours in sleet and rain on a shoot, and we still haven't *quite* forgiven him. Thinking about shooting *Son of Twister*? See Chapter 6 to find stock footage of tornadoes and do your storm chasing on the desktop.

## Lightning

We see lightning in two ways. If we're lucky, we happen to be looking at the spot where it strikes and we see the bolt. Use stock footage for this. The more common occurrence is that we see the flash on another surface. A wall is good, but a face is even better. Use an ordinary flashbulb timed with the sound of thunder. The thunderclap can be either a digital sample or an old-fashioned piece of thin sheet metal with lots of reverb added in post-production. To better control the length and intensity of your ersatz lightning, shoot the flash separately and stretch and brighten it as you need to on its own timeline track.

## Mixed stock

Film technology has evolved so quickly that each decade has its own look. To evoke the days before videotape, switch to old movie mode, either in production or in post-production. Some cameras, including our Sony, have a dedicated button for old movies. In Premiere, you can add sepia tone and funky film lines to evoke the days of 8mm film. Feel free to switch to this mode during a modern-looking video if you want to contrast today with yesterday or slickness with funkiness.

## Color seep

Remember in *The Wizard of Oz* when the screen suddenly burst into color? Or in *Pleasantville,* when the people who "got it" became colorized? Feel free to mix color and black and white freely. You can do a sudden cut, like in *The Wizard of Oz* or let the color seep in slowly and perhaps seep back out later on. Let's say you open your country music video with a sepia-toned still of an old country store. As motion begins, the characters become "real," and we are in their moment, so they take on color. After their story is told, they go back to their original positions, and the photo freezes again, back in sepia tone. In Adobe Premiere, the Black & White effect, in the Image Control video effects folder, is the simplest process for creating black-and-white clips. After you've created your black-and-white clips, you simply use the array of Premiere transitions to go back and forth between color and black and white.

## Using lens filters

Let the lens impart an overall look and feel to your video by attaching a filter that diminishes parts of the color spectrum, making other hues appear stronger. Nowadays, many videos on MTV as well as many advertising clips have an overall blue tint through the use of a *double blue* filter. This filter also imparts the illusion of moonlight. For a lovely example, see Maxwell's video for "Fortunate."

A polarizing filter, used outdoors in daylight, makes the sky look bigger and bluer, so if you're shooting in New Jersey and you want to evoke Oklahoma, this is the filter for you. Inexpensive versions of these filters are available and should be in your bag of tricks.

## Slow motion

One of the most effective special effects is slow motion. Take a look at modern soul slow jam videos, and you'll see a lot of slow-motion video. Achieving a slow-motion effect is no more complicated than defining a clip to run at a slower speed than the clips around it.

Slow motion is most effective when there's lots of movement in the clip. If the band you're taping is not very animated, you won't see any unnatural movements that slow motion magnifies. When shooting for slow motion, direct your singer to move her head enough to get her hair flying. Have her blink a few times and turn and walk or dance. Our video "Free," included on the CD-ROM, contains several good examples of slow motion. Check out a quick clip of Maura shaking out a scarf at around 1:15 into the video. That clip was shot at normal speed and then slowed down to give it a kind of psychedelic look. A few seconds later at 2:05, you see Maura throwing a couple of fists-full of yellow mums' petals at the camera. We knew in advance that it would look unimpressive at normal speed, but pretty cool sped up. The combination of the bright yellow petals flying toward the camera for depth and the unnatural velocity take the clip to another level. That trick is repeated about a minute later in the video, this time using colorful autumn leaves.

How do you lip-synch a song if you're changing its speed? Easy! Just play the song back in fast-forward mode and have your subject lip-synch more quickly while you shoot the scene. Some CD-ROM players or digital audio jukebox interfaces give you the option of playing in fast forward by clicking and releasing a button, and others will only play in fast forward if you click and hold the Fast Forward button. If this is the case, you'll need an assistant. Because your subject is still singing to the track, her vocal will stay in synch after you've slowed the video track down to match the audio. Check out where Maura starts singing 15 seconds into "Free." She's lip-synching, but somehow the facial movements don't seem to flow naturally. That clip was taped by playing the CD back at double speed while she sang along. This lip-synched track runs throughout the song. See if you can spot it each time.

## Fast motion

Recording for fast motion is similar to recording for slow motion, but exactly the opposite. To achieve this effect, you need to tape some footage and then speed it up in the Timeline. Lots of rock videos use fast motion for a hyped-up feel. This effect goes all the way back to the opening credits of The Monkees music/comedy TV series. It's no wonder they got the funniest looks from everyone they met — they were walking in fast motion!

Try this exercise for fun: Get the band together and have them play their favorite song. In the middle of the tune, direct them to switch instruments: The drummer jumps up from the throne and grabs the bass guitar. The bass player pushes the keyboard player out of the way and starts playing. The keyboard player takes the guitar away from the lead player, and she in turn picks up the drumsticks and starts smashing the skins. Now rewind the video and watch it in fast-forward mode on your camcorder. It's pretty funny, and it makes the band look like a barrel of Monkees.

To apply a fast-motion effect to a clip in Premiere, follow these steps:

1. **Select the clip in the Timeline.**
2. **Choose Clip⇨Speed.**

3. **Click the New Rate button and type in a number other than the default 100%.** A smaller number tells Premiere to play the clip slower, resulting in a longer clip duration, and a larger number tells it to play the clip faster, resulting in a shorter clip duration.

Tip    Typing a negative number in the New Rate text box makes the clip play backwards.

# Chapter Replay

After reading this chapter, you should be able to:

✦ Understand the concepts of different types of visual and audio special effects

✦ Identify various types of special effects when watching music videos, commercials, and movies

✦ Understand how to create slow- and fast-motion shots for your videos

In the next chapter, you'll find out how to import your footage into your computer using Premiere's powerful capture features.

✦    ✦    ✦

# Bringing Footage Into Premiere

**N**ow that you have great raw footage, you need to transfer it from camera to computer. In addition to using your own original footage, you may want to use clips from stock footage libraries. And because we're talking about music videos, you'll also need to import the song to your music video as a Premiere-supported audio file. In this chapter, we explain how to do all of these things as well as how to manage those clips in bins, which are organized like file folders. We also show you how to name and save your project so that you can go back and work on it at your leisure. And just to keep all the lawyers happy, we end the chapter by summarizing your rights are as a music-lover, music video maker, and (most importantly) music video distributor!

## Setting Up Your Equipment

Traditional video editing required a room full of bulky, sophisticated electronic devices. Editing video with Premiere, however, demands a smaller and more affordable setup. Although we recommend using a TV monitor as part of your Premier workstation, you can get by with as little as the Premiere software, a Premiere-compatible personal computer (see Appendix A for complete system requirements), a DV camcorder, and a FireWire cable. You can find all these items at your neighborhood electronics superstore.

### Analog or digital?

Video camcorders come in two flavors, *analog* and *digital*. Analog video cameras in formats like VHS-C, and Video8 are widely available and cost relatively little. On the other hand, digital camcorders like MiniDV and Digital8 offer broadcast-quality images and high-resolution stereo sound. If you use an analog camcorder, you need to bring your analog video into your computer by digitizing that video. When you capture video from a DV camcorder, that video is already digital — you're simply transferring the footage from your DV camcorder to your computer.

**Note**  If you have an analog camcorder or a computer without a FireWire port, you can still transfer footage to your computer, as long as your computer has a Premiere-compatible video capture card. To find out which capture cards are compatible, see the Adobe Web site at www.adobe.com/premiere.

## Monitoring your work

Before you can use Adobe Premiere to create your video, you need to set up your gear so that you can view your work on both your computer screen and a TV monitor. Viewing on your computer screen alone can suffice if you only have one TV, and your family won't give up any of their viewing time. However, monitoring on a TV gives you the benefit of actually seeing what your viewers see when they view your video.

If you monitor your Premiere project on your computer screen only, you are viewing your project using a software *codec* (compressor/decompressor), which displays your video in a jittery, pixelated form. If you connect your computer to a DV camcorder via FireWire/i.LINK and connect the camcorder's analog outputs to a TV or video monitor, you can view your video in real time at its full resolution. Why? Because the camcorder's built-in codec processes that data. Simply put, it's the best way to monitor because you can see your video at full resolution. Depending on the angle at which you are viewing the monitor, the colors, brightness, and resolution don't always represent your program accurately. Depending on the power of your computer, Premiere may slow down as your hard drive and RAM fill up. If you keep your workstation connected this way, however, Premiere sends your work through the FireWire cables, through your camcorder, and to the TV, so that your output runs smoothly on your TV monitor.

**Note**  FireWire/i.LINK is a digital connection that carries audio, video, timecode, and remote control data in both directions between DV camcorders and computers. FireWire and i.LINK are two names for the same feature, with i.LINK being Sony's own registered moniker. For our purposes here, we refer to this interface as FireWire throughout the rest of the book. If your computer is not equipped with FireWire, you can purchase hardware that adds FireWire ports to your computer for about $100 or less. This type of hardware comes in different configurations. OrangeLink offers a variety of hardware options, from their FireWire 1394 CardBus PC card to FireWire boards and Hubs. You can visit the Adobe Web site at www.adobe.com to learn about compatible hardware.

Here's what you need to monitor your project on a TV:

✦ Your computer, equipped with a FireWire port.

✦ A FireWire cable.

✦ Your DV camcorder, equipped with a FireWire port.

✦ An A/C plug from your camera to a wall outlet.

✦ An A/V dubbing cable, which is an analog cable that connects the camcorder's video/audio outputs to the TV's video/audio inputs.

✦ A TV or video monitor with analog video/audio inputs. Audio may be mono, but you will only hear your audio signal in mono. As long as you have stereo audio on your computer, you will not need stereo to monitor the video. The benefit of this monitoring system is a visual one.

If you have all the gear listed above, follow these steps to connect your hardware, as illustrated in Figure 6-1:

1. **Connect your camcorder to your computer by using the FireWire cable.**

2. **Plug your DV camcorder into the wall.** Many camcorders automatically shut off after five minutes of inactivity, but they won't do this in VTR mode when plugged into an AC socket.

3. **Switch your camcorder to VTR mode. Some models call this mode VCR.**

4. **Connect camera's A/V (audio/video) outputs to your TV or video monitor's A/V inputs.** If your camera is like ours, it has a single output that sends video as well as stereo audio. The cable splits into three (one for video, two for audio left and right). If your TV monitor only has a mono input, you'll need to buy a Y adapter to convert the stereo signal to mono.

5. **Make sure that your TV is plugged in and turned on.** You may need to follow your television's manual to set it up for video input.

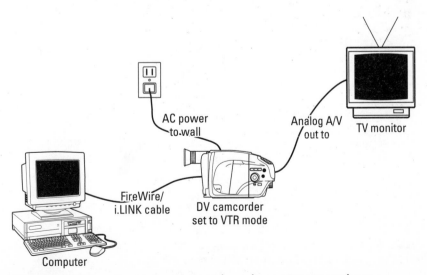

**Figure 6-1:** Connecting your computer through your DV camcorder to a television or video monitor, using FireWire cable

You're now set up to monitor through your TV. Of course, you'll still see your image on the computer screen, but as you work, you'll notice and appreciate the full resolution of the TV image. Because your camera is set to VTR mode, not to Record mode, it puts no wear and tear on the tape heads or the transport motors. You don't even need to have a tape in the machine!

# Setting Up Premiere

Before you start importing clips, you'll need to set up Premiere to work specifically with your camera and video clips. Double-click the Premiere icon to open the program. The first time you open Premiere, you are asked to select your initial workspace: either A/B Editing or Single-Track Editing. We typically work in A/B Editing mode and, because it's easier to understand than Single-Track Editing, we recommend it for beginners.

**Cross-Reference**     To find out more about the different types of workspaces and the benefits of each, check out Chapter 8.

## Loading project settings

Next, the Load Project Settings dialog box appears on your screen, and the left column lists all the available presets, as shown in Figure 6-2. Select settings from this list to tell Premiere what your camera settings are.

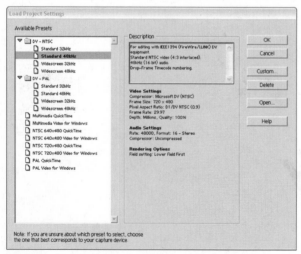

**Figure 6-2:** Check your camera's settings to make sure that you select the corresponding project settings!

*Telling Premiere what your camera settings are is the most important step that you make in creating a music video!*

We hope we got your attention with that, because we really mean it. Trust us; we are the voice of experience. Choosing the right preset determines whether your final video will be output correctly. Why doesn't Premiere just set it up for us? The answer is simple. Everyone has different equipment. Premiere makes it possible for all sizes and shapes of video and audio data to be captured and imported to Premiere, so it relies on you to know the format of your clips. Moreover, if you select the wrong presets at the start, or if there are discrepancies between your project, capture, and clip settings, you have to deal with all sorts of problems in playing your previews and final output. And who needs that? So save yourself the heartache.

**Caution** Make sure that your preset settings match the format of your *captured* video footage. If they don't match, Premiere will try to squeeze your footage and further compress it into the format you select in this window, so it behooves you now to get out the manual from your camcorder and make sure that you use the correct settings.

Take the time now to find out the following:

✦ Do you have a DV or an analog camcorder? If your camcorder is a DV model, you will be able to capture footage directly from it to your computer via a FireWire connection. If your camera is analog, you need a converter box to convert your analog signal to DV before transferring footage to the computer.

✦ Is your camcorder in the NTSC or PAL format? NTSC is the American standard, and PAL is the European standard. If you're not sure, consult your video camera's manual. Your camera may indicate on the unit whether it is NTSC or PAL.

✦ At which sample rate have you recorded? On our camera, we can choose to record 12-bit audio at 32 kHz, or 16-bit audio at 48 kHz (CD quality). Why would we choose a lower sample rate? Well, our camcorder allows us to add titles, but only if we record at a lower bit rate. Because we have much more sophisticated titling options in Premiere (see Chapter 10), we don't need to use the camcorder's titling feature, so we can record audio at the higher sample rate. If your camcorder has this option, it's good to know this: If you have the option of recording at 16 bit, you can use your camcorder as a Digital Audio Tape (DAT) recorder — in other words, you can record at CD quality. This makes a big difference if you're recording a band's live set to use in a video or live recording. You'll also need to know what sample rate you recorded at to select the appropriate preset sample rate. Most DV camcorders use standard 48 kHz as their default.

**Caution** Changing your project settings mid-video may cause some volatility in your clips and in the Timeline, so finding the right setting and sticking with it from the beginning of the project to the end is best.

To select your Project Settings, select the appropriate setting in the Available Presets list and then click OK. After you do, Premiere opens a new project.

## Customizing your desktop

Your new Premiere Project displays several windows. They may be stacked one on top of the other, but you can clean up the windows to optimize the layout by clicking Window➪Workspace➪A/B Editing (which is the workspace you selected when you first opened Premiere, as shown in Figure 6-3). At any time while working on a project, you can drag and resize windows and collapse palettes by double-clicking their tabs. The visible windows in the A/B workspace are as follows:

✦ Project window

✦ Monitor window

✦ Timeline window

✦ Effects palette

✦ Navigator palette

✦ Transitions palette

Project window          Monitor window          Palettes

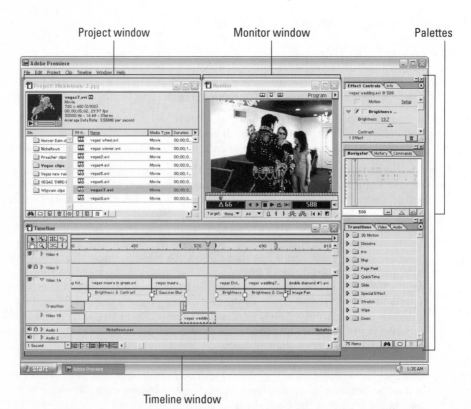

Timeline window

**Figure 6-3:** The windows of the A/B Editing workspace in Premiere offer a comprehensive approach to video editing.

As you customize your workspace to suit your needs, you can save that workspace to use on later projects. To customize and save your workspace, follow these steps:

1. **Drag and resize windows to achieve the desktop layout you want.**

2. **Double-click the tabs on any of the three palettes to collapse them, if you want.**

3. **Click the fly-out menu on the upper-right side of the Timeline and select Timeline window options.**

4. **Select the small icon to see more of the Timeline on your window.**

5. **Click OK.**

6. **Choose Window⇨Workspace⇨Save Workspace.**

7. **Give your workspace a name and click Save.**

Now whenever you start a new project or open an existing one, you can select this workspace the same way you would select one of Premiere's preset workspaces.

# Capturing Audio and Video

When it comes to capturing digital video, or DV, you must have continuous time-code striped to your videotape to get the most out of Premiere's capture features.

## Striping your tape with timecode

DV cameras use Society of Motion Picture Television Engineers (SMPTE) timecode, the industry standard. SMPTE counts hours, minutes, seconds, and frames of your video and audio material, giving each frame of audio and video a unique location point number. Most DV camcorders write timecode to tape while you shoot, but if you stop the tape or take it out of the machine and then put it back in and resume shooting, your timecode may be interrupted. This interruption could cause the camcorder to reset at zero, without rewinding. Now your camera has two zero points, two one-second points, and so on.

*Striping*, the process of formatting your tape with timecode, before you shoot ensures that your tape has one continuous timecode from the beginning to the end. Make sure that your lens cap is on and your camera is plugged into the wall. Press the Record button. Come back in an hour (or however long your tape is), rewind, and you're ready to go. After timecode is encoded onto your DV tape, it cannot be replaced, however, you can reshoot video and audio information as many times as you want over the existing timecode. Preformatting your tapes in this way takes a little more time, but it pays off in the certainty that all your location points are accurate.

## Setting up your scratch disc

Before you actually capture clips, you want to tell Premiere specifically where to save the clips on your computer. Ideally, you want to have your Premiere program along with the operating system on one hard drive, and your captured video on another AV-certified hard drive. Don't store anything else on this drive. You should save your project file to the same hard drive as Premiere and the operating system.

You will want to place your video preview files on the fastest drive, and your audio preview files on the slower one. You may specify removable media, but only if it is fast enough. To set up your scratch discs, as shown in Figure 6-4:

1. **Open the Scratch Discs and Device Control Preferences dialog box by choosing Edit⇨Preferences⇨Scratch Discs and Device Control.**

2. **In the Scratch Discs portion of the dialog box, click the Captured Movies drop-down list and select Folder to locate the drive where you want your captured clips stored.** The folder you select should ideally be located on an AV-certified hard drive where nothing else is stored. If your hard drive is not AV-certified, you can still use Premiere.

3. **Next, click the Video Previews drop-down list.**

4. **Click Select Folder to locate the drive where you want your video previews stored.** This should be your fastest hard drive, and can be the same hard drive where your captured clips are stored.

5. **Click the Audio Previews drop-down list.**

6. **Click Select Folder to locate the drive where you want your audio previews stored.** Ideally, this folder will be located on a different hard drive than where the video previews are stored. Don't worry if you only have one hard drive — Premiere will still work, but remember this option if and when you decide to upgrade your hardware.

7. **Click OK.**

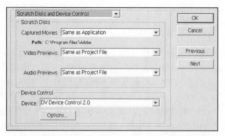

**Figure 6-4:** Setting up your scratch discs correctly optimizes Premiere's settings for your computer configuration.

## Setting up Device Control

By setting up Device Control (see Figure 6-5), the capture feature in Premiere enables you to control your camera remotely from the computer! How cool is that!

To set up the Device Control for DV cameras:

1. **Make sure that your camcorder is turned on.**

2. **Set your camcorder to VTR mode.**

3. **Choose Edit⇨Preferences⇨Scratch Discs and Device Control.**

4. **Chose DV Device Control from the pop-up menu.**

5. **Click the Options button. The Device Control Options window appears.**

6. **Select your video standard. If you're using the American standard, that's NTSC.**

7. **Select the Device Brand — that's the brand of your DV camera.** If your camcorder is not listed, you can choose Generic.

8. **Select the Device Model.**

9. **Select the Timecode Format.** The American standard is Drop-Frame.

10. **Click OK.**

**Figure 6-5:** Setting up Device Control correctly optimizes Premiere's capture capabilities for your camera model, and provides a remote control interface for your camera's transports.

## Capturing clips using Movie Capture

Now that you've hot-rodded your system and Premiere settings, you're finally ready to capture clips. To capture a clip using Movie Capture, follow these steps:

1. **Choose File⇨Capture⇨Movie Capture.** Because you set up Device Control, and your camera is connected and set to VTR mode, you should see the transport buttons enabled at the bottom of the Movie Capture window. If your camera's connections aren't established, the controls still appear there, but you can't click them. These buttons, as shown in Figure 6-6, act as a remote control for your camera, enabling you to find and capture the footage you want to use.

2. **Click Play to start your tape.**

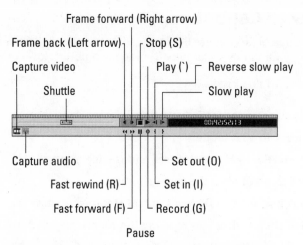

**Figure 6-6:** The transports shown at the bottom of the Movie Capture window act as a remote control for your DV camera, as long as you set up Device Control, and your camera is set to VTR mode.

3. **Use the available transport buttons and shuttle to find the clip you want to capture.**

4. **When you find the clip, click the red Record button.**

5. **Let the tape roll until you reach the end of the portion of tape you want to capture.**

6. **Press the Esc key on the keyboard to define the out point.** Premiere asks you to name the clip.

7. **Type a unique name that identifies the clip for you.** If you have more than one clip of the same subject matter, you may want to give it a number as well as a name. If you want, you can also type in a comment.

8. **Click OK to store the clip.** The clip is now visible in the Project window's default bin.

### Logging a Batch Capture list

As long as you have continuous timecode on your tape, Batch Capture enables you to go through a tape or tapes and log all your in and out points before actually capturing them. When you're done logging the clips, Premiere can capture them all at once from the information you provide in your Batch Capture list (see Figure 6-7).

Follow these steps to log the clips you want to batch capture:

1. **Click the Logging tab in the upper-right portion of the Movie Capture window.**

2. **Click the transport buttons to find the in point of the clip you want to log.**

3. **When you find that point, click the Set In button.**

4. **Let the tape roll, or you can fast forward or jog to the desired out point.**

5. **Click Set out or click the Mark Out (O) button.**

6. **Notice that the in and out points appear in timecode on the Logging tab, and the duration of the clip displays directly below.**

7. **Click the Log In/Out button and name the clip.**

8. **Name the reel using the same name you call it on the DV tape.** Why? Premiere enables you to batch capture from more than one tape in a session, but it needs to know which tape is which. Each tape will have the same timecode for different clips, so Premiere needs to know which reel of tape has the clip you want to use. In addition, you may need to go back and recapture at some point, or reference that original tape for some other reason. Being consistent pays off in the end.

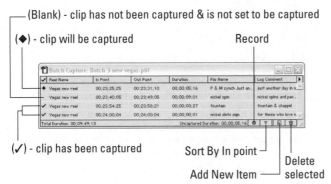

**Figure 6-7:** The Batch Capture List enables you to log the clips you want to capture as a group.

After you've logged all your in/out points to all the clips you want to capture, Premiere automatically captures everything on your Batch Capture list.

As you log your in and out points, you may notice that the Batch Capture window appears behind the Movie Capture window. This window lists all the clips, with the reel and clip names you've given them, the in and out points, and the durations. You will also notice a diamond to the left of each clip, which means that your clip is ready to be captured. If you don't want to capture a clip in the batch, click the diamond to disable the capture on that clip.

Depending on your hardware, you may experience occasional problems in Capture mode. Adobe, we're sure, has been working on this, but for now, we've gotten used to saving Batch Capture lists periodically as we go along. You're spending lots of time going through your video footage, identifying the clips you want to use and naming them, so get in the habit of saving the Batch Capture list at intervals, too.

When you save the Batch Capture list, you're not saving video. You're just saving the shopping list of in and out points that you want captured later.

## Executing a Batch Capture

To turn your Batch Capture list into actual captured files, you need to tell Premiere to find the clips defined in the Batch Capture list and save them to your computer. First, save your Batch Capture by choosing File⇨Save and name your batch list.

When you're ready to capture the clips in your Batch Capture list, do the following:

1. **Highlight all the items in the list by pressing Ctrl+A (⌘-A).**

2. **Click the red Record button at the bottom of the Batch Capture window.** Premiere tells you to insert the appropriate reel. If the reel is already in the camera, click OK.

3. **Premiere then automates your camera to find the designated clips and to capture them.** You may as well sit and practice guitar now. Premiere is doing all that time-consuming work for you!

4. **As each clip is captured, a check mark shows up to the left of each entry.**

5. **If Premiere encounters a problem while capturing a clip, no check mark appears next to the problem clip.**

6. **You should attempt to capture that clip again by highlighting just that clip and clicking Record.**

When Premiere finishes capturing your clips, you can close the Batch Capture list. Premiere then asks you if you want to save the list. A check mark now appears next to each successfully captured clip. Click Save to return view all the clips you captured in the Project window.

**Note**    If you've already shot your killer footage but didn't prestripe your tape with timecode, and now you realize that you have timecode starting from zero at more than one point in your tape, you must capture your clips manually by using Movie Capture, as opposed to Batch Capture.

## Capturing stop motion clips

If you want to incorporate stop-time animation, such as Claymation, or time-lapse footage into your video, you can capture single frames as Stop Motion clips. To capture Stop Motion clips:

1. **Close the Movie Capture window.**

2. **Choose File⇨Capture⇨Stop Motion.**

3. **Play your video by using the camcorder's controls.**

4. **Capture each clip by clicking the Capture button in the Stop Motion screen.** Alternatively, you can pause your camcorder at the frame you want and then click Capture. As you capture clips, they appear on your desktop, each in a separate window.

5. **Save the images you want to keep.**

## Capturing analog video

You may have a variety of analog material that you want to use in your digital videos. If you are a musician, someone may occasionally come up to you after a show and say, "Here's a VHS tape of that show you did last year at The Cat Club." When you view it at home, you find that it's pretty good — nice angles, good lighting, and no one walking in front of the camera. This tape is an example of the type of material you want to edit in Adobe Premiere. Perhaps you have tapes from an old VHS video camera or film from an even older 8mm machine. You can use all this material, but before you can load it into Premiere, you must first *digitize* it. The following three sections explain how you do this.

### Using a DV camcorder as a capture card

One way you can capture analog video or audio is to plug into a DV camcorder's analog inputs and record directly onto DV tape. If your camcorder has analog inputs, it has built-in analog-to-digital (A/D) converters. A/D converters come in very handy if you have footage or audio material in addition to your DV clips that you want to incorporate into your music video. Have you ever seen a music video where the singer flashes back to her childhood? Digital Video didn't exist back in 1965. Capturing analog video through a capture card or a DV camcorder is a way to get those old home movies into the digital realm. Here's how it's done:

1. **Connect the TV, VCR, or analog video camera to your DV camcorder by using the directions in your DV camcorder's manual.**

2. **Make sure that your DV camcorder is set to VTR mode.**

3. **Play the tape you want to digitize, or if you're taping off TV, wait until the part you want to tape is on.**

4. **Press your DV camcorder's Record button.** All cameras are slightly different; for details about your specific camcorder model, see its instruction manual.

You can even digitize old 8mm film or an old-fashioned slide show, if you are able to transfer it over to VHS first. Call your local photo developer. They may be able to give it to you already digitized on CD-R or DVD. In addition, there is third-party software available, which can clean up pops and clicks.

### Using a third-party capture card

With the compatible capture card, you should be able to digitize analog VHS tape, motion picture film, Hi8 tape, slides, vinyl audio recordings, cassette tape — virtually any kind of analog audio or video. See your capture card's manual for further instructions and be sure that your capture card is Adobe Premiere compatible.

### Using a media converter

If you don't have a DV camcorder with analog inputs and a FireWire output, you may consider purchasing a media converter. Sony makes one that retails at around $500, but for that kind of money, you may want to just slap down another few hundred and buy a FireWire DV camcorder.

After your analog material has been transferred to your DV camcorder, capture it as described "Capturing clips using Movie Capture," earlier in this chapter. Note that not all media converters support Stop Motion capturing. Check with manufacturer before making your media converter purchase, if you're interested in making stop time animations.

## Capturing analog audio

Your music video will need a soundtrack. In most cases, the music for your soundtrack will already exist in the form of a CD, digital audio in your camcorder, or perhaps a .WAV or other digital audio file. The process for importing these digital files into Premiere is described below, in the section entitled "Importing Audio And Video." This will cover your importing needs when the music already exists in the digital domain. There may be times, however, when you will wish to create a soundtrack using music from an analog format. This would include cassette tapes, reel-to-reel tapes, VHS and Beta videotape, and vinyl records. You might even want to dig out those old 8-track cartridges for some funky '70s music. In general, all of these formats are played back through the type of analog stereo system that has been the standard home set-up for the past few decades. The system will almost always include a number of stereo RCA jack inputs to accommodate various playback units. It will also include stereo RCA outputs to send the signal to speakers and to outboard recorders. This is the output that you will use to transfer the analog signal into your computer, as described below.

### Using a DV camcorder as a capture card

If you're using music from an analog source such as vinyl or cassette, you need to transfer it into the digital domain before you can use it in Premiere. You can capture audio in different ways. Our favorite way to capture analog audio is to plug our stereo system into the audio inputs of our DV camcorder. We always set the mic level mode to manual, so that our Sony DV camcorder's built-in compressor doesn't squash the sound. After you've recorded your audio onto DV, you can capture it the way you would capture digital video (see "Capturing clips using Movie Capture," earlier in the chapter).

If you want to digitize that old vinyl or cassette (or 8-track, even) recording of "Last Train To Clarksville" by the Monkees because you never got around to buying the CD, you can patch your stereo into you DV camcorder the same way you connected it from your VCR or TV. Too bad all those skips and scratches are still there! Maybe you *should* buy the CD, after all! We recommend that you capture analog audio only when the song you want to use is not available on CD. Not only will your song be free from defects inherent in most analog audio, you won't run the risk of clipping the audio signal by setting the audio mic/line in levels too high.

**Note**　Many DV camcorders on the European market provide FireWire output only, but not FireWire input, due to a tax imposition that classifies a unit with FireWire in/out as a VCR. Many of these camcorders can be modified to enable FireWire in/out, but that's usually provided by a third-party service, not the manufacturer.

### Using a computer's sound card to digitize analog audio

You can also capture audio by using a supported capture card and third-party sound editing:

1. **Choose File⇨Capture⇨Audio Capture.**

2. **Select the third-party capture program you want to use to record your music.**

3. **Click OK.**

4. **Use your preferred audio capture program to record and digitize your analog audio file.** (See the sound editor's literature for details.)

## A word about file size

The first time I edited a video, I was surprised and happy with the way it turned out. I knew that after I exported the final video, and before I erased all the clips and files from my hard drive to start another one, I really ought to back my video files up to CD-R disc. After all, video clips take up a lot of hard drive space, and I had to open up room for the next one. I didn't consider that I could only fit about 600MB on each CD-R. Unfortunately, some of my clips were pretty long, and they wouldn't fit. If you are going to back up all your clip files to Zip disc or CD-R, you need to keep in mind that your individual clips must, at their largest, not exceed the capacity of your storage medium. You may have to capture your clips in smaller segments. For example, if your singer lip-synched the entire song all the way through, you may still want to capture it in two parts. You can even overlap the in point of part two with the out point of part one so that you're sure to capture all the material. This way, you can also be assured that you will have a way to download the individual clips for archival purposes. Premiere regards clips larger than 2GB as large files. I regard clips larger than about 600MB as large files. Figure out how you will be storing your clips and capture clips accordingly.

Premiere can efficiently manage your project by discarding unused material, thus saving disk space. Premiere calls this process *trimming* clips. For more information on trimming clips, see Chapter 13.

# Importing Audio and Video

*Importing* files is different from *capturing* files, in that the files to be captured are not yet saved on a hard drive. Files to be imported are already on your hard drive, but are not yet in your Premiere project. Table 6-1 lists the many audio and video file types that Premiere supports.

| Table 6-1 Usable Audio and Video File Types | |
| --- | --- |
| **File Type** | **Description** |
| Digital Video Files | AVI files, DV movie files, QuickTime files, MPEG movies |
| Digital Audio Files | CD audio files, QuickTime audio files, SND and AIFF files, SoundDesigner files, WAV files, MP3 files |
| Graphics Files | JPEG files, TIFF files, GIF files, PICT files, BMP files, Targa files, Photoshop image files, Illustrator files, Generic EPS files |
| Premiere Files | Premiere's Batch Files, Premiere's Title Files, Premiere's Storyboard Files, Premiere Project |

## Importing supported file types

To import any of these file types to Premiere, choose File⇨Import. You can import a file, a folder, which comes into Premiere as a bin, or an entire Premiere project that also comes in as a bin. Note, if you only want to open a saved project, choose File⇨ Open or File⇨Open Recent Project and select the project. You import a project only if you want to pull a complete project into another one for some reason.

To import still images for use in stop-motion animation, you can set the default duration of each image by choosing Edit⇨Preferences⇨General and Still Image and then setting the number of seconds and frames you want to use as a default duration. Be sure you set the duration before importing stills, as the settings are not retroactive.

Lastly, you can import an entire Premiere project into another project. For example, suppose that you're trying out a couple of different sequences using the same clips and music. You may want to try one version of the music video with straight cuts between clips, and another version with dissolves all the way through. By opening a new project and then importing an entire music video project, you can make different versions of the same music video. Show both versions to your friends and see which one they think is the better version.

## Converting and importing audio tracks from a CD

Audio CD tracks can be brought in directly from the CD to Premiere on the Mac, but if you're working in the Windows platform, you first have to convert your CDA files (that's the CD file format) to a WAV file by using a third-party converter. We use Sound Forge Siren. Simply convert the file by using your third-party converter and save it. Then in Premiere, choose File⇨Import⇨File and find the saved, converted WAV file.

# Naming and Saving Projects

As soon as you begin loading captured digital, imported digital, or digitized analog material into Adobe Premiere, you should name and save your project.

1. **Choose File⇨Save to open the Save File dialog box.**

2. **Name your project in the File Name text box.** We usually use the name of the song.

3. **Navigate to the folder \Hard Drive\Program Files\Adobe\Premiere\ Project-Archive.**

4. **Click Save to store your project.**

When you save a project, you're not saving the individual audio and video clips. You are, however, saving edit decisions, arrangements of clips in the Timeline, and references, or pointers to, the actual clips stored on your hard drive. Here's a brief description of each element of your Premiere project:

✦ **Project (.ppj) file.** The file that stores all your edit decisions and pointers to other file types. When you open a Premiere project, this is the actual file you open.

✦ **Batch List (.pbl) files.** The list generated when you perform a batch capture. Although you don't need to save this file after your capture is complete, it's a good idea to save it, just in case you need to recapture your footage down the line.

✦ **Video (.avi, others) files.** The video files that your project file references. These are the video clips you use in your project, but they're not actually saved in the project file. This feature, which simply points to the files instead of copying them into the project file, saves an amazing amount of space on your hard drive.

✦ **Audio (.wav, mp3, others) files.** The audio file you use in your music video. You may capture the audio from your DV camcorder, if the song is from a live shoot. If you're working on the Mac platform, you can copy a CD directly into Premiere. If you're working in Windows, you must first convert the CDA (CD file) to a usable Premiere file with a third-party utility, such as Sonic Foundry's Sound Forge. If you're working with analog tape or vinyl recordings, you must first convert them to digital.

✦ **Title (.ptl) files.** A graphic file created in Premiere. When this file is placed on the superimpose track, its background is automatically set to alpha channel, so that the underlying video image shows through the transparent, non-text parts of the file.

✦ **Preview (.tmp) files.** The rendered video files. Premiere generates Preview files after you apply an effect to your Timeline. To preview your project with all applied video effects in real time, you must first create preview files.

✦ **Graphics (.tiff, .gif, others) files.** Files created in Photoshop or other graphics applications. Graphics files can be used as superimposed images that are either static or are in motion. You can create composites with multiple graphics files or titles.

✦ **Storyboard (.psq) files.** Files generated upon assembling storyboards. *Storyboards* are rough visual sketches of your project's basic video outline. They are a good way to visualize your video before actually applying the clips to the Timeline or adding effects and transitions.

✦ **Misc files.** Other files you may use in your project, including Universal Counting Leader, Bars and Tone, Black Video, and Mattes.

Get in the habit of saving your project frequently. You can configure Premiere to save at regular intervals with the AutoSave option:

1. **Choose Edit⇨Preferences⇨Auto Save & Undo.**

2. **Click the check box next to Automatically Saves Projects.**

3. **Premiere's default time interval is 5 minutes. Keep it set at 5 or set it for how often you want to Auto Save.**

If you archive your project to CD-R, Zip, or other archiving medium, with the intention of accessing it later, remember that your project file is just a set of parameters and pointers. The actual source material, in the form of captured audio and video clips, graphics, and titles must also be archived. What's more, if you upload all these files to a different computer, Premiere not only looks for the files, but it searches for their original locations. If Premiere can't find the files, a Locate File dialog box asks you for the new location.

# Organizing Your Clips Using Bins

The Project window references all your project's clips. Although the actual clips appear to be stored here, they're not really. Each clip reference serves as a pointer to the actual clip, wherever the clip is located on your hard drive.

Looking at the Project window, locate three main sections, as shown in Figure 6-8. Drag the lower-right corner of the screen to fully expand it while you learn the different features of the Project window.

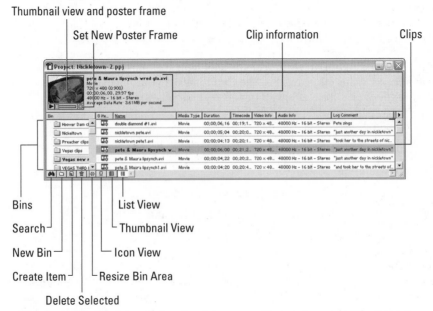

**Figure 6-8:** The Project window is where you will organize your clips. Treat the bins like folders.

## Navigating the Project window

When you work in Adobe Premiere, the Project window is always open. In fact, if you close this window, your entire project closes. You refer to this window constantly for information about your source material. The Project window displays folder icons representing the bins in which your audio, video, graphic, and title files are stored. The Project window contains three basic elements:

✦ Icon of currently selected item

✦ Bin view

✦ Currently selected bin contents view

### Icon of currently selected item

A thumbnail of the currently selected item shows up in the top portion of the Project window. If the bin is selected, a file folder displays, which is appropriate, because bins act in much the same way as file folders. Really, bins is just another name for folder in Premiere.

 Now click one of your clips and notice the still image from that clip where the folder was a moment ago. In Premiere, this identifying image is called a Poster Frame. Premiere's default Poster Frame is the first frame of each clip. Below the poster frame is a tiny Play bar, so you can play the entire clip on this tiny screen, if you like, by clicking the Play button (right-pointing arrow icon). By using this Play bar, you can change the Poster image to the frame that you feel best represents the clip. Simply scroll through your clip to find the frame that is most representative of the entire clip, and then click the Set Poster Frame button.

If you ever need to obtain technical support, you should know where to find file information on your clips. Next to the thumbnail of your clip, the Project window provides you with some technical information, including the following:

✦ Clip name

✦ Clip type

✦ Clip resolution

✦ Clip duration and frames per second (fps) rate

✦ Clip audio resolution in kilohertz (kHz), bits, and stereo/mono

✦ Average data rate

You can obtain further technical information about your clips, including image size, pixel depth, audio characteristics, by clicking on a clip to select it and choosing File⇨Get Properties For.

## Bin view

This portion of the Project window lists all the bins you have in your project. Premiere gives you a default of one bin and places all your captured files into that bin, but you can add bins and rearrange your clips. In fact, treat bins just as you treat file folders. At our studio, we usually organize bins to reflect types of shots for our music videos. For example, one bin contains all the lip-synched material, and another bin contains location shots. A third bin can contain graphics, with a fourth holding the audio clip. You don't have to follow these guidelines exactly, but use these bins in whatever way enables you to organize your clips.

You can change the way you view your clip references. If you need to see a poster frame, select either the Icon view or Thumbnail view by pressing its corresponding button at the bottom of the window or by clicking the Bin menu on the right of the window and selecting either Icon view or Thumbnail view. If you need to see only a list with the clips' filenames, select the List view from the Bin menu or click the List View button at the bottom of the Project window.

You can arrange clips in Project window in three views:

✦ **Icon view.** The Icon view is the simplest way to view your clips, but it doesn't give you very much information. We prefer to use the Thumbnail view.

✦ **Thumbnail view.** The Thumbnail view is quite versatile, because you can add notes while in this view. You can easily sort by any field simply by clicking that field's header (Name, Notes, Label, and so on). One click sorts it in ascending order. Click again to sort your clips in descending order. After you have moved your video clips around into different bins, select a bin — say, the one that contains video clips of the singer lip-synching the song. Take a look at each clip and figure out the correct sequence that the clips would appear in the video. Try numbering the clips to show the order that you will have them come into the Timeline. For example, you may have a clip of the entire length of the song lip-synched. However, you may have small segments of the song where the singer lip-synched the lyrics. Try numbering these sections in the order in which they occur in the song. In addition, you can use the Find command to search clips by any field in the Thumbnail view.

✦ **List view.** Like Thumbnail view, List view also allows you to sort by parameter, although you can't add notes or labels in this view. You can change the order by which these parameters are listed by clicking, dragging, and dropping the titles within the title bar. You can also resize each column by clicking the borders of the titles and dragging them to fit your information. If you want even more information in List view, you can add fields of information by clicking the Bin Menu button and selecting Project Window options. Here you can add Date, File Path, Reel Name, and other information, but this information only shows up in List View. You can, however, add in the Notes field that you filled in while you were in Thumbnail view.

## Creating more bins

Create new bins to better organize your clips:

1. **Choose File⇨New⇨Bin to create new bins or click the New Bin icon at the bottom of the Project window.**

2. **Name your bin appropriately.**

3. **Now click the clip that you want to move and drag and drop it into the new Bin.**

You can also create bins that you can drag other bins into, just like you would do with file folders. For example, when we make a video, we usually have a bin labeled Maura's Lip-Synched Video, one labeled Pete's Lip-Synched Video, and a third labeled Both Lip-Synch together. Then we create another bin called Lip-Synched Video into which we drag the other three bins. Do you see how you can easily arrange your clips?

## Get your kicks. . . .

**Road Diary**

Finding cool locations is largely a matter of going to interesting places and keeping your eyes open. We get lucky a lot on old Route 66 in the Southwest. The long stretches between towns have been replaced by the more modern and safer Interstate 40, however, when you hit a town, the main street is invariably a remnant of 66, the classic route of the dust bowl refugees in the *Grapes of Wrath* era. The 1950s brought an increase in automobile travel across the West. To satisfy the demand for cheap overnight lodging, motels sprang up all along Route 66. These motels were originally separate small cabins, some of which survive today. The coolest, of course, are the wigwam-style lodgings that must have been the ultimate thrill for kids from Chicago. Some of these unique and wonderful places still exist, but you have to get off the Interstate to find them. Every videographer should take a trip across Texas, New Mexico, and Arizona, and into California, on I-40, getting off at every town to find the funky old motels and shops that catered to Route 66 traffic in the 1940s and 1950s. Just shoot this stuff and develop your own library of stock "Americana" footage. If you do anything related to rock 'n' roll, folk, blues, or country music, these clips will come in handy.

For example, say that you're shooting a live gig of a local blues band at the Steak and Sausage at Mid-Suburban Mall. Begin the video by using an establishing shot of a desolate street in West Texas, auto-dollying to settle on the facade of a funky looking honky-tonk. Now cut to the band playing onstage. The viewer doesn't need to know that they're playing at the Steak and Sausage. The establishing shot says, "This is a funky honky-tonk in Texas." Come back to a shot of the desolate street, with tumbleweeds, as the last chord fades out, and you've got a video seemingly shot on location. The key is to have your camera handy at all times and shoot anything that is interesting, whether it's action or background. You will find a use for it later. To give you a real-life example, our video for the song "Free" was shot in Athens, Georgia, and Rye, New York, plus Nashville, Austin, and Los Angeles. Of course we couldn't afford to set up location trips to all those places, but over the years, as we traveled around, we kept stocking up clips for later use.

## Deleting bins or clips from your Project window

You may decide that you don't want to use one of the clips from your bin. If that's the case, select that clip or bin and click the Delete Selected button (the trashcan at the bottom of the Project window). Deleting a clip from the bin does not erase the clip from your hard drive; you simply remove it from the current project.

# Managing Source Clips and Libraries

Shooting video is habit-forming. As you develop an eye for images that look good on the screen, you may find yourself rolling tape more and more and getting an ever-higher percentage of "keeper" shots. How do you organize this mass of material into an easy-access archive? We pondered this question after several frustrating episodes of searching through cardboard boxes filled with unmarked tapes.

## Label your tapes — trust us

We had hours, and I mean *hours* of video on tape. Some of the tapes were labeled, and some weren't. By labeled, I mean that they had *really* sparse information, such as "Austin, 1998." That's it. One day, Pete decided to catalog all the keeper shots. To accomplish this, I used a database program, with fields for date, subject, location on the tape, location of the shoot, song (the music video that would best suit the clip), and so forth. Figure 6-9 shows an example. With our clips organized this way, we can search by any one of these fields. It took Pete about a week, working four hours a day, to catalog our footage this way, but it was well worth it. Now, when we sit down to edit a new video, we have an easy-to-use archive from which to draw.

**video clip file converted** — Clip Catalog

| Reel Number | Segment Start Location | Segment End Location | Segment Description | "Pick You Up" | "Free" |
|---|---|---|---|---|---|
| 05 | 34.54 | 34.59 | old radio | y | |
| 05 | 35.16 | 35.48 | diner style booth, color | | y |
| 05 | 35.48 | 37.00 | lava lamp globs closeup, in color, pans to full lamp shot | | y |
| 05 | 41.08 | 41.12 | cool posterized leopard chair with strange santa | | y |
| 05 | 41.13 | 41.30 | posterized diner booth with lava lamp, toaster(memphis) | | y |
| 05 | 42.00 | 42.13 | cowboy guitar | | |
| 05 | 2.25 (b) | 5.00 (b) | lorraine motel, Memphis, TN | | |
| 09 | .000 | 7.00 | uptown new orleans, funky neighborhood bars and shops | | |
| 10 | 38.00 | 38.30 | austin motel sign in color and old movie mode | y | |
| 10 | 41.50 | 43.00 | exploring typical thrift store --maura walking | | |
| 10 | 45.40 | 46.45 | 57 chevy in old movie, with maura | y | y |
| 10 | 51.28 | 52.15 | maura shows a row of polyester shirts | | |
| 10 | 55.20 | 55.32 | pete reflected in mirror inside lumi of gum wrapper | | y |
| 10 | 55.48 | 56.15 | old movie of statue of lady with jar--zooms in | | y |
| 11 | 01.50 | 5.24 | M. head shot singing "pick you up" b&w austin motel | y | |
| 12 | 16.10 | 17.00 | pete and maura sing not fade away at buddy holly grave. | | |
| 14 | 32.00 | 33.00 | Albuquerque: area that looks like 50's suburbia | | y |
| 15 | 51.25 | 58.00 | old movie village of cubero in NM | | |
| 16 | 10.35 | 38.20 | long interview with cross-bearing preacher walking across | | |
| 35 | 09.49 | | woman walking on glass, other tricks, cinder block at | | y |
| 36 | .000 | 3.00 | harlem, 125th st, shots of apollo theatre | | |
| 36 | 03.50 | | bombers returing from belgrade, yugoslavia, 1999 | | |
| 23 | 02.53 | 3.30 | rt 66 motels, old movie mode at nite | | |
| 23 | 03.36 | 4.50 | flagstaff pine trees. etc. | | |
| 23 | 22.45 | 28.00 | various good shots of domes, telescopes, machinery | | |
| 23 | 28.53 | 31.38 | good space shots--earth from space | | |
| 23 | 55.40 | | standin on a corner in winslow az | | |
| 23 | 56.10 | 58.00 | good desert highway shots at night | | |
| 24 | 58.46 | | knights of pythias lodge and fallout shelter--hastings NE | | |
| 25 | 34.28 | | nuclear warheads sign | | |
| 30 | 31.59 | 43.00 | rico plays his flute | | |
| 30 | 57.53 | 58.43 | good generic pete head shots | y | |

**Figure 6-9:** A typical entry in the archival database that we use for our raw footage

## Creating your own stock footage library

In Chapter 7, we tell you all about stock footage libraries and where to access them. You may recall how expensive stock footage can be. We decided long ago to create our own stock footage. We didn't know we were doing it at the time, but all that scenery that we took when we first got the camcorder — you know what I mean — cows, trucks, windmills, oil wells, more cows — at first viewing it seemed like we spent way too much time on scenery. When we developed our philosophy about stock footage, however, all that scenery went into our library. And because we cataloged it all, batch capturing like types of footage and archiving them on their own CDs became quite easy. Now we have a library — dozens of CDs of nothing but Kennedys-generated stock footage. And guess what? It's free!

# Understanding Music Rights and Legal Issues

In the MP3 age, it's become hip to say that you've ripped off the mega record labels by encoding MP3s of your favorite artists and distributing them online. MP3 advocates don't like to admit to doing this. Not only are they ripping off big corporations, but they're also cheating the very artists that they admire out of royalties that are legally owed to them. Whatever your own personal philosophy is, you need to understand that *distributing* a song that someone else wrote and recorded, without first obtaining the proper licenses, is against the law. That's not to say that you can't make your own music videos for fun to keep or to show to your friends at your next get-together. Consult a lawyer for up-to-date advice on music rights issues. The laws are complicated and change frequently. If you want to work with other people's material, get acquainted with some of the basic legal requirements.

## Obtaining music licenses

If you're making a low-budget music video segment to use in a movie, and you want to use a song recorded by the local band down the street, you can obtain a license much easier than you could for, say, a Mariah Carey recording. Of course, if you're making a music video for the band down the street, they are most likely hoping that *you* won't charge *them*. (Hey, maybe you *should!*)

If, however, you have aspirations of entering your music video in a festival, or sending it around to your local cable TV station, you need to know the legalities involved. Basically you need to obtain two different licenses or permissions:

✦ **Copyright of the song.** The songwriter and/or the publisher of the song hold the copyright to that song. Even if your little sister recorded her own version of "Tubthumping," you still need to obtain a license from the publisher.

✦ **Copyright of the recording.** The record company holds the copyright to the recording of a song. In the old days, the recording never reverted back to the artist, but that's changing more and more, so check to see who owns the master.

## Visual rights

The world is filled with copyrighted images, from corporate logos on billboards and fast food chain facades, to the brand name marking on your baseball cap (now you know why those are often fuzzed out of music videos)! If you dress up your set with items bearing copyrighted material, it's considered *fair use* as long as you don't make any of those items part of the plot, or let the camera linger on them for more than a few seconds.

## Up against the wall

**Road Diary**

A few years ago, Joe Hansard and I collaborated on a video for a song called "Nineteen in Vietnam." I wrote the song, and he directed and edited the video. It was a hard-hitting song, and we decided that the most effective location to shoot the video would be in front of the Vietnam Veterans Memorial in Washington, D.C. Joe scheduled the shoot to begin at midnight on a cold night in February. Actually, in D.C., every night in February is cold. I showed up in my stage clothes; jeans, a t-shirt, and a leather jacket, and we started shooting. Just the two of us and a boom box. No crew. Who was crazy enough to work for free outdoors, in the middle of the night, in February? Well, for starters, we were. Then it started to snow. The kind of really nasty snow that is mixed with sleet and freezing rain. "Great," said Joe. "This is gonna look fantastic on tape!" He was serious. We did take after take of me performing the song unnaturally fast, so that Joe could later slow down the playback speed, making normal time look like slow motion. It snowed harder, but I never complained. How could I? My lips were numb. I just kept acting on cue, and trying not to shiver. No one bugged us. Any sane security guard would be holed up at the local donut shop. We wrapped around 4 a.m.

There were two interesting follow-ups to that shoot. For one thing, the video was a success. It placed in several festivals, and won a few regional awards. People kept asking Joe how he achieved the haunting effect of the swirling reflective crystals in the air. It wasn't an effect, he would patiently explain. It was snowing like a dog out there. The second thing happened as Joe was working on an edit during some down time on his job as a TV sports video cutter. One of his co-workers poked his head in the door of the booth and watched for a while. "Nice job," he said, "I really like that effect that looks like snowflakes. By the way, you *did* get permission from the park service to shoot at this location, right?" Joe mumbled something. "I mean," the well-meaning but smug water cooler pundit continued, "This is the federal government we're talkin' about here. You're gonna have the FBI, the CIA, the Marines, and the U.S. Weather Service breathing down your neck if you put this out without permission." "I'm workin' on it, okay???" Joe started working on it.

A few phone calls and mounds of paperwork later, we had our permission. For "date of shoot," we gave them a day a few weeks in the future. A night, actually. If we were gonna tramp around in the snow, then they were, too. The night of the shoot came. We arrived on time. The park rangers didn't. In fact, they never showed up at all. Of course not! It was snowing again, and they were checking out a new tray of glazed donuts down the block. Oh well, at least we were now legal. By the way, I got the flu and was sick for a couple of weeks. Worth it, though. And the snowflakes did look great.

You may use trademarks in your video, as long as you don't ridicule or disparage the trademark in the video. Say, for example, that you wanted to make a video in which you're driving an SUV down the highway. The camera focuses on the brand name marking on the tires. In the next shot, the tires blow out, and the SUV flips, killing off the characters in the video. You can bet that the tire manufacturer will consider that to be trade libel. So be kind or don't use trademarks at all.

In general, you should obtain permits to film in public places, especially if they're government or commercially run.

Using clips from TV, a motion picture, or other copyrighted sources must always be cleared. Have you ever wondered how much the video for Weezer's song "Buddy Holly" cost to make? You know, the one with all the *Happy Days* clips in it. It's a brilliant video by Spike Jonze. We wondered too, but it just hurt our heads.

You're not allowed to use celebrity impersonators unless you make it obvious that that character is, indeed, an impersonator. For example, in our video for "Nickeltown," we use a clip of the Elvis impersonator who renewed our wedding vows for us in Las Vegas. We got his permission to use his image in the video, but we didn't need permission from the Elvis Presley estate, because this guy, Brendan Paul, who is in our opinion the best Elvis impersonator off the Vegas strip, is quite obviously an impersonator.

# Chapter Replay

After reading this chapter and following along with all the step-by-step instructions, you should be able to do the following things:

- ✦ Connect your camcorder, computer, and television monitor and customize Premiere's settings for your first project
- ✦ Capture audio and video material from your camcorder to your computer
- ✦ Start a new Premiere project
- ✦ Organize your clips in Bins
- ✦ Name and save your project
- ✦ Understand basic legal issues related to music and video rights

In the next chapter, you'll find out where you can obtain clips and stock footage from outside sources.

✦    ✦    ✦

# Getting Footage from Other Sources

**A**s you watch television, particularly news and information networks and music video channels, you are frequently viewing a mixture of original production footage, shot especially for the show or video, and stock footage that has been seamlessly integrated into the production by a skillful editor. Every aspiring videographer should become familiar with finding and using stock footage.

## Using Stock Footage

*Stock footage* is best defined as any footage in your final cut that wasn't shot during the making of the project. Such footage can come from a variety of sources. Corporate multimedia presenters and feature film producers buy the rights to stock footage from commercial *houses* that offer thousands of clips of every variety. Smaller houses specialize in certain genres and cater to specific types of projects. In the *gray market*, footage is offered cheaply to clients who are willing to forego exclusive rights. In the *freebie market*, indie directors and film students liberally exchange footage as a gesture of mutual support and creative solidarity.

### Benefits of stock footage

If you shoot your location shots in your own neighborhood or in places that you can easily drive to with your gear, you may never need stock footage. But if you want to leave your options open to the possibility of charging tigers, leaping flames, approaching twisters, and breaching humpback whales, you'll need to learn a little bit about hunting for footage.

# When to use stock footage

When you storyboard an idea, you want your first draft to be unencumbered by worries about the practicality of certain shots. If you picture the lead singer being charged by a moose during the second verse and the drummer falling into a volcano during his solo, don't scrap those ideas on your second draft just because they would be impossible to shoot. Start thinking of ways to combine matte and key effects with stock footage. Pretty soon you won't consider anything impossible. In general, you need stock footage when shots meet the following criteria:

✦ **Too expensive.** For example, an aerial shot from a chopper circling the Empire State Building. Other examples in this category would be a shot that would jeopardize your gear or require expensive rental gear (underwater shots of sharks or clouds of desert dust enveloping the lens), or a shot that would require travel to a remote location (Australian outback, mountains of New Zealand, Hawaiian beach, the Moon).

✦ **Too dangerous.** For example, a skydiver's point of view as he is diving over an active volcano with a tornado approaching.

✦ **Unlikely.** Some situations, such as encountering a whale, an elk, or a polar bear on the day of your location shoot, rely entirely on luck.

You could eliminate all of these possibilities by shooting only close-ups or at locations near your studio, but why limit yourself? If you can matte your singer in front of head-butting bighorn rams (this was done recently), go for it!

# Do I have to pay?

Yes, you have to pay — except when you get it free. Here's a list of the three basic types of stock footage.

✦ **Free footage.** Just like the name says. Take it. Use it anywhere you like, as many times as you like. It's a beautiful thing.

✦ **Royalty-free footage.** You pay a one-time fee, and you use the footage without paying any further royalties. You may be restricted to a single use, and you will be using footage that is available to anyone else who pays the one-time fee. In other words, your matted background may also be someone else's matted background (it's happened). Typical cost is about $15 per second, with CD packages of several dozen clips selling for $200–$400. The cost is high because you don't pay anything on the back end, no matter how much income you may generate from using the clip.

✦ **Rights-protected footage.** Obtaining this footage may require a one-time fee, and you will continue to pay royalties for as long as you use the footage. In exchange, you get exclusive rights to that footage. Think corporate branding, such as a company that uses a photo of a zebra for their logo. They don't actually rent a zebra to create the logo; they just purchase the rights to an existing zebra photo and pay royalties for as long as they use that image. Fees and royalties are negotiated based on the scale of the project, a euphemism for "How much money does the broker think that the client stands to make from using this thing?" Big bucks are usually involved.

Obviously, for the low-budget videographer, free footage is the category that grabs our attention.

# What is a stock footage house?

Nowadays, most houses are actually online brokers who manage a number of different collections. These houses may or may not have physical tapes of the footage at a brick and mortar site, but it doesn't matter. They all have delivery schemes. These systems vary greatly. Some prefer to mail out short-clip files on CD. Others download directly to you in your choice of file formats. Most still transfer video to tape and mail it, but they charge for the extra work involved. Obviously, online downloading is the quickest way for you to get your product and the most efficient way to import it into your project without leaving the digital domain. Web site interfaces vary greatly, too, with some offering lots of stills and QuickTime demos, some requiring registration before showing you samples, and others charging for demo reels to weed out cheapskate tire-kickers like us.

## Can stock footage houses sell my footage?

Yes, if it is good quality and fits into their catalogue. Different houses have their own *feels*, so hang out at their sites before approaching them. They all have their own deals, usually involving a split on the fees and royalties that they collect if someone orders your footage. Most don't pay outright front money.

## What footage is marketable?

Most houses avoid shots with people in them. Unless permission is completely secured in writing, anyone who appears in a clip can come back years later and want to be paid. The simplest guideline is this: Stock houses are interested in footage that would be impractical, expensive, or dangerous for most producers to shoot. If you travel to distant places, engage in a highly unusual occupation or hobby, or visit remote wilderness locations and encounter wildlife in their natural habitats, you may have commercially desirable footage.

# Stock footage in print

Yes. *Videography* magazine usually features a full page of ads for stock footage houses. The most complete source in print, though, is *Footage*. This aptly titled book, with more than 1,000 pages, is the bible when it comes to this confusing subject. It lists 3,000 sources for stock footage and even includes a chapter entitled "The History of Stock Footage." If you really have a lot of time on your hands, read this volume and become a world-class expert. Information on how to purchase this book is on the Web at www.footagesources.com.

When all is said and done, most of the commerce in this business happens online, and that is where we prefer to search.

## The great strobe light fiasco

**Road Diary**

In high school, my band members and I decided that we should enhance our stage show by using what was the state of the art at that time — a strobe light. These have since fallen out of favor for very good health reasons. Because we couldn't afford a professional strobe light, we built a decidedly unprofessional one. It worked great at rehearsal. We took a 150-watt spotlight bulb and mounted it inside a large cardboard box. Then we mounted an ordinary electric fan in front of the bulb. We had to duct tape a power strip in the box to accommodate the power cables. Then we made a large cardboard disc with one pie slice cut out. We duct taped this to the fan blade, painted the whole thing in day-glo colors, and voilà! We had a homemade strobe light. We tried it for a couple of tunes in the drummer's basement, with good results. We could get the same cool slo-mo and silent movie effects that the pros got. But we didn't leave it on for very long.

When we got to the gig, we decided to leave the spotlight on and just kick in the fan for the occasional psyche-out. After about 15 minutes, the bulb was melting everything in the box, and the box itself was in full flameout. And so, yet another gig ended with the fire department rushing in, as the audience fled for their lives. Don't try this at home or anywhere else, for that matter.

# Surfin' Safari: Finding the Perfect Footage

The best way to learn about stock footage is to look at it. Some stock house Web sites feature low-resolution demos of their wares. Others display stills, chosen to convey the action and color of a great clip. Because all houses have their own approach and hope to entice different types of clients, visiting a number of sites before deciding on your favorites is a good idea. A recent search for stock video footage on www.google.com turned up 800 entries. A few were bloodhound errors, such as "video footage of stock car races," or "video footage of the New York Stock Exchange." Actually, the bloodhound was cool. It was our own inaccuracy in not putting quotes around "stock video footage" that resulted in the occasional mismatch. Anyway, most were on the mark. It's a lot to wade through, but you're in luck. We did the wading for you!

We've put together a two-hour safari that takes you on the trail of high adventure without ever leaving your desk, except for the occasional bagel and latte break. Over the course of the trip, you'll get a broad overview of what stock footage is all about. Your quest is to find a stock footage house that caters to the music videographer. We're not making travelogues. We're not selling cars. We're making music videos. We need to find a site with attitude. A site that's fresh. A site that caters to our rock 'n' roll sensibilities. Most of all, we need to find a site where the footage is *free* or nearly so.

## Let's go surfin'

We begin our journey by logging onto www.google.com on the Web. This site serves as our jumping-off point on the trip. We'll check back here after visiting each site to catch our breath and search for the next port of call. With a 56 Kbps modem, each search takes about 10 or 20 seconds (an eternity to you DSL heads).

### www.footagequest.com

The junket begins here. The name just sounds right. It turns out that this is a massive clearinghouse for clips of all kinds. They are brokers who represent 14 collections. The atmosphere here is classy and corporate, and we guess that our rock 'n' roll dream won't come true here, so we move on, knowing that we may have a long journey ahead.

### www.artbeats.com

This site features royalty-free clips. See Figure 7-1. Don't confuse that term with free clips. Royalty-free means that you pay a hefty chunk to use the clips, but you pay only once when you first purchase them. Like most houses, they arrange their catalogue by category. We click the Desktop Technology link and come up with a handful of stills of hands clicking mice and pressing key commands. Nice but a little too close to what we're seeing in real-time. We scoot on over to Leather and Fabrics. This category contains some groovy clips of crushed velvet. These clips are intended as backgrounds for desktop publishing and Web sites, but they might be appropriate for music video in certain contexts. However, our quest today is for free footage, so we head on back to the Google search engine.

### www.videosource.com

This site is the home of a business called Global Village. Here's an example of a site that actively seeks to acquire new footage. I say *acquire* because they don't pay anything up front. They post it free in their catalogue. If anything sells, they do a 50/50 split with you, the vendor. Sure, there's no front money. But if you have DV tapes of the Gobi Desert sitting in a shoebox under your bed, why not post them where someone could come along and license them?

To give you an idea of typical licensing fees, Global Village charges the client $15 per second for nonbroadcast use and $30 per second for broadcast. The minimum charge is $200, so you can make $100 work-free every time someone uses your footage.

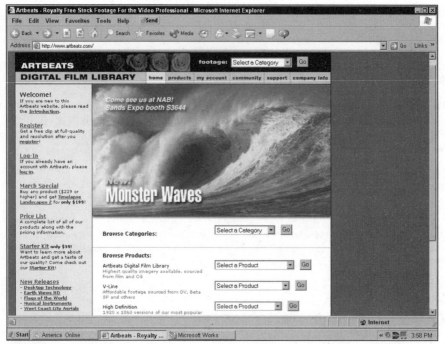

**Figure 7-1:** www.artbeats.com features a good selection of business oriented royalty-free clips.

## www.camcorderinfo.com

This site is fun, marred only by the frequent appearance of strong-armed pop-up ads that don't seem to want to be clicked away permanently. See Figure 7-2. That's okay. The site offers a fun, clubhouse atmosphere. News items, tutorials, beginners' areas, "vote for your favorite camera" boxes, and so on are all crammed into a funky attic-like space. It's colorful and kind of groovy. A button for stock footage clips catches our eye. Clicking the button takes us to a page presided over by one Robin Liss, whose picture smiles out at us from above the catalog. Turns out, the catalog clips are mostly her clips, mixed with some NASA stock footage, which is always useful stuff to have on hand. Hey, where else can you get a shot of the earth from the moon or Neil Armstrong planting the flag? We eventually discover that Robin, the videographer who created this catalog of downloadable clips, also created and maintains the entire Web site. She is an enterprising type who has traveled around and taken some good shots, which she is generously offering to share. The catalog here is small even though she is seeking more contributions, so we must continue searching for a full catalog site. This is our first taste of free stuff, and we can't be satisfied until we find more, more, more!

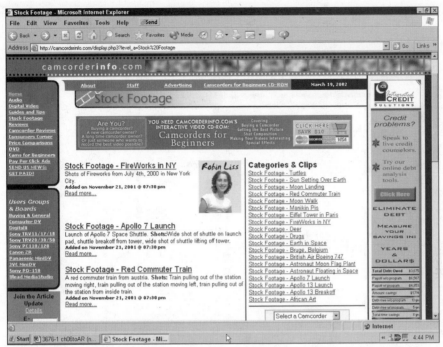

**Figure 7-2:** www.camcorderinfo.com offers a variety of downloadable stock video clips.

## www.publicdomainfootage.com

Okay, these folks have a really original idea here (see Figure 7-3). The best way to truly evoke bygone decades is to use actual footage from the era, and these entrepreneurs slapped their foreheads one day and said, "Hey, I'll bet the copyright has run out on a lot of that old stuff!" They're right. Some of it is copyright-expired. Some of it is legally mandated to become public domain. Anyway, they ran a search and developed an archive. The site promises a future online demo feature, so you'll be able to preview clips before you buy.

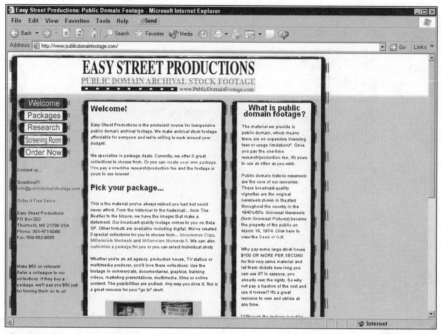

**Figure 7-3:** www.publicdomainfootage.com is a good source to go to for retro stock footage.

## www.ecofootage.com

Very pretty site, here, and a good cause as well (see Figure 7-4). These folks feature, as you might guess, footage that is useful in the presentation of ecological issues and theories of a "sustainable future." They actively seek more footage, and they seem willing to work out different kinds of profit-sharing arrangements on a case-by-case basis. If you have nature footage and you'd like to see it go to help the cause, get in touch.

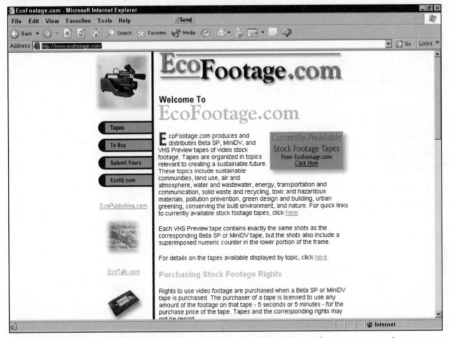

**Figure 7-4:** www.ecofootage.com provides stock footage relevant to creating a sustainable future.

## www.sourcefootage.com

Now our quest leads us to the land of specialty houses. This particular site carries a full catalog and specializes in time-lapse footage of clouds (see Figure 7-5). You've seen this effect, where speech or some other familiar motion is going on while clouds in the background pass by at an impossibly fast rate. By shooting a frame every few seconds, hours worth of cloud motion can be compressed into seconds. Is this site where Herb Ritts got his fast-moving clouds for the background of the Chris Isaac "Wicked Game" video? We don't know, but the little demo on this site is a cool miniature version of this dramatic effect.

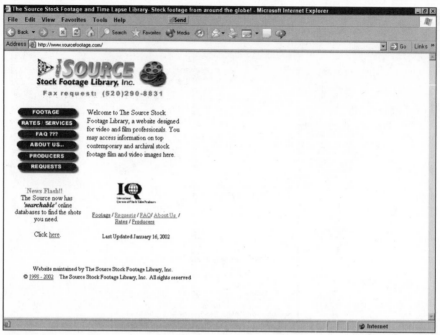

**Figure 7-5:** www.sourcefootage.com specializes in time-lapse stock footage of clouds, crowds, and cities.

## www.videocosmos.com

Wow! It's the Russian space program Web site, and these newly hatched capitalists can't wait to sell you some video (see Figure 7-6)! They offer a demo, too, that encapsulates, in a heavy accent, the history of their adventures in space. You get to see lots of big men in heavy overcoats, embracing each other, and missiles parading around Red Square. Yes, their footage is up for license, and it's certainly stuff you won't find anywhere else. They remind us repeatedly that they were the first to send men into space. We tolerate this blow to our egos and salute our overcoat-clad friends, as we continue our quest for glory and free stuff.

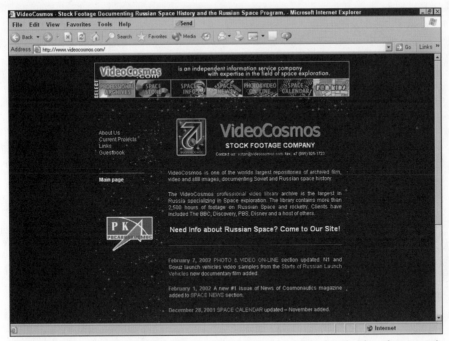

**Figure 7-6:** www.videocosmos.com is the place to go for archival video documenting Soviet and Russian space history.

## www.stormvideo.com

If you're a fan of those storm chaser shows on the Discovery Channel — and who isn't? — this site is for you (see Figure 7-7). These highly motivated researchers chase the darn things across the fields of Kansas, risking their lives to bring you this footage of tornados. Their two-minute demo is great, with the high point being one of the camerapersons yelling, "Oh my God!" as a twister bears down on them. It's a lot of thrills from the safety of your own desktop. And get this — they also carry footage of hurricanes and blizzards! This is a great example of the best stock footage — something awesome that no one else has the nerve to shoot.

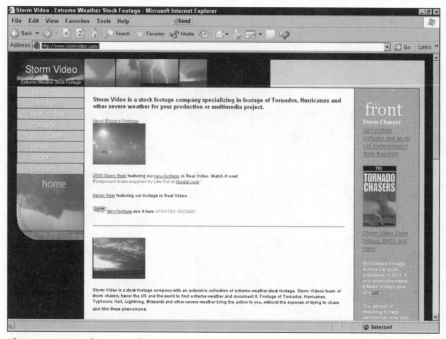

**Figure 7-7:** For footage of severe storms, hurricanes, and tornadoes, look no further than www.stormvideo.com.

## aerialextreme.com

While we're 15,000 feet up, let's check in with some dudes who are having a great time doing things that the rest of us only have nightmares about. The aerial extreme guys are stuntmen and extreme athletes who specialize in events, such as skateboarding up near the stratosphere and riding bikes off of 3,000-foot cliffs (see Figure 7-8). Their site has photos to prove their claims, and they do offer stock footage. Sadly, there's no demo to be seen, but you can contact Aerial Extreme to receive a 40-minute demo reel in the mail. This footage would definitely spice up your videos!

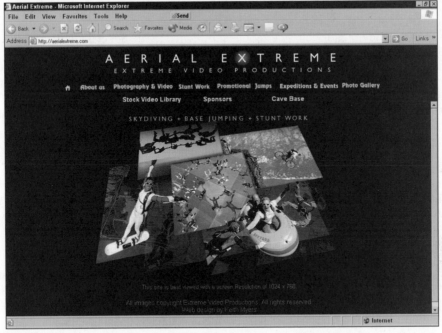

**Figure 7-8:** aerialextreme.com offers stock footage shot by skydivers.

## www.freestockfootage.com

This site has a rockin' vibe. It feels like seeing the Allman Brothers at Watkins Glen in 1973, and how many Web sites can you say *that* about? They don't seem to be trying to attract corporate clients. In fact, the first clip under "People" is entitled "Biker With Tattooed Back." Find that one on your typical stock site! Every clip is instantly playable on QuickTime. If you like what you see, you can click the still and it's yours. If you want a medium-resolution copy, click Medium and it dutifully downloads. It's all free. They offer lots of stuff, too. It all looks like real basic rock video stuff, too. Not too slick.

## www.nara.gov/research/ordering/stock.html

A surprising source for stock footage is the U.S. Government. Because all U.S. citizens pay taxes, they essentially fund all of the video shot by the government, and believe me, they've shot everything at some point. Certain shots, such as the earth from the moon, obviously can come only from government footage. As taxpayers, we've already paid for the right to use this stock. You can bet that the moviemakers who produced 1950s sci-fi classics like *Plan Nine from Outer Space* and *Mars Needs Women* knew how to tap this mother lode.

The best source for government stock footage is the National Archives and Records Administration (NARA). You can visit them on the Web at www.nara.gov/research/ordering/stock.html. The Special Media Archive Service Division on Motion Picture, Sound, and Video unit is the part of the archive that stores stock footage and makes such footage available to the public. Their archive contains over 150,000 reels of film and 20,000 videotapes. Many of these clips are government oriented, including speeches and news coverage of historical events, but the collection also contains numerous items of interest to the general public, including a large collection of film footage donated by MCA-Universal Pictures.

You can view this enormous collection, and even make dubs on your own equipment, in their research room in College Park, Maryland, or check their Web site for information on browsing through catalogs and ordering clips. If you order directly from the archive online or by mail, the service is not entirely free. If you order a copy of a film or videotape, you must cover the copying cost, but the use of this footage is royalty-free.

Certain online brokers can locate government archival material and do the paperwork for you. Check Appendix D for information about these resources.

## Using TV Clips

TV, film, and independent video are all different animals not only technically but also in a legal sense. Indie video makers can travel around the country and swap footage at will, but television producers are working under the aegis of major networks and cable channels, and the contracts outlining the assignment of copyright ownership are as long as dictionaries. It all boils down to this: You can't tape something off the TV and then stick it in one of your videos, unless you restrict your screenings to your own home and never make any money from the use.

Early TV executives didn't see any value in preserving shows for the education and entertainment of future generations. They saw the medium as ephemeral fluff that would be forgotten with the next season. Kinescopes, in which a camera was basically aimed at a screen while the program aired, were the only way shows were archived and most weren't even afforded this treatment. It's almost impossible to see most vintage TV shows in their original broadcast quality. The ones that survived in endless reruns are the exception to this rule, so classics such as *Gilligan's Island*, *I Love Lucy*, and of course, *The Honeymooners* and their animated counterparts, *The Flintstones* are still alive and well on cable. A wonderful Web site, www.tvparty.com, captures the flavor of this golden age of the small screen. You can hang out there all day and even order vintage shows on DVD. However, the site doesn't mention stock footage or copyright or royalty. In other words, there's no provision for reuse. You can enjoy Gilligan and the Skipper in the comfort of your Florida room, but you can't make them characters in your next rock video. The bottom line: Don't use TV footage unless you want corporate lawyers camping out in your front yard.

# Chapter Replay

After reading this chapter, you should be able to:

✦ Know the meaning of the term "stock footage"

✦ Understand which situations call for stock footage

✦ Find sources of stock footage on the World Wide Web

✦ Understand the significance of copyright law in the use of commercial television footage

In the next chapter, we explain how to import your footage into Premiere and begin editing your video project.

✦　　✦　　✦

# I Want It That Way: Editing Your Music Video

# Making Rough Cuts

✦ ✦ ✦ ✦

**In This Chapter**

Customizing your
workspace

Working with the
Monitor window

Placing audio and
video clips on the
Timeline

Synching your audio
and video tracks

✦ ✦ ✦ ✦

**Y**ou've got the song. You've got the clips. You've even got a cousin who works at a major music television channel. Well . . . at least you've got the song and the clips. Now all you have to do is assemble your material into a dazzling finished product. Luckily, the Premiere editing process is intuitive, after you get familiar with the tools. In this chapter, we describe the location and function of these tools and walk you through the step-by-step process of performing a rough edit.

## Understanding Workspace Elements

A workspace is a desktop layout of Premiere's windows and palettes, arranged in different ways to help you better organize the tools you work with at different stages in the process. Premiere offers three primary windows common to all preset workspaces:

✦ **Project window.** The clips that you eventually place into the Timeline are grouped here. You have the option of placing these clips into separate bins. A bin is Premiere's name for a folder. You can further organize your clips into groups and subgroups by creating new bins. See Figure 8-1.

> **Cross-Reference**
>
> Refer to Chapter 7 for details on the Project window.

✦ **Monitor window.** You view an individual video clip (shown in the Source monitor) or your whole project (shown in the Program monitor) in the Monitor window. Figure 8-2 illustrates a dual view of both the Source and Program monitors. See the section "Setting Up the Monitor Window."

✦ **Timeline.** This is the map of your program. Your clips are placed here, where you edit them and add effects and transitions. Figure 8-3 illustrates the various Audio, Video and Transition tracks available in the Timeline window.

**Figure 8-1:** The Project window

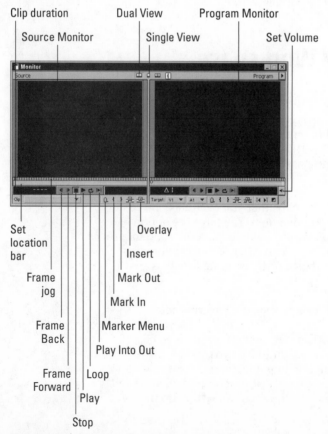

Clip duration

Source Monitor

Dual View

Single View

Program Monitor

Set Volume

Set location bar

Overlay

Insert

Frame jog

Mark Out

Mark In

Frame Back

Marker Menu

Play Into Out

Frame Forward

Loop

Play

Stop

**Figure 8-2:** The Monitor window in Dual view

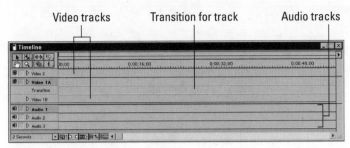

**Figure 8-3:** The Timeline window

In addition to these three primary windows, you have the option to show floating palettes containing audio effects, video effects, and transitions.

# Choosing a workspace

Choosing the workspace that's most appropriate for the task at hand and for your own working style enables you to forget about the interface so that your creativity can flow.

To select the workspace that you want to use, choose Window⟹Workspace and then select Single-Track Editing, A/B Editing, Effects, or Audio. In the following sections, we discuss the default workspaces in more detail.

## Single-Track Editing workspace

The Single-Track Editing workspace is similar to the systems used by professional video editors. Although it's called Single-Track, the Timeline actually shows two video tracks (see Figure 8-4). A track is a layer of sequenced video or audio material. You can layer material on different tracks so that they play together at the same time. In other words, you can have a song on one audio track, and a voice-over on another audio track. When you play the Timeline, you will hear them both together. You can also have a visual image on a video track and a title on another video track. When you play the Timeline, you will see the title superimposed over the video image. Premiere uses the term Single-Track because two video tracks plus a track providing transition options are collapsed into a single track on the Timeline. We've found this workspace to be helpful if you are making the transition from editing on conventional machines to editing in Premiere, however, if you are new to video editing, the A/B workspace, below, is the better choice.

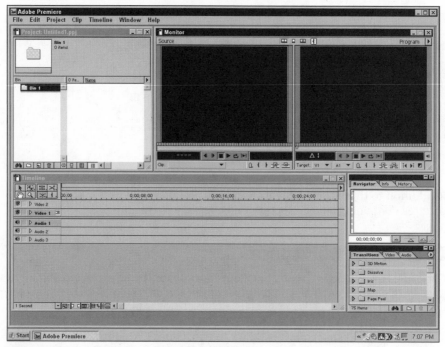

**Figure 8-4:** The Single-Track Editing workspace is similar to professional systems. Notice that there is no transition track on the Timeline and no effects palette visible.

## A/B Editing workspace

As musicians, we like using the A/B editing workspace, shown in Figure 8-5, because it's similar in some respects to multitrack audio recording. This versatile workspace may also be familiar to users with experience in traditional A/B roll videotape editing. Here's how it works: Video 1 is subdivided into two rolls, Video 1A and Video 1B. Both 1A and 1B are visible in the Timeline. A transition track runs between the two on the Timeline, enabling the user to blend the tracks by applying such transitional techniques as fades, page peels, and dissolves. See Chapter 9 for more about transitions. This workspace is the best choice if you are dragging clips from the Project window to the Timeline. It's our favorite workspace because we can edit within this workspace for the entire project from rough cuts to finished product.

Because the A/B Editing workspace is transitions-friendly, the Transitions floating palette is also displayed, which lists all of the available transitions.

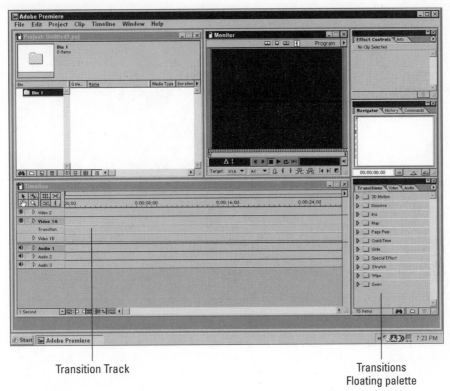

Transition Track

Transitions
Floating palette

**Figure 8-5:** The A/B Editing workspace enables you to blend effects as transitions across multiple tracks.

## Effects workspace

The Effects workspace, shown in Figure 8-6, comes in handy after you have roughed in your Timeline and you want to start adding effects, such as posterization, cropping, or color treatments.

The Effects workspace has constant Monitor, Program, and Timeline windows, just like the A/B and Single-Track workspaces, but this workspace also displays an Effects floating palette and an Effects Controls palette that shows you what clip you are applying your effect to and all of the effect's applied parameters.

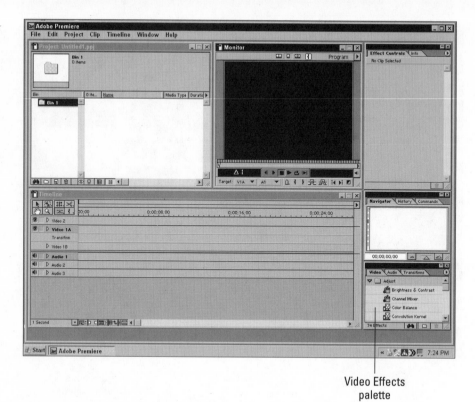

Video Effects
palette

**Figure 8-6:** The Effects workspace is a good environment for cropping clips and adding color treatments and other effects. Notice that the Video Effects palette replaces the Transitions palette as the default in this workspace. Video effects are found here.


## Audio workspace

The Audio workspace, shown in Figure 8-7, enables you to automate the volume changes of your audio tracks. The Timeline in this workspace is the same as the Timeline in the Single-Track Editing workspace and the Effects workspace.

Audio Mixer window

Audio track controls          Audio Master Volume

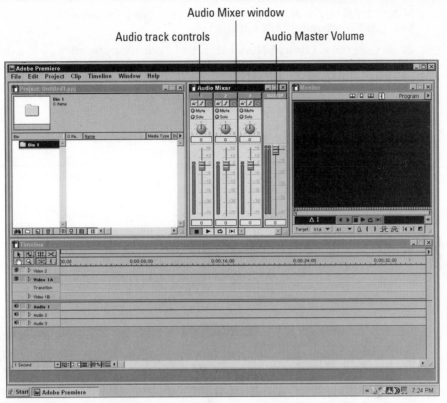

**Figure 8-7:** The Audio workspace enables you to automate the volume changes of your audio tracks with its unique Audio Mixer window.

# Optimizing Your Workspace

A/B Editing is our favorite workspace (and the most versatile), and we know you'll like it, too. Premiere enables you to customize each workspace layout to suit the way that you work. In this section, we show you how set up your workspace to resemble ours. Eventually, however, you may want to change some options. That's fine, but for now, following these steps shows you how to set those options:

1. **Open a saved project by choosing File⇨Open Recent Project and selecting the project you want to work on.** Premiere displays a Loading Project progress bar as it accesses your file settings.

**Note**
Premiere can open only one project at a time, so if you have a project open when you try to open another, Premiere will ask you if you want to save the current project before closing it.

2. **Make sure that you are working in the A/B Editing workspace by choosing Window⇨Workspace⇨A/B Editing.**

3. **Close the Effects Controls, Navigator, and Transitions palettes on the right side of your screen, so only the Project, Monitor and Timeline windows are open on-screen.**

To further optimize the layout, do the following:

1. **In the Timeline menu, select Timeline Window Options, as shown in Figure 8-8.**

2. **Click the smallest icon size box so that you can see more tracks of the Timeline by minimizing each track's size.**

3. **Click OK.**

4. **Click the Resize button on the Timeline to reduce the height of the Timeline, while still showing, from top to bottom: Video 2, Video 1A, Transition, Video 1B, and Audio 1.**

5. **Drag the Timeline so it aligns with the bottom-right side of the screen.**

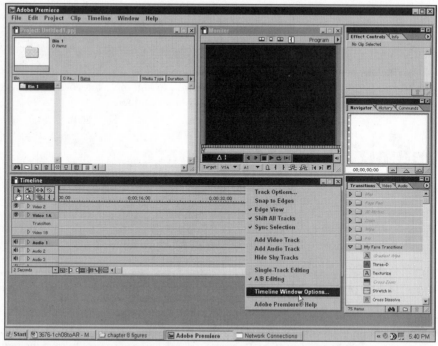

**Figure 8-8:** Change Timeline window options from the Timeline menu

6. Click the Resize button to make the Project window as small as you can and drag the resized window to the lower-left side of the screen.

7. Fine-tune the sizes of your Project and Timeline windows so that they are side by side and do not overlap.

8. Select Dual view on the Monitor window by clicking the Dual View button or by selecting Dual View from the Monitor window menu.

9. Resize the Monitor window to make it larger. Make sure that you avoid obstructing the other two windows.

This modified version of the A/B workspace is the one we use most often, so we saved and named it, as shown in Figure 8-9.

Monitor window set to Dual view and enlarged

Project window resized and moved to lower-left portion of screen

Timeline window resized

**Figure 8-9:** We custom made a workspace to accommodate our own working preferences.

## Saving your workspace

After optimizing your workspace for the way you work, you can save your workspace for use with future projects. Using your customized workspace saves you the time and hassle of arranging your workspace each time you begin a new project. To save your workspace, click Window⇨Workspace⇨Save Workspace, and then give a name to your new workspace. You will still be able to change this workspace, or change to another workspace while working on your project. As you experiment with settings, name, and store your modified workspaces in the same manner.

# Setting Up the Monitor Window

The Monitor window is an element in each type of workspace. Take a look at Figure 8-10 to get familiar with the Monitor window's controls.

How you view your masterpiece in progress can make all the difference in your efficiency and effectiveness in creating an awesome music video. You can select your preferred monitor view with one of the following three icons positioned across the top of the Monitor window:

✦ **Single view.** Displays only one monitor — the Program monitor. This monitor displays the sequence of clips as arranged in the Timeline. Double-click the clip in the bin or in the Timeline, and a Source monitor window appears, displaying the individual clip. Setting your Monitor window to Single view gives you more space on your computer screen to resize the Monitor window or display floating palettes, but the display is not as neat or as constant as the Dual view.

## The old switcheroo

**Road Diary**

Skillful clip editing can be used to create an ideal event out of composite elements, but sometimes even professional videographers leave a seam showing. In 1992, we were part of a video shoot for Nanci Griffith's "Other Voices, Other Rooms" CD project. The action was a live concert in Austin, Texas, featuring many of the guest stars who performed on the album. The final video was actually a composite of clips from two shows and was shot on consecutive nights. Emmylou Harris could only make the first night, and Jimmie Dale Gilmore could only make the second night. For the large-scale production piece "It's A Hard Life Wherever You Go," which features the entire cast on stage, the director used clips from both nights. If you look closely, in some shots Emmylou is standing next to Maura, and in others, Jimmie Dale is standing in the same spot! What makes it work is that they are both tall and slender, with long, flowing silver hair, but they're certainly not look-alikes! Nanci and the cast turned in an inspiring performance, and no one seems to have noticed (until now!).

✦ **Dual view.** Shows both the Source monitor and the Program monitor side by side, so you can edit in and out points on your Source clip and view the program without having to toggle between screens. We prefer using Dual view because we can edit our clips, drag them into the Timeline, and then press the Play button on Program monitor to see how the clip fits into the video. (Refer to Figure 8-10.)

✦ **Trim mode.** Enables you to zoom in on a particular edit to make precise adjustments. This view displays two consecutive clips from the Timeline. The bars below these two windows indicate the clip in and clip out times and durations. The corresponding adjustment buttons enable you to move the in and out points. This view is better used after you've assembled your Timeline, and you want to make minute adjustments.

For now, set your Monitor window view to Dual view.

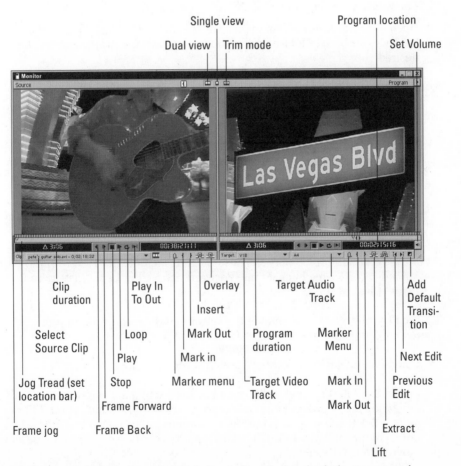

**Figure 8-10:** The Monitor window in Dual view displays both the Source and the Program monitors side by side.

# Displaying Clips in the Source Monitor

To work with your Source clips, you must be able to see them. You need to open each clip into the Monitor window to view your Source clips.

To open a video file from the Project window's bin, locate the clip you want to display. The clip should be in the bin located in the Project window. Premiere offers several ways to open a clip in the Monitor window. Do any of the following:

✦ Double-click the clip located in the Project window to make it appear in the Source view of the Monitor window.

✦ Drag the clip from the Project window's bin to the Source view of the Monitor window.

✦ Select an entire bin in the Project window and drag it to the Monitor window. The window displays the last clip in the bin.

✦ Open the Select Source Clip menu. This menu lists the last 35 clips that you have viewed in the Monitor since you last opened the project. Select the desired clip.

When you open a clip in the Source side of the Monitor window, the first frame of the clip is displayed. The Program side of the Monitor window is black because you have not yet placed a video clip into the Timeline

**Note**    After you move your clip to the Timeline, double-click the clip to make it appear in the Source monitor.

# Playing Source Clips in the Monitor Window

You've probably noticed control buttons underneath the monitor that resemble the controls on a VCR or CD player. These buttons include, from left to right: Clip Duration indicator, Frame Back, Frame Forward, Stop, Play, Loop, Play In To Out, and Current Clip Location.

Click the Play button. Notice that while your clip plays in the monitor, the Clip Location indicator tells you, frame by frame, what part of the clip you are viewing.

Take a moment and familiarize yourself with theses buttons:

✦ **Frame Back (left arrow) and Frame Forward (right arrow) buttons.** Enable you to jog backward and forward by single frames, the smallest possible increment. Click the Frame Back button a few times to see how this works. Take notice of how the monitor image and the Clip Location counter change as you move through the clip.

✦ **Stop (spacebar) and Play (L) buttons.** Function just like the stop and play buttons on a conventional tape recorder. Click the Play button, and your clip plays from start to finish, while the Clip Location counter indicates the frame location. Click the Stop button to stop playing the clip.

✦ **Loop button.** Clicking this button results in the continuous replay of your clip from beginning to end. Click this button and watch your clip loop. Click the Stop button to stop the loop.

## Using the slider bar

Directly above the Preview controls, look for a bar called the Set Location slider bar. Use this bar to jog, or navigate around your clip by following these steps:

1. **Move your mouse to position your Selection tool along the bar and click.** Notice how the Clip Location indicator changes to reflect the location of the slider while the image jumps to that frame.

2. **Click and drag the slider.** Again, the indicator reacts while the image in the screen moves along with it. Click and drag the slider both forward and backward. You can quickly find the frame you're looking for by knowing how to use the slider bar.

To move frame by frame to the desired portion of your clip, try following these steps:

1. **Click within the slider bar to a place near where you want to be.**

2. **Click the Frame Back or Frame Forward button to fine-tune your location. As a keyboard shortcut, simply click the left or right arrow, respectively.**

After you master the different ways to move around your clips, you'll be jogging like a pro!

## Customizing your clips for the Timeline

You can easily move your clip to the Timeline by dragging and dropping the image from the Monitor window to Video 1A track on the Timeline. Give this a try. Notice that a block appears on the Timeline. The block indicates that your clip has been moved. But what if you only want to use a *portion* of the clip? The clip that you captured most likely has a little extra footage on either end that you do not want to use. We call the part of the clip that you want to use the "keeper" part. You need to define the in and out points of the keeper part of the clip before you drag it to the Timeline.

Look at the bottom-most line of the Source monitor. From left to right are the following buttons: Select Source Clip, Take Video, Take Audio, Marker Menu, Mark In, Mark Out, Insert, and Overlay buttons. You'll use these buttons to customize your clip.

## Selecting only the good part

The Mark In button (I) and Mark Out button (O) mark the editing points or the frame range of the clip that you want to use in the finished video. To set Mark In and Out points:

1. **Press the Play button.** Let the clip play until you find your desired in point.

2. **Click the Mark In button while the clip is rolling.** You can use the keyboard shortcut for the Mark In button by pressing the I key.

3. **As the clip reaches the desired out point, click the Mark Out button.** You can use the keyboard shortcut for the Mark Out button by pressing the O key.

4. **When the clip is finished playing, the in and out edit points appear on the slider bar.** Click the Play In to Out button, and the clip will only play from the in point to the out point.

5. **Now click the Loop button to watch your clip play in a continuous loop from in to out points.**

6. **Click the Stop button.**

By setting these points, you are only *indicating* where you want the edit markings to be placed. These are nondestructive edits; therefore, you are only telling Premiere which segment of the clip to use, without actually throwing any part of the original clip away. This information is important to know, especially if you intend to use portions of the same clip in different parts of the Timeline. You have the option of setting different in and out points each time that you use the same clip.

## Fine-tuning in and out points

Selecting points while your video is playing will allow you to grab a general range of frames, but there are fine-tuning tools available to you. As your music video will most likely involve lip-synching audio to video, you should know how to use these fine-tuning tools.

1. **Choose Marker Menu⇨Clear⇨Clear All Markers to clear your previously set in and out points.**

2. **Click the Play button.**

3. **Near the desired in point, click the Stop button.** (You're near your desired in point but not exactly there.)

4. **Click the Frame Forward or Frame Back button or use the arrow keys to find just the right location.**

5. **When you're satisfied with the frame location, click either the Mark In button or press the I on the keyboard.**

6. **Click the Play button again to run the clip from the in point.**

7. **When you're near your desired out point, click the Stop button.** Again, use the Frame Forward or Frame Back buttons or the arrow keys to find the exact out point location that you want to use.

8. **When you're satisfied with that location, click either the Mark Out button or press the O on the keyboard.**

9. **View your modified clip by using the Play In To Out button.**

10. **When you're happy with the in and out parameters, drag your clip to Video Track 1A of the Timeline.**

## Navigating clips with counters

Premiere's counters will help you navigate along the length of your clips and your Timeline.

### Finding a Source clip's length

Because we're still just dealing with Source clips, look for the Clip Duration indicator on the bottom-left side of the Monitor window. This counter displays a number in minutes, seconds, and frames. If you are looking for just a quick cut, and you notice that the duration of the clip you want to use is 20 seconds long, you'll know that you need to set in and out points to shorten the clip before you move it to the Timeline. As the clip plays, this counter does not change, but when you open a different clip into the Monitor window, the counter will then reflect the length of the new clip.

### Finding points within a Source clip

The Clip Location indicator is the counter on the bottom-right side of the Monitor window. This counter indicates the location of the clip on the tape from which it was captured. Unless you plan on going back to your source tape for any reason, this counter is not very valuable to us as it's set up, but we can change it so that the counter starts at zero for each clip. That way, you know exactly how far into the clip you are.

Choose Monitor Window Options from the Monitor menu and select Zero Based.

## Placing Audio Clips on the Timeline

When you understand how to use the Monitor window and how to customize your clips, you're ready to move them into the Timeline (as shown in Figure 8-11) and arrange the clips into a cohesive, rocking video! First, you need to bring your audio track — the song — into the Timeline, because that's where all the video tracks get synched up to the song.

Before moving clips to the Timeline, click the Toggle Snap To Edges button at the bottom of the Timeline window. Clicking this button ensures that the sound clip snaps to the left edge, leaving no unwanted silence at the beginning of the video. Doing so also guarantees that the video clips you eventually move in will snap together, leaving no unwanted blank spaces between clips.

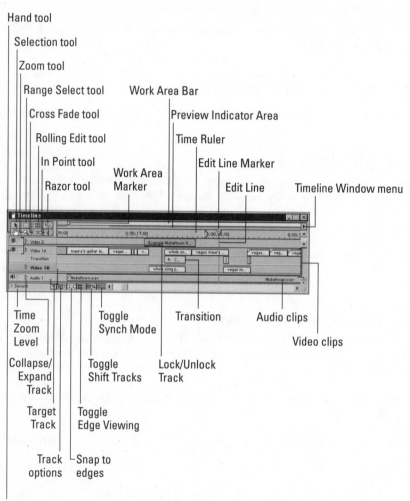

**Figure 8-11:** You will insert your clips, audio, effects, and transitions onto the Timeline.

The first step when making a music video rough cut is moving the song WAV, QuickTime audio, MP3, CD audio file (Mac), or other supported audio file to the Timeline. Here's how.

1. **Click the Project window.** This window contains your bins and clips.

2. **Find the audio track that you placed in your bin and drag it directly onto Audio 1 Track.** A blue bar labeled with the filename appears in the Audio 1 Track, and a yellow bar of equal length appears in the Work Area bar. If you cannot see the ends of these two bars, your Timeline frame range is too small.

3. **Click the Time Zoom level and select 20 Seconds.** If you still cannot see the entire bar, try 1 minute. If your audio is still too long, then your video is probably too long to get airplay on a commercial music video program!

After you've placed your audio clip in the Timeline, you want it to stay there, unchanged throughout the editing process. Premiere enables you to lock audio and video tracks. To Lock the audio track:

1. **Make sure that the audio track is snapped to the beginning of the Timeline by dragging the audio clip to the left.**

2. **Because you won't want to move or delete this track while working on the project, lock the track by clicking the Lock/Unlock Track button to the left of the audio track to select the lock icon.** As long as this track is locked, the track cannot be changed or deleted. You may later unlock any locked track, if desired.

3. **Finally, you can adjust the volume of the playback by clicking the Volume button at the bottom-right of the Monitor window.** The three settings available are soft, loud, or no sound. Some musicians have argued for a shred setting, but Adobe is holding off for the time being.

# Placing Video Clips on the Timeline

Now that your music is in the Timeline, all you have to do is arrange your video clips from the start of the song to the end.

Because you've already got the entire audio track you need for this music video in the Timeline, you only need to place the video portion of the Source clips into the Timeline. Because you'll be synching video to your audio track, click the Take Audio button in the Source monitor to turn off the audio when you're moving clips into the Timeline. Doing this tells Premiere to disregard the audio portion of your clip when activating the move.

Click the Take Audio button to tell Premiere that you do not want to use the audio portion of the clips in the Timeline. (Turning off the Take Video button tells Premiere that you only want to take the audio from a clip, but we won't be using that feature in this project.)

## Automating the bins to the Timeline

One easy way to quickly see if you have enough clips to cover the length of the song and to see if the feel of the video material fits the mood of the song is to automate the bin or bins to the Timeline (see Figure 8-12). To do so, follow these steps:

1. **Click a bin.**

2. **Click the Project window Menu button and then choose Automate to Timeline⇨Use Default Transitions**. Premiere deselects that feature.

3. **Click OK.**

4. **Select a range of clips (not a whole bin).**

5. **Click the Project Window Menu button and then click Automate To Timeline.**

6. **Under the Contents menu, choose Selected Clips.** Your clips alternate placement between tracks Video 1A and Video 1B, enabling you to add transitions between the tracks later.

7. **Click the Play In To Out button to watch your video so far.**

## Removing unwanted clips

Because you're much more artistic than letting the program automate the clips for you, remove the automated clips from the Timeline so that you can move the clips you choose into the Timeline in the order you desire.

1. **Make sure that you click your mouse within the Timeline to activate that window and select all the clips you just put into the Timeline.**

2. **Press Ctrl+A (Command-A) and Delete or Backspace to remove them from the Timeline.**

Notice that your audio track remains on the Timeline, because you locked that track earlier.

**Note**    By clearing tracks from your Timeline, you're not deleting the track from your program, bin, or hard drive. You're just deleting the pointer that tells the Timeline to play the clip at a designated point in the Timeline.

**Figure 8-12:** The Automate To Timeline feature can speedily move all the clips in a bin to the Timeline at the push of a button.

## Moving individual clips to the Timeline

In the course of creating your video, you move clips into the Timeline, move them around the Timeline, copy them, paste them, and cut them out. Creating a video is similar to using the cut and paste options of a word processor.

### Using the video track hierarchy

Video clips that you move to track Video 1A override clips on track Video 1B. Therefore, if you have a clip in track Video 1A and another clip of equal length in track Video 1B at the same point in time, Premiere's Program Monitor window will show the material in Video 1A only. That is, unless you apply a transition. Transitions are covered in Chapter 9. Likewise, clips in track Video 2 override clips in tracks Video 1A and Video 1B. Sound confusing? It's not, really, and there is a good reason for it.

For example, even though you placed the entire lip-synched clip in track Video 1B, you know that you're not going to use the entire track in your video, but you do not want it to move around in time because it's in synch with the audio track. You also know that you will be replacing portions of the lip-synched video track with other footage — perhaps the singer at a different angle, the face of someone reacting to the singer, a bit of scenery, or some other clip.

### Placing additional clips on the Timeline

You may want to move additional video clips into the Timeline's track Video 1A.

Drag the clip image from the monitor's Source view to track Video 1A on the Timeline. You are choosing track Video 1A, because the lip-synched video clip is already on track Video 1B, and you'll eventually be applying transitions between your lip-synched track and these additional clips.

Premiere enables you to move your clips around by using several different methods. For example, you can drag your clip from the Program bin directly to the Program monitor of the Monitor window. When you do that, the first frame of your video clip appears in that window, and the bar representing that clip shows up in one of the Timeline's video tracks. If you decide to move clips around in this way, be aware that you can designate the target track. Do so by following these steps:

1. **At the bottom of the Program view in the Monitor window, is the Select Video Target menu.** Select V1A, which stands for Video 1A, in this menu.

2. **Now, drag a clip from the bin to that monitor screen.** The clip is positioned in the Timeline's Video 1A track.

3. **In the Select Video Target menu, select V1B.**

4. **Drag a different clip from the Source view to the Program view.** This time, the clip is positioned in the Video 1B track.

## It doesn't get any more basic than this

**Road Diary**

We were booked to play an exclusive private school in New England, and we decided to shoot the show. We knew that we would be playing in a theater, so we figured that some good equipment would probably be on-site that we could use gratis. In the contract, we asked the school to make whatever sound and lighting gear they had on-hand available. We decided to load in early and take time to really get things set.

When we arrived, we found a bare stage. That's okay. Of course, they keep the good stuff stashed away. A couple of kids showed up to help out, and we asked them to schlep in the sound and lighting gear. They looked confused and wandered off, muttering nervously. A long time later, one of them returned. "I've got the sound system." He was carrying a tiny guitar amp. A *reeeeally* tiny guitar amp, like what you see guys playing through in the doorway of the Harvard Coop, busking for spare change. It may have even run on batteries! That's all we had for our two guitars and two voices. All we had, to fill the theatre with a flood of glorious sound. Oh well, we could make do. At least, when the lights arrived, we could set up for a top-notch video shoot, and dub in audio later. But it got better. The well-meaning kid and his well-meaning compatriot showed up a few minutes later with the piece de resistance — an overhead projector. The projector was the kind used in classrooms, the kind that casts a square of white light that illuminates the grease pencil markings on those weird clear plastic sheets. We didn't think they used them anymore, but they found one, God bless 'em. "Got your lights!" They looked relieved. Now they could get to study hall, leaving us alone with our overhead projector and our tiny, wimpy amp. So what did we do? As the seats filled, we set up, and we played the show through the mini-amp, bathed in the square glow of the overhead projector.

# Synchronizing Video to Audio

The best clip to place on track Video 1B is a performance of the lead singer lip-synching the entire song. You can cut this continuous clip into shorter clips and use portions of it throughout the video. By pasting the whole clip to the Timeline and synching it with the audio, that track will stay in synch through the whole song, provided you don't move it up or down the Timeline.

The transport controls below the Program View of the Monitor window are similar to those below the Source monitor. Click the Play In To Out button to view (and hear) your video. Unless you're *extremely* lucky, your video and audio tracks will not yet be in exact synch. Use the following steps to synch them up:

1. **Click the Toggle Snap To Edges button to deselect.**

2. **Click Play In To Out and listen to your audio.**

3. **When the track reaches the first vocal, click the Stop button.** Notice where your vocalist is in the video clip. Has he started singing yet, or is he already singing the second line of the song?

4. **Drag your clip left or right to synch up with the video.** If you need to zero in on the edit point, select 1 Second from the Time Zoom level.

5. **To start the playback, drag the slider to the point just before the video comes in and press the spacebar.**

6. **Press the spacebar again to stop the playback and make further adjustments, if necessary.**

7. **When you're fairly certain that you're in synch, click the Play In To Out button to view the entire video.** When you're sure that the video is in synch with the audio, click the Lock/Unlock Track button to lock it in place.

Congratulations! You've just made your first music video!

# Using Program Monitor Controls

The Program monitor has a few extra buttons that the Source monitor does not have. Knowing what these buttons do ultimately helps you move faster and more efficiently through the editing process.

## Following the Timeline counters

The counters below the Program monitor are quite similar to those below the Monitor view, except that they reflect the entire program as a single unit. Take a look at the Program Duration counter.

Click Play In to Out on the Program view side, and the counter won't move. It reflects the total length of the video Timeline, laterally. Similarly, the Program Location counter reflects your present location in the Timeline, but not in individual clips.

## Marking edits in the Timeline

The Program monitor has the same marker tools as the Source monitor, but they function just a little differently.

### Setting in and out points on the Timeline

If you are viewing a Source clip, and you mark in and out points for that clip, Premiere trims away the outer edges and allows only the cropped image to be moved to the Timeline.

In the Program view, however, marking in and out points tells Premiere that you want a clip to fit within the confines of those markers on the Timeline.

1. **Click the Play button on the Program view.**

2. **As the song plays, click the Mark In button.**

3. **Click the Mark Out button about five seconds later; then click the spacebar to stop the video.** Notice that the Mark In/Out notations appear along the Edit Line.

4. **Drag a clip from the Source window over to the Program window.** The Fit Clip dialog box pops up to tell you that your source and destination durations do not match. You have the option of changing your Source clip's speed or trimming the clip to fit.

5. **Click Change Speed.**

6. **Now drag the slider to the beginning of that clip in the Timeline and press the spacebar to see how the program fit your clip into the designated window.**

### Marking song parts on the Timeline

To make a video project easier, we set location points along the Edit line so that we can quickly find key sections within our song (See Figure 8-13). Doing so can be especially useful if your verse and chorus will be using different types of shots to coincide with the "scene change" that a new music section evokes. You may also want to take a different artistic approach during a guitar solo section, so marking these points is a real time-saver. We usually mark the beginning of each verse, chorus, bridge, and solo section as well as any repeated tags at the end.

1. **Click the Play In To Out button.**

2. **As the song is playing, click the Marker Menu button and select Mark.** A list of the numerals from 0 to 9 appears. As the song reaches the beginning of the first verse, click 1.

3. **As the song approaches your next section of music, be it a second verse or a chorus, repeat Step 2 but click 2 instead of 1.**

4. **Continue marking all the sections of your song until the song finishes playing.**

Markers

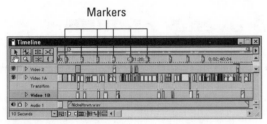

**Figure 8-13:** Use markers to set location points for important sections of your song, such as verse, chorus, and solo. In this Timeline, you'll notice markers 1 through 9 along the top of the Edit Line.

You can select unnumbered markers, but navigating the song when your markers are numbered is much easier, especially if you know which number corresponds to which section of the song. We usually keep a 3-x-5-inch card or sticky note nearby with a list of song sections and their corresponding marker numbers, for quick reference.

## Finding song parts in your video

To jump to a marked point:

1. **Click the Marker menu and select Go To.** Bullets appear next to the numbers that are being used as markers.

2. **If you know which number corresponds to the marker at verse 1, click it.** Your Edit Line Marker jumps to that point.

3. **Press the spacebar to begin playing at the marker.**

You can see how this will be invaluable when jumping from section to section within your video.

## Moving between edits

Another tool for moving around the Timeline is the Previous Edit and Next Edit buttons.

The Previous Edit and Next Edit buttons tell Premiere to jump to the previous or next clip in the Timeline.

1. **Click anywhere on your Edit line.**

2. Now click the Previous Edit button. The Edit Line Marker will jump back one edit to the previous clip.

3. Now click the Next Edit button a few times and watch the Program monitor jump ahead from clip to clip.

# Using the Insert and Overlay Features

Notice the two funny-looking yellow and black buttons at the bottom right-hand portion of the Source monitor. These buttons are the Insert and Overlay buttons.

 The Insert button works just like it does in a word processing program — it inserts the clip and moves the remaining clips to the right. We don't usually use this button when making music videos, because there is such an emphasis on lip-synching video to audio tracks. Using the Insert button in a lip-synched video would move video clips out-of-sync with audio clips. If your video is not lip-synch intensive, however, it's a useful tool.

## Inserting your clip between edits

To insert your clip into the Timeline between edits, while moving the remaining video clips to the right:

1. Position your Edit Line marker to the desired in point by using the Previous Edit button or Next Edit button in the Program monitor side of the Monitor window.

2. Make sure that the clip you want to insert is visible in the Monitor window's Source monitor and click the Insert button.

## Inserting your clip in the middle of a longer clip

To insert your clip into the middle of a clip or clips in the Timeline:

1. Move the Edit Line marker to the desired in point either by dragging it along the Edit Line or by pressing the Play button in the Project view of the Monitor window and pressing Stop at the point where you want the Edit Line marker to be positioned.

2. Make sure that the clip you want to insert is visible in the Source monitor and click the Insert button. The original video track(s) is cut at the Edit Line point. The new clip is inserted at this Edit line, and the remaining part of the track(s) is moved to the right.

The Overlay button superimposes the clip over existing clips without moving anything laterally. This option works really well when replacing a noncritical portion of the lip-synching track with a better image, while keeping the rest of the track visible and in synch with the audio. To try this feature, follow these steps:

1. **Play your program and stop it when you get to a place where you want to replace the video.**

2. **Now open the new clip in the Source monitor.**

3. **Click the Overlay button to paste that clip over the original one.** Your new clip was pasted over the same track as the old one, but it didn't erase the old track. Part of the old track that extends past the duration of the new clip is still there.

4. **Click the Previous Edit button to move back to the beginning of this overlay.**

5. **Now click the spacebar to see your changes.** Notice that when the original video segment is displayed after the new section, it remains synched up to the audio and hasn't moved laterally down the Timeline.

It's important to note that whenever you erase a clip or portion of a clip from the Timeline, the clip is not erased — just the reference or pointer to that clip. You can always get your original clip back. It's stored on your hard drive, and Premiere's clip editing functions are nondestructive to your original clips.

# Chapter Replay

After reading this chapter and following along with all the examples, you should be able to do the following:

✦ Edit in and out points of your Source clips

✦ Move your clips to the Timeline

✦ Move your clips around to get them in the order you prefer

✦ Jump from edit point to edit point

✦ Jump to any of your marked sections

In the next chapter, we explain how you can tweak your video by adjusting the in and out points and durations after they're in the Timeline. You learn to use transitions to make the cuts more cinematic. And you also learn how to fine-tune your monitor output for optimum viewing.

✦     ✦     ✦

# Tweaking Your Video

Y ou should now know how to move clips into the
Timeline window. If you don't, go back to Chapter 6 to
get up to speed.

You may be wondering why the Timeline has more than one
video track. You may also wonder if this feature enables you
to blend the tracks, creating smooth transitions in which one
clip is superimposed over another. If so, you're in luck,
because this chapter shows you how to do just that.

Before you continue, make sure that you have moved several
video clips as well as your audio song clip into your Timeline,
as described in Chapter 8.

## Cleaning Up Cuts

As you play your Timeline, you will undoubtedly see places
where your sequence is not what you want it to be. Perhaps
the timing is not quite right. We often time cuts to the beat of
the song. To clean up your cuts and transitions, you need to
know how to edit the in and out points on the Timeline and
how to move the clips around.

### Editing in and out points
in the Timeline

In Chapter 8, you learned how to edit your clips in both the
Source view monitor and the Program view monitor. After you
start adding lots of clips to the Timeline and moving them
around, however, you'll find that you probably have to make
further adjustments. You can lengthen or shorten your clips in
the Timeline by dragging their edges to the left or right.

1. **Click the Selection tool.**

2. **Position the mouse pointer over the beginning or end of a clip in the Timeline, so that the pointer's arrow image changes to the Edge Trim tool. See Figures 9-1 and 9-2.**

Selection tool

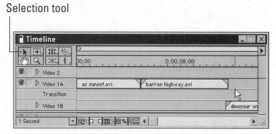

**Figure 9-1:** The Selection tool

Edge Trim tool

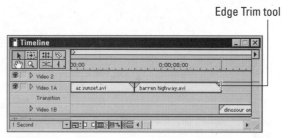

**Figure 9-2:** The Selection tool changes to the Edge Trim tool when placed over the edge of a clip in the Timeline.

3. **Click and drag the edge of the clip in to shorten it or drag it out to lengthen it, as seen in Figure 9-3.**

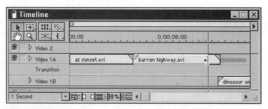

**Figure 9-3:** Click and drag the Edge Trim tool to shorten or lengthen a clip.

If the clip is expanded as far as it can go, the Edge Trim tool only points in, but not out. If there is room to lengthen a clip as well as shorten it, the Edge Trim tool shows an arrow pointing both ways (see Figure 9-4). If you want more precise editing, reduce the Time Zoom level to a smaller increment. To learn more about adjust the Time Zoom level, see Chapter 8.

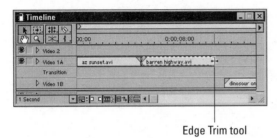

Edge Trim tool

**Figure 9-4:** The Edge Trim tool appears if the clip is not fully expanded. Notice that the arrow points both in and out, indicating that the clip can be both shortened and lengthened from its current setting.

## Moving clips around within the Timeline

You can move clips around in a given track or from one track to another. However, a video clip cannot be moved to an audio track, and an audio track cannot be moved to a video track. If a video clip is linked to an audio track, you cannot move the video clip to a place along the Timeline where there is an audio clip in the corresponding audio track. Because making music videos uses one complete audio clip of a song, overcrowding audio tracks is rarely an issue.

Premiere has a variety of Timeline tools designed to work in different editing situations. In addition to the Selection tool, Premiere provides more specialized selection tools. Take a look at Figure 9-5 to identify the different selection tools. The following list describes how you can use all of the selection tools:

- ✦ **Selection tool.** Selects a single clip in the Timeline when you click over a clip.
- ✦ **Range Select tool.** Selects a range of clips when you click and drag it over a set of clips. You can then move or delete the entire selected range of clips.
- ✦ **Track Select tool.** Selects every clip in a single track.
- ✦ **Multitrack Select tool.** Selects all clips on all tracks forward from the point where you click in the Timeline. Use this tool if you want to add bars and tone or a black screen to the beginning of your video. We describe this tool later in the chapter.

Select tool (V)

Range Select tool (M)

Track Select tool (M)

Multitrack Select tool (M)

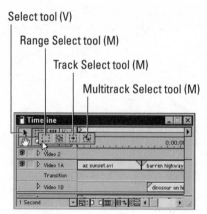

**Figure 9-5:** Premiere's selection tools

# Adjusting the Speed of Your Video Clip

We often lip-synch a song when we find ourselves in an undeniably great location. We had always thought that to have video that we could lip-synch with audio, we needed to sing to a track while it played so that we'd be at the right tempo and wouldn't be singing too fast or too slow. Too many times, however, we were in the right place but without our CD or boom box. We had to wing it. What's more, we found ourselves singing the song much faster than usual because there were strangers gawking at us and we wanted to get it over with.

## Matching audio when lip-synched without reference audio

We discovered two things: Premiere enables speed change for video clips, and speed changes look really cool.

To adjust the speed of your audio clip:

1. **Select the clip with a Selection tool.**

2. **Choose Clip⇨Speed.**

3. **Select a new rate.** A number more than 100% speeds up the click and makes the clip duration shorter; a number less than 100% slows down the clip and makes the clip duration longer.

4. **Experiment with settings to get your vocal tightly lip-synched with the vocal in the audio track.**

# Filming a lip-synched sequence specifically for slow-motion playback

Many videos use slow motion, while maintaining a perfectly lip-synched performance. How is this done? As long as you can have your computer available to you while you shoot, you can play your clip at a faster speed.

1. **Import your audio clip into your project by clicking File⇨Import⇨File and locating the clip.**

2. **Drag your audio clip from the project window to the Timeline's audio track.**

3. **Click to select the audio track.**

4. **Choose Clip⇨Speed.**

5. **Type a percentage in the New Rate text box.** A setting of 200% makes the clip play at double speed, while a setting of 50% makes the clip play at half speed.

6. **Click OK.**

Now set up your DV camcorder to shoot. Record your singer lip-synching to the double-speed audio track playing on your computer:

1. **Start the camera recording.**

2. **Click Play In To Out in the Monitor window's Program view.**

3. **While the song is playing at double speed, have the subject lip-synch to match the speed.** It may seem funny at the time, but the outcome is very cool. If the subject blinks or moves his or her hair or clothing, the slow motion effect will be more noticeable.

4. **Capture the footage and import it into the project.** (Refer to Chapter 6 for more detail on bringing footage into a Premiere project.)

5. **Line up the newly captured video with the audio.**

6. **When your clips are in synch, select the audio clip.**

7. **Choose Clip⇨Speed.**

8. **Type 100% in the New Rate text box.**

9. **Click OK.**

10. **Select the lip-synched video clip.**

11. **Choose Clip⇨Speed.**

12. **Type 100% in the New Rate text box.**

13. **Click OK.**

After you reset the speed to 100%, you may need to fine-tune the placement of video to audio.

# Adding Black Video, Color Bars and Tone, and Counting Leaders

Before you get too far in the editing process, you may consider adding a duration of black video at the beginning of your Timeline, a counting leader, or possibly even bars and tone. Why? Black video serves as a sort of tape leader — a space between your video and the previous program. The Bars and Tone feature assists viewers in calibrating their monitors before watching (and hearing) your video. Video editors typically include a counting leader when your work will be shown from a projector.

## Adding black video

Follow these steps to add black video to the beginning of the Timeline:

1. **Click the Multitrack Selection tool.** If this particular tool is not visible in the toolbox, click and hold the button next to the Selection tool to see the four sublevel tools. Click the Multitrack Selection tool.

2. **Position the Multitrack Selection tool over the beginning of the Timeline, as shown in Figure 9-6.**

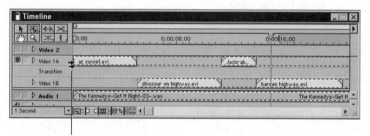

Multitrack Selection tool

**Figure 9-6:** The Multitrack Selection tool enables you to select all clips from all tracks to the right of where the tool is clicked.

3. **Click the beginning of the Timeline.** Premiere selects all the clips.

4. **Choose File⇨New⇨Black Video.** A clip entitled Black Video appears in your Project window's current bin.

5. **Drag the Black Video clip to the left edge of the first video clip in your Timeline.** See Figures 9-7 and 9-8.

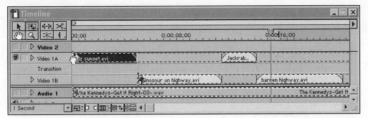

**Figure 9-7:** When you drag a clip onto the Timeline after you have used the Multitrack Selection tool, the first clip of each track displays an arrow, indicating the direction in which that track's clips will move to make room for the new clip.

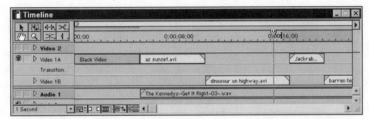

**Figure 9-8:** Premiere inserts the Black Video clip and shifts the clips of each track down the Timeline to make room for it.

## Adding color bars and tone

To add color bars and a 1 kHz tone, follow the previous steps, except select Bars and Tone rather than Black Video in Step 4. Premiere offers another way to create new objects in Premiere:

1. **Click the Create Item button on the bottom of the Project window.**

2. **Select Bars and Tone from the pop-up menu.**

3. **Click OK and notice that a clip entitled Bars and Tone appears in your Project window's current bin.**

4. **Drag the Bars and Tone clip into your video the same way you added black video.**

You can place black video, bars and tone, and counting leaders at any point within your video.

## A tale of two cities

**Road Diary**

Two of the most popular destinations in America for tourists and business travelers alike are Las Vegas and New York City. If you're in the echelon at your company where you get sent to conventions, you've no doubt been to these places on your boss's nickel. This is a great way to travel. If you're an amateur videographer, however, you can't deduct expenses for travel to locations, so you may as well throw your camera in the bag when you're on the company expense account. Oh, don't forget to go to a few meetings while you're there but use your time off to shoot some background clips and maybe some lip-synching, while you're in these two most visually engaging of American cities.

If you're staying at one of the major hotels in Vegas, you can walk up and down the entire strip in an evening. Take your time. Nothing closes here. After dark, you will be in the world's most unique artificially lit environment. It's overwhelming the first time, but don't forget to press your camera's Record button. Start out by renting a little electric car. They're available on many street corners. Now drive slowly from the north end of the strip, also known as Las Vegas Boulevard, to the south end, near the airport. Then drive slowly back. Trust me; you didn't get everything the first time. If you have a companion in the car, have one shoot while the other treats the car as a dolly. It's a lot more expensive to rent a real powered dolly than it is to rent an electric car that does the same thing. Besides, the dolly from the prop rental house won't have Love Bug decals on the hood. Don't worry about driving slowly. Everyone else will be gawking, too.

Your master shot of the Vegas strip will be different from anyone else's, even though everybody shoots this when they first get to town. There's just too much data for any two videographers to come up with identical shots. There are stock shots, though, and you should get them in your library. One caveat: Don't try to shoot footage inside the casinos. This will get you a warning, within seconds. Put on your lens cap right away, or really bad stuff might happen. But you can get great shots everywhere in this desert never-never-land. The electric cowboy at the north end of the strip is classic, and some of the newer hotel exteriors have some cool shot opportunities. I'm thinking New York, New York, with its compressed, but still massive, skyline, and Luxor, with its re-creation of the Egyptian Sphinx. After all, the skyline is one thing, but how often do you happen to be strolling by the Sphinx? The buffet in the basement is a good bargain, too, and I'll bet you can't say that about the original one in Egypt.

Speaking of New York, don't be content with the city-block-long Vegas version. Go to the real thing. Your first stop should be B&H Photo-Video-Pro Audio. This place, in midtown Manhattan, is the main supplier of gear to New York's thousands of news and entertainment media professionals. Don't be intimidated. You don't need a degree from NYU film school to fit in here. The salespeople are extremely helpful, and you may get a friendly seminar on shooting and editing technique while they show you around. Subscribe to their massive catalog, wherever you live, and you'll always be up on the latest video gear. Their prices are great, too. Tell them you're a low-budget, fledgling videographer, and they'll steer you to the right stuff at the right price. We get everything there. It's located near where the Lincoln Tunnel dumps you out and parking is actually possible.

Shooting in New York is a topic that could fill a book. The film industry started here. *The Great Train Robbery,* considered by many to be the first true feature film, was shot on location in West Orange, New Jersey near Thomas Edison's lab, and the first big studios were located in Brooklyn and Queens. A list of movies shot here would take up the rest of the book, and the same is true for video. Tune into MTV sometime and just count how many music videos are shot on location in the streets of Manhattan or in Brooklyn or Hoboken, New Jersey, with the city skyline as a dramatic backdrop. Lauren Hill even has a great video in which the city becomes a giant turntable with the Empire State Building as the spindle.

Here's a basic master shot. Bring a driver and schedule your shot for after midnight, when traffic is light. Enter the city through the Holland Tunnel, keeping the radio tuned to 1010 on the AM dial. Traffic info is crucial in this city. Coming out of the tunnel, follow signs leading uptown, and you'll find yourself in Greenwich Village. This part of town was built before the grid system was devised, and the narrow winding streets will have your driver lost in no time. That's okay. Just keep your finger on Record. Remember, simply by hanging the camera out the window, you'll be shooting the same evocative backgrounds shots as *The Godfather, Mean Streets, Annie Hall, Shaft, Moonstruck,* and so many other classic films that featured these streets as a main character. The streets tell a story, one that goes back to the arrival in America of many of our ancestors. So while you're lost, savor the streets. There's no place like it in the world.

Okay, you've made your way into The Village. You'll know because the street signs turn from green to brown. Find Sixth Avenue. It's a main drag, and it goes uptown. Roll tape and have your driver slowly dolly up Sixth Avenue. You can edit out the shrieking of cab horns behind you later. Your camera will react to the contrast between the darkened streets and the neon lights that flood them in a way that won't happen anywhere else in the world. When you get up into the fifties, cross over to Broadway and head back downtown. You'll pass the Brill Building, where the great songwriters of the '60s worked. Pull over and get a shot of the facade. Continue downtown into the maelstrom that is Times Square. This area is no longer the seedy, watch-your-back district that it once was. But it's still a riot of light, rivaled only by the Vegas strip. As you pass the MTV studios, you'll find yourself in an unreal environment of ten-story TV screens, mega video displays, and Britney Spears and Michael Jackson icons that tower higher than the Statue of Liberty. Call it excess, but it's great video content. Avoid shooting trademarked images that can land you in court. A ten-story Britney Spears is an example. Her record label owns the right to use her image for commercial purposes, and if they spend a $100,000 on a billboard, they don't appreciate you and me dropping the same image in our own little video. These guys have much bigger legal funds than we do.

But there's plenty of other stuff to shoot. The main thing is simply light. Flashing light. Pulsating light. Ten-story light extravaganzas. Take a minute and consider how much it would cost you to rent or construct flashing, pulsating, ten-story light effects at home. Using Adobe Premiere, these light flooded clips will be great raw material for you to manipulate with software-based effects. Look at it this way: If you want to create an exciting, energy filled clip, starting with an exciting, energetic image is easier than it is to solarize a shot of say, a tree in your backyard. So take advantage of your exciting life. You're in New York, so shoot everything!

*Continued*

*Continued*

You'll notice right away that you can't shoot the Manhattan skyline while you're in Manhattan. To do that, you'll have to cruise back through the Holland Tunnel and hang the first right. Doing this dumps you in Hoboken, New Jersey. Keep bearing right, and you'll wind up on Frank Sinatra Drive. Yes, you heard right. Old Blue Eyes hailed from Hoboken, and his namesake street has primo views of New York, New York. Here's where you want to shoot your skyline backgrounds.

If you have an extra day, cross the Brooklyn Bridge and auto-dolly up Bedford Avenue. Doing this takes you through every kind of neighborhood in the space of a few miles. Have lunch in the Williamsburg district and pick up the local indie video magazines. This cheaper alternative to Manhattan has become the city's most vital artist colony. If you have time, walk along the Brooklyn esplanade for more spectacular Manhattan background shots. Just remember, it's not possible to totally "do" New York in a few days. There are an infinite variety of great locations here, and if you spent the rest of your life shooting here, you'd just be following in the footsteps of great filmmakers like Martin Scorsese and Woody Allen. But come here and get clips of the city. If you want to do music video, these clips will be part of the meat and potatoes of your library.

# Transitions: Fades and More

The way your program moves from clip to clip is called a *transition*. The simplest transition is the *cut*.

## Using a simple cut transition

To perform a cut transition, all you have to do is line up two clips in the Timeline so that one clip backs up to the previous clip, leaving no space between the two. In other words, the last frame of clip number one leads directly into the first frame of clip number two. Your clips can be on different video tracks or on the same track.

The cut is the transition most often used in rock music videos. Figure 9-9 illustrates a simple cut on the Video 1A and 1B tracks.

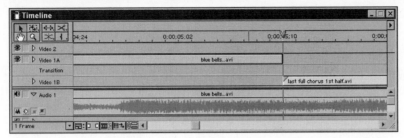

**Figure 9-9:** In a simple cut, one clip follows immediately after the other, leaving no blank video space. This type of transition can happen on a single video track or on different video tracks, as illustrated here.

## Applying a transition

In addition to the simple cut, Premiere offers 75 other transitions. To see the Transitions Palette, make sure that you are in the A/B Editing workspace by choosing Window⇨Workspace⇨A/B Editing. You can also view the Transitions palette from a different workspace by choosing Window⇨Show Transitions.

The Transitions palette contains 11 folders, and each folder contains a different type of transition, with an icon identifying each. To view a brief description of each transition, you first need to open the Info palette. Choose Window⇨Show Info.

If you click any transition, the name of that transition, an icon representing it, and a brief description will appear in the Info palette.

### Using the cross dissolve

The *cross dissolve* is our favorite transition. It's not overly noticeable, and it makes for professional-looking transitions. In a cross dissolve, the first clip fades out after the second clip fades in. See Figure 9-10.

**Figure 9-10:** Choose Animate from the Transitions palette menu to see a sample animation of the transition in the Info palette.

To apply transitions, we always work in the A/B Editing workspace. Your video clips must overlap in Video1A and 1B tracks of the Timeline for a transition to work.

1. **Click the transition you want to use from the Transitions palette.**

2. **Drag the transition to the Transition track on the Timeline, between the two clips.** The transition's duration is automatically set for the amount of time that the clips overlap, as shown in Figure 9-11. The pink bar in the Preview Indicator Area means that you must create a preview to see the rendered effect.

3. **Click Enter to generate a preview of the entire Timeline, or choose Timeline⇨Render Work Area to render just the portion of your clip that lies between the Work Area Markers.** After the Timeline or Work Area have rendered previews, the Preview Indicator Area turns green.

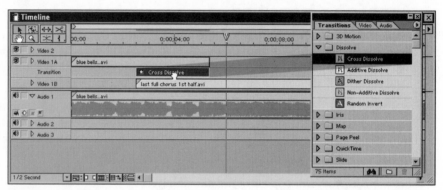

**Figure 9-11:** Click and drag the transition to the Transition track between the two clips. The transition is automatically set for the length of time that the two clips overlap.

## Checking out Premiere's other transitions

To be honest, rarely do we use any transition other than the cut or the cross dissolve in our videos. For some reason, the other transitions make video look like a cable-access infomercial. Maybe you want that look, so experiment with each transition. Don't let us tell you that more animated transitions aren't cool. Go ahead and experiment with them. You may even start a new music video trend by making one of these transitions your preferred one. Use the technique described previously to animate each of the transitions in the following folders so that you can get a better idea of what the transitions will look like. Better yet, apply each transition to your Timeline to see how they work with actual video clips. By the way, you can replace a transition with a new one simply by dragging the new transition and placing it on top of the old one. Use that technique to go through each of these transition groups:

✦ **3D Motion.** These transitions give the illusion that one clip is moving in 3D towards (or away from) the next clip. Spinning cubes, raising curtains, and swinging doors are all included in the 3D folder, along with eight others.

✦ **Dissolve.** Dissolves are the most natural type of transition, where one clip fades into the next. Cross Dissolve and Additive Dissolve are the smoothest, but three others are available, as well.

✦ **Iris.** Think of the end of the *Loony Toons* cartoons where the iris closes in around Porky Pig. That's the type of transition that's in this folder. All the variations are in the shape of the iris.

✦ **Map.** This folder contains a Channel Map and a Luminance Map. The Channel Map remaps colors. The Luminance Map replaces the brightness levels of one clip with those of the other.

✦ **Page Peel.** The page peel makes your first clip look like it's being peeled away to reveal clip number two. This folder contains five variations of the page peel.

✦ **QuickTime.** These transitions are available in this folder if you have installed QuickTime transitions. You must first drag the QuickTime Transition to the transition track before the menu of QuickTime transitions appears.

✦ **Slide.** The Slide folder contains 12 different two-dimensional slides, where portions of the first clip appear to slide into portions of the second clip. The shapes of the sliding portions of the clip vary a bit.

✦ **Special Effect.** These transitions are the most advanced of Premiere's transitions. They include a Three-D effect where the image of the clip on one track is tinted red, and the image of the other is tinted blue. The Image Mask transition masks one clip onto the other within the selected image.

✦ **Stretch.** The stretch transitions make one clip appear to stretch over another in different ways. This folder contains five stretch variations.

✦ **Wipe.** This folder contains 17 different wipes. *Wipes* are another two-dimensional type of transition, similar to slides. In fact, the Band Wipe and the Band Slide are nearly identical.

✦ **Zoom.** The zoom transitions create a zoom-like effect, zooming one clip into the other, until it takes over the whole screen. The cross zoom is cool, especially if you're going for that retro Austin Powers look.

To quickly audition many transitions on the same two clips:

1. **Place the two overlapping clips in Video 1A and 1B tracks.**

2. **Drag the first transition to the transition track between the two video clips.**

3. **Double click the transition in the Timeline.**

4. **Click Show Actual Sources in the Settings dialog box.**

5. **Click and drag the slider below either of the A or B thumbnails.** (See Figures 9-12 and 9-13.)

Click Show Actual Sources.

Slider

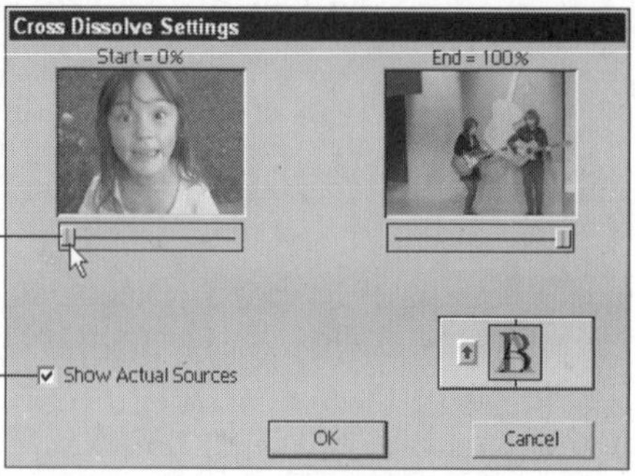

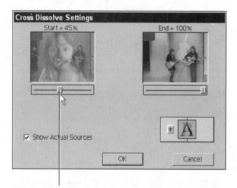

**Figure 9-12:** A typical transitions Settings dialog box

Click and drag slider to show transition effect.

**Figure 9-13:** Thumbnail shows how the transition will blend Video 1A and 1B clips.

## Changing transition settings

You can use the default transition settings that Premiere provides, or you can change the settings. In many of the transitions, you can customize your transition to run forward or backward or to transition from clip one to clip two, or vice versa. For slides, wipes, stretches, irises, and others, you can define a border width and color. You can change other transitions settings as well, and each transition has its own Settings window.

To change transition settings in one instance only:

1. **Apply your transition to the Timeline.**

2. **Double-click the transition so that the settings dialog box appears.**

3. **Adjust settings.**

4. **Click Show Actual Sources to preview.**

5. **Click OK to apply.**

To change transition settings for each use of the transition:

1. **Double-click the transition in the Transitions palette.**

2. **Make settings adjustments.**

3. **Click OK.** Whenever you apply this transition, the new settings will be applied. Changing transition settings in this way does not affect any transitions that are already in the Timeline.

## Defining and applying default transitions

Whatever your favorite transition is, you can define it as your default transition by following these steps:

1. **Click your favorite transition in the Transitions Palette to select it.**

2. **In the Transitions palette menu, select Set Selected As Default.**

3. **Set the duration.** The default setting is 30 frames, or one second, however, you can change the duration even after the transition is applied by clicking and dragging the in or out point.

4. **Set the effect alignment.** Premiere sets the effect at the center of the cut by default.

5. **Click OK.**

To apply your default transition, move your Edit Line to where both video clips overlap. Remember, one video clip should be in track Video 1A, and the other in track Video 1B. Press Ctrl+D (Command-D), and the transition appears in the Transition track for the duration that the two clips overlap.

# Using Advanced Transition Features

Premiere enables you to create and delete folders of transitions. This capability helps you arrange the Transitions palette to better suit the way you work.

## Creating a folder for your favorite transitions

You can create a new folder in the Transitions palette for transitions that you most often use. You can expand or collapse all transition folders in the palette:

1. **Click the Transitions palette menu button.**

2. **Click New Folder.**

3. **Name your folder.**

4. **Click OK.**

5. **After you create the folder, simply drag your favorite transitions into it.**

## Expanding or collapsing all transitions folders

Expand or collapse all transitions folders in the palette by clicking the Transitions palette menu and selecting Expand all Folders (to show all transitions within their folders) or Collapse all Folders (to show just the folders, but not the transitions inside them).

## Deleting folders of unused transitions

If you are sure that you will not use some of the transitions in your current project, you can delete them. Don't worry — they won't be gone forever. What's more, you can always bring them back. It's just a good way to clean up your desktop to only show usable transitions.

To delete a transition folder, follow these steps:

1. **Click the folder to select it.**

2. **Choose the Transitions palette menu.**

3. **Click Delete Folder.** The folder disappears from the Transitions menu.

If you didn't mean to do that or decide later in the project that a page peel really would make your singer appear to be more animated, you can once again display that transition folder by following these steps:

1. **Choose the Transitions palette menu.**

2. **Click Show Hidden.**

Your deleted folders show up again. Although they appear in italics, they function just the same as the folders that you didn't delete.

# Fading to Black

Many slow-jam videos as well as slow tempo country videos often use the fade-to-black transition, where each clip (often in slow motion) fades completely to black before the next clip appears. This gentler type of transition serves to add to the laid-back vibe of the song.

Although fading-to-black is a type of transition, it's not one that appears in the Transitions palette. What's more, you can't apply this transition to a clip in Video 1 (A or B) track. To perform this type of fade, you need to use the Opacity rubberbands, which are only available on video tracks two and higher. The opacity of your clip defines how much of the clip is opaque and how much is transparent. The Opacity rubberbands enable you to set the opacity at various points within your clip.

To fade a clip to black:

1. **Place the clip in track Video 2 or higher.**

2. **If it's not already expanded, expand the track by clicking the Collapse/Expand Track button to the left of the track.**

3. **If the red Opacity rubberband is not already displayed, click the Display Opacity Rubberbands button.** The default rubberband handles appear at both the beginning and the end of the rubberband.

4. **Position your pointer along the red rubberband.** The pointer changes to a pointing finger, as seen in Figure 9-14.

5. **Click the red rubberband between 5 and 10 frames from the end of the clip.** A red rubberband handle appears on the rubberband.

6. **Click the handle that appears at the end of the rubberband.**

7. **Drag the rubberband down to create the point at which your clip will be fully faded.** Figure 9-15 illustrates what a fade looks like on the Opacity Rubberband.

Opacity rubberband          Rubberband handle

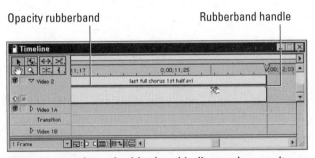

**Figure 9-14:** The red rubberband indicates the opacity of a clip.

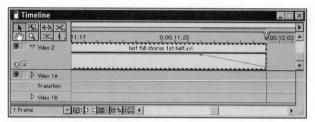

**Figure 9-15:** You can set a clip to fade out along the Opacity Rubberband.

8. **Place your next clip against this faded clip to transition from a faded clip to a fully opaque next clip.**

9. **Apply Rubberband to beginning of second clip to fade in from black.**

Opacity is explained further in the "Superimposing Images" section of Chapter 12.

## Chapter Replay

After reading this chapter and following along with all the examples, you should be able to perform the following tasks:

✦ Edit in and out points and move clips around the Timeline

✦ Adjust the speed of your clip to appear as slow motion, fast motion, or simply to get a video track to synch to the audio track

✦ Add color bars and tone and black screen to the start of your video

✦ Apply transitions between video clips and customize transitions

✦ Fade a video clip to black

The next chapter discusses how to create industry-standard video titles.

✦     ✦     ✦

# Adding Titles

**C**rafting a great song and creating a cool video to complement it is a futile endeavor if viewers can't identify the artist or song by the music and images alone. Neatly placed text labels (we call them *titles* in this book) let people know who they're hearing and seeing. Titles are valuable music video components, no matter how often they may be overlooked, because some musicians never appear in their videos at all. Due to the controversy surrounding their "Jeremy" video, grunge rockers Pearl Jam haven't actually appeared in a video since then. Other artists, such as Madonna, change their appearance from one video to the next, so titles can reassure fans that, yes, the Material Girl has a new look to match her new musical direction.

## Creating a Title

When your video is shown, whether it's on the Web, a cable-access station, or a big-name music television channel, the best way to identify the song, artist, and director is to include on-screen titles. Most music videos run a title shortly after the start and again shortly before the final fade. A music video title typically contains these elements:

- ✦ Name of band
- ✦ Song title in quotations
- ✦ Album
- ✦ Record label
- ✦ Director

The director credit is sometimes omitted, but because we're all aspiring video directors, we're certainly going to leave it in! For an example, see Figure 10-1.

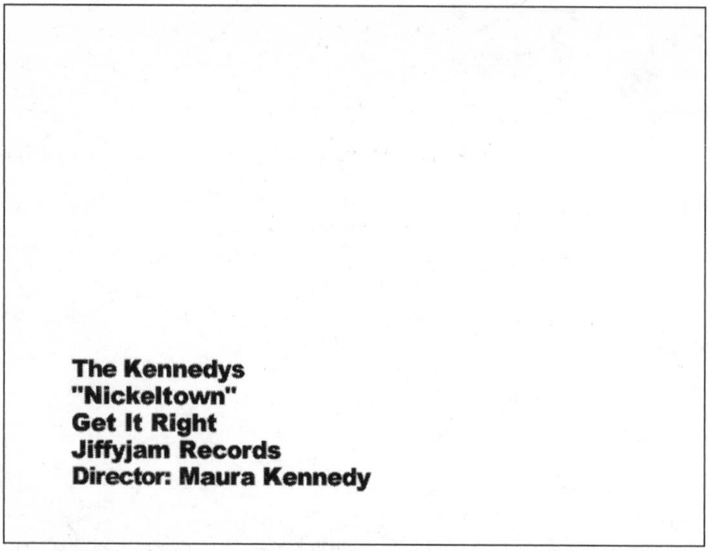

**The Kennedys**
**"Nickeltown"**
**Get It Right**
**Jiffyjam Records**
**Director: Maura Kennedy**

**Figure 10-1:** A typical music video title includes the band's name, song title, album title, record label, and director's name, in that order.

In Premiere, a title is a separate file from your program file. Think of it the way that you would think of any of your source clips or audio material.

To create a new title, choose File➪New➪Title.

## Importing a sample frame as a guide

When you create a basic title in Premiere, you're defining plain text against a solid background. The title, however, eventually gets superimposed against some video action. Premiere enables you to import a representative sample frame from one of your video's clips into your title window to use as a guide for title placement and contrast. When you create a title by using a sample frame, you see the brightness and color relationships between the title and the clip. If, for example, your title text is white, you don't want to superimpose it against a bright video. At the same time, if your video action takes place in a shadowy alley, you may need to superimpose a white title rather than use a title with black lettering. Because this frame is only a guide, Premiere does not save it in your title file. If you decide to modify a title after saving and closing it, your sample, or *poster* frame no longer shows up when you open the file. You need to reimport that frame if you still need it as a guide.

To import a sample frame into Premiere:

1. **If you haven't already created a new Title window, choose File⇨New⇨Title.**

2. **Click the Project window.**

3. **Double-click the clip in the Project window whose frame you want to use.**

4. **Set the location to the frame that you want to use as the sample frame.** You can use any frame in the clip as your sample frame.

5. **Click the Menu Marker button.**

6. **Choose Mark⇨Poster Frame.** A zero (0) at the top center of the frame indicates the marked frame.

7. **Click and drag the image from the Clip window to the Title window.** The image you drag into the Title window will be the marked sample frame, not the default first frame of the clip.

You now have a sample frame that you can use not only as a positioning guide but to make sure that your text shows up against the video's colors and resolution as well.

## Using safe zones

If you've already edited a video, you are probably already familiar with *safe zones*. They are dotted lines on your Monitor window that delineate the boundaries imposed upon your material by a typical television screen. If your titles fall outside of these lines, some TV screens may cut them off at the edge. Before you start designing your title, make sure that the safe zones are showing. If they're not, do this:

1. **While your Title window is open, choose Window⇨Window Options⇨Title Window Options.**

2. **Select Show Safe Titles.**

3. **Click OK.**

Two safe zones appear around the edges of your Title window, as shown in Figure 10-2. The outer zone is the *action-safe zone*. The one that you should be most concerned with now is the inner zone, which is the *title-safe zone*. All your text should lie within these borders. Testing the title-safe zone offers another good reason to view your work on a TV screen as you edit, as we suggest in Chapter 6.

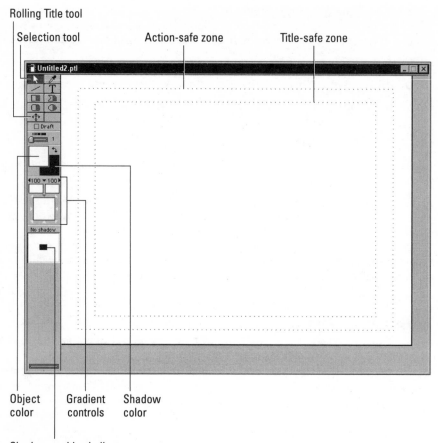

Rolling Title tool

Selection tool

Action-safe zone

Title-safe zone

Object color

Gradient controls

Shadow color

Shadow position indicator

**Figure 10-2:** The outside line is the action-safe zone; the inside line is the title-safe zone.

## Formatting title text

With Premiere, you can create rolling credits or titles with background colors. You can use any of over 150 available fonts and apply any size or style to your fonts. But because you're learning how to make titles in a specific format — the music video — you should know the industry standard configuration.

### Choosing a typeface and style

Although titles in music videos differ slightly, the basic style and elements are uniform. Because the title isn't as large as a movie title, for example, you need to make your music video title as readable as possible. The title appears only for about five seconds at the beginning and end of your video, so every detail counts. After analyzing dozens of music videos of all genres and vintages, the following conventions are most often used:

✦ Thick sans serif font typeface, such as Arial Black

✦ Bold typeface

✦ Heavy shadow to the lower right of the letters

✦ Font size around 21 or 22 points

✦ Horizontally condensed characters

✦ Vertically condensed lines of text

For a professional appearance, follow these steps to choose your font and style:

1. **Choose Title⇨Font.**

2. **Select Arial Black from the font list.**

3. **Select Bold from the Style list.**

4. **Select 22 from the Size list.**

5. **Click OK.**

6. **Now click the Type tool.**

7. **Click your cursor on the title window about two-thirds of the way down.**

Now you can type in the actual title text. See the next section to learn how.

## Adding text to your title

After you've selected a typeface and style for your title, you can type the actual text into the Title window.

Follow these steps to add title text:

1. **Type the artist's name in the first line and press Enter (Return).**

2. **Type the name of the song in quotes and press Enter (Return).**

3. **Type the name of the album (or other source) and press Enter (Return).**

4. **Type the record label name and press Enter (Return).**

5. **Type** Director: **and your name.** (Yes, you *do* get credit!)

Your text wraps to the next line if the title box is not wide enough. Click the Selection tool and then click the upper-right corner of the text box. Now drag the box to the right, until all your text fits in the appropriate lines.

## Changing text color

The standard title color for music videos is white. Videographers choose white because titles usually show up more clearly in videos if the lettering is white, as opposed to black, because the video images are in constant motion.

The Object Color icon may be set to black or another color for contrast, or if your video image is light.

To set the color of your text to white, follow these steps:

1. **Select the title text.**

2. **Click the Object Color icon in the Title window toolbar.** The Color Picker dialog box appears.

3. **Type** 255 **in the Red, Green, and Blue text boxes in the Color Picker dialog box — this is the formula for white.**

4. **Click OK.**

Your text should now be white. See Figure 10-3 for an example of a title against a sample frame.

**Caution**    If you didn't import a sample clip, you won't be able to see your text now because the white window provides no contrast to your white lettering.

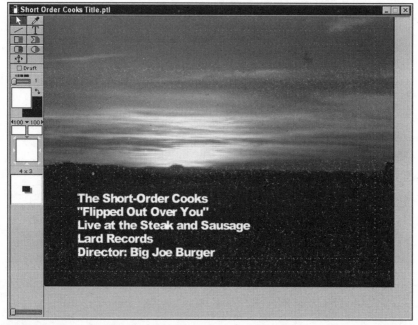

**Figure 10-3:** In the Title window, import a sample frame to see how your title will look against the video.

## Turning off gradient colors

Although you can grade colors across your typeface, that effect is not typical in a music video-style title. Make sure that the gradient colors are set to white. The Gradient Start Color, Gradient End Color, and Gradient/Transparency Direction boxes should all be white — the same color as your text. If they're not, follow these steps:

1. **Select the title text.**

2. **Select the Gradient Start Color. The Color Picker dialog box appears.**

3. **Type 255 in the Red, Green, and Blue text boxes to define white.**

4. **Click OK.**

5. **Select Gradient End Color.**

6. **Type 255 in the Red, Green, and Blue definition boxes.**

7. **Select the Gradient/Transparency Direction box.**

8. **Type 255 in the Red, Green, and Blue definition boxes.**

## Adding a shadow

White may sometimes appear in the layer beneath your title as part of the scene. To safeguard against the title lettering blending into the background, video editors usually place a black shadow to the lower right of the letters (see Figure 10-4).

To add a shadow, follow these steps:

1. **Select the title text.**

2. **Click Shadow Color in the toolbar.**

3. **Type 0 in the Red, Green, and Blue text boxes in the Color Picker dialog box.** This is the formula for black.

4. **Click OK.**

5. **Click the Shadow Position area in the toolbar.**

6. **Slowly drag the shadow positioner downward and to the right.** Notice that the two numbers above the shadow position box move as you drag. The first number is the position left to right. The second number is the position up and down. Drag the icon so that the numbers read 4 x 3.

**Figure 10-4:** The letter on the left has no shadow; the letter on the right has a shadow applied.

To modify the shadow's appearance, follow these steps:

1. **Right-click (Ctrl-click) the text.**

2. **Choose Shadow⇨Single. Notice the resultant shadow's appearance.**

3. **Right-click the text again.**

4. **Choose Shadow⇨Solid. The shadow becomes a little less noticeable.**

5. **Right-click the text one more time.**

6. **Choose Shadow⇨Soft. The shadow becomes wider but less defined.**

7. **Go back and select the single shadow.** This setting is the best standard setting for an MTV-style title.

## Using kerning and leading

The typical music video title uses *kerning* and *leading* to compact the letters and lines, respectively. See Figures 10-5 and 10-6 for examples of an uncompressed title and a title with kerning and leading applied, respectively.

To decrease the amount of space between lines, follow these steps:

1. **Choose Title⇨Leading⇨Less Leading.** Notice how the lines compress.

2. **Repeat this step six times.**

To decrease the amount of space between letters, follow these steps:

1. **Click the Type tool.**

2. **Select the whole title, and the Increase/Decrease Kerning buttons appear in the toolbar.**

3. **Click the Increase Kerning button (the left one) twice.** Watch as your text compresses.

Increase Kerning

Decrease Kerning

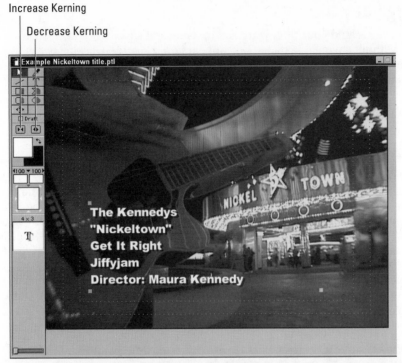

**Figure 10-5:** This title uses 22-point Arial Black font with a 4 x 3 single shadow.

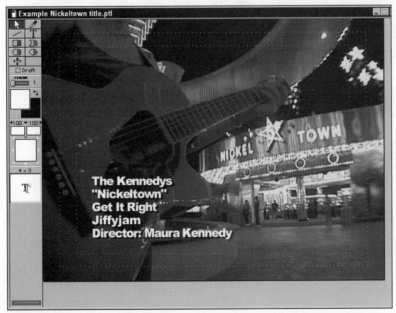

**Figure 10-6:** Here is the same title with kerning and leading applied.

## Saving your title

After you've created your title, you need to name and save it. If you close your Title window without saving it, a dialog box appears on the screen, asking if you want to save the title. If you don't save the title before closing it, your definitions and/or title changes will be lost. To name and save your title, choose File⇨Save As. Give your title a name and make sure that it's in the folder of your choice. Notice that the title file's extension is .ptl, for Premiere Title.

## Placing your title

If your title covers the lead singer's face, you'll be in trouble. This probably happened in the early days, so a conventional placement was agreed upon. The title is typically placed on the lower-left side of the screen and is usually about one third of the screen's height. Keep this in mind as you edit your opening and closing shots, and don't place any essential action in this part of the screen. Placement is easy if your title-safe zone is showing. Drag your title to line up with the bottom left of the title-safe zone, as shown in Figure 10-7.

Save your title. You can now close the title window or leave it open if you think that you may modify it later.

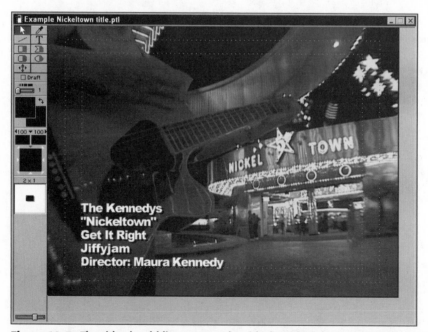

**Figure 10-7:** The title should line up exactly with the title-safe zone on the left and bottom sides.

# Importing Titles Into a Premiere Project

If you created a title with a Premiere project open, the title clip automatically showed up in the Project window's currently selected bin. If you create a title without having a project open, you need to import your title. To Import the title file, choose File⇨Import⇨File and select your newly created title.

## Superimposing your title

Because you want your title to be superimposed over the video action, you need to move it to a *superimpose* track. Superimpose tracks — video tracks two and higher — enable you to set transparency keys on the clips that they contain. They are also called super tracks. If no transparency key is defined, the clip in the higher super-impose track overrides any video clip in a lower track. In other words, you will only see the clip in the higher track. However, you can make all or part of your clip transparent or semitransparent.

See Chapter 12 for more information on alpha channels, transparency keys, and superimpositions.

The Premiere program's titles are automatically set for White Alpha Matte transparency, so Premiere detects the blank parts of the title (in this case, everything but the text) and converts those spaces — the white spaces — into transparent areas.

Commercial music videos generally play for at least five seconds before the title appears. Drag the Edit Line marker to the spot five seconds after the music begins. You can adjust this for feel later.

Drag the title clip from the bin onto the first superimpose track (the Video 2 track) of the Timeline and line it up to start at the Edit Line.

## Adjusting the title duration

By default, Premiere displays a title for five seconds. That's great, because it seems to be the industry standard, give or take a second. If the song in your music video has a slow tempo, you may make the title slightly longer than five seconds but no more than six or seven seconds. To adjust the length of the title, drag its out point on the Timeline. (See Chapter 8 for more about working with in and out points.)

## Adding fades to your title

Generally speaking, a title fades in over ten frames or so. The duration of the title is normally around five seconds, and then it fades out again over the course of another ten frames.

To add fades to your title, follow these steps:

1. **Drag the Edit Line to the front edge of the title clip.**

2. **Select One Frame on the Time Zoom level.** You'll need to count frames for the fade-in, which progresses over a very short length of time.

3. **Expand the superimpose track on which the title is placed by clicking the triangle to the left of the track.**

4. **Click the red Display Opacity Rubberbands button.** The red line that appears is the rubberband.

5. **Click the Selection tool.**

6. **Count ten frames in on your title and click the red rubberband line.** A *handle* in the form of a small red square appears on the rubberband line where you clicked it. That's the point at which the title is fully faded in.

7. **Click the handle at the title clip's very first frame and drag it all the way down.** The line's upward slope indicates that the title gradually fades in.

8. **Click the rubberband ten frames from the end of the title clip to create another handle and mark the beginning of the title's fade-out.**

9. **Drag title clip's end handle all the way down.** This lowered handle marks the point where the title is fully faded out. See Figure 10-8 for an example of a title on the expanded Video 2 track with fades defined.

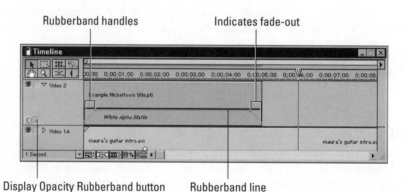

**Figure 10-8:** The red rubberband line shows where this title fades in and out over ten frames.

## Adding an end title

Your music video needs an end title to identify the song and artist for viewers who may have missed the first half. When adding an end title in Premiere, you use the same title you use at the beginning after you've assigned fades. You can drag the title from the Project window to the Timeline again if you want, but you can save a few steps by copying your edited start title to your Clipboard and then pasting it into the Timeline ten seconds from the end. Remember, the title is visible for five seconds and then the song plays for another five seconds after the title is faded out. After you paste the title clip, you may have to move it left or right in small increments along the Timeline to place it in precisely the right spot. If you follow this general formula, your video titles will look just like the ones on television.

# Previewing Titles in a Video

If you play your video program right after you've added a title, the title doesn't appear. It's right there in the Timeline, yet it doesn't show up in the Monitor window. After you add the title to the superimpose track, a pink line appears on the Timeline's Preview Indicator area, directly above the title. This pink line indicates an effect needs to be rendered for you to see the title superimposed over the clip in the Monitor window. Previewing your work can be done in a few different ways, as we discuss in the sections that follow.

## Scrubbing the Time Ruler

For a quick way to preview your video, you can *render-scrub*, which is done by dragging the Edit Line marker along the Timeline, while holding down the Alt (Option) key. The speed at which your video is played back varies with the speed at which you drag the marker. Previewing your entire video this way isn't practical, but it's useful if you want to see if your title will generally appear the way you want, without having to wait for the computer to render the work area.

If you want to see all or parts of your video with the title fully rendered, you need to render the work area, and you'll eventually need to do this before exporting the final video.

## Previewing at full playback speed

When Premiere renders your work area, it builds preview files on the scratch disk you specify when you set your project settings. To find out or change the location where Premiere stores your Preview files, follow these steps:

1. **Choose Edit⇨Preferences⇨Scratch Disks and Device Control.**

2. **The default location is Same As Project File. You can change it by clicking Select Folder and locating the folder where you want previews stored.**

To preview your video at final playback speed, viewing all your titles with fades as well as any effects that you add, you need to render the video by building a preview on your hard drive. Your previews will be built and stored on your system's disk so that after they're built, you don't need to keep rebuilding them each time you want to preview your work. Moreover, Premiere keeps the previews that have already been built while building only the latest preview files, thereby keeping the rendering time as low as possible.

To preview your movie at full playback speed, follow these steps:

1. **Choose Project⇨Project Settings⇨Keyframe and Rendering.**

2. **Select Preview From Disk.**

3. **Click OK.**

## Rendering the work area

Before you build your previews, you must first tell Premiere what part of the Timeline to include. You do this by defining the work area. Directly above the Preview Indicator area is the yellow work area bar. When you add clips to the Timeline, the work area bar automatically extends from the beginning of your Timeline to the last clip, and it expands as you add clips.

To preview your work, follow these steps:

1. **Drag the beginning and ending markers of the work area to include the part of the Timeline that you want rendered.**

2. **Choose Timeline⇨Render Work Area.** The Building Preview screen appears and indicates approximately how long your Preview will take to build. After the work area has been rendered, all the pink lines in the Preview Indicator area turn green, indicating that the Work Area is fully rendered and can be played back with all the effects applied.

3. **Click the Monitor window's Play button to play your music video.** After five seconds, the title quickly fades in for about five seconds before fading out again.

After you view the rendered video, you may decide that the title placement just doesn't feel right. You can adjust your title's placement and duration to suit your personal style, just as you would manipulate a video clip. You can also change the fade-in and fade-out simply by clicking and dragging the handles on the Opacity rubberband. Notice that after you make these changes, the Preview Indicator area above the title file turns from green (rendered) back to pink (not rendered) because you changed the file. You need to re-render the work area to see the updated title.

# Using Titles As Special Effects

Directors occasionally incorporate overlaid text into the body of the video. Text can convey literal messages, or it can be used as a pop art element. Think back to the old *Batman* TV show. Whenever the bad guy got socked in the mouth, you'd see the bubble "Pow!" pop up on the screen. Silent films sometimes used text to establish place, for example, "Egypt, 1922." In modern music videos, Director Spike Jonze used titles to make the Beastie Boys' "Sabotage" video look like the credits of a 1970s cop show. Text is also used to make the screen look like a computer monitor flashing messages at the viewer.

## Making credits fun

**Road Diary**

Why roll credits? To give credit, of course. Record labels may balk at the idea of giving up expensive production resources for such a mundane reason, but there have been instances in film where the credit roll took on a life of its own, sometimes becoming as much of an attraction as the movie. Check out Blake Edward's *The Pink Panther* series, for example. These 1960s classics are spoofs of the ever-popular James Bond films. They star British comic genius Peter Sellers as the bumbling Inspector Clouseau. Out of a half-dozen films in the original series, only one script actually mentions the "pink panther," an impossibly valuable diamond. Why are the others called the *Son of the Pink Panther, The Pink Panther Strikes Again,* and so forth? The name stuck because the audience fell in love with the opening credit roll that featured an animated panther, pink, of course, who torments a house painter by constantly swapping pink paint for whatever color is in his can. The conflict escalates into all-out war in a series of Road Runner/Wile E. Coyote-style scenarios. At certain points in the action, the credits roll, incorporated smoothly into the cartoon graphics. Amazingly, this cartoon story goes on for a full ten minutes or so before the film's actual opening scene. Edwards took a gamble by running a complete animated short before a detective movie, and it worked. Audiences of the day loved the sly panther as much as they did Sellers' hapless detective.

As artists like Gorillaz explore the full potential of animation in music video, creating modern-day equivalents to the crafty pink feline, we may see innovative use of credits as part of cutting-edge graphics.

If the best reason to roll credits is to give credit, what's the next best reason? It's one way to talk your crew into working for free! Be the first on your block to acknowledge your doughnut-earning co-workers and try using graphics to make the credit roll a fun value-add for your audience.

Essentially, superimposing text is simply a matter of blending tracks. Experiment with the different fonts, font colors, sizes, and styles, and imagine your own set of possibilities.

# Using Rolling Titles

Music videos have very standardized titles, but who says you need to stick to these conventions? Try using rolling credits to create a "mini-movie" feel.

Here's how to create rolling titles in Premiere:

1. **Choose File⇨New⇨Title.**
2. **Click the Rolling Title tool.**
3. **Drag the tool to mark the portion of the screen that will include rolling text.**

4. **To define how you want the title to scroll (up, down, left, or right), choose Title⇨Rolling Title Options.**

5. **Select Move Up, Move Down, Move Left, or Move Right to tell Premiere how you want the title to roll.**

6. **Press Enter (Windows) or Return (Mac) several times so that the first text appears to roll up from the bottom of the screen.** If you don't do this, your text will start at the top of the screen, which is generally not the desired effect of a rolling title.

7. **Type the text that you want included in the rolling title.** The text must over-fill the box for it to roll.

8. **Press the Enter (Return) key several more times so that the last word appears to roll up past the top of the screen.** If you don't do this, the title will cut off with your last text at the bottom and not fully rolled to the top.

Save the rolling title just as you would a regular title and move it to the Timeline the same way you would move a regular title.

To change the speed at which the title rolls, simply drag the title's in or out point along the Timeline.

# Chapter Replay

After reading this chapter and following along with all the examples, you should be able to:

✦ Create and save a title

✦ Import a sample frame into your title

✦ Define your title's type style and placement

✦ Import your title into your video and place it on the Timeline

✦ Fade your title in and out

✦ Preview your title over the video action

✦ Use rolling titles

Now that you understand how titles are superimposed over video, you may want to explore the possibilities of overdubbing audio material in the same way. Chapter 11 explains how this is done.

✦     ✦     ✦

# Adding Sound Overdubs, Narration, and Sound Effects

**A**lthough most music videos consist of only one stereo audio track, you have the ability in Premiere to have up to 99 tracks of audio in your Timeline. What's more, Premiere enables you to manipulate your audio tracks by applying effects, filters, and fades. Audio effects processing is very similar to video effects processing, which is described in Chapter 12. The only real difference is that when working with an audio track, you're manipulating *sound waves*, and when you're working with a video track, you're manipulating *light waves*.

Before getting into audio effects and overdubs, you should make sure that your computer's sound card and speakers aren't configured for surround sound or 3D effects. You need to hear your audio flat, with no effects so that you have a stable reference point in case you decide to add processing. In your computer's control panel and under Sounds make sure that none of these options are applied. In Windows, click Start➪Control Panel➪Sounds, Speech, Audio Devices. Select Advanced Volume Controls and click Advanced. Uncheck Apply 3D effect to digital audio. If you're using a Mac, choose Apple Menu➪Control Panels➪Monitors and Sounds. Click the Sound button. Make sure that 3D Surround Sound is not selected. If, for example, the vocal seems to be much lower in the mix than on the original source, the problem is probably in the system settings. For further information, consult your system's software manual.

# Using the Audio Mixer

When applying changes in volume and *panning* (a sound's position in the stereo sound field between the left and right speakers), you can execute these changes either on the Timeline or by using the Audio Mixer. Figure 11-1 shows all the Audio Mixer's components. If you prefer to work in a different workspace, you can open the Audio Mixer in that workspace, as well.

 **Cross-Reference**    See Chapter 8 to set up your Premiere workspace.

To open the Audio Mixer, choose Window⇨Audio Mixer.

Audio Track ID

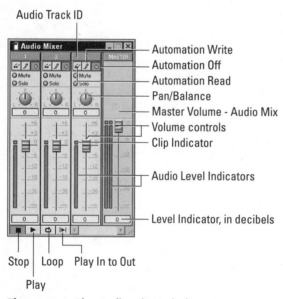

— Automation Write
— Automation Off
— Automation Read
— Pan/Balance
— Master Volume - Audio Mix
— Volume controls
— Clip Indicator

— Audio Level Indicators

— Level Indicator, in decibels

Stop | Loop   Play In to Out

Play

**Figure 11-1:** The Audio Mixer window

When processing audio in the Timeline, you can perform separate edits and apply effects to individual clips in a single track. When working in the Audio Mixer, you're manipulating the entire Track and all the audio clips that lie within it over time. The controls at the bottom of the Audio Mixer window work the same way as those at the bottom of the Monitor window. In fact, if you click the Play button in either the Audio Mixer window or the Monitor window, Premiere activates the corresponding Play button on the other window.

# Applying Simple Fades

If you've imported an audio file from a CD, the song probably has a clearly defined beginning and end. If you're using an audio clip that comes from the middle of a live concert, however, you may need to fade your clip in and out to avoid an abrupt start and ending. Figure 11-2 shows an expanded audio track, `Nickeltown.wav`, in the Timeline window. Familiarize yourself with the buttons.

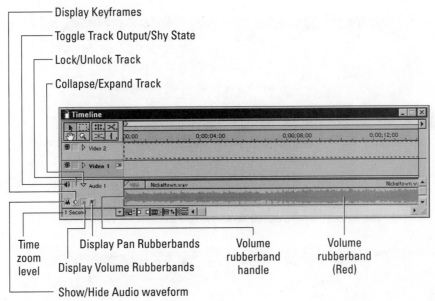

**Figure 11-2:** The expanded audio track

To fade audio, follow these steps:

1. **If you don't already have an audio clip in your Timeline, drag one from the Project window.** Only tracks marked Audio 1, Audio 2, and so on can contain audio clips.

 2. **Click the Collapse/Expand Track button on the appropriate track to see track's details.**

 3. **Click the Show/Hide Audio Waveform button.** The waveform appears in the audio track. If you don't see the waveform, click the Time Zoom Level area and select a setting that is less than four seconds. This setting enables you to see the audio waveform.

 4. **Click the red Display Volume Rubberbands icon.**

5. **Drag the Edit Line Marker left to the beginning of the song.**

6. Click the spacebar to play the song from the beginning.

7. Click the spacebar again at the point where you want the song fully faded in to stop playing the song.

8. Position your cursor over the Volume rubberband where your Edit Line marker is.

9. **Click the Volume rubberband.** Notice that the Rubberband *handle* appears, as shown in Figure 11-3.

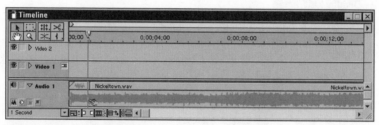

**Figure 11-3:** Click the Rubberband to create handles.

10. **Click the first rubberband handle — the one at the very beginning of your audio clip.**

11. **Drag the handle downward, as shown in Figure 11-4.**

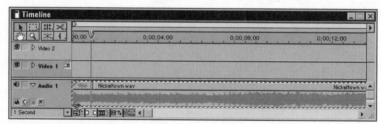

**Figure 11-4:** Drag the handle downward to decrease volume.

When the song plays across the Timeline, the volume starts at zero and fades in along the incline of the rubberband.

As long as the Audio Mixer is *not* visible on your desktop, you will hear the volume changes as you play the clip in the Timeline. If, however, you are working in the Audio workspace or are otherwise displaying the Audio Mixer, you must enable the Automation Write feature in the Audio Mixer to hear the changes, as shown in Figure 11-5.

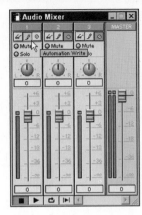

**Figure 11-5:** Click Automation Write to hear your volume changes as you play the clip in the Timeline.

# Cross-Fading Between Two Audio Tracks

Suppose you want to create a music video that's a retrospective of your favorite band, perhaps a slick montage of their tunes. You can cross-fade different audio clips to create this montage. To do this, you must have audio clips overlapping in time and in separate tracks.

1. **Import an audio clip into the project (see Chapter 6).** If you don't have a separate audio file, double-click a video clip that was captured with audio in the Project window, and the clip opens in its own window.

2. **Click the Take Video button so that a red line appears through the button.** The red line indicates that Take Video is deselected.

3. **Drag the clip to the Audio 2 track.** Only the audio portion of the clip appears in the Timeline.

4. **Click the Time Zoom Level area and select One Second.** Each hash mark along the Time Ruler now represents one second.

5. **Click the Expand Track button on each audio track that you want to cross-fade.**

6. **Drag the audio clips around in the Timeline and place them to overlap by one or two seconds.**

7. **Select the Cross Fade tool.**

8. **Click the audio clip you want to fade in the Timeline.**

9. **Click the second audio clip you want to cross-fade in the Timeline.**

Notice the new rubberband handles on both clips, as shown in Figure 11-6. Premiere fades the clips according to how long they overlap. If the audio clips overlap for 20 seconds, that's how long the cross fade will be. If you decide that the cross fade is too short or too long, simply drag the audio clips so that they loosely overlap more or less and repeat steps 7 through 9. Alternately, click a handle and drag it left or right to change its position.

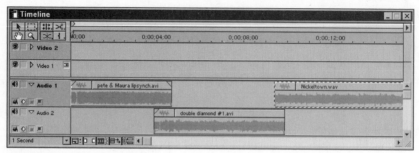

**Figure 11-6:** Two cross fades

# Using Logarithmic Fades

Because music videos emphasize the audio content, you should want your fades to sound natural. Premiere gives you the choice, in its audio project settings, of using logarithmic audio fades instead of the default linear fades. A *linear audio fade* changes the volume at a constant rate over time. A *logarithmic audio fade,* on the other hand, starts slowly but then accelerates the rate at which volume changes. Logarithmic fades more closely resemble the way we hear natural fades. You can't perform a logarithmic fade by using rubberbands in the Timeline, but you can tell Premiere to convert linear fades to logarithmic fades.

1. **Choose Project⇨Project Settings⇨Audio.** The Project Setting dialog box appears, as shown in Figure 11-7.

2. **Click the Use Logarithmic Audio Fades check box.**

3. **Click OK.**

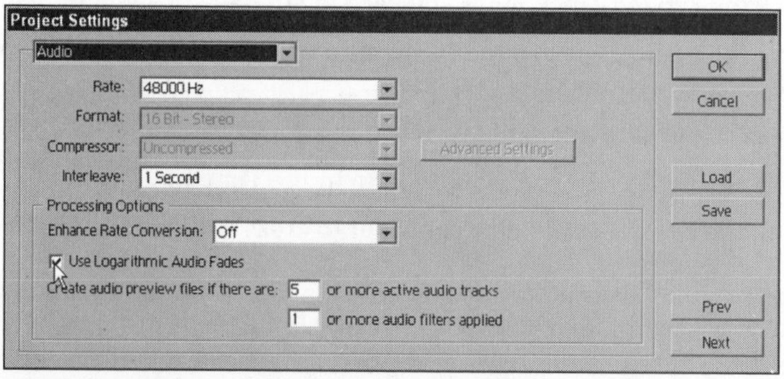

**Figure 11-7:** Select Use Logarithmic Audio Fades for more realistic-sounding fades.

## The best soundtrack we'll never use

**Road Diary**

New Orleans has a sound. That's because there's always music playing. It emanates from street corner bars and shotgun shacks, and it wafts across the French Quarter at all times of the day and night. On this particular Mardi Gras, we wound down from the parades by driving slowly through the uptown district, as the heat of the day was dissipating, and the marchers, the Wild Magnolias, the Wild Tchapatoulas, and the rest, were wending their way back home. We rolled down the windows and auto-dollied slowly down the narrow streets. Most of the time, we shot in old movie mode to create a timeless feel that would connect this Mardi Gras with the ancient heritage that is the legend of New Orleans. I thought about my dad, driving these same streets in the 1940s. Things probably hadn't changed much in this part of town. The feel was magical, dreamlike. What really made it magic for us was the music. Every block in uptown has a bar, a social club, or a house party going on. The doors are always flung open, and the music spills out into the streets. As we drove slowly around the neighborhood, this found music provided the perfect soundtrack for the funky visuals. As we came around a corner, we were bathed in a swath of "My Girl" by the Temptations. Round the next corner, it segued into "Mercy, Mercy" by Cannonball Adderly. Halfway down the block, that cross-faded into Dr. John singing "Iko, Iko." This went on all evening, as the sun set and the city settled into the never-ending song of its own nightlife.

Our video of that evening is great, but it loses a lot without the music. Bereft of its soundtrack, uptown looks like any other big city low-rent neighborhood. But we can't use the music. Why not? It's all about copyrights. Smokey Robinson wrote "My Girl," and Joe Zavinul wrote "Mercy, Mercy." No one knows who wrote "Iko, Iko." It's an African chant. But Dr. John's record label owns the rights to the master recording of his version of the song. So several rights are involved. (Refer back to Chapter 6 to learn about the rights of artists, record labels, and publishers.) Of course, we're mainly concerned with footage that will work well with our own songs, so we'll eventually use our uptown New Orleans clips with one of our tunes. But it won't, alas, be as funky as Dr. John singing "Iko, Iko."

# Panning and Balancing Audio Clips

Audio clips that are in mono can be panned full left, full right, or anywhere in between. Panning the sound places your audio clip in a specific location that coincides with the audio image. If you want to insert a voice-over but do not want to show the person speaking, you should pan that clip "up the middle." If you want to add the special audio effect of a car speeding by to go along with that visual image, you can pan the car engine sound to move with the visual image from left to right or vice versa.

Stereo clips are already set left and right, but you can adjust the balance by using the pan feature. Generally speaking, your music track should always remain balanced, with the blue pan line in the middle. To determine whether your audio clip is in stereo or mono, click that clip in the Project window. The Thumbnail view shows an audio waveform and all the audio information, including whether the clip is stereo or mono (see Figure 11-8).

**Figure 11-8:** Technical details, including stereo/mono information, are located in the Currently Selected Bin view of your Program window.

You can pan an audio clip in the Timeline using Premiere's *rubberbands*. The rubberband is the blue line that appears to run through an audio track when that track is expanded. (See Figure 11-9.)

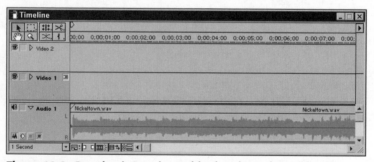

**Figure 11-9:** Premiere's Panning Rubberbands work just like the Volume Rubberbands.

To pan a mono audio clip or to balance a stereo audio clip, make sure that you can see the waveform of the expanded audio track(s) by reducing the Time Zoom level to two seconds or less. Then perform the following steps:

1. **Drag an audio clip from the Project window onto the Audio 1 track in the Timeline.**

2. **If the audio track is not yet expanded, do that now by clicking the Expand track button.**

3. **If the blue Pan rubberband is not showing, click the Display Pan Rubberband button.**

4. **Position your cursor over the Pan rubberband where you want to begin your pan.**

5. **Click the Pan rubberband, and rubberband *handle* appears, as shown in Figure 11-10.** (We call these "Panhandles!")

6. **Click that handle and drag it up to pan left or down to pan right.**

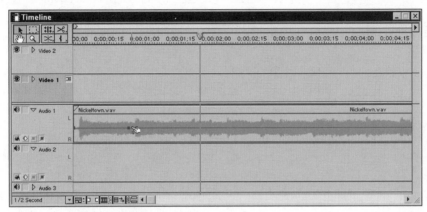

**Figure 11-10:** Panhandling with Premiere!

If you want to pan the overall audio clip and leave it in the panned position for the duration of the clip, you must set the handle at the beginning of the clip and the one at the end. To make sure that your pan is set the same at both ends, hold down the Shift key as you drag, to see the pan or balance in one-percent increments, as shown in Figure 11-11. Make sure that your pan placement is set the same at both handles.

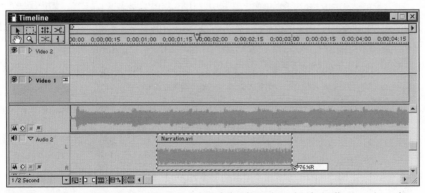

**Figure 11-11:** Hold down the Shift key while dragging the handles to view the pan or balance amount in one-percent increments.

The Audio Mixer window enables you to execute pans in real time, but you don't have as much control when you do it that way. However, you can monitor the volume and pan settings in the Audio Mixer window as you play the Timeline. Figure 11-12 shows the Audio Mixer controls for the spot marked by the Edit Line marker shown in Figure 11-11. Notice that the volume on track 1 is reduced 3.5 decibels (dB), and the panning on track 2 is 76% to the right. Remember to select Automation Write in the Audio Mixer window to hear your pan changes.

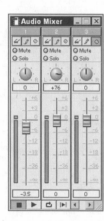

**Figure 11-12:** The Audio Mixer reflects pan and balance changes on the Timeline.

# Superimposing Sound Effects

You can superimpose incidental sounds the way a Foley sound team would add sound effects to a movie. If a rocket ship takes off in your video, you can add a track of noise — fire up the lawn mower!

To superimpose a sound effect:

1. **Make sure that your primary music clip is on track 1 of the Timeline.**

2. **Drag the Edit Line marker to where you want the sound effect to be audible.**

3. **Import the sound effect you want to use into your project by selecting File⇨Import⇨File and locating the audio file.**

4. **Drag the clip to track Audio 2 on the Timeline.**

5. **Move the sound effect clip by dragging and dropping it, placing it at the Edit Line Marker.**

6. **Listen to the track. You'll notice at this stage that both audio clips are at their normal volumes.**

7. **Make any fine-tuning adjustments to the placement of the sound effect by dragging it to the desired position in the Timeline.**

8. **Change the duration of the sound effect clip the same way you would change the duration of a video clip.** See Chapter 9 for details.

# Adding Voice-Over and Narration

Premiere's audio controls enable you to combine a variety of elements. For example, to create a presentation that includes video footage, a soundtrack song, and overlaid verbal messages, you can control the relative levels of the music and speech so that the soundtrack fades smoothly whenever the narrator speaks.

Premiere lets you easily add narration to your music video. Here's how:

1. **Make sure that your primary music clip is on track Audio 1 on the Timeline.**

2. **Drag the Edit Line marker to where you want the first narration to play.**

3. **Import the first narration clip into your project, as described in the section "Cross-Fading Between Two Audio Tracks," earlier in this chapter.**

4. **Drag the narration clip to the Audio 2 track on the Timeline.**

5. **Fine-tune the location by dragging the clip to the exact desired location.**

To make the narration stand out a bit more, you can reduce the level of the music slightly. To change the volume of the narration track:

1. **If the audio tracks are not yet expanded, do that now by clicking the Expand track button.**

2. **If the red Volume rubberband is not yet showing, click the Display Volume Rubberband button.**

3. **Position the selection tool over the rubberband at the point where the narration track begins and hold it until it turns into a pointing finger.**

4. **Click the rubberband.** A handle appears where the narration begins.

5. **Repeat Steps 3 and 4 to create another handle about five frames to the right of the first handle.**

6. **Hold down the Shift key while clicking and dragging the second handle downward.** By moving the handle this way, the volume changes display in decibels as well as in one percent increments, as shown in Figure 11-13.

7. **Create another pair of handles at the end of the Narration clip, the same way you did in Steps 3 and 4.**

8. **Repeat Step 6, dragging the handle to the same point as the one at the beginning of the clip.**

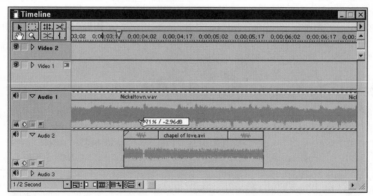

**Figure 11-13:** By holding down the Shift key while dragging a handle up or down, you can see the volume changes, in decibels, as well as 1 percent increments.

By performing the preceding steps, you can still hear the bed of your music but your voice-over narration stands out. Even though it alters the overall mix of the song, videographers occasionally use this technique to make their videos more cinematic.

## The screaming tollbooth project

**Road Diary**

Always keep the camera handy. When you're not setting up for a specific shoot, keep it loaded with a piece of trash tape that you can roll over without worrying. It's like a sketchbook. Even a simple act like getting on the New Jersey Turnpike can be worth shooting. As we approached the unmanned Exact Change booth one morning, we heard screaming. When we got there, we realized the tollbooth was screaming. Not someone inside the tollbooth but the *booth itself.* We guessed that some crackpot had planted a radio receiver in the booth, because the screaming seemed to respond to our double-take reaction. We assumed that some nut in a nearby tree was watching us.

With impatient drivers behind us, we eventually passed through the tollbooth. But you can bet that we took the first exit, and drove back to Hightstown, now filming a mock documentary loosely based on a popular low-budget horror "documentary" from a few years ago. After we passed through the still-shrieking booth a second time, Author held the camera lens up to her nose. "I'm soooo sorry," she sniffed. "I'm sooo sorry I brought everybody here, and now we're all gonna die." Although that footage won't be a blockbuster, we've got clips to cut away to if a band ever comes to us with a song about a screaming tollbooth!

# Chapter Replay

Now, after reading this chapter and following along with all the examples, you should be able to:

✦ Apply fade-ins and fade-outs to audio clips

✦ Cross-fade between two overlapping audio clips

✦ Pan and balance audio tracks

✦ Superimpose sound effects and voice-overs

In the next chapter, you discover how to apply Premiere's built-in video effects to your clips, and you see how similar the process is to applying audio effects.

✦　　✦　　✦

# Using Built-In Premiere Effects

◆ ◆ ◆ ◆

**In This Chapter**

Using video effects

Using keyframes

Superimposing images

Creating special effects with mattes

Using motion settings

◆ ◆ ◆ ◆

**P**remiere includes 74 different effects that you can use to impart style to your videos. In this chapter, we discuss how you can hype colors, posterize a clip, apply different types of distortion to an image, add a lens flare, modify the viewer's perspective, and more!

## Applying Video Effects

As shown in Figure 12-1, Premiere arranges effects within folders. You can click the Find Video Effect button, indicated by a binoculars icon, to search for a particular effect. You can even create a folder of your favorite effects by clicking the New Folder button. First, however, you should understand how to apply these effects to your video clips.

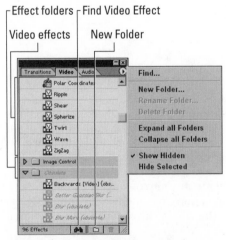

**Figure 12-1:** The Video Effects palette contains 14 folders with all types of video effects.

To apply a video effect to a clip, follow these steps:

1. **Choose Window➪Show Video Effects.**
2. **Drag the effect to the desired video clip on the Timeline.**

## Adjusting effect settings

Premiere gives you precise control of all effect parameters in your music video. Right after you drag an effect from the Video Effects palette, the Effect Controls palette offers options for you to tweak. Depending on the effect you use, the Effect Controls palette displays various sliders, buttons, setup options, and other controls, which you can use to customize your video effect settings (see Figure 12-2).

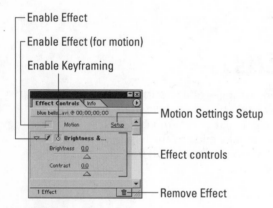

**Figure 12-2:** The Effect Controls palette pops up after you apply a video effect. Change settings in this window.

When working with video effects, you should expand your video track because a lot of information about the applied effects is visible only when the track is expanded. You can expand and collapse tracks at any time while working in Premiere. Figure 12-3 identifies all the elements of the Timeline that apply to video effects.

You can apply more than one video effect to any clip on any track in the Timeline. When you apply multiple effects to a clip, a pop-up menu appears on the left edge of the clip, listing all the effects applied to the clip in the order that they are rendered.

To change the order in which effects are rendered, perform the following steps:

1. **Select the video clip by clicking the clip in the Timeline with the Selection tool.**

2. **The Effect Controls palette displays controls for each effect that is applied on the selected clip. Click an effect in the corresponding Effect Controls palette.**

3. **Drag the effect to a new position in the list of effects.**

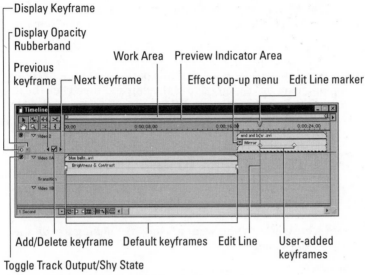

**Figure 12-3:** Keyframe elements of the Timeline.

## Previewing effects

Before you can see your video with all its applied effects, Premiere has to render the *work area*, the space between the work area bar markers in the line above the Preview Indicator area. When rendering, Premiere builds preview files for each clip that has an effect applied to it. When you apply an effect, the Preview Indicator area turns pink, indicating an effect that has not yet been rendered. You can simply press Enter (Return) to render the work area, or choose Timeline⇨Render Work Area from the menu. After Premiere renders the work area and builds a preview, the Preview Indicator area turns green, indicating that you can view the video with the rendered effect. After you've built the preview once, you don't have to build it again.

Depending on the number and complexity of the effects, the rendering process may take several minutes to complete. You can audition your effects by holding down the Alt (Option) key and dragging the Edit Line marker over the length of the clip. Your clip will not run smoothly, but it will give you an idea of how the effect looks using its current settings. You can then adjust the settings. When you're sure that the settings are correct, you can go through the more lengthy rendering process.

Cross-Reference    To adjust effect settings, see the section "Adjusting effect settings" earlier in this chapter.

## Deleting video effects

To delete a video effect, follow these steps:

1. **Select the clip by clicking it in the Timeline with Selection tool.**

2. **Click the Remove Effect button, indicated by a trashcan icon in the Effect Controls palette.** A dialog box appears asking if you want to delete the effect.

3. **Click Yes.**

If you have more than one video effect applied to a particular clip, select the effect from the Effect pop-up menu on the left edge of the clip and then click the Remove Effect button in the Effect Controls palette. Clicking Yes in the resulting dialog box deletes the effect.

## Copying effect and settings to another clip

If you're using an effect or set of effects whose settings you want again, you can copy the settings to another clip by following these steps:

1. **Select the clip whose effects you want to copy by clicking it with the Selection tool in the Timeline.**

2. **Choose Edit⇨Copy.**

3. **Select the clip or clips into which you want to paste the effects.**

4. **Choose Edit⇨Paste Attributes.** To perform this task on more clips, choose Edit⇨Paste attributes again until you've adjusted all the clips you want.

We use this feature a lot in our music videos, especially when *color hyping*, or saturating the colors, so that they are brighter than natural. Flashy music videos are more exciting (to us, anyway), so we often saturate colors. If you're using a lip-synched video clip and portions of the clip keep reappearing throughout the video, it's much simpler to set the Brightness and Contrast effect one time and use the Paste Attributes command than it is to redefine the settings in each of the clip's instances.

## Temporarily turning off effects

If you're applying more than one effect to a clip, you may want to temporarily turn off all effects other than the one whose attributes you're currently setting. To do this, follow these steps:

1. **Select the clip in the Timeline by clicking it with the Selection tool.**

2. **In the Effect Controls palette, click the Enable Effect button to disable the effect you want to disable.**

When you want to turn the effect back on, click the Enable Effect button again. The letter *f* reappears in the box.

## The great smoke bomb debacle

**Road Diary**

Some teenage buddies of ours are in a band. They were inspired by footage of The Who, back when they were in their prime. Their shows would end with an apocalyptic version of "My Generation," during which the action on stage would degenerate into unorchestrated, destructive chaos. It was wonderfully cathartic, back in the day, but would it play today at the local Steak and Sub? Our boys decided to try. They figured out the essential elements. Singer swings microphone into crowd. Guitarist switches to cheap pawnshop guitar and smashes it into the stage. While this is going on, the drummer kicks his drums over. And the bass player? He just keeps playing. The roadies, meanwhile, set off a small smoke bomb that sends a cloud wafting over the wreckage. That's where our local heroes ran into trouble. They decided to shoot a video of themselves at a local teen center. It was a small room that held maybe 50 or 60 people. They found old instruments worthy of sacrifice, and their drum tech volunteered to steal a smoke bomb from his granddad, a retired Naval Ordinance expert who kept a few Korean War souvenirs on a high shelf in the garage. These unfortunate lads violated rule number one: Never, *never* let the drum tech volunteer to do anything, especially if it involves theft. Forgetting this cardinal rubric, they bashed away merrily toward their big climax. When the time came, the guitarist smashed his pawnshop plank, the drummer kicked over his floor tom, and the drum tech? He'd neglected to read the specs printed on the smoke bomb. Remember, they were in a 50-seat club. The bomb was meant to completely blanket a battlefield of say, 30 acres, with impenetrable black smoke. Within seconds, well . . . use your imagination. The crowd ran out of the club as the fire department ran in, the video shoot was over, and the drum tech was in deep trouble with his grandpa. The moral of the story is, if you want to use pyrotechnics, don't. Feature films spend ungodly sums on insurance for this sort of thing, and The Who were climbing out of debt for several decades after their reign of terror. Besides, it's dangerous. Instead, have an actor look off screen and yell "Holy cow! There's a huge cloud of smoke headed this way!" Everybody runs. Study low-budget horror films for real examples.

You can also experiment with Premiere's effects. After you have read this chapter and have learned how to apply effects and set transparencies, try this:

1. Add the Brightness and Contrast effect to your clip, then set brightness keyframes to simulate a quick flash of light.

2. Now download the free *ReelFire 1* stock footage from Premiere's Web site at http://studio.adobe.com/expertcenter/premiere/goodies.html.

3. Place the stock footage in a superimpose track (2 or higher).

4. Key out the black background by setting a luminance key, and render the effects.

Voilà! A flash of a smoke bomb and resulting fire appears, all without necessitating any calls to the fire department!

# Types of Effects

Each effect has a different set of controls, and the best way to find out how they work is to use them. Although teaching the finer points of each effect lies outside the scope of this book, we attempt to describe our favorite effects to you here and give step-by-step instructions on using them.

## Adjust

The Adjust folder contains eight effects, including: Ripple, Brightness and Contrast, Channel Mixer, Color Balance, Convolution Kernel, Extract, Levels, and Posterize.

### Setting Brightness and Contrast

We use this effect frequently to enhance a clip's brightness. It's best used when you are trying to fit a low-contrast clip into a series of high-contrast clips. For example, Figure 12-4 shows a clip of an eel that was recorded inside a dark aquarium. We brightened up this clip by applying the Brightness and Contrast effect (see Figure 12-5). If you use too much of this effect, your clip will look grainy. If you look at any video shown on MTV today, chances are pretty good that the brightness and contrast have been adjusted.

**Figure 12-4:** This clip is so dark that the cute little eel in the frame is almost invisible.

Set the Brightness and Contrast effect by following these steps:

1. **Select the clip in the Timeline to which you want to apply this effect, by clicking the clip with the Selection tool.**

2. **Choose Window⇨Show Video Effects if that palette is not already visible on your desktop.**

3. **Drag the Brightness and Contrast effect from the Video Effects palette onto the clip in the Timeline.** The Effect Controls window pops up on your screen to reveal a Brightness slider and a Contrast slider, both with default settings at zero. To apply this effect, you have to change one or both of these slider settings.

4. **Make sure that the Enable Effect button is on.** The letter *f* indicates that it is on.

5. **An *x* appears in the Monitor window.** This *x* indicates that the preview must be rendered before you can see the final effect in motion. Hold down the Alt (Option) key while you slide the Edit Line over the clip to render-scrub, or manually scrub through the clip or program viewing effects. Render-scrubbing enables you to view the effect without having to wait for Premiere to fully render the effect in your program.

6. **Make any further adjustments, if desired.**

7. **To render the preview, drag the yellow work area bar in the Timeline over the portion of the program that you want to preview.**

8. **Press Enter (Return).** You can't view your clips with applied effects in real time until you render the preview.

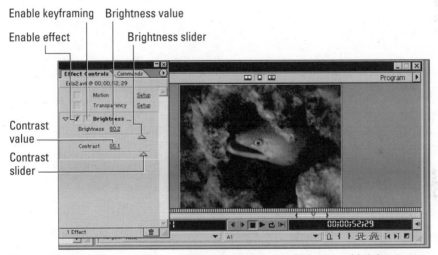

**Figure 12-5:** Use the Brightness and Contrast effect to lighten and brighten a dark clip.

## Setting Color Balance

You may choose to make the overall tone of your video heavy on one color. The TV series *Twin Peaks* was heavy on red. The movie *The Godfather* was heavy on yellow. You can adjust a clip that does not fit in to that scheme naturally by using the Color Balance effect. This effect has three Color sliders — Red, Green, and Blue — with ranges of 0–200. The default setting is 100 for each color. By increasing the value of any color, you increase the amount of that color in the clip. Moreover, if you want a purer red, you can increase the red while decreasing the green and blue. Experiment with mixing colors the way a painter would mix paints on a palette.

## Setting Levels

If you want more flexibility when adjusting brightness and contrast than you get when using the Brightness and Contrast effect, look no further. The Levels effect settings look a little more confusing, but after you get to know them, you'll probably use this effect more than the Brightness and Contrast effect.

In Figure 12-6, you can see that there's plenty of dark signal in our image. You can tell both by looking at the image in the screen on the right, and by looking at the graph itself. The bulk of the wave is down around the region of the black arrow. When you use the Brightness and Contrast effect, the adjustments you make affect the entire image. In other words, if you want to lighten an image, you don't necessarily want to lighten up the parts that are supposed to be dark, but that's what will happen. Using this effect, you can keep the shadows dark, while lightening up the midtones. Move the gray slider to change the midtone input levels.

Follow these steps to achieve proper brightness and contrast:

1. **Drag the Levels effect to a dark video clip that you want to lighten or brighten.** The Effect Controls window appears.

2. **Click Setup.** The Settings dialog box appears. Here you can select a channel whose levels you want to set. If you want to set the overall levels, select RGB Channels. A graph displays a black waveform on a white background. This wave indicates the levels from shadows (the section above the black arrow on the Input Levels slider), midtones (the section above the gray arrow in the middle of the Input Levels slider), and highlights (the section above the white arrow).

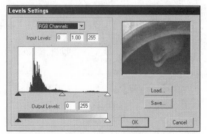

**Figure 12-6:** The Levels effect offers much more control when setting brightness and contrast than the Brightness & Contrast effect.

3. **Drag the white slider to change the highlight input levels.**

4. **Drag the black slider to change the dark input levels.**

5. **On the Output Level slider, drag the black arrow to set the dark output level.**

6. **Drag the white arrow to set the light output level.**

# Blur

The Blur folder contains seven different blurring effects, including our favorites: Camera Blur, which simulates the way a camera blurs images that come in and out of focus, Fast Blur, which is the best overall blur to use due to its high quality and quick rendering time, and Radial Blur, described here.

The Radial Blur makes your figure look like it's in the center of a cyclone. The default amount of blur is 10, and the default center of the blur is the center of the clip. You can change both of these settings. You can also change the Blur Method to a Zoom blur, rather than the default Spin blur.

To apply a Radial Blur effect, follow these steps:

1. **Drag the Radial Blur effect from the Video Effects Palette to the clip on the Timeline.** The Radial Blur pop-up menu appears on your screen.

2. **Make the desired settings adjustments and click OK.** See Figure 12-7 for Radial Blur controls.

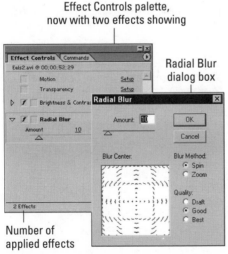

**Figure 12-7:** Radial Blur controls

3. **If your Effect Controls palette was not showing before, it appears, revealing the newly added effect.** Any other effect previously applied to the clip — in our case Brightness and Contrast — is indicated in the Effect Controls palette.

4. **Render-scrub or render preview by holding down the Alt (Option) key while you drag the Edit Line marker over the clip.**

5. **Make any further adjustments.**

6. **Press Enter (Return) to render the preview,**

## Distort

The ten effects in the Distort folder bend the image in some way. The Distort folder contains the Bend, Lens Distortion, Mirror, Pinch, Polar Coordinates, Shear, Spherize, Twirl, Wave, and ZigZag effects. Our favorite effect in this folder is Mirror, described here.

The Mirror effect is our favorite Distort effect. The Mirror effect enables you to define a reflecting center and a reflecting angle of your clip to produce a mirrored image within your clip. This effect excels at livening up a scene and providing visual interest where it is lacking.

To apply the Mirror effect to a clip, follow these steps:

1. **Drag the Mirror effect to the clip you want to alter in the Timeline.**

2. **Click the Reflection Center grid, as shown in Figure 12-8.** A crosshair appears in your Monitor window.

**Figure 12-8:** Mirror controls include a Reflection Center coordinates setting and a Reflection Angle setting.

3. **Drag the crosshair to the desired reflection center.** Wait while Premiere processes this effect. Figure 12-9 shows the results of using this effect.

4. **Now click the Reflection Angle number in the Effect Controls palette.** The Edit Reflection Angle dialog box appears.

5. **Type the desired reflection angle in the Value text box.**

6. **Click OK.**

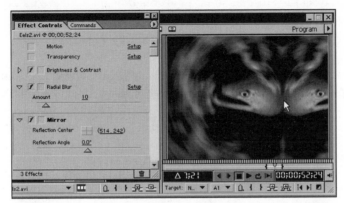

**Figure 12-9:** Set the Reflection Center by clicking the desired coordinates in the Monitor window.

# Image Control

The Image Control folder contains eight effects: Black & White, which turns any color clip into a black-and-white clip, Color Balance, which enables you to adjust hue, lightness and saturation of a clip, Color Pass, which allows a defined color to pass through, while rendering all other colors to black and white, and Color Replace. All of these effects control color and shading.

## Setting Color Pass

This effect works really great if you shoot a scene in which you know in advance you're going to apply a Color Pass effect. A Color Pass effect removes all colors but the specified color that it is allowed through. All the other colors are converted to grayscale. To apply this effect dramatically, first shoot a scene where you carefully select only one item of its color to be included in the shot. Perhaps, for example, the lead singer has bright red lipstick, but there is no other bright red in the shot. Maybe there's a red rose. In editing, if you apply a Color Pass effect to convert everything but bright red to grayscale, you end up with a pretty dramatic shot.

Follow these steps to apply the Color Pass effect:

1. **Place a clip on the Timeline that has one highly contrasting color that is easily isolated.** (See Chapter 8 to learn about placing clips on the Timeline.)

2. **If the Video Effects palette is not visible on your computer screen, choose Window⇨Show Video Effects.**

3. **Apply the Color Pass effect by dragging it from the Effects palette onto the clip.** The clip in the Monitor window then turns to grayscale before you can make any adjustments.

4. **Click and drag the Edit Line marker across the clip until the natural color is restored.**

5. **Click the Eyedropper tool in the Color Pass Effects palette.** If the Eyedropper tool is not visible, scroll down the Effects palette.

6. **Move the Eyedropper tool over the Program monitor, and click the one color that you want to remain in the shot while all the other colors convert to grayscale.**

7. **Now drag the Similarity slider until you achieve the desired result.**

We love this effect. Check out Maxwell's video for "Fortunate" sometime to see a great example of this kind of filtering.

## Color Replace

By using the Color Replace effect, you can select any color within the clip, such as the drummer's dingy, gray T-shirt and replace it with something that looks, well, cleaner . . . like a nice mauve. Follow these steps to use the Color Replace effect:

1. **Choose Window⇨Show Video Effects, if the Video Effects palette is not visible on your computer screen.**

2. **Drag the Color Replace effect to your clip in the Timeline.** The Effect Controls palette reveals the Color Replace settings. The default Similarity setting is 8, and the available range is 0–100. Premiere provides a Target Color picker and a Replace Color picker, with an Eyedropper next to each. Premiere's default Target Color is red, and the default Replace Color is blue, but you can change both of these default color settings.

3. **Click the Target Color Eyedropper tool, shown in Figure 12-10.**

4. **Move the Eyedropper tool over your clip in the Monitor window and click the color that you want to target.**

5. **Now click either the Replace Color swatch or the Replace Color Eyedropper tool and pick the color with which you want to replace the target color.**

6. **Drag the Similarity slider right to allow for color replacement of a broader shade range of the target color.** If desired, you can make the replacement colors solid by clicking the Setup link beside Color Replace. Click the Solid Colors button in the Color Replace Settings dialog box. You'll see your original image in the left screen, and your edited image in the right screen. You can also make further adjustments, if needed.

7. **Click OK in the Color Replace Settings dialog box.**

**Figure 12-10:** Click the Eyedropper tool to select a color from your clip.

When working with effects, after you have applied two or more effects, the effect you're adjusting reflects the effects you've already applied. You can turn these off without erasing the image by clicking the Enable Effect box (the one with the *f* in it). You can leave the effects disabled until you're done tweaking and then turn them on again with a single mouse click.

## Perspective

The five effects in the Perspective folder deal with various forms of 3D settings, including: Basic 3D, and Drop Shadow. Use these two effects on images that contain an alpha channel, like text or line art created in another graphics program. You can also use these effects on Premiere titles.

### Basic 3D

Follow these steps to apply a Perspective effect, Basic 3D:

1. **Choose File⇔New⇔Title.**

2. **Click the Type tool.**

3. **Position the Type tool in the window and type** Wow!

4. **Click Object Color swatch.**

5. **Click the white box to change the type from black to white.** The text appears to have disappeared, but it's still there.

6. **Click Save, and name the file.**

7. **Choose File⇔Close to close the Title window.**

8. **In the Project window, drag that Wow! title clip onto the Timeline's Video 2 track.** Make sure that another clip is at the same point in the Timeline on track Video 1.

9. **Open the Video Effects palette by choosing Window⇔Show Video Effects.**

10. Drag the Basic 3D effect to the "Wow!" title.

11. Click the Enable Keyframes button so that a stopwatch appears in the box.

12. Drag the Swivel slider all the way to the left.

13. Drag the Distance to Image slider all the way to the right.

14. Click the Next Keyframe arrow to advance to the end keyframe.

15. Slide the Swivel slider all the way to the right.

16. Click the Distance To Image value (the underlined number) and type -80.

17. Render-scrub, or perform a full render by pressing the Enter (Return) key.

Now watch the word Wow! spin up and out of your video clip!

### Drop Shadow

By applying a Drop Shadow effect to a title, you're adding the contrast you need around the lettering to make it stand out from the clip.

1. **Choose Window⇨Show Video Effects to open the Effects palette.**

2. **Drag the Drop Shadow effect from the Video Effect palette onto a title clip in the Timeline.**

3. **You can adjust opacity, direction, distance, and softness and pick a color besides black for the shadow.** Keep the default settings for now.

4. **Render-scrub or perform a full render to see the resulting effect.**

## Pixillate

The Pixillate folder has three effects — Crystallize, Facet, and Pointillize — that texturize the video image. You can adjust the cell size in both the Crystallize and Pointillize effects, but the Facet effect is either on or off and has no further adjustments available.

You can see a good example of a pixillating effect used with a keyframe, which gradually applies the effect, in our video "Pick You Up," found on the CD-ROM included with this book. At 2:18, a shot of a vintage mixing console slowly crystallizes before your eyes. This is the effect that we used.

## QuickTime

The QuickTime folder contains only one effect, but if you apply that effect to a video clip, a Select Effect dialog box containing 15 QuickTime-supported effects appears. Some of the effects are redundant to Premiere's effects, but some, like Film

Noise, Fire, and Cloud, are useful. These are all animated effects. Film Noise super-imposes lines to make your video look like old stock movie footage, while changing the image to black and white. Both the Fire and Cloud effects can be applied to an image. For you to be able to see the fire or clouds moving on top of your image, you'll need to set a key to key out the background. Fire needs a black background, and Cloud needs a blue background.

**Cross-Reference**

See the section "Creating Special Effects with Mattes" to learn how to use keys.

## Render

The Render folder contains only one effect, Lens Flare. The Lens Flare effect makes your clip look like you filmed your shot aiming toward the sun. You can define the lens type, the level of brightness of the flare, and the placement of the flare on your image. If you wanted to shoot a video of, say, a surf musician, but he wouldn't come out of his sand-filled bedroom, you could apply a lens flare to give the illusion that he was really at the beach. To do this:

1. **Choose Window⇨Show Video Effects to open the Effects palette.**

2. **Drag the Lens Flare effect to your clip on the Timeline.** If the Effect Controls palette was not already opened, it will appear. Leave Brightness set at 100 for now.

3. **Choose the Lens Type options that you prefer.**

4. **In the Flare Center area, drag the crosshair to where you want the flare to shine.**

5. **Click OK.** Figure 12-11 illustrates the Lens Flare controls and the finished effect using them produces.

**Figure 12-11:** Lens Flare effect settings include Brightness, Flare Center, and Lens Type.

# Stylize

The Stylize folder contains 12 varied effects — Alpha Glow, Find Edges, Replicate, and Strobe Light.

## Alpha Glow

You can use the Alpha Glow with good effect on text or other images containing an alpha channel. This effect adds a glow around the edges of the alpha channel

To apply the Alpha Glow effect, follow these steps:

1. **Choose Window⇨Show Video Effects to open the Effects palette.**

2. **Drag the Alpha Glow effect from the Video Effects palette onto a Title clip in the Timeline.**

3. **You can adjust the Glow and Brightness settings, but the defaults should work fine for now.**

4. **If you want a glow other than white, select one from the color picker or from the Eyedropper tool.**

5. **Render-scrub to see the results.**

## Find Edges

This effect is pretty cool. It renders a kind of line drawing from an image. The look is quite impressionistic. Although overuse of this effect is not a good thing, it may have a place in your personal favorite effects folder.

To apply the Find Edges effect, follow these steps:

1. **Choose Window⇨Show Video Effects to open the Effects palette.**

2. **Drag the Find Edges effect to your clip. The Effect Controls palette opens, if it was not previously.**

3. **Drag the Blend with Original slider to the right for a more natural, blended look or keep it at zero for the most radical effect.** The default setting is 0%, and the available range is 0–100.

4. **Click the Invert button to invert colors.**

5. **Render-scrub or render preview to view.**

**Cross-Reference**

See "Previewing effects," earlier in this chapter, for more information on previewing effects.

## Replicate

The Replicate effect is fun and easy to use. What's more, this is an effect that we've seen from time to time on MTV videos and shouted, "I can do that!" Remember those old Breck shampoo commercials? One lady tells her two friends about Breck, and they tell two friends, and so on? That's the Replicate effect at work in all its retro glory.

To apply the Replicate effect, follow these steps:

1. **Choose Window⇨Show Video Effects to open the Effects palette.**

2. **Drag the Replicate effect from the Video Effects palette to your clip.** The default count is two, which means that there are two figures by two figures, for a total of four replicants. The range is 2 to16.

3. **Drag the slider to add more replicants.** See Figure 12-12 for a truly frightening image of four replicated eels with lens flare!

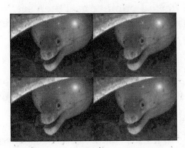

**Figure 12-12:** By choosing a count of 2 in the Replicate Settings window, you are defining your image to display two across and two down, or a total of four. Likewise, a 3 count results in nine images, and a 4 count results in 16 images.

## Strobe Light

The Strobe Light has been used as a rock and roll video effect since the '60s, when light show-loving hippies discovered the Chaplinesque effect it had on stage movement. There are quite a number of settings in this effect, including Strobe Light Color, where you can pick a color from the picker or with the Eyedropper tool), Blend With Original, Strobe Duration, Strobe Period, Random Strobe Probability, Strobe setting (Operates on Color or Makes Layer Transparent), and Strobe Operator. The default settings of one half-second strobe every second are not nearly frenetic enough for rock and roll.

Try these settings for a classic look:

1. **Choose Window⇨Show Video Effects to open the Effects palette.**

2. **Drag the Strobe Light effect to your clip.**

3. **In the Effect Controls palette, click the Strobe Color picker and select black.** The reason we do this is because with a natural strobe light, bright, white light is flashed on a subject, illuminating it quickly and then just as quickly turning off so that we're temporarily blinded — everything seems to go black for an instant. With the Strobe effect, the default setting is white but when the white "light" flashes, it doesn't illuminate anything. In a sense, it's backwards from a traditional strobe light. By picking black as our strobe color, we can simulate that moment where everything is suddenly black. Using a brightly lit image with the Strobe effect is best because it too simulates the strobe light hitting the subject.

4. **Keep blend with original at 0%, the default setting.**

5. **Double-click the underlined Strobe Duration number and select .09 seconds in the resulting Edit Strobe Duration dialog box.** *Strobe duration* is the amount of time that the black strobe will last each time it flashes.

6. **Click OK.**

7. **Double-click the underlined Strobe Period number and then set your strobe to flash every .15 seconds in the resulting Edit Strobe Period dialog box.** *Strobe period* is the time cycle of the strobe.

8. **Keep all other settings at their default values.**

9. **Because render-scrubbing doesn't give you a very good idea of how your strobe will look, you have to render a preview by dragging the Work Area bar over your clip and then pressing Enter (Return).**

Tip

To enhance your Strobe Light effect, add in a Lens Flare effect as described earlier in this chapter's "Render" section. You will need Premiere to process the Lens Flare before the Strobe, or else the flare will be superimposed not only on the video clip but on the black strobes, as well. You can easily rearrange the effects in the Effect Controls window. Simply click the effect you want to move, and drag it up or down.

# Transform

This folder contains ten extremely useful effects, including our favorites: Crop, Horizontal Flip, Image Pan, Roll, and Vertical Flip. Transform effects enable you to film from one vantage point, but make your footage look like it came from more than one camera simply by cropping, panning, or changing the camera view. We've used this effect quite a bit.

## Crop

If you're making a video of the neighbor kids' band and you find out during editing that Dad's banjo was left in the corner of the shot, tell the kids not to worry! You can crop it out by doing the following:

1. **Choose Window⇨Show Video Effects to open the Effects palette.**

2. **Drag the Crop effect from the Video Effects palette to the clip you want cropped.**

3. **Drag the sliders until you get the right cropping.** You have controls to crop the top, bottom, left, and right. In general, you need two perpendicular controls to the same percentages to keep the images ratios in tact. In other words, if you crop the top 10 percent, you should crop either the right or left side the same amount. If you crop the right side 15 percent, you need to crop the top or bottom the same amount.

4. **Render-scrub or render a preview to see the clip in action with the cropping applied.**

### Horizontal and Vertical Flip

These effects contain no controls — they're either applied (on) or not (off), so set up is easy. Simply drag the effect to the clip and render as usual. See our "Nickeltown" video on the CD-ROM for an example of using Horizontal Flip. At 00:50, Pete points his hand. The hand is coming from the right side of the screen. This exact shot is revisited 1:42, but this time, the hand sticks out from the left side of the screen.

### Image Pan

Image Pan is a wonderful tool to use if you only have one camera on a tripod, but you want to give the footage different depth. Because we shoot our own videos, we use this tool quite often. In the video for "Free" (included on this book's companion CD-ROM), all the shots of us in front of the colorful TV studio set were shot on a single tripod. We set up the tripod, pressed Record, and then lip-synched the song. The panning effect was achieved during editing.

To set the Image Pan effect, follow these steps:

1. **Choose Window⇨Show Video Effects to open the Effects palette.**

2. **Drag Image Pan from the Video Effects window to the desired clip in the Timeline.**

3. **Click the underlined Setup link in the Effect Controls window.**

4. **Drag the handles from the Source window until you have the desired end pan shot.**

5. **Click OK.**

If you render the preview now, you will still have a static shot, but the image is cropped. But how do we make the clip appear as though the camera is panning? By setting a *keyframe*. We discuss keyframes later in this chapter in detail (see "Using Keyframes"), where we describe how you set motion to an Image Pan effect.

### Roll

We used the Roll effect in our video for "Free," which you can play on the companion CD-ROM. At about six seconds into the song, drummer Vinnie Santoro seems to roll across the screen while he plays. You can set the Roll effect to move the clip left to right, right to left, top to bottom, or bottom to top.

## Video

This folder contains three technical effects: Broadcast Colors, Field Interpolate, and Reduce Interlace Flicker. The Broadcast Colors effect is one that you should know about. Computers can reproduce colors at a far greater resolution than can consumer video equipment. If your videos are for CD-ROM, Web streaming, or download only, you don't need to worry about this feature. However, if you plan to export your music video to tape or distribute it to television stations, you absolutely need to know about this feature.

When we asked music video producer and television editor Joe Hansard to tell us the number one problem to avoid when mastering a video he said, "Make sure that the video colors aren't saturated. The video should be clean and bright but never hot or overmodulated." Joe knows what he's talking about. He produced an Emmy winning music video in the early 1980s and is one of Washington, D.C.'s most in-demand television editors.

Luckily, Premiere provides the Broadcast Colors effect. Television signal amplitude is measured in IRE units, with 120 IRE being the maximum possible level for transmission.

To apply the Broadcast Colors effect to a clip, follow these steps:

1. **Choose Window⇨Show Video Effects to open the Effects palette.**

2. **Drag Broadcast Colors effect to any clip that you think you may have over-saturated with effects.**

3. **Select NTSC for Broadcast Locale, if your video will be formatted and viewed in North America or Japan.** Select PAL if your video is for Western European or South American audiences.

4. **Select the Reduce Luminance option in the How To Make Color Safe box.** This is Premiere's default setting and offers the most transparent result.

5. **The default setting for Maximum Signal is 110.** We told you that 120 is the maximum possible level, but you should bring that level down a tad. Adobe chose 110 as the default level because it is conservative but effective.

Be sure to render the preview before exporting to tape.

# Using Keyframes

You can choose to either apply an effect to the entire clip or to have it change over time with the use of *keyframes*. Keyframes are markers that contain sets of values for each of the effect's controls and apply those values to the clip at a specific point in time. By default, Premiere applies a beginning and ending keyframe to each clip after the effect is applied. These keyframes have the same values, so they don't change over the duration of the clip. But you can set the values differently at different keyframes so that they change over time. What's more, Premiere automatically blends the settings over time so that the changes happen smoothly.

You can apply keyframes to most of Premiere's video effects, but some of them are not keyframeable. For example, both the Black & White and Ghosting effects are either on or off, but you can't change the effect over time. You can tell if an effect is keyframeable by looking at the Effect Controls palette. If it is keyframeable, a small Enable Keyframing box is displayed next to the name of the effect in the Effect Controls palette. When you click this box, a stopwatch icon displays.

If you apply an effect to a clip on track Video 1, a light blue keyframe line appears along the length of the clip with the name of that effect appearing above the line. If you apply an effect to a clip on track Video 2 or higher, you need to click the Effect Keyframe button to see the Keyframe line (and name of effect). You cannot see the Opacity rubberbands and the Keyframe line at the same time, but you can toggle between the two by clicking the appropriate button.

If you add more than one effect to a single clip, the Effect pop-up menu appears at the left edge of the clip. When you click this menu and select the effect you want to work with, the Effect Controls palette displays the controls for that effect, and the Keyframe line of the clip in the Timeline displays only the keyframes for the selected effect.

## Increasing or decreasing an effect over time

If you want to slowly add in an effect over time, you only need to use the two default Keyframes — one at the beginning of the clip, and one at the end. Premiere represents the default keyframes as white rectangles at both ends of the clip. The default setting is the same for both Keyframes when you first apply an effect. To change the settings:

1. **Click the Previous Keyframe or Next Keyframe arrow to move the edit line to the Keyframe at the beginning of the clip.**

2. **Make sure that the Enable Keyframing button is selected in the Effect Controls palette (a stopwatch displays in the box if it is).** When you enable Keyframing, the rectangular Keyframe buttons turn into half-diamonds.

3. **Now make the desired settings adjustments to the first keyframe.** Tweak it until you're happy with the way that the first keyframe looks.

4. **Now click the Next Keyframe arrow to move your edit line to the end keyframe.**

5. **Make the necessary settings adjustments in the Effect Controls palette.**

Remember, you're setting the way the very last moment in the clip will look. Premiere will automatically interpolate the effect between keyframes so that the effect will gradually progress from the first Keyframe effect settings to the second Keyframe effect settings.

If you don't want your effect to kick in right away, you can move the starting keyframe laterally in the Timeline by dragging it. The blue line turns black to the left of the Keyframe button and remains blue to the right, indicating that the effect is applied starting at the Keyframe button (see Figure 12-13).

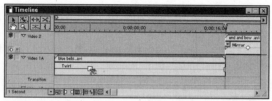

**Figure 12-13:** To start the video effect at a point other than the first frame of the clip, click and drag the first Keyframe button. The black line to the left of the button indicates that the effect does not affect that portion of the clip.

This exercise shows how to set an Image Pan effect into motion and enables you to give panning motion to a stationary shot.

1. **Choose Window⇨Show Video Effects to open the Effects palette.**

2. **Apply the Image Pan effect to the video clip of your choice.**

3. **In the Effect Controls palette, click the Enable Keyframing box.** It's the one just to the left of the words Image Pan. You should see a tiny stopwatch appear in the box.

4. **Expand the Video Track, if it's not already expanded, by clicking the triangle to the left of the track so that it points down and displays hidden information about the track.**

5. **If your clip is in Video Track 1, you'll see a blue Keyframe line that runs the length of the clip.** If your clip is in Video Track 2 or higher, you'll need to click the Display Keyframes button to toggle from the red Opacity rubberband, to the blue Keyframes line.

6. **Now click the first Keyframe handle. That's the little white triangle at the beginning of the blue Keyframe line.**

7. **Click Setup in the Effect Controls window under the Image Pan effect.**

8. **Set the first clip so that it contains the entire shot.** In other words, make sure that all handles are fully extended to the borders of the shot.

9. **Click OK.**

10. **Now click the Next Keyframe arrow (that's the one on the right) to move to the ending keyframe.**

11. **Click Setup in the Effect Controls window under the Image Pan effect again to set controls for the final frame of the clip.**

12. **Drag the handles to contain the final clip.**

13. **Click OK.**

14. **Render-scrub the preview by holding down Alt (Option) and dragging the Edit Line across the clip in the Timeline.**

15. **Make any tweaking adjustments to your starting or ending keyframes.**

16. **Render the preview to watch the clip with full effects applied in real time, by pressing the Enter (Return) key.**

## Creating complex effect changes over time

You can set multiple keyframes of different values anywhere within a clip. Your effect can increase and decrease, or you can fade one keyframed effect in while another one fades out. Premiere does not limit the number of effects or keyframes for each effect that you use.

To set additional keyframes within your clip, follow these steps:

1. **First make sure that the enable Keyframing button is selected and showing the stopwatch in the Effect Controls palette.**

2. **Move the Edit Line marker to the point in the clip where you want to change the Keyframe settings.**

3. **Now make the appropriate settings changes in the Effect Controls palette.**

You will have to wait a second or two while the keyframe is set. After it's set, you'll notice a diamond along the Timeline at the point of your Edit Line. You can set as many keyframes as you want in this way. You can also adjust the placement of the keyframes simply by dragging them left or right along the Timeline.

### Adjusting keyframe values

After you set the keyframes, you can adjust their values by clicking the Previous Keyframe or the Next Keyframe arrow on the left side of the Timeline. The video clip must be selected for these arrows to be displayed. The Effect Controls palette reflects the settings values for the current keyframe.

### Changing effect settings by adding keyframes

You can also add a keyframe by placing your edit line at the point where you want to add a keyframe and clicking the Add/Delete Keyframe button.

## Deleting keyframes

You can delete a single keyframe by moving the edit line to the keyframe you want to delete (by using the arrows) and clicking the Add/Delete Keyframe button between the arrows.

 If you want to delete all keyframes, aside from the default keyframes at the beginning and end of a clip, click the Enable Keyframing button to make the stopwatch icon disappear.

# Superimposing Images

You can adjust the opacity of any clip in track Video 2 or higher. (You cannot, however, adjust Video 1's opacity.) By adjusting opacity, you can create transitions between tracks, make composites of two or more video tracks, or create special effects by keying out portions of one clip so that a track underneath it shows through. The opacity is set by selecting the clip and then choosing Clip⇨Video Options⇨Transparency. Opacity set to 100% means that nothing shows through the track, and 0% provides full transparency. By adjusting the opacity to somewhere in between, you can create interesting composites.

## Fading transparencies into a clip

If you have clips in both the Timeline's Video 1 and Video 2 tracks, only the clip in track Video 2 appears when you press Play in the Monitor window. Premiere calls the Video 2 track a *superimpose track*, and any clip in the superimpose track takes priority because the default Opacity setting for superimpose tracks is 100%.

Nothing shows through the clip on the superimpose track unless you decrease the track's opacity. After you adjust the superimpose track's opacity, you will only be able to view the clip on the Video 1 track until the preview files have been rendered.

If you created a title in Chapter 10, you may recall that Titles use alpha channels, which are transparent. In that case, only the text is at 100% opacity. You can learn more about alpha channels and other types of keys in "Creating Special Effects with Mattes" later in this chapter.

To see transparencies fade into an effect, take a look at the QuickTime video for "Pick You Up" on the CD-ROM. Play the video until you get to the first verse (42 seconds into the video). As the figure walks down the long hallway, a face is superimposed over the clip. It seems to fade in and fade out, in a kind of ghostly manner. Although this device doesn't move you from one clip to another, it fades into a composite and back out again.

Follow these steps to superimpose a clip over another:

1. **In the Timeline, place a clip in track Video 1.**

2. **Place another clip in track Video 2 at the same point.** You may adjust the lengths of the video clips to have the same duration if you choose. (See Chapter 9 to learn about editing clips in the Timeline.)

3. **Expand the Video 2 track (see Chapter 9).**

4. **Click the red Display Opacity Rubberbands icon.** The red Opacity rubberband appears along the Video 2 track.

5. **Locate both the beginning and ending Opacity rubberband handles, as shown in Figure 12-14.**

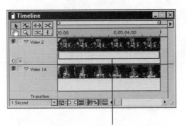

**Figure 12-14:** Premiere automatically places two default Opacity rubberband handles on all clips in the superimpose tracks. The default opacity setting is 100%.

Default Opacity rubberband handles

6. **While holding down the Shift key, click the starting Opacity rubberband handle.** You should see a percentage of 100 appear next to the pointing finger icon.

7. **Drag the handle down to 0% opacity.**

8. **Drag the cursor over the Opacity rubberband until it turns into a pointing finger.**

9. **Click the Opacity rubberband with the pointing finger a couple of seconds into your video clip.** A new Opacity Rubberband handle appears.

10. **While holding down the Shift key, drag this new handle upward until the opacity percentage reaches around 50.**

11. **Click the Opacity rubberband a second or two from the end of the clip to create a new handle.**

12. **While holding down the Shift key, drag this handle downward until it, too, reaches 50% opacity.**

13. **Finally, drag the end Opacity rubberband handle to the bottom to 0% opacity.**

14. **Press the spacebar to play the video clip.** A small *x* appears in a box in the upper-left corner of your Monitor window, indicating that the work area needs to be rendered before you can view the composite clip. Figure 12-15 shows you what your Timeline and Monitor windows should look like up to this point.

**Figure 12-15:** The clip in the Video 2 track is set to gradually superimpose the clip in track Video 1A before fading out.

To remove an Opacity rubberband handle, click the handle and drag it up or down and beyond the borders of the clip's track.

You're surely wondering how this composite looks! You have two choices as to how to do this. If you think you may have more tweaking to do, you can save some rendering time by performing a render-scrub. Do this by holding down the Alt (Option) key while dragging the Edit Line marker across the Timeline. Render-scrubbing shows you how the two clips blend. If you like what you see, you can press Enter (Return) to generate a preview so that you can see the composite in fully rendered motion. The *x* disappears from the Monitor window when the preview has been built.

When you click the spacebar to play the video, track Video 1's clip plays by itself, and the Video 2 track's clip gradually fades in and holds, creating a composite between the two video clips. Finally, the Video 2 track's clip slowly fades out at the end.

## Make composites of two or more video tracks

You don't need to use fades with your composite tracks, although fades are quite effective. If you want to adjust the overall opacity of a clip in the Video 2 track or higher, follow these steps:

1. **Select the clip.**

2. **Select the Fade Adjustment tool.**

3. **Move your cursor over the Opacity rubberband until it changes into the Fade Adjustment tool.**

4. **Drag the rubberband to the setting you want.** If you hold down the Shift key while you do this, you can see the opacity percentage.

You can preview your work in two ways. First, render-scrub by holding down the Alt (Option) key while dragging the Edit Line marker across the clip. Alternatively, you can press the Enter (Return) key to render a preview.

# Creating Special Effects with Mattes

Do you remember the old *Superman* TV shows where the hero flies through the air? You probably know that having the actor lie on a table in front of a blue background created that special effect. The blue was later keyed out in post-production, and the sky, birds, planes, and treetops were added in where the blue screen had been. This technique demonstrates another type of transparency. Only clips in the *superimpose* tracks — track Video 2 and higher — can have keying applied to them.

## Compositing, keys, and mattes

Keys and mattes can be a little confusing, so here are the definitions and example of uses for the terms used in this section.

*Compositing* is a method of combining tracks to make one clip look natural in a new setting. Sometimes you can composite a scene that looks supernatural by placing a rock singer, for example, on the planet Mars or Superman flying across the sky. In either case, you shoot the subject in front of a solid screen and then key out that screen. This particular video clip must be placed in the Video 2 track or higher. You simply place a clip of scenery on track Video 1, render the previews, and voilà!

You'll be swimming with Ringo in his Octopus' Garden in the waves, flying like Superman with R.E.M., or hitching a ride on the Galaxy Express with The Kennedys! If you want to see a great example of a composite being built, rent the video *It's A Mad, Mad, Mad, Mad World.* Make sure that you get the one with bonus behind-the-scenes footage at the end.

*Keys* are tools that make defined parts of the clip transparent while maintaining the other part of the clip at full opacity. You define keys in several ways, including using color, brightness, and other factors. When you key out a color or level of brightness, you make that color or level of brightness transparent while maintaining the opacity of the rest of the clip. Premiere provides 15 key types, found in the Transparency Settings dialog box. To open this dialog box, your clip must first be placed in a transparency track (Video 2 track or higher), and selected with the Selection tool. Choose Clip⇨Video Options⇨Transparency.

*Mattes* are areas defined to be transparent, behind which a background video clip plays. You can use an image that you have created in any program that can save the image in a Premiere-supported format. See Table 6-1 in Chapter 6 for supported graphics files.

## Chroma key

A chroma key enables you to define a color or range of colors to key out. This type of key helps you when you're using footage shot against a shadowy screen, or, say, a relatively uniform sky. The Chroma key controls include Similarity, Blend, Threshold, Cutoff, and Smoothing.

To apply a chroma key, follow these steps:

1. **Shoot a clip of your subject against a uniform background.** For example, try shooting an airplane in the sky on a day when the colors look fairly uniform — not a lot of cumulonimbus.

2. **Shoot any other scene that you would like to place the subject into.** Try taping a shot of the band running across a field.

3. **Start a new project in Premiere by choosing File⇨New Project.**

4. **Capture the clips from your camcorder (see Chapter 6).**

5. **Drag the subject clip to the Video 2 track.**

Note    The clip you place in Track 2 can be either a motion clip or a still image.

6. **Drag the shot of the band running across the field in the Video 1 track.**

7. **Click the subject track.**

8. **Choose Clip⇨Video Options⇨Transparency.** See Figure 12-16 for the Transparency Settings window.

9. **Select Chroma from the Key Type drop-down list.**

10. **Move your mouse pointer into the Color window.** The pointer turns into an Eyedropper tool.

11. **Click the background (any part of the clip other than the subject).** If you shot video of an airplane as your subject, click on the surrounding blue sky.

12. **Drag the Similarity slider to the right until the clip of the band running across the field comes into view where the blue sky once was in the Sample window.**

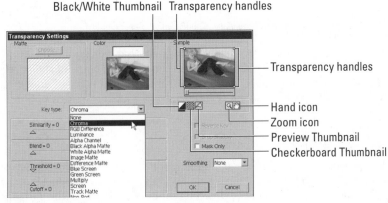

**Figure 12-16:** The Transparency Settings dialog box enables you to select one of fourteen different key types.

 13. **Click the Black/White thumbnail to toggle between white and black.** When you do this, Premiere replaces the transparent areas with either white or black, depending on where the thumbnail is toggled. Doing this helps you set transparency levels by enabling you to see the effect in black and white.

 14. **Now click the Checkerboard thumbnail.** This does the same thing as Step 13, except that it enables you to see your transparent areas with a checkerboard fill.

 15. **Now click the Preview thumbnail.** This comps the underlying track into the transparent areas. Remember, Steps 13 through 15 are performed simply to assist you in setting levels.

16. **Now click the Mask Only check box.** Selecting this option turns your image to black and white, where the black represents the defined transparent portion of the clip, and the white shows the opaque area.

17. **Make final adjustments by dragging the Similarity slider.**

18. **Deselect the Mask Only check box.**

19. **When you're done, click OK.** You must render-scrub or build a preview to see your composite.

## RGB Difference key

This key is like the Chroma Key but is better for footage shot against a brightly lit screen. The RGB Difference Key controls include Similarity and Smoothing. To apply an RGB Difference Key, follow the same instructions given in this chapter's "Chroma key" section. The main difference is that in this case, you don't have controls for Blend, Threshold, and Cutoff.

## Blue Screen and Green Screen keys

This type of key is for use specifically on footage that was shot in front of a brightly lit blue or green screen, respectively. Since you pick the color of the screen by selecting these keys, you can't further control the color. You can only control the Threshold and cutoff, so you can compensate for various shades of blue.

## Non-Red key

This key is also for use on footage shot in front of a green or blue background, but it also allows for the blending of clips. Use this key when the Green Screen or Blue Screen key does not give you the desired result. In addition to the Threshold and Cutoff controls that are adjustable with Blue and Green Screen keys, Non-Red key also gives you the option to adjust blending.

## Luminance key

A Luminance key will enable you to key out dark areas. Doing so is best when you have high contrasting light and dark footage. High-quality black velvet is our screen of choice when shooting against a backdrop because luminance mattes have four times the resolution as color mattes. This method diminishes that cheesy staircase effect, or aliasing, that is inherent in DV video chroma keys, and is usually a dead giveaway that your clip is digital. Luminance key controls include Threshold and Cutoff, and because you're keying out luminance, you don't have a color-picking option.

## Alpha Channel key

In addition to digital video's three grayscale channels (red, green and blue, or RGB), a fourth channel called the *alpha channel* defines the transparent areas of the video.

The Alpha Channel key in Premiere's Titles, for example is the background (wherever there is not text). That's why the text of the title only, at 100% opacity, lays over the video clip, and the rest of the video shows through the transparency of the alpha channel background. Photoshop files and After Effects files also contain alpha channels. You would not use this key to create composites of regular video clips.

## Black Alpha Matte and White Alpha Matte

Use these to key out a black or white background, respectively, from a Premiere-supported graphics file that contains a premultiplied alpha channel. See Table 6-1 in Chapter 6 for supported graphics files.

## Image Matte

*Image Mattes* are images that create transparent areas in the footage on another video track. You would create the still image — preferably grayscale — in a program, such as Photoshop. The still image is called the *Matte*. The image determines the transparent areas in the underlying clip. The clip shows through all of the black parts of the image but not through the white parts. Image Matte controls include Choose Matte and Reverse Key.

Use the following steps to create an Image Matte:

1. **First, create a simple grayscale image in Photoshop, if you have it.** If you don't, use a Premiere title. (See Chapter 10 to learn how to create Titles.)

2. **Place an image in the Video 2 track or higher.**

3. **Click the clip to select it.**

4. **Choose Clip➪Video Options➪Transparency.**

5. **Select Image Matte from the Key Type drop-down list.** The Matte window appears.

6. **Click the Choose button to select the image (or title) you want to define as your image matte.** Your composite displays in the Sample window.

7. **Click the Reverse key to change from keying out the white portions of the image to keying out the black portions.**

8. **Click OK.** Render-scrub or build a preview to see the final result.

## Difference Matte

A Difference Matte makes a comparison between two clips and identifies information that is identical in both clips. Enabling the matte hides this information, leaving only the difference visible, hence the name. For example, you could start by shooting a static shot of your empty garage. Then have your band set up their gear and play a song in the garage. During this shot, leave your camera and tripod in the same position you used for the static shot. In the editing process, when you apply the Difference Matte to the band clip, the matte will compare the clip with the static shot and hide all identical data, in this case the garage background. You can now choose a new background from your clip archive, or from stock footage.

## Track Matte

Track Mattes can help you create traveling mattes. A traveling matte gives motion to an image. Track Mattes utilize at least three video tracks: the lowest track (Video 1) for the background clip, the next highest track for the traveling image, and the highest for the image that provides the Matte for the traveling image to show through. The traveling image is usually a graphic containing an Alpha Channel. You can create the Matte in any program that allows you to save it in a format that Premiere supports (see Table 6-1 in Chapter 6), or as a Premiere Title. After you place the Matte image in the topmost video track, you then select Motion Settings so that you can animate the Matte. For an excellent example of a traveling matte, check out the Basement Jaxx video "Where's Your Head A?" in which video faces of band members play through mattes shaped like monkeys' heads, which travel along with monkey bodies.

## Garbage Matte

If you film a band against a plain blue screen and you later key that blue out and place the band in front of a carnival, it will be unconvincing if there's a white lamp cord running in front of the ferris wheel. (It was in the house when you shot the band, but you didn't notice it then.) Well, it's not too late. You can drag the handles of the image in the Sample window to exclude that cord but keep the band. Then when you key out the rest of the blue screen, that cord will be gone too!

## Creating split screens

You can create a split screen by using the Transparency feature. To create a split-screen effect, follow these steps:

1. **Place a clip in the Timeline's Video 1 track.**

2. **Place another clip in the same place on the Timeline, but on the Video 2 track.**

3. **Select the clip in track Video 2.**

4. **Choose Clip⇨Video Options⇨Transparency.**

5. **Click the image's handles (there's one in each corner) and drag the handles to the middle of the Sample thumbnail to reveal the image below.**

6. **Adjust the placement of the handles until you achieve the composite you want.**

7. **Drag the slider under the thumbnail image to see how your composite will look along the length of your video clip.**

Now that you know about mattes, keys, and split screens, check out the video "Free" on the CD-ROM included in this book. The scene at 01:43 is a good example of a matte (see Figure 12-17). In this example, we used a still image of three TVs, and defined a portion of the image — the three TV screens — as transparent. Because this is our matte image, it must be placed on the highest video track (in this case, Video 5 track). Video 4, 3, and 2 tracks contain the images that show through each of the three TV screens. You can change the sizes and screen placement of any image with the Camera View and Transform video effects (see Figures 12-18 and 12-19). You must also set split screen transparencies for each of the Video 4, 3, and 2 tracks to enable the lower tracks to show through (see Figures 12-20 – 12-23).

**Figure 12-17:** This figure illustrates how a Track Matte works. In this scenario, we defined the square areas inside each TV screen as the alpha channel matte, that is, the areas through which the underlying videos appear.

**Figure 12-18:** The centered image, as shown in the Sample thumbnail of the Transparency Settings dialog box.

**Figure 12-19:** The same image with Transform effect applied to move the image.

**Figure 12-20:** Transparency settings for image in the Video 2 track.

**Figure 12-21:** Transparency settings for the image in the Video 3 track.

**Figure 12-22:** Transparency settings for the image in the Video 4 track.

**Figure 12-23:** Split screen composite, showing through alpha channel portion of the clip in the Video 5 track.

# Using Motion Settings

You can give any clip additional motion by making the clip travel across the screen in any direction or zigzag across your screen using the motion settings. The clip you apply motion to can be either a still clip or a video clip. Either way, you use the same process. This effect works best on superimposed clips.

## Setting the motion's path

A *motion path* is the user-defined path along which your clip travels. Figure 12-24 shows the Motion Settings dialog box.

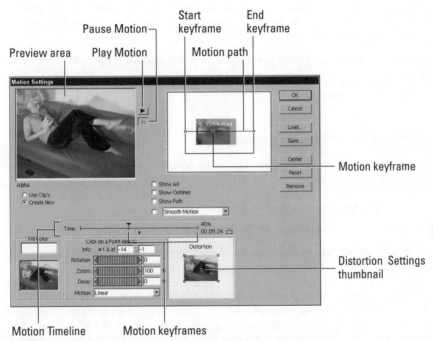

**Figure 12-24:** The Motion Settings dialog box contains all the controls you need to set up animation. Drag the Time slider to change the timing of the keyframes.

To set a motion path, follow these steps:

1. **Place the clip that you want to give motion to in the Timeline.** You can apply motion to a clip in any video track.

2. **Select the clip in the Timeline using the Selection tool.**

3. **Choose Clip⇨Video Options⇨Motion.**

4. **When you first open the Motion window, your clip travels from left to right across the Preview area.** You should click the Show All check box before you go any further.

5. **Move your cursor over the motion path line until it turns into a pointing finger.**

6. **You'll see two motion keyframes on the motion path: one at the beginning of the line, and one at the end.** Click the first keyframe and drag it to the top corner of the Visible Area preview.

7. **Next, click anywhere along the motion path to create more keyframes.**

8. **Drag these keyframes around the screen to set up a switchback path.** These keyframes are similar to video effect keyframes because they affect the motion setting over time.

9. **Notice that the preview area reflects the motion changes that you made.**

10. **To delete any motion path keyframe, click and drag it out of the region of the Visible Area box.**

## Setting the motion's rotation

You can make your image tumble across the screen by defining rotation settings. The default setting is 0 degrees To set the rotation, follow these steps:

1. **Click the Start keyframe.**

2. **Type** 90 **in the rotation box to achieve a 90-degree spin.**

3. **Repeat this process for each keyframe to watch your image tumble smoothly, while zigzagging across the screen.**

Motion settings are most useful for superimposing objects, making them blend into the track. Imagine a video in which the lead guitarist breaks a string. Miraculously, a shiny new guitar, complete with six fresh strings, tumbles from the heavens! He fumbles for a pick, and a beautiful glowing pick tumbles his way from above. Not Spielberg, we know, but it's a start!

## Setting the motion's zoom

You can make your image zoom into or out of the screen by defining the Zoom settings. The default setting is 100%, or completely filling the screen.

1. Click the Start keyframe.

2. Type 0% in the Zoom text box.

## Setting the motion's distortion

You can distort your image by dragging the handles of the Distortion thumbnail in the lower-right corner of the Motion Settings dialog box. Experiment with this.

## Loading motion presets

Premiere has some predefined motion settings that you can apply to your images. While in the Motion Settings dialog box:

1. Click Load.

2. Select the Motion folder.

3. Select one of the motion presets.

After you define your own motion settings, you can save them to this folder.

Play around with motion settings. When you understand how motion settings work, you can spot these kinds of animations while you watch music videos on VH1 or MTV. Motion settings are best used on objects created with alpha channels, rather than video clips.

# Chapter Replay

After reading this chapter, you should be able to:

✦ Understand and apply video effects and keyframes

✦ Superimpose images by defining transparencies

✦ Create special effects with mattes and keys

✦ Use motion settings to animate your clips

In Part IV, you learn all about outputting your finalized music video as well as how to promote and distribute it to your target audience.

✦    ✦    ✦

# It Ain't Over 'Til It's Over: Formatting and Distributing Your Video

# Preparing Your Video for Tape Output

**C**ongratulations! Your first music video is ready for viewing on your TV. If you set up your computer to enable you to monitor your Premiere projects through your camcorder and onto your television set, as we recommend in Chapter 6, you've already seen how your video looks on the tube. But right now, however, you can watch your video only while your computer is hooked up to the TV/VCR. You want to be able to copy your video to VHS tape so that it can play back on any VCR.

In this chapter, you find out how to export your video to both DV and VHS videotape. You also learn how to archive your video, both as an AVI movie and as individual clips and files. In addition, we give you pointers on how to duplicate tapes of your music videos.

## Formatting for VHS Output

First, make sure that your computer is hooked up to your DV camcorder, TV, and VCR as follows:

1. **Connect your digital camcorder to your computer by using the FireWire cable.**

2. **Plug the power cable of your DV camcorder into the electrical outlet.** Many camcorders automatically shut off after five minutes if they're not engaged, but they don't do this in VTR mode if they're plugged into an outlet.

3. **Switch on your camcorder to VTR mode.**

4. **Connect the camera's A/V (audio/video) outputs to your VCR's A/V inputs.** Make sure that your VCR is hooked up to your television, as described in your owner's manual. If your camera is like ours, it has a single output that sends video as well as stereo audio. The cable splits into three — one for the video signal and one each for left and right audio signals. If your VCR has only a mono audio input, you need to buy a Y-adapter cable to convert the stereo signal to mono.

5. **Make sure that your TV is plugged in and turned on.** You may need to follow your TV's manual to set it up for video input.

Premiere provides several different ways to export your video to tape:

✦ Record to tape while you play the video from the Timeline

✦ Export to tape

✦ Print to video

## Record to tape by playing the Timeline

Play the video from the Timeline while manually enabling the Record button on the VCR. When you record the video to tape this way, the first frame of your video appears as a still until the Timeline starts.

When you record to tape from the Timeline, Premiere uses the settings defined in the Project Settings dialog box.

1. **Hook your computer up through your camcorder and into a VCR, as described earlier in the section "Formatting for VHS Output."**

2. **Insert a blank VHS tape into your machine.**

3. **Cue the tape to the position on the VHS tape where you want your music video copied.**

4. **Press your VCR's Record button.**

5. **Wait several seconds to give the VCR transports some black leader and some time to stabilize the tape.**

6. **Play the Timeline by clicking the Play In To Out button in Premiere's Program Monitor window.**

7. **Stop the VCR when the video has finished playing.**

Following these steps is an easy way to get your video on tape, but you don't have as much control as you do when exporting to tape or printing to video, which we explain later.

# Exporting to camcorder tape

Use this export option when recording from the computer to the camcorder using DV Device Control.

1. **Connect your computer to your DV camcorder using a FireWire cable.**

2. **Plug your camcorder's power supply into an electrical outlet.**

3. **Turn your camcorder on.**

4. **Make sure Device Control is set for your camcorder model in Premiere's preferences (see "Setting up Device Control" in Chapter 6).**

5. **Cue your DV tape to the location you want to record, by using your camcorder's transport controls.**

6. **Choose File⇨Export Timeline⇨Export to Tape.** The Export To Tape Settings dialog box appears, as shown in Figure 13-1.

7. **Select Activate recording deck.**

8. **Click Record.**

**Figure 13-1:** The Export to Tape Settings dialog box gives you the choice of starting your DV deck manually, or having the DV Device Control activate it for you.

By selecting Activate recording deck, Premiere's interface starts the recording feature on your DV camcorder by sending the command through the FireWire connection. Your camcorder stays in record mode until the video is finished playing, and then the camcorder automatically stops.

# Printing to video

The third way to record from your computer to VCR is by using the Print to Video command. Use this option for exporting without Device Control.

1. **Hook your computer up through your camcorder and into a VCR, as described earlier in the section "Formatting for VHS Output."**

2. **Insert a blank VHS tape into your machine.**

3. **Cue the VHS tape to the location where you want your music video copied.**

4. **Choose File⇨Export Timeline⇨Print to Video.** The Print to Video dialog box, shown in Figure 13-2, appears.

**Figure 13-2:** The Print to Video dialog box gives you the options of playing color bars and black screen before the video starts to record.

5. **In the top text box, type in the number (in seconds) of how long you want Premiere to play color bars before the video starts, if desired.**

6. **In the bottom text box, type in the number in seconds of how long you want Premiere to play a black screen before the video starts, if desired.** The color bars and black screen won't actually print to tape, but they will be displayed on your computer monitor before the video starts to play. We like this feature because it's a good way to gauge when to start recording (after the color bars, during the black screen).

7. **Drag your Edit Line left to the beginning of the Timeline.**

8. **After the color bars have been displayed, manually start recording on your VCR.** You'll record black screen before your video starts.

9. **Play the Timeline by pressing the Play In To Out button in your Premiere project's Program Monitor window.**

10. **Stop recording when the video has finished playing.**

If you experience playback problems when exporting using one of the above methods, try another method to see which works best for your equipment.

# Backing Up to DV

You should have backups of your final video in a couple of different forms, just to be safe. If you export only to an analog VCR, you won't have a digital-quality master of your work from which to make copies. Still, you don't want to keep your project and all its elements stored on your hard drive just to make dubs, so you should have a digital master of your video outside your computer.

Making a digital backup is as simple as playing the Premiere video program on your computer, while simultaneously recording on both your DV camcorder and your VCR. You should press the Record buttons on both the DV camcorder and the VCR, and let the tape roll for a few seconds before pressing Play on the source device, just to be sure that you don't cut off the beginning of the video. Use any of the three methods described earlier in the chapter to back up to DV. Instead of simply playing the video through your DV, enable recording on the camcorder at the same time that you record to the VCR.

## Home of tackiness

**Road Diary**

Anyone who has driven Interstate 95 from New York down to Florida knows that "South of the Border" doesn't refer to our neighboring country, Mexico. It's actually a place just across the border in northern South Carolina. Okay, picture it this way. You've been driving through North Carolina for a few hours, heading south for that long-awaited vacation in Fort Lauderdale. You still have long way to go, and the kids are getting restless. Washington, D.C., turned out to be bumper-to-bumper beltway traffic, with not a monument in sight from the highway, and the rest of the trip has been relieved only by a few stops at outlet malls. By now, everyone has stocked up on factory-second socks, and it's time for a new diversion.

Some entrepreneurial genius realized that this stretch of highway could be hazardous to the sanity of parents, and thus was born the ultimate tacky tourist trap — South of the Border. The border, of course, is the North Carolina/South Carolina border. This place makes Vegas look like Versailles. It's indescribably tacky. It's kitsch on a massive, drive-thru scale. The maddening thing is, it's on a stretch of road so boring that you actually welcome it! We had the good fortune to drive through on the day we bought our video camera. That's the day when you shoot everything. We didn't yet have the concept of short clips, so we shot two or three hours of the highway. Trucks. Cars. More trucks. Two or three hours of this. We have plenty of cutaway shots of trucks, should we ever need them.

We were so relieved to arrive at South of the Border. Finally, something to shoot besides trucks! And oh, is there a lot to shoot. This place is truly strange. Everything is out of scale, and it was all concocted in the early 1960s to appeal to kids. This was before it became clear that what the kids liked was the Beatles and the Rolling Stones not giant chickens and eight-foot ice cream cones. But the chickens and the ice cream cones were put there, and by gosh, they're still there, scaring the heck out of unsuspecting tourists who thought that such things existed only in 1950s B-movie monster flicks. Disney World it's not. This is the land of bad taste and bad puns. The miniature golf course, for example, is called the Golf of Mexico.

What does all this represent to the shoestring videographer? Free props, of course! Where else can you find a seven-foot chicken, unless your brother-in-law has a key to the Warner Bros. prop lot? Heck, even they probably don't have one! But it's all here. Best time to shoot is late at night, when no one seems to be in charge. If you ever shoot a video for a song that's just a little bit quirky, this is the place to find your ready-made props.

Okay, don't make a special trip. It's not Route 66, which you should make a special trip to shoot. If you miss South of the Border, life will go on, but you won't have that clip of the giant sombrero when you really need it.

# Archiving Your Video as an AVI File

Having a DV videotape master is great, but you should have an AVI master, too. You'll need this file if you ever want to create additional DV masters, or other versions in Web-based video file formats. It's always a good idea to have more than one kind of backup. Saving your video as an AVI file to CD-R is beneficial because CD-R is a more stable medium than DV videotape.

When you export a movie to DV or VHS tape by using the methods in the previous sections — recording to tape by playing the Timeline or by using either the Export To Tape or Print To Video commands — Premiere uses the settings defined in the Project Settings dialog box. However, when you export a movie to AVI or other file formats by using the File➪Export Timeline➪Movie command, Premiere uses the settings defined in the Export Movie Settings dialog box.

## Optimizing Premiere's export settings

You won't want to mess with most of your project's settings in the middle of a project, although you may want to review the section on loading project settings in Chapter 6. You should, however, get in the habit of checking the export settings when you're ready to export. This chapter deals with exporting to tape and AVI. The next chapter shows how you export to CD and to the Web. The export settings are different for these different scenarios, so be sure to go through the following steps when you're exporting to tape:

1. **Choose Project➪Settings Viewer.** The Settings Viewer dialog box appears, as shown in Figure 13-3.

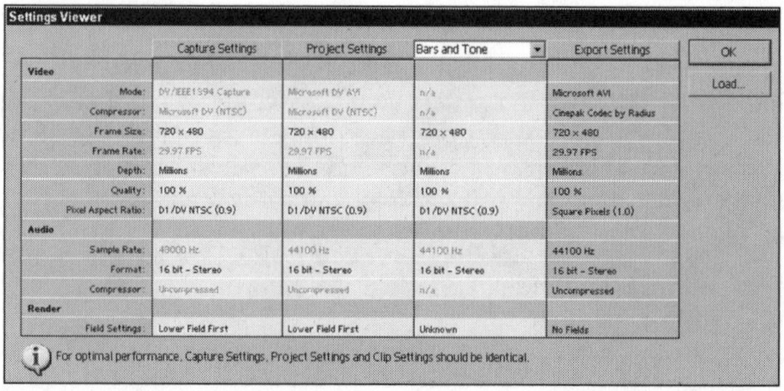

| Settings Viewer | | | | | |
|---|---|---|---|---|---|
| | Capture Settings | Project Settings | Bars and Tone | Export Settings | OK |
| **Video** | | | | | Load... |
| Mode: | DV/IEEE1394 Capture | Microsoft DV AVI | n/a | Microsoft AVI | |
| Compressor: | Microsoft DV (NTSC) | Microsoft DV (NTSC) | n/a | Cinepak Codec by Radius | |
| Frame Size: | 720 x 480 | 720 x 480 | 720 x 480 | 720 x 480 | |
| Frame Rate: | 29.97 FPS | 29.97 FPS | n/a | 29.97 FPS | |
| Depth: | Millions | Millions | Millions | Millions | |
| Quality: | 100 % | 100 % | 100 % | 100 % | |
| Pixel Aspect Ratio: | D1/DV NTSC (0.9) | D1/DV NTSC (0.9) | D1/DV NTSC (0.9) | Square Pixels (1.0) | |
| **Audio** | | | | | |
| Sample Rate: | 48000 Hz | 44100 Hz | 44100 Hz | 44100 Hz | |
| Format: | 16 bit – Stereo | 16 bit – Stereo | 16 bit – Stereo | 16 bit – Stereo | |
| Compressor: | Uncompressed | Uncompressed | n/a | Uncompressed | |
| **Render** | | | | | |
| Field Settings: | Lower Field First | Lower Field First | Unknown | No Fields | |

ⓘ For optimal performance, Capture Settings, Project Settings and Clip Settings should be identical.

**Figure 13-3:** The Settings Viewer enables you to compare Capture Settings, Project Settings, individual Clip Settings, and Export Settings.

2. **Click the Export Settings column heading.** The Export Movie Settings dialog box appears, as shown in Figure 13-4.

3. **Choose Microsoft AVI for an AVI file export.**

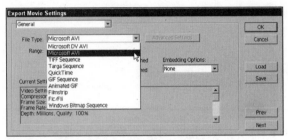

**Figure 13-4:** Export Settings has five pages. The General settings page is the first page that displays when you click Export Settings in the Settings Viewer.

4. **Click the Next button to move to the Video settings panel (see Figure 13-5) and make your video export settings selections.** If you chose Microsoft AVI filetype in Step 3, you'll see that the compressor is set for Cinepak Codec by Radius. You may use the default codec, but if you want to preserve your video at the highest quality, and if you have sufficient disk space to store the uncompressed AVI file, choose the None compressor (no compression).

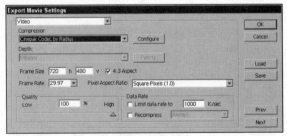

**Figure 13-5:** You can change your video compressor settings in the Video Settings page of Export Settings.

5. **Click the Next button to move to the Audio settings dialog box (see Figure 13-6) and make any audio export settings changes.** We normally use the Microsoft AVI audio defaults.

6. **Clicking the Next button again displays the Keyframe and Rendering panel; clicking Next one more time displays the Special Processing panel.** The defaults are fine for both of these panels too, so click OK to apply your preferences and close the Export Movie Settings dialog box.

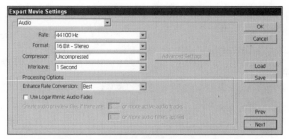

**Figure 13-6:** Audio settings should be the same as capture, project, and clip settings for maximum quality.

## Exporting your music video as an AVI file

After making the export settings adjustments, you're ready to export your movie as an AVI file. To do so, follow these steps:

1. **Choose File⇨Export⇨Movie.** The Export Movie dialog box appears.

2. **Type a name for your movie in the File Name text box.**

3. **Click Save.** A task bar appears on your screen, telling you how long it will take to export the movie. When the process is complete, the AVI movie opens in its own window. Click the Play button to see the saved video.

### Thrift shop romance

**Road Diary**

One day we were bumping around the Nob Hill neighborhood in Albuquerque, New Mexico, when we stumbled upon a cool little out-of-the-way thrift store. The owner seemed glad to have some company. She was the main supplier of vintage clothes for all the swing dancin' kids in town and, like a lot of thrift shop keepers, she needed little prompting to launch into her life story. We got the tape rolling. She'd come from the Northwest and had bummed around the country for years before winding up in this desert oasis. Today was her last day in business. Tomorrow she would, well, resume bumming around. She was a little wistful about leaving, though. Just a few days before, she had finally met a guy at a local swing dance who could have made her stay in town. Trouble was, she hadn't heard from him since then. This potential Mr. Right didn't give her his number, and it seemed like he may have simply hit the road. People tend to do that in desert towns.

Well, we listened to her story, punctuating it with the occasional "awww" at the sentimental parts. The afternoon wore on, and still no customers came in to liven up her last day in business. Just before closing time, the front bell jingled. Can you guess who walked in? You got it. None other than Mr. Right himself! And he was carrying flowers! As he handed her the dozen roses, we discreetly slipped out the door, ruining our chance to shoot the ending of this thriftshop romance. Well, we imagine the story had a happy ending, and if we ever reshoot it with actors, by gosh, we'll give it one!

# Archiving Clips and Timeline

After you've completely finished editing and exporting your music video, you'll want to remove all the files for that project to open up room on your hard drive to start another project.

**Cross-Reference**   If you want to make QuickTime or other Web-based copies, skip to Chapter 14 before archiving your project.

## Taking stock of all related files

If you're archiving to CD-R, expect to use around eight discs per three-to-four-minute music video to hold all the files associated with your project. Hard drives are becoming cheaper and cheaper, and you may want to look into purchasing removable hard drives to store your projects. You must not only archive your project file. Here are all the elements you must save:

✦ The video project (.ppj extension)

✦ All video clips used (.avi extension)

✦ All previews rendered, unless you don't mind rebuilding previews in the future (.avi extension)

✦ Your audio files (WAV or MPEG files)

✦ All titles (.ptl extension)

✦ Any batch lists you may have created when capturing clips (.pbl extension)

✦ A storyboard, if you have created one (.psq extension)

✦ A File List, if you created one (.txt extension)

✦ Any still images that you may have created in Photoshop, Illustrator, or another supported program

When you store your files, you should take notes as to where they are on your computer before you download them. In the event that you need to reload the files, they must be placed in the same disk and folder that they were in before you offloaded them for Premiere to find them.

## Creating a trimmed version of your project

A great way to save archiving space is by trimming your clips of unused frames. You should only do this when all of your editing is complete. Make sure that your project is open and then:

1. **Choose Project⇨Utilities⇨Project Trimmer.** See Figure 13-7 for the dialog box.

**Figure 13-7:** The Project Trimmer first creates a new Batch List of only the clips and frames used in the final project, and then it makes trimmed copies of the source files. You can also specify how many frames you want retained on either side of each clip's edit for further minute tweaking.

2. **Select Create Trimmed Batch List.** This command tells Premiere to create a new batch list that only includes the clips that are in the final Timeline.

3. **Select Copy Trimmed Source Files.** By copying the files, Premiere leaves the original clips in tact. When you're certain that you want to keep only the trimmed versions of your clips, you can discard the originals.

4. **Type the number of frames you want to keep on the front and back end of each clip in the Keep Frame Handles box.** A second of video is approximately 30 frames. If you type 30, Premiere will leave one second of slack on both ends of each clip, so you can make further minor adjustments, if needed.

5. **Click Create Project.**

6. **Type in the name and location of the new project.** Make sure that it's in a different location than the original. If it's not, your originals and copies will be in the same folder, making it labor-intensive to go through and separate the trimmed clips from the originals.

7. **Choose File⇨Open.**

8. **Find the trimmed version PPJ file and open it.**

9. **Play the trimmed Timeline to make sure that it's satisfactory.** After it's met your approval, you can archive that version and discard the old version and original clips.

By performing a Project Trim on the video "Nickeltown," we reduced the size of our video from 5.5GB to less than 2GB. Trimming projects makes archiving much less memory-intensive. What's more, all your files are now in a single folder. You do need to rebuild previews after you trim your project. When you're sure that you have all the files you need for your video, you can save them to CD-ROM, an external disk drive, or any other available form of storage.

We've included a QuickTime version of the "Nickeltown" video on the CD-ROM that comes with this book.

# Duplicating Your Videos

When we make one-off copies of our videos, we dub from the DV videotape backup to analog VHS tape. This way, we don't have to reload all the clips, title, project, and preview files into Premiere and go through the entire export process each time we need to make a first-generation copy. When we need more than a handful of copies, we take it to a video duplication house.

## Taping one-off copies from DV

When you export your video to DV tape, that export stays in the digital domain, and you don't lose anything in the transfer. Because the quality is in tact at its highest level, you can make copies directly from the DV camcorder to your VHS machine.

Follow these steps to make one-off VHS copies from a DV tape:

1. **Plug your DV camcorder into an electrical outlet.**

2. **Switch your camcorder on to VTR mode.**

3. **Connect camera's A/V (audio/video) outputs to your VCR's A/V inputs.** Make sure that your VCR is hooked up to your television as described in your owner's manual.

4. **Make sure that your TV is plugged in and turned on, so you can monitor the transfer image and sound.**

5. **Insert the master DV into the camcorder and cue it up.**

6. **Insert a blank VHS tape into the VCR and rewind it to the beginning of the tape.**

7. **Press Record on the VCR and let a few seconds go by before pressing your camcorder's Play button to be sure that you don't cut off the beginning of the video.**

8. **Stop the VCR a few seconds after the song has ended.**

9. **Stop the camcorder.**

## When to use a duplication service

The previous process is fine if you're only going to be making a copy or two at a time, but because the transfer happens in real time, it's not the best way to make multiple copies. If you've decided to compile a list of cable access music shows across the country and send your video to each and every one of them, you'd better look into having copies made at a video duplication house.

You can find advertisements for many video duplication services in the backs of video magazines. A good videotape duplication service will be able to bulk copy your video, ensure clean signal processing, and minimize generational loss. In addition, most video duplicators should be able to provide CD-ROM and DVD-ROM copies of your video in MPEG, MPEG-2, AVI, QuickTime, and other digital formats. Turnaround time and cost differ from facility to facility, so shop around. Rates are typically based on the length of the video and how many copies you order. Prices generally get cheaper as the quantity rises, so buying in bulk saves you money. Duplication houses should also be able to print artwork for your video packaging, including labels and shells. In general, you should expect to pay between a dollar and a dollar-fifty per unit for 100 copies of your videotape. DV tape copies are much more expensive, because the format is relatively new. If your band has already released a CD and your audience still wants more, why not produce a music video compilation and sell it on VHS?

# Chapter Replay

After reading this chapter and following the step-by-step instructions, you should be able to:

✦ Export your video to DV and VHS tape

✦ Archive your video as an AVI file

✦ Create a duplicate of your project, with unused clips and frames trimmed

✦ Archive project elements

✦ Make VHS duplicates from a DV master

✦ Know when you need to take your project to a duplication service

In the next chapter, we show you how to export your video as a QuickTime, RealPlayer and other Web-based file types to use as streaming, downloadable, and CD-ROM files.

✦    ✦    ✦

# Preparing Your Video for Distribution on CD and the Web

The World Wide Web has put independent artists like you and us on somewhat of an even playing field with the big guys in that we finally all have an outlet for our music, our artwork, our writings, and our videos. As long as there is that mysterious, seemingly endless universe of Web storage available to us all, and it is accessible to anyone with a computer and a phone line, information can be passed across the globe in a matter of seconds. Now that cable, DSL, and T1 lines are making their way into personal computer setups, transfer times are becoming quicker and quicker.

In this chapter, you learn how to save your music videos in formats that can be played on a computer, distributed over the Internet, and posted on the Web.

## Formatting Video for CD or DVD-ROM

One fun way to distribute music videos is by recording, or *burning* them to CD. The last chapter told you how to create an AVI file as a digital backup. This section takes that process a step further by showing you ways to format and compress your videos into files that can be stored and sold or passed around on CD-ROMs.

CD-ROM drives differ from unit to unit, and older models have a lower data transfer rate. If you set the data rate too high, your video may not run as smoothly on older drives as it does on newer, faster drives.

Premiere's Movie Export options enable you to export your video by using your designated export settings. Adobe also provides a simpler way to export videos to a variety of file formats by including three plug-ins: Cleaner EZ 5, Windows Media Export, and Advanced RealMedia Export.

## Using Cleaner EZ 5 plug-in

The easiest way to save your music video for use on a CD-ROM drive is to use the Cleaner EZ 5 plug-in. This plug-in offers the choice of saving your video as an AVI CD-ROM or a QuickTime CD-ROM. You should know ahead of time what CD-ROM video player format your audience is most likely to use. QuickTime is the most widely used format for both Mac and PC CD-ROMs, and the format integrates seamlessly with other popular video players. Windows offers built-in support for AVI files, so if you know that your audience is only using Windows, you may opt for this format.

Cleaner EZ 5 offers a choice of encoding for different target speed drives. See Figures 14-1 and 14-2 for menu options.

To export your music video as an AVI or QuickTime file for CD-ROM, open your video in Premiere and follow these steps:

1. **Choose File⇨Export Timeline⇨Save For Web.** The Save for Web dialog box, shown in Figure 14-1, appears.

Pull-down menu lists settings options.

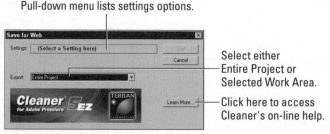

Select either
Entire Project or
Selected Work Area.

Click here to access
Cleaner's on-line help.

**Figure 14-1:** The Save For Web dialog box

2. **Under Settings, select either AVI CD-ROM or QuickTime CD-ROM, depending on the file type you prefer using.** (See Figure 14-2.)

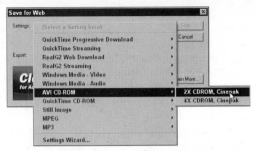

**Figure 14-2:** The Save For Web Settings options

3. **Select the speed from the resulting pop-up menu (2x, 4x Cinepak for each plus CD-ROM Sorenson option for QuickTime).**

4. **From the Export list, select the portion of the project you want to export by choosing either Entire Project or Selected Work Area.**

5. **Click the Start button.**

6. **Type a name for your video in the File name text box.**

7. **Click the Save button.**

8. **An Output dialog box appears on your screen, as shown in Figure 14-3, which shows the frame of the video that is being encoded and other valuable statistics.**

**Figure 14-3:** The Cleaner EZ 5 Output dialog box displays the video frames as they're being exported, the length of time elapsed and remaining to export, the average data rate, and the amount of time each minute of video will take to encode.

To further explore the Cleaner EZ 5 features, click the Learn More button in the Save for Web dialog box to connect to the Cleaner Web site. You can also choose Settings Wizard instead of AVI or QuickTime CD-ROM (as described in Step 2) to walk through and customize settings for your specific needs. When you use the Wizard, you'll be able to set CD-ROM speed, file format, quality settings, codecs, frame rate, display size, bit depth, and more. If you are going to burn your movie to DVD-ROM, the Settings Wizard enables you to optimize for DVD.

After you've saved your movie, you can burn it to a CD-R or DVD-R. Depending on the export settings, you should be able to fit many music videos on one CD-R. CD-Rs can hold up to 650MB (standard) or 700MB (newer format), so if your QuickTime video is 60MB, you can easily fit 10 videos of the same length.

## Using QuickTime videos to enhance an audio CD

Today's recording artists can now add video to conventional audio CDs as enhancements. Our latest CD, *Get It Right,* is an "enhanced CD" that includes video and still pictures as well as other visual enhancements, such as lyrics, liner notes, and Web links, in addition to the full album of music. If your band (or the band whose video you're making) plans to release a CD, they should seriously consider adding video material to their disc. See Chapter 15 for more information about putting together an enhanced CD.

When an audio CD has been recorded and mixed, the CD is then sent to a mastering facility, where the mastering engineer sets the sequence and gaps between songs and sweetens the final audio with varying amounts of compression and equalization before sending it off to the pressing plant. Ask your mastering engineer if they have the ability to master an enhanced CD. Most mastering facilities should be able to do this, but it's best to ask first. Typically, you provide them with your visual content, and they can master the material into the disc. The audio content cannot use up the entire 800MB of disc space or else no room will be left for the visual material.

Enhanced CDs often include:

✦ Music video

✦ Interview video

✦ Liner notes (some releases don't include printed liner notes but do include them as part of the enhanced CD)

✦ Lyrics

✦ Photos

✦ Flash files

# Formatting Video for Internet/Web Movies

When we post videos on our Web site, we like to give our audience a choice of formats and connection speeds. You may decide to do the same. Before you do, contact your Web hosting company to see what your memory limitations are. The more file types you post, the more memory you use, and the more you may have to pay each month.

Premiere offers several options for exporting videos for use on the Web. The rate of Internet data delivery varies depending on Internet traffic, your Web host's hardware and software, and the user's computer hardware and software. Some users rely on the latest broadband technology, while others still count on a 28K modem. When you format your music video for Web distribution, it's important to consider whom your target audience is. If you know, for example, that almost all of the people who will download your video consist of your film 101 class, all of whom have access to the university's broadband connections, then you won't have to worry about uploading a slower streaming video. If you're like us, and you have people all over the world with varying degrees of Internet speed, you may want to consider creating multiple bit rate video.

You can use the Premiere program's Movie Export options by choosing File⇨Export Timeline⇨Movie to use the export settings, but we like using any of the three plug-in options: Advanced Windows Media (only available in Windows version of Premiere), Save For Web, and Advanced RealMedia Export because they offer lots of great presets. Use one of these options to take advantage of all the homework that Adobe has already done for you!

## Advanced Windows Media

Use this Windows Media Export Plug-in for Adobe Premiere for creating video as a Windows Media file (.wm file extension) for use on the Web. Windows Media files can be played over the Web using the Windows Media Player, which comes with Microsoft Windows and is available as a free download at http://microsoft.com. The high-quality video files you can create with the Advanced Windows Media plug-in can be downloaded or streamed, depending on the settings you choose.

You can choose from one of 32 preset packages that will enable you to provide audio and video to targeted audiences of varying bandwidths, including dial-up modems, ISDN, LAN, Cable, DSL, Web servers, and broadband NTSC.

To export your video as Advanced Windows Media, open your video in Premiere and follow these steps:

1. **Choose File⇨Export Timeline⇨Advanced Windows Media.** The Windows Media Export Plug-in for Adobe Premiere dialog box appears on your screen (see Figure 14-4). The Profile menu includes several presets. To see further information on each preset, click a profile and read the description and details in the boxes below the Profile menu.

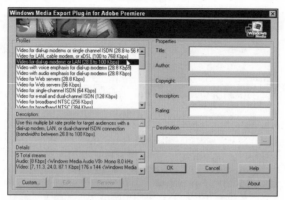

**Figure 14-4:** The Windows Media Export Plug-in offers a variety of streaming profiles for your Windows Media movies.

2. **Select the desired profile.**

3. **Type a filename in the File name text box.**

4. **Click OK.** The Exporting window pops up and shows the progress of the export, as shown in Figure 14-5.

This plug-in offers a comprehensive help feature that can help you understand all of its features.

**Figure 14-5:** Windows Media export status window

## Save for Web

The Save for Web option is a good place to start, when exporting video for a number of different applications. Of the three available export plug-ins, this is the one we prefer and most often use. By choosing this option, you can access the Terran Media Cleaner EZ 5 plug-in. Export presets include QuickTime, RealMedia, Windows Media, ASF, MPEG-1, DV stream, and more. Streaming video delivers the video frame by frame, so that the viewer does not have to wait for the file to download before viewing it. If the connection is slow, like a 28 Kbps or 56 Kbps modem, the download can take a half hour or more for a three-minute music video. By posting your video on your Web site as a streaming file, the video starts playing right away. Video download files, however, must be completely downloaded before they can be viewed. You must decide if you want your audience to be allowed to keep the video on their hard drive (as a download), as opposed to being able to just watch the video but not retain a copy. Available download and streaming preset options include the following:

✦ QuickTime Progressive Download

✦ QuickTime Streaming

✦ Real G2 Web Download

✦ Real G2 Streaming

✦ Windows Media Video

✦ Windows Media Audio

✦ AVI and QuickTime CD-ROM (covered in section above)

✦ Still Image (as JPEG, PICT, or BMP files — no audio)

✦ MPEG

✦ MP3 (audio only)

To use the Save for Web option to export a QuickTime video, open your video in Premiere, click within the Timeline to activate it, and follow these steps:

1. **Choose File⇨Export Timeline⇨Save For Web.**

2. **You may either select the preset that you desire or select Settings Wizard.** For this exercise, choose the Settings Wizard.

3. **Click Start.** The Cleaner EZ plug-in application starts, and the Settings Wizard Delivery Medium displays on your screen.

4. **Select WWW, as shown in Figure 14-6.**

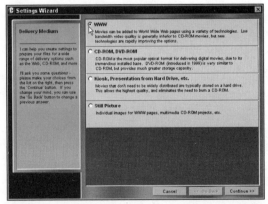

**Figure 14-6:** The Settings Wizard offers the choice of saving for the Web, CD-ROM or DVD-ROM, presentation from kiosk or hard drive, or saving as a still picture.

5. **Select Continue.**

6. **Select the format you want to save your file as.** Your choices are QuickTime, Real, or Windows Media. To make a QuickTime file, select QuickTime.

7. **Select Continue.**

8. **Select Progressive Streaming (high quality) for a typical three-to-four-minute music video.** There will be a delay on the viewer's end before the video starts playing, but the quality will be better than the other two choices would provide, if the connection speed is slow.

9. **Click Continue.**

10. **Select the connection(s) your viewers are most likely to use.** The more options you select, the longer it will take to prepare your music video.

11. **Click Continue.**

12. **In the Soundtrack dialog box, select Audio & Video Equally Important.**

13. **In the same dialog box, select Soundtrack Is Mostly Music.**

14. **Select Continue.**

15. **Select High Quality Image, in the Optimize dialog box.**

16. **Select Continue.**

17. **Select Show Controller and Start Playing Automatically, as shown in Figure 14-7.**

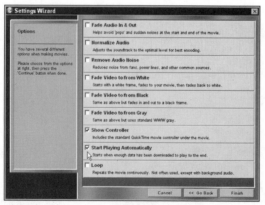

**Figure 14-7:** The Settings Wizard Options dialog box

18. **Select Finish.**

19. **Select a destination folder in which to output the video.** The Output dialog box appears on your screen and displays export status.

20. **View the movie to see if it's at the quality you want.**

You may opt to use the Cleaner EZ 5 presets. To save a QuickTime movie by using presets, open the Premiere file, activate the Timeline and follow these steps:

1. **Choose File⇨Export Timeline⇨Save For Web.**

2. **Under Settings, select QuickTime Progressive Download.** (Only select QuickTime Streaming, if you plan to stream from a QuickTime server.)

3. **Select Medium-size Movie in the Settings menu.**

4. **Select the project range (entire project or work area) in the Export menu.**

5. **Click the Start button.**

6. **Name the file.**

7. **Once again, the Output dialog box appears on your screen, telling how long the encoding process will take.**

The presets in this step-by-step example export your QuickTime movie at a higher bit rate than in the previous example, producing a better-quality video in a larger file. Experiment with the various options to find the settings that are right for you and your audience.

## Advanced RealMedia Export

The Advanced RealMedia Export plug-in enables you to create RealMedia (.rm extension) files for streaming or Web download. RealMedia files can be played back using the RealPlayer application, which is available as a free download at http://real.com. You can export the movie as either a single-rate streaming file or as a multirate SureStream file. If you intend to broadcast multirate SureStream files, you must do so by using a RealNetworks RealServer. The Advanced RealMedia Export offers a comprehensive help feature that connects you to the Advance RealMedia Export Plug-in User's Guide for Adobe Premiere on the Web.

Because you can export your movie as a RealMedia file using both this plug-in and the Cleaner EZ 5 plug-in, experiment with both plug-ins to decide which one you prefer using.

# Batch Processing

You may have realized that the best way to make your video available to as many people as possible is to save it in several different file formats and consider your target audience's varying bandwidth availability. Premiere thought of that, too, and made it easy to perform a series of exports all at once by defining a batch-processing job.

Batch processing saves you lots of time and headaches, especially if you do a batch process on your very first music video. If you're exporting for the Web, the only way to really see the quality and size of your finished exported file is to export it. As you know by now, the export process for a three-minute music video can be close to a half-hour. By setting up a batch-processing job, you can create a list of export files, all with different settings, and run the batch job while you sleep. In the morning, check the different versions of the file to see which ones you prefer.

To perform a batch export, follow these steps:

1. **Choose Project⇨Utilities⇨Batch Processing.** The Batch Processing window appears on your screen (Figure 14-8).

**Figure 14-8:** Batch Processing window

2. **Click the Add button to add a video project to the batch list.**

3. **Find the Premiere project you want to add to the list and select it.**

4. **Click Open.** The buttons along the bottom of the Batch Processing window that were inactive before you added a project now become active.

5. **While that project is selected in the Batch Processing window, click Target.**

6. **Find the folder where you want to place the exported file and name it.**

7. **Click Save.**

8. **Click the Settings button to open the Export Movie Settings window.**

9. **Click the Load button to load in preset settings, or you can change settings manually.** You may save any modified settings by clicking Save and then naming the settings. When you perform your first batch-processing job, you may want to give each file a name that reflects the settings you use. This way, you'll know which settings work best in the future.

10. **Repeat Steps 3 through 10 for each export you want add to the list.**

11. **Select the entire list and click the Check button.** Premiere checks to make sure that it can find all related files. If any files are missing, you will be alerted.

12. **To perform the batch process, click the Make button and specify whether you want to make all the files in the list or just the selected ones, as shown in Figure 14-9.**

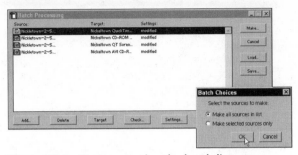

**Figure 14-9:** Start processing the batch list.

13. **Click OK, and your batch-processing job begins.**

14. **Get some sleep!**

# Chapter Replay

After reading this chapter and following all the step-by-step instructions, you should be able to:

✦ Format your music video to a number of files that can be burned to CD-ROM or DVD-ROM

✦ Format your music videos for placement on the Web

✦ Know a variety of formats that are available to most Web surfers and be able to make copies of your videos in all these formats

✦ Perform a batch-processing job while you sleep

✦     ✦     ✦

# Promoting and Distributing Your Video

**W**ell, you've conceptualized your video. You've storyboarded it. You've drawn floor plans and set marks. You've coaxed temperamental musicians into smiling for the camera, and you had good weather on your location shoot. You've even preserved friendships with your long-suffering crew, and no animals were harmed in the making of your video. You've edited it like a pro in Adobe Premiere, and the results look a lot like the big-budget videos on VH1. So now you can relax. Your work is done, right? *Wrong!* It's only just begun. Now you've got to get people to look at it!

Many great videos have been made that no one has ever seen. Why? One reason is that they featured artists who weren't part of a major-label marketing plan, which took them out of network competition. But is featuring an artist on a marketing manager's list the only way to get seen? Is there another fate for a good indie video besides enforced obscurity? Actually, you have lots of options, and the number is increasing every day. Independent filmmakers have become expert at devising strategies for supporting each other and getting seen, and the music video world has been taking some lessons from them. The Internet, of course, is a prime resource, and a number of other avenues are available as well. (See Figure 15-1.) Let's explore.

**Figure 15-1:** Here are 16 possible destinations for your completed music video.

# Putting Your Press Kit Together

Most people get information about entertainment options, such as music videos, from the media. In broad terms, the media includes news programs, radio programming, newspapers and magazines, arts and entertainment guides, and so forth. If they get excited about something, they may tell their friends and co-workers about it, resulting in a word-of-mouth buzz. This is a great form of free advertising, but it happens only through a combination of luck and circumstance. No one launches a project with the assumption that word of mouth alone will make it popular. It always comes down to contacting the media first. Even if your project develops a buzz, you will have to get the ball rolling, and to do so, you need a press kit.

Media people are typically overworked and underpaid and are under pressure to make impossible deadlines. They are inclined to give coverage to press releases that make their job easy. Packages that threaten to eat up precious time often end up in the circular file. Know what to send and what not to send, and you've won half the battle.

# What's in a press kit?

A good press kit contains only a few elements. These items should be striking and attention getting, and each element should reinforce the visual image of the project. A folder is the first object that a reporter should see when she opens your envelope. Spend a little extra at the copy shop and get a glossy folder. Bright colors are okay. Design a label with your logo and the simple, catchy name of your production company. Your contact info should be on this label. Put this label on the videotape, as well. Contact info has to be on every item in the envelope, because, although you have packed it all with great care, the components probably will become separated very quickly at the destination office. Videotapes go in a separate pile from folders, and if the busy executives happen to like the video when they finally view it a few weeks later, the two items may be completely separated by that time. More than once, acquisitions people have fallen in love with a demo tape, only to find that it doesn't have contact info. Straight into the circular file! They don't have time for detective work.

Opening the folder, the reporter should see a black-and-white 8x10-inch glossy of the act featured in the video. You may want to include one or two stills from the video as well. Underneath these stills, you'll find a *one-sheet*. This sheet is literally a one-page description of the video, no longer. Three short paragraphs will suffice. The first should announce the video's existence and say why it is newsworthy. It could be "long-awaited," or it may be the "first live video from so and so," or whatever. This is called the *hook*. The stronger the hook, the more likely you are to get coverage. The second paragraph may go into a little more detail but not enough to make the reporter's eyes glaze over. The final, one- or two-sentence paragraph should sum things up neatly.

## The hook

When you read the Sunday newspaper, you don't literally read every line. You scan the headlines and stop at any that catch your eye. Media pros do the same thing as they go through their stacks of demos for the day. They want to finish quickly so that they can pick up their kid at the dentist at four, so they look for a headline at the top of each one-sheet. Sheets without headlines will probably get chucked. Keep the headline simple and make every word informative.

SPRINGFIELD HEAVY METAL BAND *POISON LION* RELEASES FIRST VIDEO

If you have a hook, set it right away with a single line sub-headline:

DIRECTOR SURVIVES NASTY BITE, BRINGS PROJECT IN ON TIME

A new hair band video may not grab the arts and entertainment editor, but a director who survives is news. Was there a real lion? Was it really poison? Now her interest is piqued, and she'll probably read the one-sheet. If there is no room in the entertainment section, maybe you'll get a blurb on the medical page! You don't have to get bitten by a lion to have a hook. "Springfield accountant ventures into world of video production" might grab the editor, too.

If you have ever received good press, include a couple of quotes, not entire articles, on the same one-sheet. Don't reprint articles and include them. If you have a good folder, label, one-sheet, and a tape, stop! Don't put anything else in the media kit. Cover letters are not required. Arts and entertainment editors read press releases for a living, and they expect all the info to be included in the one sheet.

### The cardinal rule

Don't waste anybody's time. You're dealing with overworked people, and they will love you if you acknowledge that and respect their crazy schedules. If someone gets you some "ink," e-mail a brief thank-you note. They'll remember you, and your material will get their attention in the future.

## Electronic press kits

Provide a link on your Web site to a downloadable version of your press kit. This electronic press kit, or EPK, will not be accessible to your fans. Besides your press kit and photos, post QuickTime versions of your video. See Chapter 14 for more on converting your video to QuickTime format. Avoid overly technical or time-consuming downloads and go for the lowest common denominator. The music editor of a community paper may be running a Powerbook 165, and you want her to be able to get your material with minimal hassle.

### Content is king

If you've got the HTML chops, coordinate the look of your Web site to match the look of your latest video or create a new page devoted to each video. The graphics will make an impression, even for those who don't have the time or gear to view the videos themselves. Check out Beck's Web site (www.beck.com) or the Austin Powers Web site (www.austinpowers.com) for examples of cool graphics and animation.

### Screeners versus trailers

In the world of film, a *screener* is a videotape (usually VHS) of the entire movie. It gets sent to people who are likely to take the time to view the whole thing. A *trailer* is a compilation of highlights from the film that puts across its best qualities in less than five minutes. Music videos themselves are less than five minutes long, so trailers are not generally needed. But consider this sobering fact: Reviewers, hard pressed for time, frequently watch the first 30 seconds of a video and then write their review. It's harsh but true. If your first 30 seconds is an establishing shot of a cornfield, and your spaceship doesn't land until 4:30 into the video, consider making an action-packed trailer to post on your EPK.

# Getting on Television

The ultimate goal of a video is to be shown on television. That's why it's called a *video* and not an *audio*. It's not uncommon to hear inexperienced bands and video directors complaining that they send their unsolicited tapes to MTV and never get played. This shows a bit of a misunderstanding of what MTV is all about. It's not a public service to give exposure to deserving artists. It's a paid advertising medium, like a Times Square billboard. And just as the billboard is only affordable to mega-corporations, so is MTV affordable to the same corporate giants.

Unless you are mounting a million-dollar ad campaign for your act, MTV is probably the wrong venue, anyway. Imagine that we are going to stage a garage sale next Saturday. Would we sit down and say, "Okay, the first thing we'll do is take out full-page ads in *Time* and *Newsweek*?" Of course not, that would be, as our friend Kevin Welch once said, like taking a 747 to 7-11. Instead of giving up because MTV is a different playing field, take the opportunity to look around at what is available to us no-budget, would-be moguls. As a matter of fact, there is a TV medium mandated as a public service to give exposure to deserving artists. It's called *public access television*.

## Using public access television

Although some sectors of the corporate world have become more and more monopolistic (radio, for example), television has become less so, and with the meteoric rise of cable, the medium now exists in a pleasant state of anarchy. Boutique cable channels, such as CNN, ESPN, and HBO, have risen up to challenge the "big three" networks, which no one really considers the big three anymore. At the same time, cable channels appealing to small audiences are readily available as part of multichannel packages, so recent immigrants, aspiring chefs, bass fishermen, and soccer fans can all find the content they desire with a little bit of surfing. The United States Government, as part of the 1984 Cable Communications Policy Act, declared that every American should have the opportunity to exercise her First Amendment right to free speech on the booming medium of cable television.

### What is public access TV?

The 1984 Act enabled local governments to negotiate with cable providers to set aside part of their profits to provide equipment and training for any citizen who might want to use the airwaves. Cable companies are not bound to comply but many of them do, and at last count, about a thousand public access television (PATV) channels were available across the U.S.

**Cross-Reference**　To find some of the PATV stations in your area, turn to Appendix D for great Web resources.

## How does the public get access to it?

We, the public, must simply contact our local PATV channel and inform them that we want to express ourselves in the form of a TV show. We then become supporting members, that is, we pay a small fee. Then we sign up for training classes, typically two or three sessions for each class, in various skills including camera, sound and lighting techniques, location shooting, and simple "cuts only" editing. If you bought this book, you will undoubtedly see the value in getting cheap training in these skills. The quality of the gear varies widely depending on location, but in many cases, it's first-rate. At the end of the classes, we sign up on a waiting list, either to serve as crew members, or to produce our own show. If we're putting our own show together, we can find a crew on the crew waiting list, or, better yet, assemble a "gang" beforehand, and have everybody go through training together.

## Produce your own show

However, you can also assemble your own TV show and submit tapes to the PATV channel, rather than go through the channel's classes. If you're working with Premiere, you may want to go this route, because you may have more sophisticated editing capabilities than the station, especially if you are running After Effects. Do you have enough videos, "making of" footage, interviews, and live clips for a half hour, or a series of half hours? If so, congratulations, you're a TV producer!

## Are you ready for reality TV?

Here's a twist on the "produce your own show" concept. Follow a band around for a while (with their consent, of course) and shoot them just being themselves. Bob Dylan, Radiohead, Fugazi, and the Beatles have all done this. On gig days, you can meet them when they arrive at the gig and ride with them to the next gig. They'll probably get pretty irritated with you at times, but that makes for some good footage!

## Finding programs that will air your video

If all this seems too much like work, then consider being a content provider for another PATV producer who airs music videos. Find out from the channel access coordinator who produces the "Wednesday Video Bash," and approach her in a businesslike way. "Hi, I'm a local video producer, and I've done professional-quality videos of six local bands. I think I could talk them into coming down to the studio for live interviews, and I have some exciting live footage from top clubs in the area. How about running a weekly segment on local bands? I'll provide the content." She may be relieved to know that someone else is willing to account for five minutes of her show every week. When you get that going, of course, then it's time to go online and repeat the process on the other 999 PATV channels across the nation.

## Get on your bicycle

If you produce your own show, you can get it aired in other cities. It's called *bicycling*. If you have a devoted fan in another town, and they have the time and willingness to get involved in PATV, ask if they would like to executive-produce your show in their city. They would go through the process of "supporting" the station and taking training classes, but you would supply the content. Even better, have them round up local video talent and start a loose national network of local video shows with a common concept.

## Taking a look at Manhattan Neighborhood Network

The unofficial flagship of PATV channels is Manhattan Neighborhood Network. The staggering cultural diversity of New York, and the general attitude of tolerance for the arts and free speech, makes for a variety of homegrown TV. A quick glance at their online program guide (www.mnn.com) reveals the following music shows:

✦ *Hanging Out and Jamming*

✦ *New Flavor Videos*

✦ *Music Madness*

✦ *Teenavision*

✦ *Local Vision*

✦ *Pandemonium*

✦ *Gospel Today*

✦ *All This Jazz*

✦ *Jazz Bytes*

✦ *International Women of Jazz*

✦ *Latin Jazz, Alive and Kickin'*

✦ *Feels Good* ("uplifts viewers")

✦ *Family, Inc.* ("A family singing group born and raised in Harlem")

✦ *The Music Sampler*

✦ *The Art of Jazz*

As you can see, it's pretty open-minded. In fact, by federal law, there is no censorship. After all, PATV is part of our exercise of the right to free speech (and music video). Forget *Wayne's World*. That was then. This is now, and public access is there for the taking. Sure, you'll see some stuff that's so tacky it's frightening, but your half hour is what you make it. PATV is a brave new world, and it's free!

Of course, if you watch *The Sopranos* or *Six Feet Under*, you know that you're not watching freebie public access. Have you ever noticed, though, that late at night, sandwiched between two classy reruns, you'll see those half-hour infomercials for ab rollers, free government money, fishing rods that fit in your pocket, and so forth? Obviously, someone bought that time on the cheap. Inexpensive airtime is out there.

### Leased access: Going commercial

Commercial cable channels sometimes offer time at a reduced rate. One station in Cleveland offers half-hours for as low as $250. Because it is commercial TV, slots are included for ads, so if you can line up two sponsors to buy two ads each on your show, you're covered. Keep in mind that you now have the responsibility to keep the sponsors happy and, in a sense, you are hostage to them, as all commercial shows are.

### Jump on the infomercial bandwagon

Infomercials used to be the realm of TV's bottom-feeders. The lowest of the low, the tackiest of products, hawked by the dorkiest of pitchmen. Check out Handsome Devil's video for "Makin' Money" to see a hilarious spoof of this genre. In the last decade, however, changes have occurred. David Letterman and Conan O'Brien have made late night TV a hip place to hang out, and the venerable Time/Life organization now airs infomercials for their great music compilations, complete with rare video footage, where Vegematics once roamed. We even saw a cool and classy late night commercial for Bob Dylan's *Love and Theft* CD. More and more advertisers are realizing that cheap airtime is not a bad thing. This once-scorned time slot may well be a new frontier for cutting edge artists who can't afford prime time prices, and who cater to an audience that stays up late, anyway.

### Satellite TV: Taking it nationwide

Did you know that in India, relatively few people ever had dial telephones, but now almost everyone carries a cell phone? In countries around the world where cable-based infrastructure was never installed, cheap wireless technology catches on very fast. In techno-intensive cultures, such as the U.S., consumers want all modern conveniences available in their cars. For these two reasons, wireless technologies will soon replace cable. Then, computers and multichannel TV and radio systems will join cell phones in the car and in homes across the world. Satellite TV dishes are already commonplace, of course, and there are a couple of satellite networks that broadcast to homes across the country. Channel America reaches 25 million sets, and they sell time. Rates are reasonable, but you will need sponsors. Watch for public access to go satellite someday. Then we'll all be able to tune into "The life and times of two fellas doing whatever. . . ."

## It's All About Networking

When you're promoting your video, you're in the marketing business. It's been said that marketing is not about selling stuff; it's about relationships. As the relationships blossom, stuff gets sold. It's all part of the same process. If you approach your promotional campaign this way, you can actually enjoy it. You may experience some rejection, some unfair competition, and some rude bumps along the way, but you'll also be making friends with people who will become long-time supporters and co-workers.

# Join the Alliance for Community Media

Free speech is guaranteed in the United States Constitution, and we can assume that it will always be a part of American life. But what about public access television? Will it always be around? Will it keep pace with the technological changes that are sweeping the information industry? Well, PATV was legislated into existence, and it could be legislated back out. It could come under attack from special interest groups, who may interpret free speech according to their own agenda, or it could be viewed as competition by the very cable providers who now support it, should it ever really take off. A resource this fragile needs a watchdog on Capitol Hill. Fortunately, PATV has a very proactive one — the Alliance for Community Media or simply, the Alliance.

The Alliance is a nonprofit organization devoted to helping the public get the most out of public access television. Membership is yearly, and various levels of participation have different annual fees, starting as low as $35. The Alliance is located at 666 Eleventh Street, NW, Washington, DC 20001; phone (202) 393-2650.

## Making use of the Alliance Web site

The Alliance Web site (www.alliancecm.org) is a useful source of information on PATV. If you're planning a national promotional campaign for your videos, check out the Alliance's Community Media Yellow Pages, a nationwide listing of public access stations.

The Web site also provides links to the official Web sites of various alternative channels, including Deep-Dish Television, a national satellite network, and Paper Tiger Television. These two networks are primarily politically oriented but also provide some arts coverage.

 **Note**  Don't confuse PATV with PBS. The public broadcasting system is a listener- and government-supported network of stations that provides community-related programming produced by industry professionals.

## Taking part in the Hometown Video Festival

The Alliance sponsors the Hometown Video Festival. Under the motto, "Think globally, produce locally," the festival gives out awards in over 40 categories, including category 28, Music Video. Special categories for k-12 students are also available. Alliance members receive discounts on festival entry fees.

# Join the Music Video Production Association

Music video producers have always known that they were creating an art form, not just churning out ad agency hackwork. But it's only lately that they've become organized into a forum to let the rest of the world know. That forum is the Music Video Production Association, or MVPA.

Founded by working producers, the MVPA was set up to further video as an art form, and to recognize the best work in the medium on its aesthetic merits, without consideration of the role of video in major-label marketing. Log on to www.mvpa.com at least once a week to keep up with current events and issues on the cutting edge of video.

### Making use of the MVPA Web site

On the MVPA site, you'll find interviews with top producers, up-to-date news items, and many links to useful sites for videographers. Although it's geared toward professionals, amateurs can learn much from hanging out at this site. One page offers downloadable contract forms for music video directors, a rare peek into the business side of the medium. From here, you can also link to www.musicvideoinsider.com, an e-zine for video directors, and www.mvdbase.com, the video equivalent of www.imdb.com, the Internet Movie Database.

### Keeping up with MVPA-sponsored events

The MVPA sponsors several major events every year. Artfest is a showcase for the most artistic, not necessarily commercial, videos by directors both known and unknown. The Director's Cut Festival, held in Los Angeles in July and New York in October, airs cutting edge videos by top directors displaying their own concepts, unencumbered by "guidance" from label executives and managers.

The MVPA Annual Awards are aiming to be the Oscars of video, and they seek to recognize excellence not just commercial impact (MTV Awards, anyone?).You may be surprised to find that awards are given for Best Hair in a Video and Best Make-up in a Video. Then again, you may not. Recent winners include pioneering directors Jean-Baptiste Mondino and Spike Jonze.

# Using Web Resources

A little over a decade ago, a home-cooked video had no chance of being seen by anyone outside the director's immediate family. Cable TV and the Internet have changed all of that forever. A few hours surfing the Web can turn up all kinds of opportunities to be seen and also to learn.

## Get on the wire

Music Video Wire is a terrific Web site that posts interviews and news items of interest to videographers both great and small. Like the MVPA site, it's geared toward the professional. There aren't any fans contributing gushing reviews, but plenty of information is available to help you keep up with behind-the-scenes events in the world of video.

You can find the Music Video Wire Web site www.musicvideowire.com. From there, you can link to a number of other cool sites. Most of these sites are oriented toward the music video professional but none are too esoteric for amateur viewing.

## I'm gonna wait 'til the magic hour

**Road Diary**

Taos is one of our favorite towns. It's a little artists' colony, tucked way up in the Sangre de Christo Mountains of northern New Mexico. You can get there by driving up the Rio Grande gorge from Santa Fe, a beautiful route, or you can take the spectacular ride over Cimarron Pass, which brings you up around ten thousand feet and then drops you into the high Rocky Mountain meadow called Angel Fire. Best way to do that is to drive down from Denver to Cimarron on Day One, and spend the night at the only motel in this little town of four hundred people and fifteen hundred elk, not to mention the cattle. Cimarron is the real Old West, and it's too out of the way to be touristy. Anyway, get up at dawn and have coffee and a couple of eggs, and then set out across Cimarron Canyon. The road will take you up to the pass described above, after which you'll want to stop at Angel Fire for a little rest and altitude adjustment. Continue on down the creek into Taos and wind your way down the narrow streets. Take the Paseo to Kit Carson Lane, or Martyrs Lane, and stop in at a little gallery or bookstore. We usually hole up at the Kachina Lodge, where we can relax in the pool during the afternoon and huddle around the mesquite campfire at night.

Taos has been a center for artists since the turn of the 20th century, and there's a good reason why they flock to this aerie high in the mountains. The light. The light is totally unique here. Just as a light in Venice is reflected off the canals, the light here is reflected off adobe and red rock. Everything is a slightly different color here. The light is warmer, in a funky, pastel way. This is Georgia O'Keefe country. It's film country, too. *Easy Rider*, *Lonesome Dove*, and many other movies were shot on location in this area. In fact, there are several ranches devoted to serving the film industry. This is a great place to shoot video.

One evening, we were strolling around town after dinner. It was the time that cinematographers call the "magic hour." The magic hour, actually only a few minutes, is when the sun has set but it's still light out. It's light out, but a completely different light than the direct light of daytime. All natural light is, for a few minutes, reflected light, bathing objects in a kind of visual softness. It's also known as, of course, twilight. This is a time to get special shots. On this particular evening, twilight teamed up with an unexpected partner. One small dark cloud was lurking in an otherwise clear sky. As sometimes happens out West, this one little cloud decided to precipitate, and though it was still early in the fall, the temperature was just right for the droplets to turn to snow as they fell on the town plaza. The whole phenomenon lasted maybe five minutes, but it was a real treat for lovers of light. Not only was it the magic hour, but also each snowflake reflected the pinkish light off its own unique surface, creating a walk-through kaleidoscope where the air seemed to cycle through various shades of pink, red, and orange. Every adobe wall was a different color than it was a few minutes before, and the whole process was like liquid flowing over the town. No one spoke, but everyone celebrated. Maura and I started dancing in the street. Look for the light, said the old man in Oklahoma. Look for the light.

## Get on the databases

Several sites exist on the Web, where you can go and hunt for archived videos, streaming videos, stills, biographies of directors, and so forth. If you produce videos, you should be included in these databases. Most of them have a "contact us" button that you can click to ask for information about being included on the Web site's lists of videos and directors.

### Using mvdBase.com

Before going to the mvdBase.com Web site, go to www.imdb.com, the Internet Movie Database. This site is truly awesome, one of the cooler accomplishments to be found online. You may stop in for a quick visit and end up spending a whole day here. The goal is to provide information on every movie ever made. You can search in a number of different ways, and you can become a Trivial Pursuit grand master, at least in the movie category.

Okay, now on to www.mvdb.com. The Music Video Database is still growing, and it's certainly not on the titanic scale (no pun intended) of the Internet Movie Database, but its goal is equally noble: to provide information, and eventually perhaps streaming video when DSL is everywhere, on all videos in general circulation. A very useful site for looking up "who-directed-what" and other hard to find information. You can link to this site from www.mvpa.com, as well.

### A ticket to clipland.com

Clipland is yet another great archive of video clips and information. Located at www.clipland.com, this site claims to have 12,000 downloadable videos and 2,400 streaming clips. If you just got a high-speed line, come to this site and bring plenty of Twinkies; you'll be here for a while.

### The big one: launch.com

If high-speed streaming video is your thing, www.launch.com is your source for thousands of archived videos. Easy searching and lots of fan-oriented extras, such as photos and bios make this Yahoo! spin-off a pleasant place to while away the hours.

# Selling Your Video

We recently read an interview with a video project coordinator for a major label. She stated, matter-of-factly, that the big labels routinely spend $300,000 to $600,000 to produce a promotional video. A bit more than we spend on our desktop masterpieces, eh? But there is some cost involved for us. After all, we do buy hardware and software and wonderful books that teach us how to use the stuff. It would be nice to recoup a little bit of this outlay by selling a few copies of the video, wouldn't it? Here are a few ideas and a little rumination on a basic problem shared by all video producers.

## Ponder public perception

Have you noticed that people will buy tickets to see a movie? Of course you have. They'll also buy tickets for a live concert (Michael Jackson recently sold seats for $2500 at a Madison Square Garden show), but have you ever seen anyone line up to buy tickets for a video? Videos may be movies in miniature, but from a marketing standpoint, they are two different animals. The movie industry grew to satisfy an insatiable demand for a new technology that completely revolutionized the notion of entertainment. Records, and later, CDs, have been churned out by the millions to meet the demand of a public that can't get enough. But videos were born as an advertising tool. They were always intended to entice customers to go out and buy records not videos. People don't pay to look at a billboard, and they don't expect to pay to watch videos. Someday, when videos are recognized as an art form, they will be a destination purchase, just like a book or a CD. In the meantime, we've got to be resourceful in coming up with ways to make music fans see videos as an item of value.

## Sell your own QuickTime CDs

As you know by now, QuickTime is a nifty little compression format that enables the huge file size of a video to be reduced enough to fit on a standard CD. It's not exactly broadcast quality, but it looks great, provided the video was well produced in the first place. Our friends, The Nields, recently released a QuickTime video compilation on CD that captures their charm and onstage charisma, without elaborate special effects. Their fans love it. In between shows, fans can boot up their computers and watch their favorite band in action in the comfort of their home. What's not to like? Begin with the assumption that it won't be the same quality as, say, a new Steven Spielberg flick in 70mm, and you can really have fun with this format.

**Tip**
If you're going to sell the thing, put it in an attractive package. Make your CD jewel box or eco-pak look competitive with the audio CDs on the rack at Tower Records. If you're not expert at graphic design, have a professional do it for you. They may exchange time for a credit, if they're looking to break into more music work.

## Create an enhanced audio CD

Consumers are used to the idea that when they unwrap a CD, they are getting about 45 minutes of entertainment. There's no logical reason for this. It could be 70 minutes or 20 minutes. Book buyers, for example, don't buy books by the page. They buy for the content. But the fact remains that if your buyers open their CD and get one four-minute video, they may feel short-changed. Of course, QuickTime is a very small file format, and you could put a lot of video content on there, but most of us aren't like veteran producer Nigel Dick, who just logged his 250th video. We might do better to piggyback a few videos with some live footage, an interview, some stills, and lyric pages to create a package to enhance a standard length CD. There's plenty of disc space left after a typical pop music CD has been burned, and compact-file visuals are a great way to give buyers an added value.

Figure 15-2 illustrates the typical file structure of an enhanced CD. The enhancement files may include:

✦ The interface file, which contains audio files, text including lyrics and liner notes, and photo images

✦ ReadMe files for both Mac and PC platforms

✦ QuickTime movies

✦ Other necessary technical files

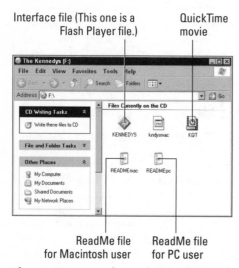

Figure 15-2: An enhanced CD contains several files, combining audio, video, and text elements.

Figure 15-3 shows how the interface from Figure 15-2 looks, when opened. You may elect to have a computer graphics designer or mastering lab (see below) assemble your audio and visual elements for you.

## Navigating the manufacturing waters

If you choose to go the indie route and produce your own package of audio and visual information on CD, you'll need to deal with a mastering lab that has done this type of project before. Check out Airshow Mastering, with studios in Washington, D.C. and Boulder, Colorado, for enhanced CD mastering.

## Looking ahead to DVD

As soon as low-cost DVD burners are readily available, and the price of media comes down, the rules will change once again. Higher-quality audio and video will be in our hot little hands. Watch for new developments on this front.

Link to band Web site

Play video

Link to lyrics

Link to liner notes

Return to start    Exit    Background image of band

**Figure 15-3:** You should arrange all the added visual content on your enhanced CD by creating an easy-to-use, cross-platform interface, like the one shown here.

## Sell through distributors

You can still sell analog VHS tapes through traditional brick and mortar stores, but this avenue is fast disappearing for two reasons. First, retailers didn't have a lot of success selling music videos (most major chain video stores don't even have a music section anymore). Second, VHS is being phased out. As soon as manufacturers feel that most people have DVD players, VHS will go the way of audio cassettes.

### Compete with the big guys at your local video store

If you do want to slug it out with middle-of-the-road mega-fare, including Hollywood features, get your product listed in the Major Concept Video Catalogue (800-365-0150). This catalog is where buyers for video stores find their product. Be forewarned — they will be looking for music videos on the Garth Brooks/Sting level of popularity, and besides, VHS is on the way out, so why make a big investment in it? Our advice is to stick with DIY, small distributors, and online resources until the DVD dust settles.

### Is Canyon Cinema for you?

In the indie world, small is beautiful. If you go with a boutique distributor, their customers will be hardcore video fans, the kind who seek out the good, hard-to-find stuff like yours and ours. Canyon Cinema is a Bay Area indie-friendly film distributor. Will they handle your video compilation? Doesn't hurt to ask. It costs $40 to get listed in their catalogue (415-626-2255).

### Join the Filmmakers Cooperative

This venerable artist's co-op lists independent films in their biannual catalogue for a yearly fee of $35. If anything sells, you take 60 percent, and they take 40 percent (212-889-3820).

### Exploring the Amazon

This online powerhouse seems to have an almost pathological willingness to deal with small accounts. If you sell two units a month, they are happy to pay you and order two more. You can find Amazon.com (www.amazon.com) and their competitor, Barnes and Noble (www.bn.com), just about everywhere on the Web. They pop up on our AOL home page, and if we go from there to the Google search page, they pop up there, too. So you'll have no trouble finding them. Set yourself up as a vendor, and follow this bit of advice. After your product is available, it may be reviewed by Amazon customers. Get the jump on this process by encouraging your enthusiastic and well-informed fans to post reviews.

Even people who spend very little time online know to search for media on Amazon.com, so it's important to have a presence there, even if it doesn't amount to a lot of income from sales.

## Sell to stock footage houses

You can recoup your costs in other ways, too. *El Mariachi* director, Robert Rodriguez, volunteered to be a subject at a medical testing lab to raise money for his no-budget film. You don't have to go that far, but explore ways that you can raise funds by using resources already available to you.

### Don't throw away those outtakes!

If you're incredibly efficient, most of what you shoot ends up on the screen. If, however, you're like most of us, you shoot a lot more footage than you use in the final cut. That's okay. Major studio pictures often have a shooting ratio of 10 minutes to every 1 minute used. B-movie legend Ed Wood worked on a 1:1 ratio. He used every bit of film that he shot, but his movies are often cited as the worst ever made, so efficiency isn't everything.

If you're on a really tight budget, you'll want to dump your usable footage into the computer, and then blissfully reuse the same tape, blithely erasing everything on it as you shoot. If you can afford tape, though, you probably have reels lying around that you will never use. What's on those reels? Recent ads for stock footage houses touted available clips of sharks, Yellowstone, Hawaii, hot water vents, clouds, desert, snow, storms, and so on, endlessly. One ad simply offers "every subject." If you have footage, especially scenes without people, you may be able to recoup some costs by selling it to a stock footage house.

### Where to find buyers

To find buyers for all of your stock footage, click on www.clipclick.com and look for acquisitions. In addition, *Videography* magazine features a monthly full page of ads for stock footage houses. See Appendix D for Stock Footage Library Information.

# Promoting Your Video Guerilla-Style

We're guessing that you didn't spend $300,000 to $600,000 on your latest video, and we're willing to bet that you don't have that kind of money earmarked to promote it, either. That's what puts you, and us, on a different playing field than the majors. It's a field where networking, imagination, and ingenuity count more than cash outlay. Let's explore some options for a down-low-to-the-ground promotional budget.

## Use your Web site: It worked for Blair Witch!

To a major label, a word-of-mouth buzz is the icing on a promotional cake. To a no-budget videographer, it may be the only promotions we get. You can boost the buzz, and even control it to a certain extent, by carefully managing your Web site. The producers of *The Blair Witch Project*, one of the best known rags-to-riches indie success stories, got it's buzz going by setting up a simple but highly imaginative Web site that convinced everyone weeks before the film's release that it was a true story.

We strongly recommend that you learn enough about Web site construction through the use of simple templates to maintain your own site. Doing so frees you from being held hostage to the schedule of your Web*meister* who gets busy doing something else and doesn't update your site for six months.

### Establish a fan base headquarters

Your Web site should be a place where your fans gather, such as a local coffee shop. Make the site a comfortable place for them. Use a simple URL and make your site friendly to the primitive hand-me-down computers that your younger fans may be stuck with. Don't get carried away with cutting edge technology that requires the latest hardware. Your fans come to the site for information and inspiration, not a technical morass that their computer may not be able to navigate quickly. Have an easy-to-return-to home page that sums up who you are for first time visitors.

### Get a fan to edit a newsgroup

If your fans gather at your Web site, shouldn't they be able to talk to each other? Have a computer savvy fan set up and edit an online discussion group about your work. Your one fan in Norway will really enjoy reading the set list from last night's Boston gig, and if he can see a QuickTime of your latest video, that's even better. A newsgroup is a total value-add for your fans. Don't participate in it yourself, though. It will make them self-conscious about voicing their opinions. Feel free to lurk once in a while. You'll learn a lot about how you're perceived, and you'll find out about other artists and videographers that they discuss online.

## Pump up your e-mail list

E-mail is the cheapest and most effective way to publicize your work. It has a great advantage over traditional advertising, in that you have an actual address for each potential fan/consumer.

### Why e-mail is more powerful than the Web

E-mail also has a big advantage over a Web site. Your site just sits there, waiting patiently for someone to search for it or link to it. It's a passive entity until someone actually hits it. With e-mail, you proactively reach out to your fans. You have a specific message for them, and you give it to them. What's more, after you see "Your mail has been sent," you know they got it. We can think of a million reasons why people get too busy to visit your Web site, but most people with e-mail check it daily.

### Strategies for building up your e-mail list

Rule Number One is — don't abuse anybody's privacy. Let people sign up voluntarily on your list. Don't put people on it, thinking that they might consider it a great thing. How many involuntary lists have you been put on that you thought were great? Going through music business directories and convention rosters and putting everyone on your list is a good way to get everyone in the music business simultaneously thinking of you as a nuisance, which is probably not a great career move.

If you play gigs, that's the best time to collect addresses. We keep a clipboard right next to the stage for e-mail sign up, and we get addresses at every show. At some shows, we give away a free CD in a simple raffle. The raffle ticket is a slip of paper with entries for name and e-mail address. The audience knows that we will put them on the list, but if they're competing for a free CD, we know they won't mind. By the way, restrict your promotional mailings to once or twice a month. You don't want to be thought of as Spam, do you?

# Go link-crazy

We first heard about the Web about 10 years ago, when we bought our first little Mac. Our friend Gareth Branwyn told us excitedly, "Now you'll be able to get on the World Wide Web. It's this amazing resource that links people together."

### Links are what the Web is all about

A Web site alone is a groovy thing, but it's the ability to link to any other Web site in the world that opens up the door to unlimited possibility. After all, it's called the *Web*, not the *Site*. It's the interconnection that matters. Make the most of this interconnection by linking to any friendly site that would interest your visitors.

### Make your site a portal to other cool sites

Don't be afraid that links will lead your visitors away from your site. On the contrary, having lots of fun links encourages them to start surfing at your site, and they will visit it that much more often.

### Use your imagination

Don't limit your links to sites that are similar to yours. If your fans are interested in film as well as video, make sure that they can get to the Internet Movie Database from your site. There's no doubt that they're into music, so provide links to your own favorite artists. This promotes the original spirit of camaraderie that characterized the Web back in the early, smaller-scale days.

### It never hurts to ask

Asking to establish a link is a great way to make contact with your peers. It's a compliment and an acknowledgement of common interests and goals. Ask some professionals who are further along than you. Even if you only get ten hits a day, that's ten more links that they might pick up, and your site becomes a more interesting destination with each link.

# You're newsworthy!

So *Entertainment Tonight* isn't ringing your phone off the hook, begging for an interview? Hey, who needs them? Here's a tip: They don't ring anybody's phone off the hook. They sit back and wait for press agents to pitch stories to them. So take the initiative. Is your story interesting? How would the headline read? If a short story on you and your video work appeared in the local paper, how would you want it to read? While you're picturing this, sit down and write the story. Write it in the short, concise style of a good news piece and make every word focus on an interesting point. No rambling allowed.

## Compose a short news item

Let's say your piece reads like this:

SPRINGFIELD ACCOUNTANT DIVES INTO WORLD OF VIDEO

"When Joe Miller's clients sit across from his desk, going over their tax receipts and asking questions about 401k plans, they have no idea that they're talking to an aspiring director of rock videos. The soft-spoken accountant's low-key style belies his moonlighting job, as official videographer to Springfield's burgeoning hard-rock scene. 'It's all in a day's work,' says Joe, who sometimes works all night at his video editing desk, wrapping only minutes before his first client arrives. The music scene has taken notice. Miller was nominated for three 'Springies' last year, including an award for Video of the Year for Poison Lion's 'Pet Me at Your Own Risk.' Accountants may be thought of as conservative, but Joe Miller proves that you can't judge a bookkeeper by looking at his cover."

## Make it easy on them

Okay, this story isn't going to be fighting for front-page newspaper space, but it may get printed in the local interest section. To Joe's surprise, the fact that an accountant is an aspiring rock videographer is newsworthy. In fact, this story might appear as a human-interest piece on the financial page. The point is that Joe did the reporters' work for them. He wrote the story and sent it in with his press kit. All they had to do was print it. It's much easier for an overworked individual to copy something and print it than it is to compose an original story based on some sketchy information. The community interest editor of Joe's local paper isn't trying to be Woodward and Bernstein. She just wants to get a few interesting press releases that she can reprint virtually as is.

## Get to know the local media

Find out the names of the local editors and reporters who deal with your type of non-life-threatening stories. When you send out a press release, don't include a cover letter. Just put a sticky note on the cover of the folder with a very short message, such as "Becky — Loved your piece on the Slovakian dance troupe. I've got a new video airing on *Springfield Rocks* Tuesday night. Information's enclosed. Thanks!"

You get off to a good start by offering a quick, nonfawning compliment. Then cut to the chase by saying exactly what you're sending her and when you hope to have a mention in print. This short burst of information shows that you appreciate how little time she has to devote to each submission. She'll appreciate that. If she runs a mention in the "What's Happening in the Arts" column, send her an e-mail saying simply "Becky — Thanks for the ink. Response was really good. Columbia Records is sending a talent scout to check out Poison Lion. I'll keep you posted, Joe Miller."

Becky, the overworked arts editor, will always remember you as someone who doesn't waste her time, and that's a good thing.

### Make sure that they know what's happening

Don't send out regular press releases. Send one when something is happening. But don't lose track of your contacts between events. Create a simple database of contact information, with a field to flag "friendly" reporters who actually give you coverage, as opposed to the ones you send to, hoping to get coverage. Don't underestimate the importance of an enthusiastic reporter at a small paper. The music editor at the Springfield community college *Fightin' Falcon* might be writing a regular sidebar for *Rolling Stone* by this time next year. Remember, she's working to advance her career just as you are.

### Enter film festivals and awards shows

Don't be disappointed if you're not invited to Sundance after your first video is released. They don't officially air music videos, and besides, Utah's cold in January! Check the online archive of your local paper for the Annual Guide to Film Festivals. While you're there, search for Festivals of the Arts and Music Awards. Get entry information for all of these events. When we first got into video, we were known in our hometown as musicians, and we surprised a few people, including ourselves, by winning Video of the Year at the local music awards show the first time that we ventured into that category. Join the local music organization, if there is one. It's a great way to network with bands who may become your future video clients.

## Use your video to seek new gigs

This tried-and -true use for video is still the second best way to sell your act to club owners and concert bookers. The best way, of course, is to have them actually see you live, but a video clip is worth a thousand 8x10-inch photographs.

### Approach venue bookers

Some venue bookers are happy to see your latest artful, conceptual video creation. Others are mistrustful of all that new-fangled editing stuff and insist on getting only raw live footage. There's no consensus on this, so have both on hand and check with bookers first before you send out your kit.

### Attend showcase conventions

Performance videos are an important feature of the exhibit booths at conventions. Concert bookers have their own conventions, just as do dentists, teachers, and book publishers. Check online for your state government's council for the arts. They probably sponsor an annual showcase of talent for bookers who present government funded shows. On the national level, Association of Performing Arts Presenters (APAP) and National Association for Campus Activities (NACA) are two organizations that host major convention/showcases for talent buyers. Find out how you can rent booth space to hawk your video skills or promote your band with expertly shot live footage looping all day on a monitor.

## Use your video to promo upcoming gigs

If you're going to approach local video programs, time your campaign to coincide with an important live gig. When the band books the show, they can tell the club owner, "We'll be interviewed on *Springfield Rocks* the Tuesday before the gig, so we can plug it then." They can tell *Springfield Rocks*, "We're gonna be at the Roxy on Saturday the fifteenth, and our new video is in the can, so we can premiere it and talk about the upcoming gig." The show is happy. The club is happy. The band is happy. Everybody's happy. And that's a good situation.

## Get press information for a "DIY" campaign

When the act is playing out of town, you may need to make new press and TV contacts. The best source for this information is the club itself. They know who their friendly media people are, and they probably keep a list that they can fax you. Don't depend on the club to promote the gig for you. A few do. Most don't. But they are extremely happy if you ask for a media list. This shows them that you are serious about promoting the gig. Twelve weeks in advance is not too far out to start making contacts.

## Use professional publicists

Have you ever noticed that, when a new album by, say, Madonna or No Doubt is released, their photogenic faces are splashed across the newsstand on a dozen different magazines, all in the same week? Is it just that the magazine editors are all so excited about the new CD that they coincidentally all ran cover photos the same week? Not exactly. The record label, hoping to recoup expenses as soon as possible, hires a high-powered public relations firm to work the album, starting several months in advance to ensure that the cover shots will all be timed with the release date. It's not a spontaneous burst of enthusiasm, but it's designed to induce a burst of enthusiasm among potential record buyers, who, seeing the same face everywhere, say to themselves, "This has got to be hot."

Publicists range in cost from expensive to Madonna-level. In every town, though, there are people who know the music scene and might be eager to break in by playing a supporting role as a publicist. Freelance reporters who get assigned to city council meetings and zoning hearings are often music fans who would love to use their contacts to do a little gratis work that supports local musicians.

If you have the budget, hire a professional, someone who already has his Rolodex together. These people are found in New York, Los Angeles, and Nashville, with the price being a little lower in Nashville. Don't blow your budget on one week of Madonna's publicist (also called a "flack"). She'll be working Madonna and will assign your project to an intern. Find someone who's up and coming and eager to build a client base.

If you're planning a full-fledged tour, you may want to log onto www.rockamericamusic.com and click promotions. They will handle publicity for a tour and get your video to the right people. Of course, it'll cost ya.

# Use your video to break into the profession

From where we're sitting, we can't tell if you're *really* good or not. It's also hard for you to know, yourself, as the huge number of mediocre videos out there will attest to. One way to gauge is if a lot of people *outside* of your friends and family are blown away by your work. Sometimes academic types who teach film classes are good judges but beware. Some are failed filmmakers themselves, and they don't hand out encouraging words to up and comers. If you encounter a teacher with this attitude, move on. Encouragement fosters art; discouragement kills it. Seek out the former and simply walk away from the latter.

If you believe strongly in your work and you've gotten a lot of ecstatic feedback from non-family members and a few media professionals, you may already be considering a real gig in the video world. Film school is one way that up-and-comers have broken in. Photography school is another. Public access TV is a good way to learn the gear. (See "Using Public Access Television" earlier in this chapter.) And you may be surprised to learn that most professional videographers do a lot of work in advertising.

## The marriage of video and advertising

Have you ever noticed that the music and video content of TV commercials is frequently a lot hipper than the shows themselves? The shows have to hold an audience of widely varying tastes for a full half hour. Commercials, on the other hand, launch a full-scale assault that lasts only 30 seconds. The goal of a TV ad is to raise the on-screen energy level in a short burst, so that the viewer will remember the product even after watching a full-length, plot-driven show. It makes sense that the same directors who are expert at packing sensory data into a 30-second package are also highly skilled at music video. Many of the top directors regularly turn out spots for visually progressive companies including Nike, Levi's, Intel, and Coca-Cola. If you're taping videos off the air for your own study, don't forget to capture any commercials that catch your eye. In fact, some of the online music video archives also feature well-stocked departments for TV ads and movie trailers.

## Think globally, start out locally

If you're skilled at shooting and editing music video, you may have your ticket into cutting edge media advertising. Your Premiere skills, especially if you are an avid After Effects user, may enable you to start right in working on the progressive end of the advertising field. Don't look down your nose at advertising work. The top music video directors don't.

## Contact the major video production houses

Many of the top video directors work in the stable of an independent film company. Most of these companies are located in Hollywood, and many have an office in New York as well. For an updated list, log on to the Music Video Production Association Web site at www.mvpa.com. Click links and then click Production Company List. If you want to send a demo reel to a company, get familiar with their work first. If you feel that your stuff is really right for them, contact the acquisitions manager and ask if she would be interested in seeing a short demo reel. *Don't* send unsolicited tapes to any production company. To avoid spurious copyright lawsuits, they don't even open tapes that haven't been prescreened. Your time and tape would be better spent applying for entry to video festivals. Production companies recruit new talent from these events, not from cold calls.

## Get thee to a library

Although we live in an age in which vast stores of knowledge are available on the Web, many people still like to go to the library. It's a good place to get some work done, a good place to find peace and quiet, and a good place to score free books. Of course, you have to return them after you've read them, but you knew that already.

### Get reviewed in library catalogues

It wouldn't hurt to have your video or full-length compilation available in any library that wants to stock it in its collection. Make the libraries aware of your work by submitting a review copy to *Booklist*, a national publication that librarians use to keep up with new releases. Inclusion in library collections will certainly make your work available to thousands of potential viewers, and more and more libraries are expanding their collections to encompass various types of visual media, including music video.

### You are a local interest item

Your local library probably has a small section devoted to artists and writers who live in the region. Find out who the librarian is and let him know that you're producing video work that would interest their patrons. Some libraries, like the 53rd Street Donnell branch of the New York Public Library, are designated media centers that specialize in film and video as well as books.

### Subscribe to everything

Stay up with the cutting edge of your medium. Check in with the Music Video Wire at www.futureffects.com every week. Do the same with the Music Video Production Association Web site, at www.mvpa.com. Go through all their links and find out what's happening.

Subscribe to the top print magazines, including *Res*, *Videography*, *Videomaker*, and *Indie Slate*. If you can only afford one, get *Res*. It's the most music oriented of the bunch, and its graphic style can give you visual inspiration. Magazines are cheap, up-to-date knowledge. For more expensive up-to-date knowledge, subscribe to *Billboard*, as well. It's the music industry bible.

### Write your own local column

Your local paper probably doesn't have a weekly video review column. Volunteer to write it. Better yet, volunteer with a partner. You can each review two new videos a week, and your partner can review your stuff. You won't get paid, but they may allow you access to their high-speed DSL line for a couple of hours a week. This can give you time to plumb deeply into the online streaming video archives, such as www.launch.com, www.clipland.com, and www.mvdbase.com. You may also convince record labels to put you on their promo list. (Free stuff!)

# Have you ever tried four walling?

No, *four walling* is not when you take your SUV off-road. It's a term that's used in independent film and means, creating your own venue. You find a room, you invite people, and you show your video.

## Rent a room

Register at a major film conference. You don't have to submit anything. Just go as a participant. Rent a small suite instead of a room at a nearby hotel within walking distance from the conference site. Drive to the conference so that you can bring a trustworthy monitor and VCR. Schedule showings and announce the time and place on your e-mail list. Send individual e-mails to press people who will be attending. Also approach agents and acquisitions managers. Be brief. Tell them that you know that their schedules are crazy. You're just letting them know. Free food helps. (Mention the food.) If it's the South by Southwest film conference in Austin, serve Tex-Mex food. If it's Sundance, serve caribou. On second thought, chips and salsa is probably okay.

## Be the opening act

When your video band is playing at a venue that provides a video projector and screen, volunteer to come out and open the show with their video. The audience, having watched the band onscreen, is really pumped when they finally appear in person. They're mythological TV creatures! We went to a private Indigo Girls gig a few years ago. The show opened with a 15-minute video retrospective of their career. It was great. We showed our homegrown video of our Elvis wedding in Las Vegas before a show at Wolf Trap, and by the time we came onstage, the audience was already loosened up.

Another variation on this theme is to run video during a show, projected on the rear scrim. Sonic Youth ran cool footage of a Greenwich Village Street corner throughout a show at the 9:30 club in Washington, D.C., transplanting us all right to NYC for an hour and a half.

## Get in the house

Another cheap four-wall strategy is to simply throw a press party in your house or apartment development community room. Free food and music attracts low-paid reporters. If the band is an unknown start-up, double up with them and stage a house concert/video party. Get a buzz going. Did we mention that free food helps?

# Chapter Replay

After reading this chapter, you should be able to:

✦ Assemble an effective press kit

✦ Understand the basics of public access television

✦ Be familiar with organizations that enable videographers to network with each other

✦ Understand how to sell and promote your video through various outlets

Congratulations on finishing the book! You now have all you need to shoot, edit, distribute, and promote professional-looking music videos. To help you on your journey, we've included loads of supplemental information in the appendixes that follow, so you can use this book as a handy resource.

✦ ✦ ✦

# Valuable Information

# What's on the CD-ROM

**T**his appendix provides you with information on the contents of the CD-ROM that accompanies this book. For the latest and greatest information, please refer to the ReadMe file located at the root of the CD-ROM. Here is what you will find:

✦ System requirements

✦ Using the CD-ROM with Windows and Macintosh computers

✦ What's on the CD-ROM

✦ Troubleshooting

## System Requirements

Make sure that your computer meets the minimum system requirements listed in this section. If your computer doesn't match up to most of these requirements, you may have a problem using the contents of the CD-ROM.

**For Windows 9x, Windows 2000, Windows NT4 (with SP 4 or later), Windows Me, or Windows XP:**

✦ Intel Pentium II processor (300 MHz or faster)

✦ Microsoft Windows 98, Windows 2000, Windows ME, Windows NT 4.0 with Service Pack 6, or Windows XP

✦ 64MB of RAM (128MB or more recommended)

✦ 85MB of available hard-disc space required for installation (40MB for application)

✦ 256-color video display adapter

✦ Large-capacity hard disk or disk array

✦ CD-ROM drive

Additional requirements for DV:

✦ Intel Pentium III 500MHz or faster (Pentium III 700MHz recommended)

✦ Windows 98 Second Edition, Windows ME, or Windows 2000

✦ 128MB RAM (256MB or more recommended)

✦ Dedicated large capacity 7,200 rpm UDMA 66 IDE or SCSI hard disk or disk array

✦ Microsoft-certified OHCI IEEE-1394 interface

✦ Microsoft DirectX-compatible video display adapter (for Windows XP)

✦ DV Devices Compatibility Matrix

Additional requirements for third-party capture cards:

✦ Adobe Premiere-certified capture card

**For Macintosh:**

✦ PowerPC processor

✦ Mac OS software Version 9.0.4

✦ 32MB of available RAM (128MB or more recommended)

✦ 50MB of available hard drive space required for installation

✦ Apple QuickTime 4.1.2

✦ Large-capacity hard disk or disk array

Additional requirements for DV:

✦ PowerPC processor (at least 300 MHz)

✦ Apple FireWire 2.4

✦ QuickTime-compatible FireWire (IEEE 1394) interface

✦ Large-capacity hard disk or disk array (capable of sustaining 5MB/sec)

# Using the CD-ROM with Windows

To install the items from the CD-ROM to your hard drive, follow these steps:

**1. Insert the CD-ROM into your computer's CD-ROM drive.**

**2. A window will appear with the following options:**

**Install.** Gives you the option to install the supplied software and/or the author-created samples on the CD-ROM.

**Explore.** Allows you to view the contents of the CD-ROM in its directory structure.

**Links.** Opens a hyperlinked page of Web sites.

**Exit.** Closes the autorun window.

If you do not have autorun enabled or if the autorun window does not appear, follow the steps below to access the CD-ROM.

1. **Choose Start⇨Run.**

2. **In the dialog box that appears, type** $d$:\setup.exe, **where $d$ is the letter of your CD-ROM drive.** The autorun window described above displays.

3. **Choose the Install, Explore, Links, or Exit option from the menu.** (See Step 2 in the preceding list for a description of these options.)

# Using the CD-ROM with the Mac OS

To install the items from the CD-ROM to your hard drive, follow these steps:

1. **Insert the CD-ROM into your CD-ROM drive.**

2. **Double-click the icon for the CD-ROM after it appears on the desktop.**

3. **For those programs that come with installers, simply open the program's folder on the CD-ROM and double-click the Install or Installer icon.** Note: To install some programs, just drag the program's folder from the CD-ROM window and drop it on your hard drive icon.

# What's on the CD-ROM

The following sections provide a summary of the software and other materials you'll find on the CD-ROM. The CD-ROM contains lots of valuable tools, including trial versions of Adobe Premiere, Photoshop, and After Effects. The CD-ROM also includes three complete QuickTime videos as well as video and audio clips that you will need for the video tutorial in Chapter 1.

## Author-created materials

All author-created material from the book, including code listings and samples, are on the CD in the folder named "Nickeltown Tour."

### Audio clips for tutorial

The Nickeltown Tour folder includes a 30-second segment of the song "Nickeltown," which you need for Chapter 1's QuickStart tutorial. Instructions on how to load files from the CD are included in Chapter 1. "Nickeltown" was written by Pete and Maura Kennedy (© 2002 Cherry Lane Music/Cherry River Music, BMI) from the 2002 Jiffyjam release, *Get It Right. Get It Right* and other Kennedys' CDs are available in fine stores, or on their Web site, www.KennedysMusic.com.

### QuickTime videos for study

Three music videos written, played, sung, directed, shot, and edited by The Kennedys are in the main directory on the CD-ROM, including the Washington Area Music Association (WAMA) voted Best Video of 2000 winner, "Free," starring Sissy and Duke Allman as well as "Pick You Up" both from The Kennedys' CD *Evolver* (Zoe Records). Winner of the 2001 WAMA for best music video, "Nickeltown," is also included on this disc.

### Video clips for tutorial

The Nickeltown Tour folder contains seven video clips and a title, all of which you need for Chapter 1's QuickStart tutorial. The tutorial shows you how to build the first 30 seconds of The Kennedys' full-length music video, "Nickeltown."

### Web site links

✦ **QuickTime.** You need QuickTime installed to view the QuickTime (MOV) files on the CD-ROM. You can download the latest version of the QuickTime software from Apple Computer, Inc. at www.apple.com/quicktime/download/.

✦ **The Kennedys.** If you like the music videos in this book, you may want to visit the authors' Web site at www.KennedysMusic.com.

## Applications

The following applications are on the CD-ROM:

### Adobe Photoshop, from Adobe Systems Incorporated

*Thirty-day tryout version for Macintosh and Windows.* Professional-quality image-editing software. For more information, visit the Adobe Web site at www.adobe.com/products/photoshop/main.html.

### Adobe Premiere, from Adobe Systems Incorporated

*Thirty-day tryout version for Macintosh and Windows.* Powerful, professional digital video editor. For more information, visit the Adobe Web site at www.adobe.com/products/premiere/main.html.

**Adobe After Effects, from Adobe Systems Incorporated**

*Thirty-day tryout version for Macintosh and Windows.* After Effects lets you create visual effects and motion graphics for film, video, multimedia, and the Web. For more information, visit the Adobe Web site at `www.adobe.com/products/ aftereffects/main.html`.

*Shareware programs* are fully functional, trial versions of copyrighted programs. If you like particular programs, register with their authors for a nominal fee and receive licenses, enhanced versions, and technical support. *Freeware programs* are copyrighted games, applications, and utilities that are free for personal use. Unlike shareware, these programs do not require a fee or provide technical support. *GNU software* is governed by its own license, which is included inside the folder of the GNU product. See the GNU license for more details.

*Trial, demo, or evaluation versions* are usually limited either by time or functionality (such as being unable to save projects). Some trial versions are very sensitive to system date changes. If you alter your computer's date, the programs will "time out" and will no longer be functional.

# Troubleshooting

If you have difficulty installing or using any of the materials on the companion CD, try the following solutions:

✦ **Turn off any anti-virus software that you may have running.** Installers sometimes mimic virus activity and can make your computer incorrectly believe that it is being infected by a virus. (Be sure to turn the anti-virus software back on later.)

✦ **Close all running programs.** The more programs you're running, the less memory is available to other programs. Installers also typically update files and programs; if you keep other programs running, installation may not work properly.

✦ **Reference the ReadMe:** Please refer to the ReadMe file located at the root of the CD-ROM for the latest product information at the time of publication.

If you still have trouble with the CD, please call the Hungry Minds Customer Care phone number: (800) 762-2974. Outside the United States, call (317) 572-3994. You can also contact Hungry Minds Customer Service by e-mail at `techsupdum@ wiley.com`. Hungry Minds will provide technical support only for installation and other general quality control items; for technical support on the applications themselves, consult the program's vendor or author.

✦　　✦　　✦

# Upgrading Your Computer

**APPENDIX**

**B**

**W**hen working in Adobe Premiere, you will be using memory-intensive clips. A three-minute music video might take up several gigabytes (GB) of space. This includes all of the clips you use in the video as well as those you have only used portions of. We have found that the ideal setup is to have a dedicated computer just for editing video. Having a dedicated computer reduces the likelihood of compatibility problems between programs. Of course, you can still run other programs, but you may want to eschew computer games and memory/processing-intensive programs.

When we started using Premiere, we used a Sony VAIO desktop, which included Premiere in its software package. The computer was optimized for video editing. The only problem we encountered was that our extensive touring schedule kept us away from our desk. We yearned for a beefy laptop that could handle video processing. We now use a Sony VAIO laptop, also optimized for video editing, and it's even more powerful than that ancient, three-year-old desktop machine.

We've tried several other computers, and found that you should look for certain qualities when purchasing a computer for video editing with Premiere. This appendix can help you in purchasing a new computer or upgrading your old one.

Your computer has three basic aspects that determine its speed, functionality, and storage:

+ The processor (speed)
+ The memory, or RAM (functionality)
+ The hard drive (storage)

# Processor

The *central processing unit,* or CPU, is the engine that runs your software. The faster the CPU, the better the performance of your software, and the less time you'll spend waiting for your computer to process data. When working with audio and video files, this becomes extremely important. If your processor is not fast enough, your data may have to "wait around" to be processed. When you're exporting a video to tape, you can't afford to wait around.

We recommend that when purchasing a new computer, you opt for the fastest CPU you can afford to buy. If you're sticking with your old machine, you can upgrade to a faster processor if your computer has a processor upgrade slot. Even if your machine doesn't have a processor upgrade slot, there are some processor upgrades available that plug into alternate card slots on your computer. Check with the manufacturer for compatibility.

Computer superstores, such as CompUSA and Circuit City, have comprehensive Web sites where you can search for product information and compatibility. Check out www.compusa.com or www.circuitcity.com. Bizrate.com (www.bizrate.com) is also a great site that compares stores and prices by product.

# Memory

Premiere processes all of your editing in RAM. When you add memory, you install *random access memory,* or RAM, modules that expand the functionality of your computer, not the storage space. Computers are often sold with less than the maximum RAM that the computer will accommodate. See your computer owner's manual to see how much you can upgrade your RAM. We recommend that you upgrade the RAM to the computer's limit. Processing is all-important when editing and exporting video.

Your owner's manual should tell you what's involved with upgrading your RAM. If you've never done it before, be sure that you read all the directions carefully or have a professional install it. Most computer dealers have a service department that offers RAM installation. Electrostatic discharge can damage the RAM module, so if your computer is in a carpeted room, and you get a shock every time you walk across the room and grab the fridge handle, you'll want to be extra careful.

# Hard Drive

When purchasing a hard drive upgrade, don't just look at capacity and price. Speed is important, too, and many times the cheaper hard drives have slower disk speed. For video editing, a disk speed of at least 7,200 rpm is essential. Research hard drives on the Web before you buy. Find out if the hard drive you're interested in is optimized for audio and video applications.

## AV-certified hard drives

When you are looking for a computer, make sure that you have two separate hard drives. One drive should be an AV-certified hard drive, which means that the drive is capable of spinning fast enough to keep up with the processing of large multimedia files without skipping or stalling. Store captured video on this drive and your program and operating system on the other one.

## Partitioned hard drives

We used a 30GB computer for a trial run, but it only had one hard drive, with one partition, and the computer could not handle the storage and processing. You would think that a 30GB hard drive would be sufficient, but you need to pay attention to a couple of details. Some computers come with hard drives *partitioned*, meaning that the drive is divided into two parts. Your operating system is on one partition, and you can put your captured video on the other partition. This is a good compromise, but it's better still to have two separate hard drives.

## External hard drives

These days, large (multi-gigabyte), inexpensive hard drives are cheap and plentiful. You can pick up an external hard drive for a fraction of what they cost just a year ago, and they're much larger in capacity.

## Internal hard drives

Internal hard drives are also much cheaper and larger than they were, even a year ago. You can buy an 80GB, 7,200 rpm hard drive for around $150! Check with the manufacturer or the dealer for compatibility.

## Removable hard drives

Many computers, like the Sony VAIO, have removable hard drives. Because they're so inexpensive, you can archive your video files on removable drives. If you have a band that wants you to shoot and edit their hour-long retrospective, you can put their entire project on its own hard drive (that's *their* expense, not yours). When they're done with the project, you can pull the hard drive out and pop in a shiny new one for the next project.

Swappable drives cost about twice as much as internal drives, but you pay for the convenience of holding lots of data in a removable, portable drive.

## Other storage options

When you're done editing a movie, you should archive the files associated with that video. You may need to access it in the future, whether to edit the movie further or to export it to a different format. The removable hard drive is becoming more and more affordable. You can also use a Jaz drive, which stores 2GB of data. You can store the files to CD-R media, but you'll need several CD-R discs per project. Saving to CD-R is a slower process than the other options.

# IEEE 1394 Card or Capture Card

If you have a camera that has a FireWire connection, but your computer does not, you can purchase an IEEE 1394 PCI card or a capture card. These cost around $50 and will enable you to transfer video and audio directly out the FireWire port of a digital camera into your computer, keeping your digital footage in the digital domain.

✦     ✦     ✦

# Other Helpful Equipment

**A**lthough you should be able to make a professional-quality music video using only your computer, DV camcorder, and Adobe Premiere, you may want to consider purchasing some additional equipment to give yourself more flexibility and to simplify the process.

## Tripods

A tripod is the first accessory you should purchase, if you don't already have one. The lightweight tripods found in low-end camera shops are fine for still photography, but for video work, the heavier tripods will provide more stability and minimal shaking. A *fluid head* allows for less jerky panning. All sorts and sizes of tripods are available, from small desktop tripods, to those that can hold your camera up over the heads of a crowd in a rock club. Monopods can be useful if you want to stabilize your camera vertically but still have the ability to quickly pick up and move to another location. Shoulder supports give your camcorder stability as you shoot while walking. Monopods can cost as little as $30, and as much as $700, while tripods range in price from around $60 for basic, no-frills DV camcorder tripods, to $800 for professional heavy-duty, fluid-head tripods.

## Lights

You can choose from all kinds of lighting, and the first time that you go into a professional camera/lighting shop, you may be overwhelmed. You can spend as little as $150 for a simple system, or into the thousands for high-quality professional gear. Just remember, light is light. You might consider starting with an inexpensive system. Use it until you decide what additional features you need. These might include barn doors, umbrellas, and other diffusers, and light stands.

Many DV camcorders can accommodate a single light that attaches to the accessory shoe of the camera. The shoe is a coupling device built into the camera's casing. Some shoes have hot patches that will allow your light to draw on the camera's battery power. If you don't have this feature on your camera (usually only the high-end camcorders have it), you'll need to purchase battery packs and other attachments. Ask your dealer what setup is best for your camera. These lights typically cost anywhere from $35 to $100.

Cross-Reference    See Chapter 4 for a complete description of the three-point lighting system.

# Lenses

You can shoot solely with the lens that comes built into your camcorder, but you may eventually want to invest in some additional lenses. Make sure when you purchase your lenses that they are made for video camcorders, as opposed to still cameras.

## Wide-angle lenses

Fitting a whole band into a single shot can sometimes leave too much headroom. When shooting indoors, it's hard to get the "feel" for the room you're shooting in, because you can't "see" enough of it in your lens. If you want to pack as much as you can, laterally, into a shot, consider purchasing a wide-angle lens. Wide-angle lenses come in varying degrees. We found that a good all-purpose wide angle, that doesn't noticeably distort the image (unless filmed extremely close-up), is the .5x lens. You can opt for more radical distortion with a fish-eye lens.

## Polarizer filters

If you need a good all-purpose outdoor lens, consider purchasing a polarizer filter lens. It's a great lens to use if you want to deepen and intensify blue skies and saturate colors shot outdoors. It also cuts down on unwanted nonmetallic reflections, which comes in handy if you're shooting through a window, for example. The circular polarizer enables you to choose the desired amount of the effect by rotating the filter.

## Color correcting and light balancing filters

These filters compensate for shooting under florescent and other forms of artificial lights as well as under daylight, sunlight, and various types of natural light. These come in handy when you find a good-looking location that has less-than-ideal available light.

## Special effects filters

Special effects filters come in all forms and include:

✦ **Soft focus.** Gives wedding portraits that hazy look.

✦ **Star effect.** Turns lights, flames, and water gleams into star-shaped designs.

✦ **Enhancing filter.** Brings out reddish colors without noticeably changing others.

✦ **Fog filter.** Adds a foggy haze over your image to mimic natural fog.

✦ **Sepia tone filter.** Gives shots an old-fashioned look.

## Color gradation filters

Color gradation filters are clear on the bottom, with a graduated blend of color on the top, and are usually used to change the appearance of the sky. They come in different colors for use on blue skies, sunrise/sunset, and sky to foreground balancing.

## Contrast filters

Contrast filters even out the brightly lit and shadowy contrasts you find outdoors. Use them so that nothing in your composition is severely over-exposed or under-exposed.

# Dollies

As we mentioned in Chapter 4, it's better to dolly a shot than to zoom. You can certainly spend lots of money buying rolling tripods and dolly tracks, but we have a few low-budget recommendations. One of the more common low-budget methods of getting dolly shots is to borrow or buy a used wheelchair. Don't use an electric wheelchair yourself, because you won't be able to navigate it and shoot at the same time. Have someone push you as you shoot. You can also use an auto mechanic's creeper dolly (the ones with ledges on the sides) along with your tripod. Set the tripod on the dolly and roll it along. It's best to use rolling dollies on smooth surfaces, of course. You can also use a baby stroller, shopping cart, or anything with wheels that can securely hold your camera.

# Backdrops

If you want to incorporate composites into your videos, you'll need to have a color screen to shoot against. Blue and green backdrops are common for this use because there is typically little blue or green in human skin tone. However, you should have a variety of colors to use as screens so you have the appropriate contrasting color to the figure you will be shooting.

You may also want to have different colors on hand to diminish the aliasing staircase effect that is inherent in DV video chroma keys. The color you choose will depend on the color of your composite background. A cheap, high-quality option is to use a black backdrop as a luma key. Luminance has four times the resolution as color mattes. The darkest black velvet you can find is the best stuff to use. You may need to use a garbage matte around parts of your foreground figure that are black — dark eyes, for example — to avoid drop out.

# Microphones

If you're using your camcorder to record live concerts, consider purchasing a good microphone or two. All DV camcorders come with a built-in microphone, but although the recording quality of the camcorder is 16 bit, the quality of your built-in microphone is not always the best. Talk to your dealer to find out what microphone is best for your camcorder and be sure to find out if you need an external power source or special adapters.

Microphones fall into two basic types — dynamic and condenser. *Dynamic* microphones are cheaper, connect to your mic input with a simple audio cable (although you may need an adapter to fit the mini-jack on your camera), and require no power supply. *Condenser* microphones have a wider frequency response but are delicate and need an appropriate power supply. This is a specific voltage commonly referred to as *phantom power*. If you want to go this route, make sure that you will be able to power your mics at remote locations. If your camera is equipped with a hot accessory shoe, the manufacturer may offer a specialized high-quality microphone that can take its power directly off the camcorder's battery.

# Camera Bags

Unless you shoot everything within the confines of your home, you'll need to carry your camera around outside. Protective luggage options range from the simplest of canvas bags to airline-approved flight cases that would withstand an angry elephant or possibly even an airport baggage handler. Somewhere between these two extremes is the typical camera case. A briefcase-style carrier with interior foam blocks that can be arranged to snugly fit your gear are standard. Keep in mind that thieves have their eyes peeled for the silver colored briefcases that professional photographers carry their expensive cameras in. Don't be afraid to disguise your gear in something more prosaic. We went to the local discount store and got a fishing tackle box. It doesn't look like something a CNN correspondent would use, but it's carried our DV safely across the country several times. Even if you go this route, get a hard case, too. When you're packing gear for a location shot, remember that the camera is the main reason you're going. Protect it like it is the most valuable piece of gear on the shoot, because it is.

✦   ✦   ✦

# Resources

**T**his appendix contains miscellaneous information to enhance your knowledge of music videos.

## Studying Video

The best way to learn about music videos is by watching them. We've put together some lists that will help you seek out some of the most instructive and inspiring ones.

### Groundbreaking videos of the 1980s

The 1980s was the classic period when music video came into the public consciousness as both an entertainment outlet and an art form.

- ✦ Michael Jackson, "Billie Jean" (Directed by Steve Barron)
- ✦ Peter Gabriel, "Sledgehammer" (Directed by Nick Park)
- ✦ Dire Straits, "Money for Nothing" (Directed by Godley and Crème)
- ✦ The Police, "Every Breath You Take" (Directed by Godley and Crème)
- ✦ Don Henley, "Boys of Summer" (Directed by Jean-Baptiste Mondino)
- ✦ Chris Isaak, "Wicked Game" (Directed by Herb Ritts)
- ✦ Herbie Hancock, "Rock-it" (Directed by Godley and Crème)
- ✦ Eurythmics, "Sweet Dreams are Made of This" (Directed by Derek Burbridge)
- ✦ The Buggles, "Video Killed the Radio Star" (Directed by Dennis Mulcahy)

### Groundbreaking videos of the 1990s

The 1990s saw the rise of new musical styles, and a fresh crop of video visionaries who kept the screen alive with new ideas.

✦ Nirvana, "Smells Like Teen Spirit" (Directed by Samuel Bayer)

✦ The Breeders, "Cannonball" (Directed by Spike Jonze)

✦ The Beastie Boys, "Sabotage" (Directed by Spike Jonze)

✦ Lenny Kravitz, "Fly Away" (Directed by Paul Hunter)

✦ R.E.M., "Everybody Hurts" (Directed by Jake Scott)

✦ The Smashing Pumpkins, "Tonight, Tonight" (Directed by Jonathan Dayton and Valerie Faris)

✦ Janet Jackson, "Runaway" (Directed by Marcus Nispal)

✦ Björk, "Human Behavior" (Directed by Michel Gondry)

✦ Madonna, "Ray of Light" (Directed by Jonas Akerlund)

✦ TLC, "No Scrubs" (Directed by Hype Williams)

## Groundbreaking videos of the twenty-first century

In the present day, the explosion of digital technology has made the evolution of video technique an ever-quickening process.

✦ Apex Theory, "Shh . . . (hope diggy)" (Directed by VIM and Tony)

✦ Maxwell, "Fortunate" (Directed by Francis Lawrence)

✦ Aterciopelados, "El Estuche" (Directed by Marina Zurkow)

✦ Coldplay, "Trouble" (Directed by Tim Hope)

✦ Gorillaz, "19-2000" (Directed by Jamie Hewlett and Pete Candeland)

✦ Angie Stone, "Brotha" (Directed by Chris Robinson)

✦ Lauren Hill, "Everything is Everything" (Directed by Sanji)

✦ Nortec Collective Featuring Bostich, "Polaris" (Directed by Matthew Amato and Sal Ricalde)

✦ Tenacious D, "Wonderboy" (Directed by Spike Jonze)

✦ Mary J. Blige, "No More Drama" (Directed by Sanji)

## Video directors to check out

From 1980 right up until today, an unbroken line of innovators has continued to push the video envelope.

✦ Hype Williams (TLC/Missy Elliot/Faith Evans)

✦ Paul Hunter (Lenny Kravitz/Puff Daddy/Will Smith)

✦ Spike Jonze (Beastie Boys/Fatboy Slim/Tenacious D)

✦ Tim Pope (Coldplay/The Cure)

✦ Jean Baptiste Mondino (Don Henley)

✦ Michel Gondry (Björk/Foo Fighters)

✦ Dave Myers (Mary J. Blige)

✦ Chris Robinson (Alicia Keyes/Angie Stone)

✦ Godley and Crème (The Police/Herbie Hancock)

✦ Sanji (Mary J. Blige/Lauren Hill)

## Films that have influenced music video

Cinematic technique has greatly influenced music video, and over the last two decades the influence of music video has had an impact on the movies.

✦ *A Hard Day's Night* and other Richard Lester films

✦ *2001: A Space Odyssey* and other Stanley Kubrick films

✦ *Down by Law* and other Jim Jarmusch films

✦ *Paris, Texas* and other Wim Wenders films

✦ *Blue Velvet* and other David Lynch films

✦ *Do the Right Thing* and other Spike Lee films

✦ *Dazed and Confused* and other Richard Linklater films

✦ *Rock and Roll High School* and other Roger Corman films

✦ *Spinal Tap* (Directed by Rob Reiner)

✦ *Head* (The Monkees, Directed by Bob Rafelson)

✦ *Shaft* (Directed by Gordon Parks)

✦ *Being John Malkovich* (Directed by Spike Jonze)

✦ *Easy Rider* (Directed by Dennis Hopper)

✦ *Blow Up* (Directed by Michelangelo Antonioni)

✦ *Repo Man* (Directed by Alex Cox)

✦ James Bond films (Opening credits)

✦ *This Was Rock,* also known as The TAMI/TNT Show

# Where to See Music Videos

Music videos seemingly play everywhere today, from dedicated television networks to department store displays. After reading this book, we hope that you can evaluate videos with a critical eye and an appreciation of everything involved in creating them.

## Music television

The best place to see videos is on TV! Make sure that your cable plan provides the following:

- ✦ MTV2, which airs the latest music videos 24/7.
- ✦ VH1CL, which airs old and new videos from artists in all genres.
- ✦ VH1SO, the urban channel, which airs a mix of hip-hop, slow jams, and soulful R&B.
- ✦ VH1CT, the country channel (if country music is your area of interest).
- ✦ MTVX, which specializes in hard-edged rock, features many technically advanced videos.

Pay special attention to the on-air promotions. These are short clips that feature the network logo, along with some innovative footage and graphics. MTV's on-air promotions department is considered a cutting-edge workshop for up-and-coming videographers.

## Music videos online

Online videos are best viewed with a high-speed connection. If you want to study them in anything approaching the quality that the director was hoping for, make sure that your system can deliver dense files at high speed. Even at high speed, a compressed file will lose some of its original quality, but online archives are still a valuable resource. Because videos are promotional materials, most of them are deleted from TV airplay after the record has run its course. Despite the compromise in quality, online archives are still the only way to view many older videos, and also many independent videos that don't get aired on the big networks. Sputnik7 is a great site to view the latter. Also check out the following:

- ✦ http://launch.yahoo.com (home to thousands of streaming videos)
- ✦ www.MTV.com
- ✦ www.VHI.com
- ✦ www.sputnick7.com
- ✦ www.musicvideos.com
- ✦ www.egads.com/nemceff2/resources.htm (A general clearinghouse for music video information)

And check out these free, or almost free, video streaming servers:

- ✦ www.iclips.com
- ✦ www.playstream.com
- ✦ www.imagestation.com

✦ www. singlereel.com

✦ http://spotlife.com

# Where to Post Your Videos

If you're just starting out, you will find the warmest reception at various online virtual festivals. These sites may be willing to post your video, collect viewer reviews, and get you the exposure that you need to kick it to the next level. Plus, they're fun, and you can't beat the travel expenses!

✦ **http://launch.yahoo.com.** You must submit your video on Beta or 3/4-inch tape. See Web site for further submission details and address.

✦ **www.imdb.com.** The Internet Movie Database is a great resource for all kinds of information about independent film and video. While you're there, register yourself so that you can get the site's full benefits.

✦ **http://us.imdb.com/Help/.** This is the IMDb University page, which is one of the most comprehensive help sections we've ever seen. It's organized like college courses, arranging information in the form of a syllabus. Click How To Sell Videos in the Orientation column. You'll be provided with several useful marketing links. Go back to the previous page and click Adding/Correcting Data in the Senior Year column to register yourself in the directory as a video director. From there, you can send in a press release whenever you submit a new video. Video fans searching this site will want to know about you!

✦ **www.DFILM.com.** This site is an archive of independent video. It also sponsors an ongoing traveling festival. You must submit your video on VHS tape, DVD, or as a QuickTime movie burned onto CD or DVD. There is no submission fee, but you need to fill out a form posted on their Web site. DFILM specifically seeks films made with computers and digital gear. Some films screened by DFILM have been picked up by MTV!

✦ **www.thesync.com/festival.** An online showcase of experimental shorts that describes itself as a "never ending" festival.

✦ **www.amazon.com.** Click the Join Advantage button at the bottom of the page. Amazon's 10 million browsers will have access to your wares. Put your video up for sale!

# Contests and Festivals

Start your search at www.marklitwak.com/filmfes.htm. Mark maintains a clearinghouse of film festival information, with links to many festival Web sites, including fests that only exist online.

✦ **www.sxsw.com/film/.** The South by Southwest festival, held in Austin, Texas every March, is a major gathering for both music and film aficionados. Plus, the food and weather are great. So apply!

✦ **ResFest.** Visit `www.resfest.com` for info about this festival sponsored by RES, a cutting-edge print magazine and online archive.

✦ **Sundance Film Festival.** Although this festival is not yet video-friendly, it is the major showcase for independent filmmakers. Hits like *The Blair Witch Project* and *Reservoir Dogs* were discovered here, and music industry types are starting to consider this one an essential "hang."

✦ **www.nitrateonline.com/ffilmfest.html**. This site features reviews from most of the major festivals.

# Stock Footage Libraries

Say that you want to start your next video with an establishing shot of the earth from space. Kind of a tough location shoot, and that spinning globe in your bedroom looks pretty bogus. Well, don't sweat it. The U.S. government already did the dirty work for you. And because you're a taxpayer, you've already paid for it! This site tells you how to obtain dirt-cheap video footage, all rights included, from the government. It's not just Army hygiene training films, either. The U.S. government has shot almost everything, at one time or another, and because it was all done on the taxpayer's dime, we can use it for next to nothing. Go ahead; storyboard your lead singer walking on the Moon. Armstrong, Aldrin, and Collins already got the location shot, and with the space suit on, who can tell? In fact, MTV uses just such a shot for one of their classic network logos. How do you get in on this bonanza? Do not pass Go. Do not collect $200. Go straight to:

✦ **www.nara.gov/research/ordering/stock.html**. This is the quickest route to get information about the National Archives and Records Administration's motion picture and video collection. See Chapter 7 for more information about this extensive archive of stock footage.

✦ **www.videouniversity.com/disk1.htm.** This site, maintained by Oak Tree Press, is a goldmine of stock footage and learning resources. They also offer a huge library of informational pamphlets dealing with every aspect of shooting and editing video. Check it out.

✦ **www.adobe.com.** This is Adobe's official Web site. Follow the links to Adobe Premiere's Expert Center for free stock footage. Set a bookmark for this page. Adobe offers tutorials and other training resources.

✦ **www.dvpa.com.** This is the official Web site for the Digital Video Professionals Association. By purchasing an annual membership for around $150, you get their DVPA Stock Video Footage Collection Volume 1 (a $1,000 value). Renew your membership for $100, and you get Volume 2.

# Recommended Reading

The following two books give an excellent overview of the theory, history, and techniques of music video:

✦ *You Stand There: Making Music Video*. David Kleiler and Robert Moses, Three Rivers Press, 1997.

✦ Thirty Frames per Second: The Visionary Art of the Music Video. Steve Reiss and Neil Feineman. Harry N. Abrams, Inc., 2000.

Music video is such a young art form that there are as yet only a few books specifically devoted to the discipline. Videographers glean information from the many fine books available on the craft of filmmaking. All the titles below are useful to video makers:

✦ *Film Production: The Complete Uncensored Guide to Film Making.* Greg Merritt, Lone Eagle Publishing Company, 1998.

✦ *Digital Moviemaking*. Scott Billups, Michael Wise Productions, 2000.

✦ *The Computer Videomaker Handbook*. Various authors, Focal Press/Butterworth-Heineman, 2001.

✦ *Film Directing: Killer Style and Cutting Edge Technique*. Renee Harmon, Lone Eagle Publishing Company, 1998.

✦ *Cinematography/Screencraft*, Peter Ettedgui, Focal Press, 1999.

✦ *Clearance and Copyright: Everything the Independent Filmmaker Needs to Know*. Michael C. Donaldson, Silman-James Press, 1996.

✦ *The Technique of Film and Video Editing*. Ken Dancyger, Focal Press, 1997.

✦ *Rebel Without a Crew*. Robert Rodriguez, Plume, 1995.

✦ *How I Made a Hundred Films in Hollywood and Never Lost a Dime*. Roger Corman, Random House, 1990.

✦ *The Man Who Framed the Beatles, a Biography of Richard Lester*. Andrew Yule, Donald I. Fine and Co, 1994.

✦ *Jamming the Media*. Gareth Branwyn, Chronicle Books, 1997.

✦ *Film*. Andrea Gronemeyer, Barron's Educational Series, Inc., 1998.

## Where to find video books

All the books we mention here and many others on the subject are available at the following bookstores:

✦ Drama Bookshop, 723 Seventh Avenue, New York, New York (212-944-0595)

✦ Samuel French Bookstore, 7623 Sunset Boulevard, Hollywood, CA (213-876-0570)

If a road trip to one of the above shops is out of the question, check online at:

✦ www.amazon.com

✦ www.focalpress.com

## Video magazines

Consider subscribing to one or more of these periodicals to keep up with the latest industry developments:

✦ *RES*, 601 West 28th St, 11th Floor, New York, New York, 10001 (www.res.com)

✦ *Indie Slate*, 10134 Hammerly, #178, Houston TX, 77080

✦ *Independent Film and Video Monthly*, 304 Hudson St., 6th Floor, New York, New York, 10013 (www.virtualfilm.com)

✦ *Videography*, P.O.Box 0513, Baldwin, New York, 11510 (www.videography.com)

✦ *Camcorder and Computer Video*, 4800 Market Street, Ventura, CA, 93003 (www.CandCV.com)

✦ *Computer Videomaker*, P.O.Box 3780, Chico, CA, 95927 (www.videomaker.com)

# Recommended Elvis Impersonator

The Elvis impersonator who appears in the video "Nickeltown," included on the companion CD-ROM and mentioned in Chapter 1, can be contacted for bookings.

Brendan Paul
1960 Papago Lane
Las Vegas, NV 89109

Telephone: 702-450-9548
Fax: 702-450-9549

E-mail: brendanpaul@lvcm.com

Web site: www.bestelvis.com

✦    ✦    ✦

# Index

*Continued*

# Hungry Minds, Inc.
# End-User License Agreement

**READ THIS.** You should carefully read these terms and conditions before opening the software packet(s) included with this book ("Book"). This is a license agreement ("Agreement") between you and Hungry Minds, Inc. ("HMI"). By opening the accompanying software packet(s), you acknowledge that you have read and accept the following terms and conditions. If you do not agree and do not want to be bound by such terms and conditions, promptly return the Book and the unopened software packet(s) to the place you obtained them for a full refund.

1. **License Grant.** HMI grants to you (either an individual or entity) a nonexclusive license to use one copy of the enclosed software program(s) (collectively, the "Software") solely for your own personal or business purposes on a single computer (whether a standard computer or a workstation component of a multi-user network). The Software is in use on a computer when it is loaded into temporary memory (RAM) or installed into permanent memory (hard disk, CD-ROM, or other storage device). HMI reserves all rights not expressly granted herein.

2. **Ownership.** HMI is the owner of all right, title, and interest, including copyright, in and to the compilation of the Software recorded on the disk(s) or CD-ROM ("Software Media"). Copyright to the individual programs recorded on the Software Media is owned by the author or other authorized copyright owner of each program. Ownership of the Software and all proprietary rights relating thereto remain with HMI and its licensers.

3. **Restrictions On Use and Transfer.**

   (a) You may only (i) make one copy of the Software for backup or archival purposes, or (ii) transfer the Software to a single hard disk, provided that you keep the original for backup or archival purposes. You may not (i) rent or lease the Software, (ii) copy or reproduce the Software through a LAN or other network system or through any computer subscriber system or bulletin-board system, or (iii) modify, adapt, or create derivative works based on the Software.

   (b) You may not reverse engineer, decompile, or disassemble the Software. You may transfer the Software and user documentation on a permanent basis, provided that the transferee agrees to accept the terms and conditions of this Agreement and you retain no copies. If the Software is an update or has been updated, any transfer must include the most recent update and all prior versions.

4. **Restrictions on Use of Individual Programs.** You must follow the individual requirements and restrictions detailed for each individual program in Appendix A of this Book. These limitations are also contained in the individual license agreements recorded on the Software Media. These limitations may include a requirement that after using the program for a specified period of time, the user must pay a registration fee or discontinue use. By opening the Software packet(s), you will be agreeing to abide by the licenses and restrictions for these individual programs that are detailed in Appendix A and on the Software Media. None of the material on this Software Media or listed in this Book may ever be redistributed, in original or modified form, for commercial purposes.

### 5. Limited Warranty.

**(a)** HMI warrants that the Software and Software Media are free from defects in materials and workmanship under normal use for a period of sixty (60) days from the date of purchase of this Book. If HMI receives notification within the warranty period of defects in materials or workmanship, HMI will replace the defective Software Media.

**(b)** **HMI AND THE AUTHOR OF THE BOOK DISCLAIM ALL OTHER WARRANTIES, EXPRESS OR IMPLIED, INCLUDING WITHOUT LIMITATION IMPLIED WARRANTIES OF MERCHANTABILITY AND FITNESS FOR A PARTICULAR PURPOSE, WITH RESPECT TO THE SOFTWARE, THE PROGRAMS, THE SOURCE CODE CONTAINED THEREIN, AND/OR THE TECHNIQUES DESCRIBED IN THIS BOOK. HMI DOES NOT WARRANT THAT THE FUNCTIONS CONTAINED IN THE SOFTWARE WILL MEET YOUR REQUIREMENTS OR THAT THE OPERATION OF THE SOFTWARE WILL BE ERROR FREE.**

**(c)** This limited warranty gives you specific legal rights, and you may have other rights that vary from jurisdiction to jurisdiction.

### 6. Remedies.

**(a)** HMI's entire liability and your exclusive remedy for defects in materials and workmanship shall be limited to replacement of the Software Media, which may be returned to HMI with a copy of your receipt at the following address: Software Media Fulfillment Department, Attn.: *Make Your Own Music Videos with Adobe® Premiere®*, Hungry Minds, Inc., 10475 Crosspoint Blvd., Indianapolis, IN 46256, or call 1-800-762-2974. Please allow four to six weeks for delivery. This Limited Warranty is void if failure of the Software Media has resulted from accident, abuse, or misapplication. Any replacement Software Media will be warranted for the remainder of the original warranty period or thirty (30) days, whichever is longer.

**(b)** In no event shall HMI or the author be liable for any damages whatsoever (including without limitation damages for loss of business profits, business interruption, loss of business information, or any other pecuniary loss) arising from the use of or inability to use the Book or the Software, even if HMI has been advised of the possibility of such damages.

**(c)** Because some jurisdictions do not allow the exclusion or limitation of liability for consequential or incidental damages, the above limitation or exclusion may not apply to you.

### 7. U.S. Government Restricted Rights.
Use, duplication, or disclosure of the Software for or on behalf of the United States of America, its agencies and/or instrumentalities (the "U.S. Government") is subject to restrictions as stated in paragraph (c)(1)(ii) of the Rights in Technical Data and Computer Software clause of DFARS 252.227-7013, or subparagraphs (c) (1) and (2) of the Commercial Computer Software - Restricted Rights clause at FAR 52.227-19, and in similar clauses in the NASA FAR supplement, as applicable.

### 8. General.
This Agreement constitutes the entire understanding of the parties and revokes and supersedes all prior agreements, oral or written, between them and may not be modified or amended except in a writing signed by both parties hereto that specifically refers to this Agreement. This Agreement shall take precedence over any other documents that may be in conflict herewith. If any one or more provisions contained in this Agreement are held by any court or tribunal to be invalid, illegal, or otherwise unenforceable, each and every other provision shall remain in full force and effect.

# The Kennedys
## Get It Right

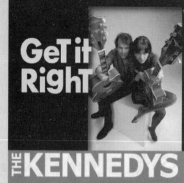

*Masters of the three-minute pop gem, this duo returns to the scene with their first studio album in two years. **Get It Right** has a rootsy, organic feel that harkens back to their breakthrough CD, **Life Is Large**. Vinnie Santoro returns on drums, and special guest Nanci Griffith appears on two cuts, as vocalist on "Ride Angel Ride," and as co-writer on "Pearl's Eye View." As usual, Pete and Maura pay sonic tribute to a wide variety of influences, ranging from Gram Parsons to Marvin Gaye and from The Ramones all the way to Antonio Carlos Jobim. Includes "Nickeltown" from the award-winning video. This enhanced CD also features visual material, including photos, video, liner notes, and lyrics.*

### Order your copy of The Kennedys' Get It Right and receive 20% off!
Fax this order form to 415-329-1828 or mail your check to The Kennedys. Call 1-800-864-3962 for address.

| CD Title | Reg. Price | Sale Price | Quantity | Total |
|---|---|---|---|---|
| **Get It Right (2002)** | **$15.00** | **$12.00** | | |
| *Other Kennedys CDs available:* | | | | |
| Positively Live! (2001) | $15.00 | $13.00 | | |
| Evolver (2000) | $15.00 | $13.00 | | |
| Angel Fire (1998) | $15.00 | $13.00 | | |
| Life Is Large (1996) | $15.00 | $13.00 | | |
| River Of Fallen Stars (1995) | $15.00 | $13.00 | | |
| *Shipping & Handling: Add $1.50 for the first CD, $1.00 for each additional CD:* | | | | |
| *Total:* | | | | |

| Name as it appears on credit card: | | | |
|---|---|---|---|
| Address: | | E-mail address: | |
| City: | State: | Zip: | Phone: |
| Credit card *number* (Visa/Mastercard only): | | Expiration date: | |
| CDC code (3- or 4-digit number located on the back of your credit card. It's the last set of numbers and is typically located on the signature strip.): | | | |
| Signature: | | | |

*Visit The Kennedys' Web site at www.KennedysMusic.com*

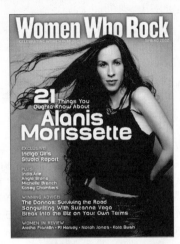
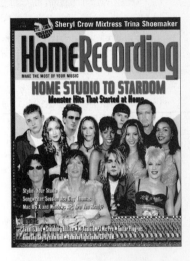

# SPECIAL OFFER: Stream Your Videos Online!

Once you've made your music video, submit it for all the world to see and download! From now through June 1, 2003, readers of *Make Your Own Music Videos with Adobe® Premiere®* will be able to submit videos at no charge to a special Web site created especially for them by JTL Networks.

Wiley and JTL will review your submitted video, and if it meets technical and legal requirements, it will be put in a queue for posting on JTL's site. You'll be notified by e-mail before the video is scheduled for viewing.

When the video "goes live" online, you'll be able to direct fans, friends, and family to the site's Web address, where they'll be able to download and view your cool creation.

In order to qualify for posting, videos must not infringe on any copyrights or trademarks, and must not be libelous or offensive in the judgment of Wiley or JTL Networks. Submitted videos will be posted on a first-come, first-serve basis, and will remain available for a period of time. Wiley and JTL cannot guarantee that every submitted video will be posted, but will make every effort to display all qualifying videos within the promotional time period!

Videos should not exceed 8MB in size, and should be between 2 and 4 minutes in length. They should be submitted in Windows Media Player, Real Networks, or QuickTime format.

To submit your video, go to:

## http://videopromo.jtlnet.com

---